JOHN MAY was born in Llwynypia, Rhondda. After graduating in History at University College, Cardiff, and gaining a teaching qualification at the University of London, he spent twenty-five years as a lecturer in further education before becoming a full-time writer. He is author of some sixteen school and college textbooks and has scripted a large number of schools broadcasts for BBC radio. Between 1987 and 1990 he was editor of the Welsh news digest *Wales Monthly Monitor*. He is also author of the recently published history book *A Chronicle of Welsh Events* (1994).

REFERENCE WALES

Compiled by

JOHN MAY

CARDIFF
UNIVERSITY OF WALES PRESS
1994

British Cataloguing-in-Publication Data

A catalogue record for this book is available from the British Library.

ISBN 0-7083-1234-9

Cover design by Design Principle.
The cover portraits are: (front) Neil Kinnock, Sir Anthony Hopkins, J. P. R. Williams; (back) Siân Phillips, Tanni Grey, Bryn Terfel.

Printed in Wales by Dinefwr Press, Llandybïe

For my wife Lesley

CONTENTS

ACKNOWLEDGEMENTS

In assembling the information in this book, I have had to consult a great range of publications – far too many, in fact, to be listed here although a select bibliography has been included. Without the rewarding mining of all these rich seams the present work could not have been attempted.

I am grateful to the scores of individuals and organizations who responded so readily to my requests for information. My thanks also go to the readers who examined the original typescript for correcting my errors and for making valuable suggestions.

Liz Powell, Editor at the University of Wales Press, deserves my special thanks for seeing what was a difficult production so expertly through its different stages. My thanks also to Susan Jenkins, Senior Editor at the University of Wales Press, who was involved in the project from the start.

Any inadequacies that remain in these pages, of course, are entirely the responsibility of the compiler.

Cardiff   JOHN MAY
October, 1994

1

PHYSICAL CHARACTERISTICS AND FEATURES

Wales is an irregular-shaped peninsula bounded in the north by the Irish Sea, in the south by the Bristol Channel, in the west by Cardigan Bay and St George's Channel, and in the east by the English counties of Cheshire, Shropshire, Hereford and Worcester, and Gloucester for 150 miles (240 km.).

The country is only some 40 miles (64 km.) wide at its narrowest, is 100 miles (160 km.) across at its widest, and has a maximum length of 140 miles (225 km.).

About 60 per cent of the country is over 500 feet (152 metres) high, 25 per cent is over 1,000 feet (305 metres) high and 6 per cent is over 1,500 feet (457 metres) high. There are 168 summits over 2,000 feet (610 metres) and 15 which are over 3,000 feet (914 metres).

Approximately 5 per cent of the population of the United Kingdom live in Wales which comprises just over 8 per cent of the total area of the UK.

GEOLOGY

Nearly all of Wales is composed of hard rock over 200 million years old, but large parts of Anglesey are 650 million years old, making it the most extensive area of pre-Cambrian rock in the British Isles. The oldest rock in Wales is a Gabbro from the Stanmer–Hanter area of Powys and is 702 million years old.

The last glacier in Wales, in Snowdonia, disappeared about 10,000 years ago.

AREAS

	Square miles	Square kilometres	Percentage of the area of Wales
Wales	8,017	20,763	
Welsh counties (from 1974)			
Clwyd	937	2,427	11.7
Dyfed	2,226	5,765	27.8
Gwent	531	1,375	6.6
Gwynedd	1,493	3,867	18.6
Mid Glamorgan	393	1,018	4.9
Powys	1,960	5,076	24.4
South Glamorgan	161	417	2.0
West Glamorgan	315	816	3.9
Old Welsh counties (to 1974)			
Anglesey	276	715	3.5
Brecon	733	1,890	9.1
Caernarfon	569	1,474	7.1
Cardigan	692	1,792	8.6
Carmarthen	920	2,383	11.5
Denbigh	669	1,733	8.3
Flint	256	663	3.2
Glamorgan	818	2,118	10.2
Merioneth	660	1,709	8.2
Monmouth	542	1,404	6.8
Montgomery	797	2,064	9.9
Pembroke	614	1,590	7.7
Radnor	471	1,220	5.9

Islands

Anglesey (Môn)	261 square miles (676 square kilometres)
Holy Island (Ynys Gybi)*	28 square miles (73 square kilometres)
Skomer*	722 acres (292 hectares)
Ramsey (Ynys Dewi)*	625 acres (253 hectares)
Caldey (Ynys Bŷr)	500 acres (203 hectares)
Bardsey (Ynys Enlli)*	498 acres (201 hectares)
Skokholm*	263 acres (106 hectares)

Flat Holm (Ynys Hafren)*	95 acres (38 hectares)
Puffin Island (Ynys Seiriol or Priestholm)*	78 acres (32 hectares)
Ynys Llanddwyn*	70 acres (28 hectares)
Ynys Feurig*	63 acres (25 hectares)
Bishops and Clerks*	41 acres (17 hectares)
Cardigan Island	40 acres (16 hectares)
The Skerries (Ynysoedd y Moelrhoniaid)	38 acres (15 hectares)
Sully Island*	28 acres (11.3 hectares)
St Margaret's Island	27 acres (11 hectares)
St Tudwal's East	24 acres (10 hectares)
Grassholm (Gwales)*	22 acres (9 hectares)
St Tudwal's West	21 acres (8.5 hectares)
Gateholm (Goat Island)	20 acres (8 hectares)
Middleholm (Midland Island)*	20 acres (8 hectares)
Ynys Gifftan	18 acres (7 hectares)
Ynysoedd y Gwylanod*	15 acres (6 hectares)
Thorn Island	8 acres (3 hectares)

Barry Island (Ynys y Barri)* was 170 acres (69 hectares) in area before being joined by causeway to the mainland in the 1880s with the building of Barry Dock.

* Indicates a Site of Special Scientific Interest (SSSI). (See below.)

Islands of five acres (two hectares) or less:

The Bitches	Ynys Cantwr
Black Scar	Ynys Dulas
East Mouse (Ynys Amlwch)	Ynysoedd Duon
Green Scar	Ynys Gorad Goch
Maen Piscar	Ynys Meibion
Middle Mouse (Ynys Badrig)	Ynys Moelfre
South Bishop (Em-Sger)	Ynys Traws
Stack Rock	Ynys yr Adar
St Catherine's Island	Ynys y Charcharorion
The Smalls	Ynys y Cranc
West Mouse (Maen y Bugail)	Ynys y Fydlyn
Ynys Bery	

COASTLINE LENGTHS BY COUNTIES

Clwyd:	34 miles (55 km.)	Mid Glamorgan:	17 miles (27 km.)
Gwynedd:	290 miles (467 km.)	South Glamorgan:	30 miles (48 km.)
Dyfed:	280 miles (450 km.)	Gwent:	22 miles (35 km.)
West Glamorgan:	59 miles (95 km.)		

Total coastline 732 miles (1,178 km.).
(Equivalent to some 17 per cent of the British coastline.)

NATURAL FEATURES: HIGHEST AND LARGEST

Highest Peaks

The 15 peaks in Wales over 3,000 feet (914 metres) are:

Snowdon (Yr Wyddfa)	3,560 ft. (1,085 m.)
Crib y Ddysgl (Carnedd Ugain)	3,494 ft. (1,065 m.)
Carnedd Llywelyn	3,485 ft. (1,062 m.)
Carnedd Dafydd	3,424 ft. (1,044 m.)
Glyder Fawr	3,278 ft. (999 m.)
Glyder Fach	3,262 ft. (994 m.)
Pen yr Ole Wen	3,208 ft. (978 m.)
Foel Grach	3,202 ft. (976 m.)
Yr Elan	3,152 ft. (961 m.)
Y Garn	3,104 ft. (946m.)
Foel Fras	3,092 ft. (942 m.)
Carnedd Uchaf	3,038 ft. (926 m.)
Elidir Fawr	3,030 ft. (923 m.)
Crib Goch	3,023 ft. (921 m.)
Tryfan	3,010 ft. (917 m.)

All the above peaks are in Gwynedd. The highest peak in south Wales, and the nineteenth highest in Wales, is Pen y Fan (2,907 ft./886 m.) in the Brecon Beacons of Powys. It is the highest mountain in Britain south of Cadair Idris (2,926 ft./892 m.) and the highest Old Red Sandstone peak in Britain.

Highest Passes

The highest mountain pass in Wales is Bwlch y Groes (path of the Cross) at 1,790 ft. (545 m.) on the road between Llanuwchllyn and Dinas Mawddwy,

Gwynedd. The highest pass in south Wales is Bwlch yr Efengyl (Gospel Pass) at 1,778 ft. (542 m.) between Hay and Capel-y-ffin, Gwent.

Highest Crag and Sea Cliffs

The highest crag is the 800 ft. (244 m.) north face of Lliwedd, Gwynedd. The highest sea cliffs in Wales are on Ramsey Island and are some 450 ft. (137 m.) high.

Highest Waterfalls

Pistyll Rhaeadr, Llanrhaeadr-ym-Mochnant, Clwyd: 240 ft. (73 m.)
Pistyll-y-Llyn, Dyfed–Powys border: 230 ft. (70m.) in cascades.

Pistyll Rhaeadr is the highest waterfall in England and Wales.

Highest Sand Dunes

Merthyr Mawr, Mid Glamorgan: over 200 ft. (61 m.) high – the highest in Britain and the second highest in Europe.

Caves: Largest and Deepest

The deepest cave in Wales – and also in Britain – is Ogof Ffynnon Ddu, Powys, at 1,010 feet (308 m.). It is 28 miles (45 km.) long making it the second longest cave in Britain.

The largest passage in a British cave is the 'Time Machine' in Ogof Daren Ciliau, Mynydd Llangatwg, Gwent – 65 feet (20 m.) wide by 65 feet high and 1,312 feet (400 m.) long.

Largest Meteorite

21 September, 1949: a meteorite weighing 25½ ounces (723 grammes) fell at Beddgelert, Gwynedd.

RECENT EARTHQUAKES

25 January 1974	Shock felt in many parts of Wales; epicentre in south Gwent. 4.4 on the Richter scale.
15 April 1984	Shock felt throughout mid-Wales; epicentre in Newtown– Hay area. 3.3 on the Richter scale.

19 July 1984	Shock felt in many parts of Wales; epicentre Nefyn, Llŷn. 5.4 on the Richter scale – the most intense shock in Britain in the twentieth century.
2 April 1990	Shock felt throughout Wales, epicentre Newtown, Powys. 5.1 on the Richter scale.
29 July 1992	Shock felt within a 50-mile radius of the epicentre near Caernarfon. 3.0 on the Richter scale.
10 February 1994	Shock felt throughout Gwynedd, epicentre Bangor. 2.9 on the Richter scale.
18 March 1994	Shock felt within a 30-mile radius of the epicentre in the Newtown–Caersws area. 3.1 on the Richter scale.

RAINFALL, SNOW, TEMPERATURE AND SUNSHINE

Annual Rainfall at Selected Places (1961–1990 averages)

Cardiff (Rhoose)	961 mm. (37.8 in.)	Loggerheads, Clwyd	910 mm. (35.8 in.)
Colwyn Bay	761 mm. (30.0 in.)	Pen-y-ffridd, Gwynedd	1,107 mm. (43.6 in.)
Dale Fort, Dyfed	828 mm. (32.6 in.)	Swansea	1,178 mm. (46.4 in.)
Gogerddan, Dyfed	1,009 mm. (39.7 in.)	Trawsfynydd, Gwynedd	1,677 mm. (66.0 in.)

Annual Rainfall for the Whole of Wales

1983–91 average	1,385 mm. (54.2 in.)
1990	1,366 mm. (53.8 in.)
1991	1,273 mm. (50.1 in.)
1992	1,448 mm. (57.0 in.)

The highest rainfall in Wales is on the summit of Snowdon with an average of 4,500 mm. (180 in.) although 6,200 mm. (246 in.) were recorded there in 1922. This is the wettest place in the British Isles.

The least rainfall ever recorded in Wales in a calendar year was at St Asaph, Clwyd, in 1955 when only 477 mm. (18.8 in.) were recorded.

The greatest rainfall in a 30-minute period to be recorded in the British Isles was at Cowbridge, South Glamorgan, on 22 July 1880 when 73.6 mm (2.90 in.) fell.

The highest rainfall in a month ever recorded in Britain was 1,435 mm. (56.5 in.) at Llyn Llydaw, Snowdonia, in October, 1909.

Snow and Frost

Snow has been estimated to cover areas over 3,000 feet high in Snowdonia for an average of about 100 days a year. Although there are no peaks in Wales above the permanent snow line, there are some spots where snow does not melt during most summers including Ffos Ddyfn near the summit of Carnedd Llywelyn. Outside Scotland, no other part of the British Isles has snow lying so late.

Between 22 January and 17 March 1947, there was a record accumulation of 60 inches of snow on the Denbigh Hills.

Frost has been recorded as late as the beginning of June and from early September.

Temperatures and Sunshine (1961–1990 averages at selected sites)

	Average January temperatures	*Average July temperatures*	*Average daily sunshine hours*
Cardiff, Rhoose	4.5°C (39.6°F)	16.0°C (60.4°F)	4.34
Dale Fort, Dyfed	6.2°C (42.8°F)	15.6°C (59.9°F)	4.70
Loggerheads, Clwyd	3.0°C (36.9°F)	14.1°C (57.4°F)	3.68
Pen-y-ffridd, Gwynedd	4.8°C (40.6°F)	15.4°C (59.2°F)	3.74

The highest January and November temperatures ever recorded in Britain were in north Wales:

Aber, Gwynedd:	18.3°C (64.9°F), 10 January 1971
Prestatyn, Clwyd:	21.7°C (71.0°F), 4 November 1946

The highest temperature ever recorded in Wales was 35.2°C (95.4°F) at Hawarden Bridge, Clwyd, on 2 August 1990.

The lowest temperature ever recorded in Wales was -23.3°C (-10°F) at Rhayader, Powys, on 21 January 1940.

The lowest daytime maximum temperature ever recorded in Wales was -8.0°C (17.6°F) at Trecastle, Powys, on 12 January 1987.

Growing Season

Over nine months
The west coast of Wales. The growing season in south-west Dyfed (Pembrokeshire) is approximately 365 days a year at sea level.

Seven–eight months
The hill country, along the east and coastal plateaux of south and south-east Wales, the Dee estuary and the Welsh hills around the main upland areas.

Five–six months
The main upland areas from Snowdonia to the Brecon Beacons.

The arrival of spring, as measured by the flowering of 12 wild flowers, varies between 27 April in west Pembrokeshire, the tip of Gower and the coastal strip of the Vale of Glamorgan, to after 11 May in the mountainous hinterland of Wales.

INLAND WATER

There are over 400 natural lakes and over 90 reservoirs in Wales covering a total of about 50 square miles (130 square kilometres).

The largest natural lake in Wales is Lake Bala (Llyn Tegid) 1.69 square miles (4.38 square kilometres) in area, slightly smaller than the Lake Vyrnwy reservoir (Llyn Llanwddyn), Powys, 1.75 square miles (4.53 square kilometres) created in 1894.

The largest natural lake in south Wales is Llan-gors Lake (Llyn Syfaddan) in Powys, 0.58 square miles (1.5 square kilometres) in area.

The highest lake in Wales is Llyn y Cwrt at 2,500 feet (762 m.) and the deepest is Llyn Cowlyd, 222 feet (67.7 m.), both in Snowdonia.

There are 57 dams in Wales.

The Largest Lakes and Reservoirs

(By capacity in megalitres)

Celyn	71,200	Clywedog	49,900	Llandegfedd	22,600
Brenig	59,600	Claerwen	46,500	Pontsticill	25,200
Brianne	58,700	Bala (Tegid)	45,000	Usk	12,200
Vyrnwy	51,000	Caban Coch	32,000	Alwen	11,900

Rivers

The 20 longest rivers wholly in Wales are:

Usk (Wysg)	85 miles (137 km.)	Clwyd	40 miles (63.9 km.)
Teifi	73 miles (117 km.)	Dovey (Dyfi)	37 miles (60 km.)
Tywi	68 miles (110 km.)	Ithon	37 miles (60 km.)
Taff	41 miles (66.7 km.)	Alyn	36 miles (58 km.)

Rhymney (Rhymni)	36 miles (58 km.)	Ebbw	29 miles (47 km.)
Conwy	35.5 miles (57 km.)	Neath (Nedd)	29 miles (47 km.)
Taf	35 miles (56 km.)	Loughor (Llwchwr)	28 miles (45 km.)
Cothi	34 miles (54 km.)	Rheidol	28 miles (45 km.)
Elwy	30 miles (48 km.)	Ely (Elái)	26 miles (41.5 km.)
Tawe	30 miles (48 km.)	Irfon	26 miles (41.5 km.)

There are some 15,000 miles of rivers in Wales.

There are three major rivers which have their sources in Wales but which also flow through England. Their overall lengths are:

		Sources
Severn (Hafren)*	220 miles (354 km.)	Plynlimon (Pumlumon, Dyfed)
Wye (Gwy)	130 miles (209 km.)	
Dee (Dyfrdwy)	111 miles (179 km.)	Lake Bala (Llyn Tegid)

*The longest river in Britain.

The River Monnow (Mynwy), 35 miles (57 km.) long, is not wholly in Wales as it forms the boundary between England and Wales along a part of its length.

WIND

The most powerful gusts of wind ever recorded in Wales were 113 m.p.h. at St Anne's Head, Pembrokeshire, 18 January 1945, and 107 m.p.h. at Aberporth, Dyfed, on 25 January 1990.

On the Welsh coast, wind speeds average 15–17 m.p.h. on Anglesey, Llŷn and Pembrokeshire to 10–15 m.p.h. elsewhere.

NATURE RESERVES AND PROTECTED AREAS

National Parks

Snowdonia: 838 square miles (2,170 square kilometres), Gwynedd. The first national park to be designated in Wales (1951).

Pembrokeshire Coast: 225 square miles (583 square kilometres), Dyfed. Designated in 1952.

Brecon Beacons: 519 square miles (1,344 square kilometres), located in parts of four counties – Dyfed, Gwent, Mid Glamorgan and Powys. Designated in 1957, it was the last of the 10 national parks of England and Wales to be established.

Country Parks

(Areas in hectares and years of designation shown in brackets)

Clwyd: Erddig Park (83.1; 1977), Loggerheads (25.5; 1974), Moel Famau (961; 1074), Tŷ Mawr (20.8; 1984), Waun-y-Llyn (29.6; 1972), Wepre Park (66; 1980), Greenfield Valley (24;1989).

Dyfed: Gelli Aur (39.1; 1979), Llys-y-Frân Reservoir (124.7; 1971), Scolton Manor (16.2; 1976), Pembrey (211; 1978)

Gwent: Bryn Bach (510; 1979), Caldicot Castle (20; 1974), Pen-y-Fan Pond (13.8; 1976), Sirhowy Valley (260; 1978), Tredegar Park (40.3; 1976).

Gwynedd: Llyn Padarn (129.6; 1970), Great Orme (291; 1978), Glynllifon (25.8; 1985), Breakwater Quay (20.2; 1989).

Mid Glamorgan: Bryngarw (18.4; 1981), Dare Valley (193; 1973), Parc Cwm Darren (84; 1989).

Powys: Craig-y-Nos (18; 1974).

South Glamorgan: Cosmeston Lakes (87; 1979), Parc Cefn Onn (64; 1972) Porthkerry Park (91.9; 1972).

West Glamorgan: Afan Argoed (56.7; 1972), Clyne Valley (280; 1983), Margam Park (321.5; 1976), Vale of Neath – The Gnoll (86.5; 1989).

Areas of Outstanding Natural Beauty

Anglesey: 83 square miles (215 square kilometres). Designated in 1966.

Clwydian Range: 60.2 square miles (156 square kilometres). Designated in 1985.

Gower: 73 square miles (189 square kilometres). Designated in 1956 – the first AONB in Britain.

Llŷn: 59.8 square miles (155 square kilometres). Designated in 1956.

Wye Valley: 45.2 square miles (117 square kilometres). Designated in 1971, there is a further part in England.

Heritage Coast Areas

(Years of designation shown in brackets)

Gwynedd:		
	Great Orme (1974)	4.4 miles (7 kilometres)
	North Anglesey (1973)	18 miles (29 kilometres)
	Holyhead Mountain (1973)	8 miles (13 kilometres)
	Aberffraw Bay (1973)	4.9 miles (8 kilometres)
	Llŷn (1974)	54.7 miles (88 kilometres)

Dyfed:	Ceredigion Coast (1983)	21.7 miles (34 kilometres)
	St Dogmaels and Moylgrove (1974)	13.7 miles (22 kilometres)
	Dinas Head (1974)	11.2 miles (18 kilometres)
	St David's Peninsula (1974)	51 miles (82 kilometres)
	Marloes and Dale (1974)	26.7 miles (43 kilometres)
	South Pembrokeshire (1974)	41 miles (66 kilometres)
	St Brides Bay (1974)	4.9 miles (8 kilometres)
West Glamorgan:	Gower (1973)	34.2 miles (55 kilometres)
Mid and South Glamorgan:	Glamorgan (1973)	13.7 miles (22 kilometres)

Heritage Coast areas make up over 40 per cent of the Welsh coastline.

National Nature Reserves

Area in hectares

Dyfed:	Allt Rhyd y Groes	70
	Coedmor	33
	Coed Rheidiol	43
	Cors Caron (Tregaron Bog)	792
	Corsydd Llangloffan	40
	Rhos Llawr Cwrt	35
	Skomer	307
	Stackpole	199
	Coed Tŷ Canol	69
Gwent:	Coed y Cerrig	11
	Cwm Clydach	24
	Penhow Woodlands	24
Gwynedd:	Cadair Idris	430
	Ceunant Llennyrch	9
	Coed Camlwyn	64
	Coed Cymerau	26
	Coed Dolgarrog	69
	Coed Glanllwyd	24
	Coed Gorswen	13
	Coed Tremadoc	20
	Coed y Rhygen	28
	Coedydd Aber	170
	Coedydd Maentwrog	68
	Cors Bodeilio	6
	Cors Erddreiniog	66

	Cors Geirch	15
	Cwm Glas Crafnant	15
	Cwm Idwal*	398
	Hafod Garregog	87
	Morfa Dyffryn	202
	Morfa Harlech	884
	Newborough Warren/Ynys Llanddwyn	1,297
	Rhinog	598
	Yr Wyddfa/Snowdon	1,677
	Ynys Enlli/Bardsey	180
Mid Glamorgan:	Kenfig Pool and Dunes	518
Powys:	Cors y Llyn	17
	Craig Cerrig-gleisiad	282
	Craig y Ciliau	64
	Nant Irfon	142
	Ogof Ffynnon Ddu	413
	Rhos Goch	45
	Stanner Rocks	5
West Glamorgan:	Crymlyn Bog	63
	Gower Coast	47
	Whiteford	782
	Oxwich	289
Dyfed/Gwynedd/Powys:	Dyfi	2,095
Gwent/Gloucester:	Lady Park Wood	45

* Cwm Idwal was the first reserve to be designated in Wales, in 1955.

Marine Nature Reserves

Skomer Island   1,500 hectares

There are also two Voluntary Marine Conservation areas in Wales: Bardsey Island and the Menai Strait.

Royal Society for the Protection of Birds Nature Reserves

Clwyd:	Point of Ayr	Gwynedd:	Mawddach Valley
Dyfed:	Dinas/Gwenffrwd		South Stack Cliffs
	Grassholm		Valley Lakes
	Ynys-Hir		

Powys: Dyffryn Wood
                Lake Vyrnwy
West Glamorgan: Cwm Clydach

Local Nature Reserves

(Years of designation shown in brackets)

		Area in hectares
Dyfed:	Carreg Cennen Woodlands (1976)	16
Gwent:	Cleddon Bog (1970)	15
	Coed y Cerrig (1977)	6
Gwynedd:	Coed Dinorwig (1976)	36
	Great Orme's Head (1981)	195
	Traeth Lafan (1979)	2,200
Mid Glamorgan:	Kenfig Pool and Dunes (1978)	575
	Taf Fechan (1975)	40
Powys:	Tal-y-bont Reservoir (1975)	198
South Glamorgan:	Cliff Wood (1970)	5
	Flat Holm (1977)	38
	Glamorgan Canal (1981)	23
	Hermit Wood (1985)	1
	Howardian (1991)	11
West Glamorgan:	Bishops Wood (1976)	14
	Cwmllwyd Wood (1981)	7
	Mumbles Hill (1989)	21
	Pant-y-Sais (1984)	18
	Swansea Canal (1987)	4

Special Protection Areas

(Conservation areas for wild birds under a European Community Directive)

1. Aberdaron coast and Bardsey Island
2. Burry Inlet
3. Cemlyn Bay, Ynys Feurig, The Skerries
4. Dee Estuary
5. Grassholm
6. Holy Island coast
7. Skomer and Skokholm
8. Traeth Lafan (Conwy Bay)

Ramsar Sites

(Wetlands of International Importance)

Burry Inlet	Dee Estuary
Cors Caron	Llyn Idwal
Cors Fochno and the Dyfi	Llyn Tegid (Lake Bala)
Crymlyn Bog	

Sites of Special Scientific Interest (SSSIs)

There are some 870 SSSIs in Wales classified as being of biological interest (about 630), geological interest (about 150) or mixed (about 90). The numbers in each county are shown below. Details may be obtained from the Countryside Council for Wales, Penrhos Road, Bangor, Gwynedd, LL57 2LQ.

Clwyd	59	Mid Glamorgan	34
Dyfed	247	Powys	204
Gwent	65	South Glamorgan	24
Gwynedd	199	West Glamorgan	38

Environmentally Sensitive Areas (ESAs)

ESAs are those which might be damaged or destroyed by existing farming methods. Farmers are encouraged to adopt methods which help conservation and incentive payments are made for this purpose.

There are six ESAs in Wales: Anglesey, the Cambrian Mountains, Clwydian Range, the Llŷn Peninsula, Preseli, Radnor.

Biogenic Reserve

Rhinog (Gwynedd), 598 hectares, designated 1992.

Biogenic reserves are intended to guarantee that Europe preserves a cross-section of various kinds of habitat and ecosystems to safeguard a pool of genetic diversity.

Biosphere Reserve

Dyfi Estuary (Dyfed/Gwynedd/Powys), 2,097 hectares, designated 1977.

Biosphere reserves have been established to conserve examples of major types of ecosystems.

NATIONAL TRAILS

Pembrokeshire Coast: 185 miles (298 km.) from Amroth to Cardigan. Opened in 1970.

Offa's Dyke: 168 miles (270 km.) from Chepstow to Prestatyn. Opened in 1971.

Other Long-distance Trails

Glyndŵr's Way:	120 miles (193 km.) circular route linking Knighton, Welshpool, Machynlleth and Llanidloes.
Landsker Borderlands Trail:	60 miles (96 km.) circular route around South Pembrokeshire.
Taff Trail:	55 miles (88 km.) from Cardiff to Brecon.
Coed Morgannwg Way:	36 miles (58 km.) from Merthyr Tydfil to Margam Country Park near Port Talbot.
Rhymney Valley Ridgeway Walk:	27 miles (43 km.) circular route around southern part of the Rhymney Valley.
Ffordd y Brenin Ridgeway Walk:	21 miles (34 km.) from Mynydd y Gaer near Pencoed to Caerphilly Common.
Afan Valley:	14 miles (22.5 km.) from Blaengwynfi to Pontrhydyfen.
Ogwr Ridgeway Walk:	13 miles (21 km.) from Margam Country Park to Mynydd y Gaer near Pencoed.

LAND USE

Categories of Land Use

Agriculture	81 per cent
Woodland	12 per cent
Urban	7 per cent

Almost 80 per cent of the agricultural land is within the European Community's Less Favoured Area category so qualifying for assistance to counter rural depopulation and maintain farming practices.

Forest and Woodland

Approximately 12 per cent of Wales or some 247,000 hectares is covered by forest and woodland. Some 53 per cent of this woodland is in the hands of the Forestry Commission with the rest privately owned.

Changes in the Forest Cover

From 8,000 to 2,000 BC:	about 90 per cent
During the Roman occupation:	about 50 per cent
By the sixteenth century:	about 10 per cent
By the First World War (1914–18):	about 4 per cent
At present:	about 12 per cent (70 per cent coniferous)

Until the eighteenth century the native woodland of Wales was almost exclusively broadleaf with the yew the only native coniferous tree.

Land Reclamation (1981–1992)

Year	No. of schemes	Total area (hectares)
1981	30	143
1982	25	248
1983	43	167
1984	20	209
1985	36	248
1986	27	153
1987	56	405
1988	69	633
1989	49	324
1990	61	417
1991	76	772
1992	43	210

Since 1966, when land reclamation began after the Aberfan disaster, over 7,500 hectares of land have been reclaimed and in 1993 work was in progress, planned or awaiting approval on a further 4,000 hectares. This land reclamation scheme in Wales is the largest in Europe.

2

POPULATION

POPULATION FROM ROMAN TIMES TO THE 1800s

Most estimates of the population of Roman Britain vary between one and two million, making the population of what is now Wales probably somewhere between 50,000 and 100,000. However, one fairly recent estimate has put the population of Roman Britain at over five million which would indicate a population of about 250,000 in the 'Welsh' part of the Roman province.

At the time of the Edwardian conquest of Wales in the late thirteenth century, it has been estimated that the population was some 300,000 but such was the devastating effect of the Black Death ('Y Farwolaeth Fawr') in the next century, when it seems that between 70,000 and 100,000 could have died, that it took about two hundred years for the population to recover to 250,000–300,000 by the time of the Acts of Union of 1536 and 1543.

During the Civil War of the seventeenth century, a figure of at least 350,000 has been calculated and by the mid-eighteenth century the Welsh population was probably between 450,000 and 490,000.

Until the eighteenth century, Wales was overwhelmingly rural with no large urban centres of population. Estimates show only three towns with populations of over 1,000 in 1300 (Cardiff the largest), nine with over 1,000 in 1400 and only 12 with over 1,000 by 1550. At the latter date three towns seem to have had over 1,500 inhabitants – Carmarthen, 2,150, Brecon, 1,750, Wrexham, 1,515, with Haverfordwest at 1,496. By the late seventeenth century, Wrexham was the largest Welsh town with 3,225 inhabitants, followed by Carmarthen with 2,195, Brecon and Haverfordwest with about 2,000 each, Caernarfon, Cardiff and Swansea with some 1,700 each and Pembroke with some 1,200 inhabitants.

Since 1801, census returns have given accurate population statistics for Wales. By that date, the largest town in Wales was Merthyr Tydfil with over 7,700 inhabitants.

The population of the country became increasingly concentrated in the south-east as industrialization gathered momentum during the nineteenth century. By the beginning of the twentieth century, over 50 per cent of the population was to be found in the two counties of Glamorgan and Monmouth and this distribution persisted through the rest of the century. Rural depopulation became evident from the 1851 census.

THE POPULATION OF WALES, 1801–1991

	1801	1811	1821	1831
Anglesey	33,806	37,045	45,063	48,325
Brecknockshire	32,325	37,735	43,826	47,763
Caernarfonshire	41,521	49,655	58,099	66,818
Cardiganshire	42,956	50,260	57,784	64,780
Carmarthenshire	67,317	77,217	90,239	100,740
Denbighshire	60,299	64,249	76,428	82,665
Flintshire	39,469	45,937	53,893	60,244
Glamorgan	70,879	85,067	102,073	126,612
Merioneth	29,506	30,854	34,382	35,315
Monmouthshire	45,568	62,105	75,801	98,126
Mongomeryshire	48,184	52,184	60,245	66,844
Pembrokeshire	56,280	60,615	73,788	81,425
Radnorshire	19,135	20,417	22,533	24,743
WALES	587,245	673,340	794,154	904,400

	1841	1851	1861	1871
Anglesey	50,891	57,327	54,609	51,040
Brecknockshire	55,603	61,474	61,627	59,901
Caernarfonshire	81,093	87,870	95,694	106,282
Cardiganshire	68,766	70,796	72,245	73,441
Carmarthenshire	106,326	110,632	111,796	115,710
Denbighshire	88,478	92,583	100,078	105,102
Flintshire	66,919	68,156	69,737	76,312
Glamorgan	171,188	231,849	317,753	397,859
Merioneth	39,332	38,843	38,963	46,598
Monmouthshire	134,368	157,418	174,633	195,448
Montgomeryshire	69,607	67,335	66,919	67,623
Pembrokeshire	88,044	94,140	96,278	91,998
Radnorshire	25,458	24,716	25,382	25,430
WALES	1,046,073	1,163,139	1,312,834	1,412,583

	1881	*1891*	*1901*	*1911*	*1921*
Anglesey	51,416	50,098	50,606	50,928	51,744
Brecknockshire	57,746	51,393	54,213	59,287	61,227
Caernarfonshire	119,349	115,886	123,481	122,588	128,183
Cardiganshire	70,270	63,467	61,078	59,879	60,881
Carmarthenshire	124,864	130,566	135,328	160,406	175,073
Denbighshire	111,740	118,979	131,582	144,783	154,842
Flintshire	80,587	77,041	81,485	92,705	106,617
Glamorgan	511,433	687,758	860,510	1,121,840	1,253,728
Merioneth	52,038	48,859	48,852	45,565	45,087
Monmouthshire	211,267	257,593	297,497	394,789	449,547
Montgomeryshire	65,718	58,003	54,901	53,146	51,263
Pembrokeshire	91,824	88,296	87,894	89,960	91,978
Radnorshire	23,528	21,791	23,281	22,590	23,517
WALES	1,571,780	1,771,451	2,012,876	2,420,921	2,656,474

	1931	*1951*	*1961*	*1971*
Anglesey	49,029	50,660	51,705	59,761
Brecknockshire	57,775	56,508	55,185	53,377
Caernarfonshire	120,829	124,140	121,767	123,064
Cardiganshire	55,184	53,278	53,648	54,882
Carmarthenshire	179,100	172,073	168,008	162,564
Denbighshire	157,648	170,726	174,151	185,192
Flintshire	112,889	145,279	150,082	175,769
Glamorgan	1,229,065	1,202,581	1,229,707	1,258,730
Merioneth	43,201	41,465	38,310	35,330
Monmouthshire	431,610	425,105	444,700	462,171
Montgomeryshire	48,473	45,990	44,165	43,119
Pembrokeshire	87,206	90,906	94,124	98,968
Radnorshire	21,323	19,993	18,471	18,279
WALES	2,593,332	2,598,675	2,644,023	2,731,204

In 1974 the 13 old counties of Wales were replaced by eight new ones in local government reorganization.

	1981		1991	
	Number	*%*	*Number*	*%*
Clwyd	385,600	14.0	408,090	14.4
Dyfed	323,041	11.7	343,543	12.1
Gwent	436,506	15.9	432,063	15.6
Gwynedd	222,279	8.1	235,452	8.3
Mid Glamorgan	533,574	19.4	534,101	18.8
Powys	108,125	3.9	117,467	4.1
South Glamorgan	376,743	13.7	392,780	13.9
West Glamorgan	363,772	13.2	361,428	12.7
WALES	2,749,640	(79.5% born in Wales)	2,835,073	(77.2% born in Wales)

Percentages do not add up to 100 per cent because of individual rounding.

THE POPULATIONS OF WELSH DISTRICTS IN 1991

Clwyd
Alyn and Deeside	73,494
Colwyn	55,070
Delyn	67,850
Glyndŵr	41,870
Rhuddlan	54,555
Wrexham Maelor	<u>115,521</u>
	480,090

59.6% born in Wales

Dyfed
Carmarthen	55,119
Ceredigion	63,094
Dinefwr	38,547
Llanelli	74,698
Preseli Pembrokeshire	70,193
South Pembrokeshire	<u>41,892</u>
	343,543

74.6% born in Wales

Gwent
Blaenau Gwent	76,122
Islwyn	66,177
Monmouth	76,068
Newport	133,318
Torfaen	<u>90,527</u>
	442,212

81.8% born in Wales

Gwynedd
Aberconwy	52,972
Arfon	53,296
Dwyfor	27,070
Meirionydd	32,965
Ynys Môn/Anglesey	<u>69,149</u>
	235,452

67.4% born in Wales

Mid Glamorgan		Powys	
Cynon Valley	65,171	Brecknock	41,145
Merthyr Tydfil	59,317	Montgomery	52,692
Ogwr	132,442	Radnor	23,630
Rhondda	78,344		117,467
Rhymney Valley	103,400		
Taff Ely	93,427		
	534,101		

89.2% born in Wales   60.5% born in Wales

South Glamorgan		West Glamorgan	
Cardiff	279,055	Lliw Valley	63,099
Vale of Glamorgan	113,725	Neath	65,040
	392,780	Port Talbot	51,023
		Swansea	181,906
			361,428

78.2% born in Wales   86.5% born in Wales

AGE DISTRIBUTION OF THE POPULATION
(in thousands)

	1871	1901	1931	1961	1981	1991
Under 14	519.6	684.4	690.2	618.1	573.1	542.8
15–59	775.2	1,191.5	1,625.2	1,560.7	1,601.1	1,646.7
60 and over	117.8	137.0	277.9	465.2	575.8	645.6
	1,412.6	2,012.9	2,593.3	2,644.0	2,750.0	2,835.1

DEATHS, BIRTHS, MARRIAGES AND DIVORCES, FROM 1980

	Deaths	Legitimate live births	Illegitimate live births	Marriages	Divorces
1980	35,149	33,461	3,896	21,071	9,183
1981	35,010	31,820	4,022	19,760	9,070
1982	35,152	31,106	4,614	19,029	9,326
1983	35,242	30,349	5,145	19,981	9,475
1984	33,652	29,835	6,026	19,174	9,969
1985	35,536	29,807	6,964	19,148	10,618

	Deaths	Legitimate live births	Illegitimate live births	Marriages	Divorces
1986	34,712	29,215	7,823	19,513	10,096
1987	33,919	29,988	8,828	19,528	9,864
1988	33,981	28,711	10,113	19,309	10,107
1989	35,134	27,301	10,718	19,453	10,628
1990	33,963	27,466	11,400	18,438	10,785
1991	34,636	25,780	12,229	16,638	10,331
1992	33,792	24,769	12,754	n/a	10,750

POPULATIONS OF THE LARGEST CITIES AND TOWNS, 1991

(Approximate figures)

Cardiff	269,000	Port Talbot	40,000	Ebbw Vale	21,000
Swansea	177,000	Pontypool	36,000	Buckley	17,000
Newport	130,000	Aberdare	32,000	Prestatyn	16,000
Neath	50,000	Bridgend	32,000	Abergavenny	15,000
Barry	47,000	Pontypridd	30,000	Bargoed	15,000
Llanelli	46,000	Colwyn Bay	27,000	Carmarthen	15,000
Cwmbran	45,000	Rhyl	23,000	Connah's Quay	15,000
Wrexham	41,000	Maesteg	22,000	Llandudno	15,000
Merthyr Tydfil	40,000				

3

GOVERNMENT AND POLITICS
LAW COURTS • THE POLICE

DATES OF SIGNIFICANCE AND INTEREST

1542   The first 27 MPs representing Wales were returned to the House of Commons.

1680   The first Welsh Speaker of the House of Commons was Sir William Williams, MP for Chester.

1685   The first Speaker of the House of Commons representing a Welsh constituency was Sir John Trevor, MP for Denbigh.

1727   A majority of Whig MPs was returned for Welsh constituencies for the first time.

1830   During this year the last general election was held in which not a single seat in Wales was contested.

   The Courts of Great Sessions were abolished making the legal system as well as the political system in Wales identical with that in England.

1841   William Edwards standing as a Chartist candidate in Monmouth Boroughs did not receive a single vote – the only time this has happened to a Parliamentary candidate in Wales.

1852   Walter Coffin became the first Nonconformist MP to be elected in Wales (for Cardiff Boroughs).

1859   This year saw the most unopposed candidates in a general election in Wales since the 1832 Reform Act – 28 in 32 constituencies.

1868   A majority of Liberal (Radical) MPs were returned for the first time in Wales.

1885   The first general election was held in which the Liberal Party had candidates in every Welsh constituency.

1886   The first Welsh working-class MP was elected – William Abraham ('Mabon'), Liberal, representing Rhondda.

1888   A Welsh Parliamentary Party was formed by Liberal MPs.

1898	The first Labour councillor elected in Wales was David Williams, Swansea Town Council.
1900	The first Labour MP in Britain was elected – Keir Hardie became one of the two MPs for Merthyr Tydfil.
1905	David Lloyd George first entered the Cabinet as President of the Board of Trade.
1906	No Conservative MPs were elected in Wales for the first and only time.
1907	A Welsh Parliamentary Committee was established for dealing with the commmittee stage of bills concerned only with Wales.
1910	The January election was the first one in which all Welsh seats were contested.
1911	A short-lived Liberal-dominated Welsh Nationalist League was founded in Caernarfon to campaign for Welsh home rule in a federal UK parliament.
1914	E. T. John, Liberal MP for East Denbighshire, unsuccessfully introduced a Welsh Home Rule Bill.
1916	David Lloyd George became the UK's first Welsh Prime Minister.
1918	The University of Wales became represented by its own MP.
	The first woman parliamentary candidate in Wales was Mrs Millicent Mackenzie contesting the University of Wales seat.
	Home Rule for Wales was included in the Labour Party election manifesto.
1922	A Communist Party candidate stood for election for the first time anywhere in Britain at a by-election in Caerphilly.
1924	James Ramsay MacDonald, MP for Aberavon, became the first Labour Prime Minister.
1925	Plaid Genedlaethol Cymru – later Plaid Cymru – was founded.
1929	A Plaid Cymru candidate first contested a Parliamentary seat (Caernarfonshire).
1929	This was the first general election in which all seats in Wales were contested by the Conservatives.
1929	Megan Lloyd George, Liberal, representing Anglesey, became the first woman MP to be elected in Wales.
1930	The Conservative Party established an area organization in Wales.
1932	Self-government became the official policy of Plaid Cymru.
1937	South Wales Regional Council of Labour formed.
1944	The first Welsh Day debate took place in the House of Commons.
1945	The last general election took place in Wales in which a candidate was returned unopposed – Will John (Labour), Rhondda West.
	In the Neath by-election, a Trotskyist candidate stood for the first time in a British parliamentary election.

1949   The Welsh Republican Movement was founded in Cardiff.

1950   The Labour Party contested all seats in Wales for the first time.

The University of Wales ceased to be represented by its own MP.

Three women MPs were elected – the largest number ever in Wales: Megan Lloyd George (Liberal), Anglesey; Dorothy Rees (Labour), Barry; and Eirene White (Labour), Flint East.

1951   The first Minister for Welsh Affairs was appointed – Sir David Maxwell Fyfe.

1956   A petition for a Welsh Parliament with 250,000 signatures was presented to the House of Commons.

1957   The first Minister of State for Welsh Affairs was appointed – Lord Brecon.

1958   The first Welsh life peer was Granville West, former Labour MP for Pontypool.

1960   The Welsh Grand Committee was established.

1964   The office of Secretary of State for Wales was created and the Welsh Office was established. Welsh Question Time was introduced in the House of Commons.

The first woman MP from Wales to be given a ministerial appointment was Mrs Eirene White (Labour) who became Parliamentary Under Secretary at the Colonial Office.

1966   The first Plaid Cymru MP was elected – Gwynfor Evans representing Carmarthen.

In the general election, a record number of Labour MPs was returned in Wales – 32 from 36 constituencies.

An autonomous Welsh Liberal Party was created.

1966,   In the general elections of these two years, there were eight Communist
1970   Party candidates on both occasions – the maximum ever to stand in Wales.

1970   The last two NUM-sponsored MPs in Wales were elected – S. O. Davies (Merthyr Tydfil) and Elfed Davies (Rhondda East).

The first general election was held in which all Welsh seats were contested by Plaid Cymru.

The first National Front candidate stood in Wales.

1974   Following the February general election this year, MPs were allowed to take the oath in Welsh as well as in English and 11 of the 36 MPs for Wales did so.

In the October general election, Alec Jones (Labour), Rhondda, was elected by the largest majority ever recorded in Wales – 34,481.

1976   The Welsh Regional Office of the European Community was opened in Cardiff.

1979	In the devolution referendum, a Welsh Assembly was rejected by four to one.

1979   In the devolution referendum, a Welsh Assembly was rejected by four to one.

A Select Committee on Welsh Affairs was established.

A record number of 67 deposits was lost in this year's general election.

This was the first general election with Green (Ecology) Party candidates in Wales.

The first elections for the European Parliament were held: Wales had four MEPs.

1980   First public session of the Select Committee on Welsh Affairs held in Cardiff Castle.

1983   A record number of Conservative MPs this century was returned in Wales – 14 from 38 constituencies.

Neil Kinnock (Islwyn) was elected the first Welsh leader of the Labour Party.

1991   A joint Plaid Cymru–Green Party candidate stood for the first time in Wales in a by-election in Monmouth.

1992   A record number of 180 candidates stood in the general election in Wales, among them a record 24 women candidates but only one woman, Ann Clwyd (Labour), Cynon Valley, was elected.

1992   A record number of four Plaid Cymru MPs was elected including one Plaid Cymru/Green MP.

1992   Dafydd Elis Thomas became the first Plaid Cymru life peer.

1993   Welsh Grand Committee met in Cardiff for the first time.

The first three Welsh representatives on the European Community's Committee of the Regions were selected.

1994   Wayne David was elected Leader of the Labour European Parliamentary Group and Neil Kinnock became a European Commissioner.

Prestatyn-born John Prescott was elected deputy leader of the Labour Party.

PARTY LEADERS AND PRIME MINISTERS

Prime Ministers Representing Welsh Constituencies

David Lloyd George (Liberal) Caernarfon Boroughs: Prime Minister, 1916–22
James Ramsay MacDonald (Labour) Aberavon: Prime Minister, 1924
James Callaghan (Labour) Cardiff South-East: Prime Minister, 1976–79

Labour Party Leaders Representing Welsh Constituencies

Keir Hardie:	MP for Merthyr Tydfil 1900–1915. Chairman of the Parliamentary Labour Party 1906–1908.
James Ramsay MacDonald:	MP for Aberavon, 1922–29. Leader of the Parliamentary Labour Party, 1922–31.
James Callaghan:	MP for Cardiff South-East and Penarth, 1945–87. Leader of the Parliamentary Labour Party, 1976–80.
Michael Foot:	MP for Ebbw Vale then Blaenau Gwent, 1960–92. Leader of the Parliamentary Labour Party, 1980–83.
Neil Kinnock:	MP for Bedwellty then Islwyn from 1970. Leader of the Parliamentary Labour Party, 1983–92.

Liberal Party Leaders Representing Welsh Constituencies

David Lloyd George:	MP for Caernarfon Boroughs, 1890–1945. Leader of the Liberal Party, 1926–31.
Clement Davies:	MP for Montgomery, 1929–62. Leader of the Liberal Party, 1945–56.

Welsh Deputy Party Leaders

Labour Party

James Griffiths:	1955–58
Aneurin Bevan:	1959
Roy Jenkins:	1970 and 1971
John Prescott:	1994–

Liberal Party

Lady Megan Lloyd George: 1949–51

Conservative Party

Sir Geoffrey Howe: Deputy Prime Minister 1989–90

Welsh Labour Party Leaders in House of Lords

Lord Cledwyn of Penrhos:	1982–92
Lord Richard:	1992–

Welsh Liberal Democrat Leader in House of Lords

Lord Jenkins of Hillhead: 1988–

THE WELSH ELECTORATE SINCE THE FIRST REFORM ACT, 1832

Years shown are ones in which general elections were held. Figures in brackets show the percentage voting where seats were contested.

1832	41,763	(76.2)	1922	1,236,653	(79.4)
1835	42,426	(75.1)	1923	1,259,208	(77.3)
1837	49,706	(71.1)	1924	1,289,924	(80.0)
1841	54,683	(68.7)	1929	1,602,138	(82.4)
1847	55,251	(65.1)	1931	1,629,529	(79.3)
1852	54,858	(74.5)	1935	1,692,821	(76.4)
1857	55,686	(68.1)	1945	1,810,046	(75.7)
1859	56,033	(73.1)	1950	1,802,356	(84.8)
1865	61,656	(76.0)	1951	1,812,664	(84.4)
1868	127,386	(74.8)	1955	1,801,217	(76.6)
1874	137,143	(71.3)	1959	1,805,586	(82.6)
1880	149,841	(78.3)	1964	1,805,454	(80.1)
1885	282,242	(82.8)	1966	1,801,735	(79.0)
1886	282,242	(74.5)	1970	1,958,778	(77.4)
1892	314,647	(75.6)*	1974 (Feb.)	1,998,764	(80.6)
1895	322,784	(79.3)	1974 (Oct.)	2,008,744	(76.6)
1900	340,290	(76.4)	1979	2,061,108	(79.4)
1906	387,535	(82.6)*	1983	2,113,855	(76.1)
1910 (Jan.)	425,764	(84.9)*	1987	2,151,352	(78.9)
1910 (Dec.)	425,764	(78.3)*	1992	2,195,029	(79.7)
1918	1,170,048	(65.9)			

* The turnout of voters in general elections in Wales was higher than the UK as a whole in every year except for the four indicated.

After 1832, there were further extensions of the franchise in 1868, 1886, 1918, 1929 and 1970.

UK Poll Comparisons (1992)

Wales	79.7%	Northern Ireland	67.0%
England	75.4%	United Kingdom	75.3%
Scotland	75.1%		

Votes Cast in Wales in 1992

Electorate: 2,195,029

Votes cast: 1,748,677
Labour: 862,663 (49.5%), 38 candidates, 27 elected
Conservative: 499,577 (28.6%), 38 candidates, 6 elected
Liberal Democrat: 217,457 (12.4%), 38 candidates, 1 elected
Plaid Cymru: 154,439 (8.8%), 35 candidates, 4 elected
Others: 11,590 (0.7%), 31 candidates, 0 elected

UNOPPOSED ELECTIONS

Unopposed Elections Before 1832

In the 71 general elections that took place between the Acts of Union and the Reform Act of 1832, there were 16 in which no seats at all were contested in Wales as far as can be ascertained from the incomplete records for early parliaments. The maximum number of seats contested in any election during these three centuries was 14 in 1727.

Unopposed Elections Since 1832

(Total Welsh constituencies shown in brackets)

1832	22 (32)	1874	12 (33)	1910 (Dec)	11 (34)
1835	22 (32)	1880	10 (33)	1918	11 (36)
1837	17 (32)	1885	4 (34)	1922	4 (36)
1841	24 (32)	1886	12 (34)	1923	5 (36)
1847	27 (32)	1892	4 (34)	1924	8 (36)
1852	21 (32)	1895	2 (34)	1929	0 (36)
1857	27 (32)	1900	11 (34)	1931	6 (36)
1859	28 (32)	1906	12 (34)	1935	11 (36)
1865	27 (32)	1910 (Jan)	0 (34)	1945	1 (36)
1868	14 (33)				

There have been no uncontested parliamentary elections in Wales since 1945.

The University of Wales seat is included in the total number of constituencies from 1918 to 1945.

SPEAKERS OF THE HOUSE OF COMMONS FROM WALES

Sir William Williams (MP for Chester)   1680
Sir John Trevor (MP for Denbigh Boroughs)   1685

Robert Harley (MP for Radnor Boroughs)   1701
George Thomas (MP for Cardiff West)   1976

MINISTERS FOR WELSH AFFAIRS

(From 28 October 1951)

Sir David Maxwell Fyfe: 1951–54 ⎫
Gwilym Lloyd George: 1954–57 ⎬ Jointly with the Home Office
Henry Brooke: 1957–62 ⎭
Sir Keith Joseph: 1962–64 Jointly with Housing and Local Government.

All the above ministers were Conservative.

SECRETARIES OF STATE FOR WALES

(From 18 October 1964)

James Griffiths (Labour):	1964–66
Cledwyn Hughes (Labour):	1966–68
George Thomas (Labour):	1968–70
Peter Thomas (Conservative):	1970–74
John Morris (Labour):	1974–79
Nicholas Edwards (Conservative):	1979–87
Peter Walker (Conservative):	1987–90
David Hunt (Conservative):	1990–93
John Redwood (Conservative):	1993–

DEVOLUTION

Result of the referendum held on 1 March 1979, on the establishment of an elected Welsh Assembly in Cardiff.

Question: Do you want the provisions of the Wales Act, 1978, put into effect?

	Yes	*No*	*Percentage poll*
Clwyd	31,384	114,119	51.62
Dyfed	44,849	114,947	65.43
Gwent	21,369	155,389	55.83
Gwynedd	37,363	71,157	65.40

Mid Glamorgan	46,747	184,196	59.40
Powys	9,843	43,507	66.87
South Glamorgan	21,830	144,186	59.48
West Glamorgan	29,663	128,834	58.22
TOTALS	243,048	956,335	58.30
	(20.3%)	(79.7%)	

THE WELSH OFFICE

Cathays Park, Cardiff, CF1 3NQ.
Gwydyr House, Whitehall, London, SW1A 2EB.

Ministerial Responsibilities

Secretary of State: Overall responsibillity for the whole department, with a special interest in economic matters; agriculture; industry; regional policy; Welsh Development Agency; Citizens' Charter; local government reorganization; Rural Initiative; environment policy; Programme for the Valleys; financial and revenue support grant issues; European Community issues; consitutional issues; Cardiff Bay; West Wales Task Force.

Minister of State: Education; training; enterprise; small businesses; rural affairs; tourism; transport; Welsh language; arts and culture; broadcasting (Welsh interests); Development Board for Rural Wales; CADW; historic buildings and ancient monuments; Countryside Council for Wales; national parks; forestry; conservation; youth issues including the Wales Youth Agency; women's issues; general issues relating to public appointments.

Parliamentary Under-Secretary of State: health; community care; personal social services; housing; Land Authority for Wales; Housing for Wales; fisheries; water and environmental protection; general issues involving local government; sport; land-use planning; energy; urban affairs.

Extension of Welsh Office Responsibilities

1965   Housing and local government; roads; 'oversight' of agriculture, fisheries and food; education; health; transport; labour and the Board of Trade.

1968   Historic buildings; water.

1969	Ancient monuments; health; some agriculture, some welfare services.
1970	Planning; primary and secondary education.
1975	Virtually all the powers of the Department of Industry.
1978	Remaining agriculture and fishing responsibilities; further and higher education; negotiating directly with the Treasury for the Block Grant for local authorities.
1992	University education; special protection areas.
1993	Financing the arts; industrial training.

In 1974 the Welsh Office was upgraded, its head becoming a Permanent Secretary (Grade I) instead of a Permanent Under-Secretary (Grade II).

PARLIAMENTARY COMMITTEES

Welsh Grand Committee (Established 1960)

This is a standing committee of all 38 MPs representing Welsh constituencies, plus up to five other MPs, which meets four or five times a year, normally in London. It considers such matters relating entirely to Wales which are referred to it by the House of Commons, including all public bills relating exclusively to Wales. It can pass motions but cannot bind the House of Commons itself.

Select Committee on Welsh Affairs (Established 1979)

This is a departmental committee of 11 members (six Conservative, three Labour, one Liberal Democrat and one Plaid Cymru in 1994) which meets about 20 times a year, usually in London, to scrutinize the policies and administration of the executive and of associated public bodies. It is composed only of back-bench MPs with the party balance reflecting that of the House of Commons. It can compel witnesses to attend its meetings if necessary and it issues a number of annual reports.

Chairs of the Select Committee

| Leo Abse | 1979–81 | Gareth Wardell | 1984– |
| Donald Anderson | 1981–83 | | |

WELSH QUESTION TIME

This normally takes place every fourth Monday when Parliament is in session and lasts for some 40 minutes after prayers at 2.20. MPs submit their questions in a ballot two weeks in advance and those successful in the ballot are allowed to put an additional supplementary question to the Welsh Office minister replying. Welsh Question Time was introduced after the setting up of the Welsh Office in 1964.

QUANGOS IN WALES

There are about 100 'quasi-autonomous non-governmental organizations' (quangos) in Wales which carry out functions assigned to them by the government. They are permanent, non-elected bodies whose members – some paid, some unpaid – are appointed by the Secretary of State for Wales and are not part of any government department or public corporation but which are publicly funded. In the mid-1990s, Welsh quangos had a total annual budget of over £2 billion.

In 1992, quangos in Wales had 1,679 members – 1,397 males and 282 females – and employed over 57,000 people.

Examples of Welsh quangos are the Cardiff Bay Development Corporation, the Development Board for Rural Wales, the Higher Education Funding Council, the Land Authority for Wales, the Sports Council for Wales, Tai Cymru (Housing for Wales), the Wales Tourist Board, the Welsh Development Agency and the Welsh Language Board.

WELSH REPRESENTATION IN THE HOUSE OF COMMONS

From 1542:   27 MPs
except for 1653: 6 MPs (Barebone's Parliament), all nominated, not elected, and 1656 (Cromwell's Parliament) and 1659: 28 MPs
From 1832:   32 MPs
From 1867:   33 MPs
From 1885:   34 MPs
From 1918:   35 MPs
From 1950:   36 MPs
From 1983:   38 MPs

In addition, the University of Wales was represented by its own MP from 1918 to 1950 when all university seats were abolished.

Under current legislation, Wales may not be represented in the House of Commons by less than 35 MPs.

Boundary Commission for Wales

The address of the Boundary Commission for Wales is St Catherine's House, 10 Kingsway, London, WC2B 65P.

The Commission is required by law to keep both Westminster and European parliamentary constituencies under review.

The Parliamentary Commissioner (Ombudsman)

The Commissioner investigates complaints referred to him by MPs where someone claims to have suffered an injustice as a result of maladministration by a government department and certain non-government departments.

The address of the Ombudsman is Church House, Great Smith Street, London, SW1P 3BW.

GENERAL ELECTION RESULTS IN WALES THIS CENTURY
(University of Wales MPs excluded from the lists)

1900
Liberal	26
Conservative	6
Labour	1
Lib/Lab	_1
	34

1918
Liberal Coalition	18
Labour	10
Conservative	3
Liberal	2
Conservative Coalition	1
National Democratic and Labour Party	_1
	35

1906
Liberal	28
Lib/Lab	4
Independent Lib/Lab	1
Labour	_1
	34

1922
Labour	18
National Liberal	8
Conservative	6
Liberal	2
Independent Labour	_1
	35

1910 (January)
Liberal	27
Labour	5
Conservative	_2
	34

1923
Labour	19
Liberal	11
Conservative	4
Independent Labour	_1
	35

1910 (December)
Liberal	26
Labour	5
Conservative	_3
	34

1924
Labour	16
Liberal	10
Conservative	_9
	35

1929

Labour	25
Liberal	9
Conservative	1
	35

1931

Labour	15
Liberal	8
Conservative	6
National Liberal	4
National Labour	1
Independent Labour	1
	35

1935

Labour	18
Conservative	6
Independent Liberal	4
National Liberal	3
Liberal	2
National Labour	1
National	1
	35

1945

Labour	27
Liberal	4
Conservative	3
National Liberal and Conservative	1

1950

Labour	27
Liberal	5
Conservative	3
National Liberal and Conservative	1

1951

Labour	27
Conservative	5
Liberal	3
National Liberal and Conservative	1
	36

1955

Labour	27
Conservative	5
Liberal	3
National Liberal and Conservative	1
	36

1959

Labour	27
Conservative	6
Liberal	2
National Liberal and Conservative	1
	36

1964

Labour	28
Conservative	6
Liberal	2
	36

1966

Labour	32
Conservative	3
Liberal	1
	36

1970		*1983*	
Labour	27	Labour	20
Conservative	7	Conservative	14
Liberal	1	Liberal	2
Independent Labour	1	Plaid Cymru	2
	36		38

1974 (February)		*1987*	
Labour	24	Labour	24
Conservative	8	Conservative	8
Liberal	2	Plaid Cymru	3
Plaid Cymru	2	Social Democrat/Liberal Alliance	3
	36		38

1974 (October)		*1992*	
Labour	23	Labour	27
Conservative	8	Conservative	6
Plaid Cymru	3	Plaid Cymru	3
Liberal	2	Plaid Cymru/Green	1
	36	Liberal Democrat	1
			38

1979	
Labour	21
Conservative	11
Plaid Cymru	2
Liberal	1
The Speaker	1
	36

University of Wales MPs

1918 Coalition Liberal	1,066 electorate, 85.8% poll
1922 National Liberal	1,441 electorate, 87.2 % poll
1923 Christian Pacifist (Labour)	1,922 electorate, 83.1% poll
1924 Liberal	2,252 electorate, 79.0% poll
1929 Liberal	3,623 electorate, 74.4% poll
1931 Liberal	5,121 electorate, 61.4% poll
1935 Liberal	7,325 electorate, 62.3% poll
1945 Liberal	11,847 electorate, 58.5% poll

Note: University of Wales MPs were elected by a system of proportional representation.

GENERAL ELECTION RESULTS, 1992

Welsh Constituencies, MPs and Majorities

General Election, 9 April 1992 (Electorates in brackets)

		Majority	*%Poll*
Aberavon (51,650)	John Morris (Labour)	21,310	(77.6)
Alyn and Deeside (60,477)	Barry Jones (Labour)	7,851	(80.1)
Blaenau Gwent (55,638)	Llewellyn Smith (Labour)	30,067	(78.1)
Brecon and Radnor (51,509)	Jonathan Evans (Conservative)	130	(85.9)
Bridgend (58,531)	Wyn Griffiths (Labour)	7,326	(80.4)
Caernarfon (46,468)	Dafydd Wigley (Plaid Cymru)	14,476	(78.2)
Caerphilly (64,529)	Ronald Davies (Labour)	22,672	(77.2)
Cardiff Central (57,716)	Jon Owen Jones (Labour)	3,465	(74.4)
Cardiff North (56,721)	Gwilym Jones (Conservative)	2,969	(84.2)
Cardiff South and Penarth (61,484)	Alun Michael (Labour)	10,425	(77.3)
Cardiff West (58,898)	Rhodri Morgan (Labour)	9,291	(77.6)
Carmarthen (68,887)	Dr Alan Williams (Labour)	2,922	(82.7)
Ceredigion and Pembroke North (66,180)	Cynog Dafis (Plaid Cymru/Green)	3,193	(77.4)
Clwyd North West (67,351)	Rod Richards (Conservative)	6,050	(78.6)
Clwyd South West (60,607)	Martyn Jones (Labour)	4,941	(81.5)
Conwy (53,576)	Sir Wyn Roberts (Conservative)	995	(78.9)
Cynon Valley (49,695)	Ann Clwyd (Labour)	21,364	(76.5)
Delyn (66,591)	David Hanson (Labour)	2,039	(83.4)
Gower (57,231)	Gareth Wardell (Labour)	7,018	(81.8)
Islwyn (51,079)	Neil Kinnock (Labour)	24,728	(81.5)
Llanelli (65,058)	Denzil Davies (Labour)	19,270	(77.8)
Meirionnydd Nant Conwy (32,413)	Elfyn Llwyd (Plaid Cymru)	4,613	(81.5)
Merthyr Tydfil and Rhymney (58,430)	Ted Rowlands (Labour)	26,713	(75.8)
Monmouth (59,147)	Roger Evans (Conservative)	3,204	(86.1)
Montgomery (41,386)	Alex Carlile (Liberal Democrat)	5,209	(79.9)
Neath (56,392)	Peter Hain (Labour)	23,975	(80.6)
Newport East (51,603)	Roy Hughes (Labour)	9,899	(81.2)
Newport West (54,871)	Paul Flynn (Labour)	7,779	(82.8)
Ogmore (52,195)	Ray Powell (Labour)	23,827	(80.6)
Pembroke (73,187)	Nick Ainger (Labour)	755	(82.9)
Pontypridd (61,685)	Dr Kim Howells (Labour)	19,797	(79.3)
Rhondda (59,955)	Allan Rogers (Labour)	28,816	(76.6)
Swansea East (59,196)	Donald Anderson (Labour)	23,482	(75.6)
Swansea West (59,785)	Alan Williams (Labour)	9,478	(73.3)

Torfaen (61,104)	Paul Murphy (Labour)	20,754	(77.5)
Vale of Glamorgan (66,672)	Walter Sweeney (Conservative)	19	(81.9)
Wrexham (63,720)	Dr John Marek (Labour)	6,716	(80.7)
Ynys Môn/Anglesey (53,412)	Ieuan Wyn Jones (Plaid Cymru)	1,106	(80.6)

Welsh Parliamentary Constituencies Ranked by Majorities

1.	Llewellyn Smith (Labour) Blaenau Gwent	30,067
2.	Allan Rogers (Labour) Rhondda	28,816
3.	Ted Rowlands (Labour) Merthyr Tydfil and Rhymney	26,713
4.	Neil Kinnock (Labour) Islwyn	24,728
5.	Peter Hain (Labour) Neath	23,975
6.	Ray Powell (Labour) Ogmore	23,827
7.	Donald Anderson (Labour) Swansea East	23,482
8.	Ron Davies (Labour) Caerphilly	22,672
9.	Ann Clwyd (Labour) Cynon Valley	21,364
10.	John Morris (Labour) Aberavon	21,310
11.	Paul Murphy (Labour) Torfaen	20,754
12.	Dr Kim Howells (Labour) Pontypridd	19,797
13.	Denzil Davies (Labour) Llanelli	19,270
14.	Dafydd Wigley (Plaid Cymru) Caernarfon	14,476
15.	Alun Michael (Labour) Cardiff South and Penarth	10,425
16.	Roy Hughes (Labour) Newport East	9,899
17.	Alan Williams (Labour) Swansea West	9,478
18.	Rhodri Morgan (Labour) Cardiff West	9,291
19.	Barry Jones (Labour) Alyn and Deeside	7,851
20.	Paul Flynn (Labour) Newport West	7,779
21.	Win Griffiths (Labour) Bridgend	7,326
22.	Gareth Wardell (Labour) Gower	7,018
23.	Dr John Marek (Labour) Wrexham	6,716
24.	Rod Richards (Conservative) Clwyd North West	6,050
25.	Alex Carlile (Liberal Democrat) Montgomery	5,209
26.	Martyn Jones (Labour) Clwyd South West	4,941
27.	Elfyn Llwyd (Plaid Cymru) Meirionnydd Nant Conwy	4,613
28.	Jon Owen Jones (Labour) Cardiff Central	3,465
29.	Roger Evans (Conservative) Monmouth	3,204
30.	Cynog Dafis (Plaid Cymru/Green) Ceredigion and Pembroke North	3,193
31.	Gwilym Jones (Conservative) Cardiff North	2,969
32.	Dr Alan Williams (Labour) Carmarthen	2,922
33.	David Hanson (Labour) Delyn	2,039

34.	Ieuan Wyn Jones (Plaid Cymru) Ynys Môn/Anglesey	1,106
35.	Sir Wyn Roberts (Conservative) Conwy	995
36.	Nick Ainger (Labour) Pembroke	755
37.	Jonathan Evans (Conservative) Brecon and Radnor	130
38.	Walter Sweeney (Conservative) Vale of Glamorgan	19

Largest and Smallest Majorities by Party

Labour	Largest – Llewellyn Smith (Blaenau Gwent)	30,067
	Smallest – Nick Ainger (Pembroke)	755
Conservative	Largest – Rod Richards (Clwyd North West)	6,050
	Smallest – Walter Sweeney (Vale of Glamorgan)	19
Plaid Cymru	Largest – Dafydd Wigley (Caernarfon)	14,476
	Smallest – Ieuan Wyn Jones (Ynys Môn/Anglesey)	1,106
Liberal Democrat	One seat only – Alex Carlile (Montgomery)	5,209

Largest and Smallest Electorates (1992)

Largest: Pembroke – 73,187
Smallest: Meirionnydd Nant Conwy – 32,413

Highest and Lowest Polls (1992)

Highest: Monmouth – 86.06%
Lowest: Swansea West – 73.34%

Lost deposits in 1992

Of the 180 candidates who contested the 38 Welsh seats, 52 failed to obtain 5 per cent of the vote and so lost their £500 deposits.

Deposits lost by parties

Plaid Cymru	20	Plaid Cymru/Green	3
Green Party	10	Liberal Democrats	1
Natural Law Party	10	Others	8

No Labour Party or Conservative Party candidates lost their deposits.

Sponsored MPs from Wales

Donald Anderson (Swansea East)	Rail, Maritime and Transport Workers
Ann Clwyd (Cynon Valley)	Transport and General Workers' Union
Ron Davies (Caerphilly)	UNISON
Roy Hughes (Newport East)	Transport and General Workers' Union
Barry Jones (Alyn and Deeside)	Transport and General Workers' Union
Martyn Jones (Clwyd South East)	Transport and General Workers' Union
Dr John Marek (Wrexham)	Rail, Maritime and Transport Workers
Alun Michael (Cardiff South and Penarth)	Co-operative Party
John Morris (Aberavon)	General, Municipal and Boilermakers and Allied Trade Unions
Paul Murphy (Torfaen)	Transport and General Workers' Union
Ray Powell (Ogmore)	Union of Shop, Distributive and Allied Workers
Alan Rogers (Rhondda)	UNISON
Ted Rowlands (Merthyr Tydfil and Rhymney)	Union of Shop Distributive and Allied Workers
Gareth Wardell (Gower)	General, Municipal and Boilermakers and Allied Trade Unions

SMALLEST MAJORITIES AND FEWEST VOTES SINCE 1832

Smallest Majorities in Parliamentary Elections in Wales this century (under 100)

1974 (February)	G. G. Jones (Labour) Carmarthen	3
1910 (December)	Hon. W. G. A. Ormsby-Gore (Conservative) Denbigh	9
1910 (January)	Hon. W. G. A. Ormsby-Gore (Conservative) Denbigh	10
1923	C. H. L. Davies (Labour) University of Wales	10
1910 (January)	Sir J. D. Rees (Liberal) Montgomery Boroughs	13
1910 (January)	C. L. D. V. Llewelyn (Conservative) Radnorshire	14
1900	General J. W. Laurie (Conservative) Pembroke and Haverfordwest Boroughs	15
1992	Walter Sweeney (Conservative) Vale of Glamorgan	19
1910 (December)	Sir Frank Edwards (Liberal) Radnorshire	42
1922	T. A. Lewis (National Liberal) University of Wales	46
1928 (by-election)	W. N. Jones (Liberal) Carmarthen	47
1910 (December)	E. Pryce-Jones (Liberal) Montgomery Boroughs	54
1987	R. Livsey (Liberal) Brecon and Radnor	56

| 1959 | E. White (Labour) Flint East | 75 |
| 1906 | J. D. Rees (Liberal) Montgomery Boroughs | 83 |

Fewest Votes for Parliamentary Candidates in Wales since 1832 (under 100)

1841	W. Edwards (Chartist) Monmouth Boroughs	0
1989 (by-election)	D. Black (Independent) Vale of Glamorgan	32
	Lindi St Clair (Correction Party) Vale of Glamorgan	39
1985 (by-election)	C. L. Genillard (Independent) Brecon and Radnor	43
1989 (by-election)	D. Black (Independent) Pontypridd	57
1992	M. Beresford (Natural Law Party) Gower	74
1974 (October)	B.C. D. Harris (Communist Party of England) Cardiff South-East	75
1992	D. Palmer (Natural Law Party) Cardiff North	86
1841	J. M. Child (Liberal) Pembroke Boroughs	95

BY-ELECTION RESULTS SINCE THE 1945 GENERAL ELECTION

	Constituency	*Date*	*Winning candidate*	*Winning party*
1.	Monmouth	30 Oct. 1945	G. E. P. Thorneycroft	Con. (Held for Con.)
2.	Ogmore	4 June 1946	J. Evans	Lab. (Held for Lab.)
3.	Pontypool	23 July 1946	D. G. West	Lab. (Held for Lab.)
4.	Aberdare	5 Dec. 1946	D. E. Thomas	Lab. (Held for Lab.)
5.	Abertillery	30 Nov. 1950	Revd. L. Williams	Lab. (Held for Lab.)
6.	Aberdare	28 Oct. 1954	A. R. Probert	Lab. (held for Lab.)
7.	Wrexham	17 March 1955	J. I. Jones	Lab. (Held for Lab.)
8.	Newport	7 June 1956	Sir Frank Soskice	Lab. (Held for Lab.)
9.	Carmarthen	28 Feb. 1957	Lady Megan Lloyd George	Lab. (*Gain* from Lib.)
10.	Pontypool	10 Nov. 1958	L. Abse	Lab. (Held for Lab.)
11.	Ebbw Vale	11 Nov. 1960	M. Foot	Lab. (Held for Lab.)
12.	Montgomery	15 June 1962	H. E. Hooson	Lib. (Held for Lib.)
13.	Swansea East	28 March 1963	N. McBride	Lab. (Held for Lab.)
14.	Abertillery	1 April 1965	A. C. Williams	Lab. (Held for Lab.)
15.	Carmarthen	14 July 1966	G. E. Evans	Plaid (*Gain* from Lab.)
16.	Rhondda West	9 March 1967	T. A. Jones	Lab. (Held for Lab.)
17.	Caerphilly	18 July 1968	A. T. Evans	Lab. (Held for Lab.)

Constituency	Date	Winning candidate	Winning party
18. Merthyr Tydfil	13 April 1972	E. Rowlands	Lab. (*Gain* from Ind. Lab.)
19. Gower	16 Sept. 1982	G. C. Wardell	Lab. (Held for Lab.)
20. Cynon Valley	3 May 1984	Ann Clwyd	Lab. (Held for Lab.)
21. Brecon and Radnor	4 July 1985	R. Livsey	Lib. (*Gain* from Con.)
22. Pontypridd	23 Feb. 1989	Dr K. Howells	Lab. (Held for Lab.)
23. Vale of Glamorgan	4 May 1989	J. Smith	Lab. (*Gain* from Con.)
24. Neath	4 April 1991	P. Hain	Lab. (Held for Lab.)
25. Monmouth	16 May 1991	H. Edwards	Lab. (*Gain* from Con.)

WOMEN PARLIAMENTARY CANDIDATES

Westminster Parliament

1918*	1 in 36 constituencies	Not elected
1922	3 in 36 constituencies	None elected
1923	1 in 36 constituencies	Not elected
1924	1 in 36 constituencies	Not elected
1929	3 in 36 constituencies	One elected
1931	3 in 36 constituencies	One elected
1935	3 in 36 constituencies	One elected
1945*	3 in 36 constituencies	One elected
1950	4 in 36 constituencies	Three elected
1951	4 in 36 constituencies	One elected
1955	5 in 36 constituencies	One elected
1959	5 in 36 constituencies	One elected
1964	6 in 36 constituencies	Two elected
1966	4 in 36 constituencies	Two elected
1970	4 in 36 constituencies	None elected
1974 (Feb)	5 in 36 constituencies	None elected
1974 (Oct)	6 in 36 constituencies	None elected
1979	7 in 36 constituencies	None elected
1983	14 in 38 constituencies	None elected
1987	18 in 38 constituencies	One elected
1992	24 in 38 constituencies	One elected

*From 1918 to 1945 the total number of constituencies includes the University of Wales seat.

Women Candidates by Party, 1992

Liberal Democrats	8	Conservative	2
Plaid Cymru	7	Others	3
Labour	4 (one elected)		

European Parliament

1979	4 in 4 constituencies	Two elected
1984	4 in 4 constituencies	One elected
1989	3 in 4 constituencies	None elected
1994	10 in 5 constituencies	Two elected

Women Candidates by Party, 1994

Conservative	2	Plaid Cymru	1
Labour	2 (both elected)	Others	3
Liberal Democrats	2		

WALES IN THE EUROPEAN COMMUNITY

Referendum

The result of the European Community Referendum held on 5 June 1975.

Question: Do you think the United Kingdom should stay in the European Community ('The Common Market')?

	Yes	*No*	*Majority*
Clwyd	123,980	55,424	68,556
Dyfed	109,184	52,264	56,920
Gwent	132,557	80,992	51,565
Gwynedd	76,421	31,807	44,614
Mid Glamorgan	147,348	111,672	35,676
Powys	38,724	13,372	25,302
South Glamorgan	127,932	56,224	71,708
West Glamorgan	112,989	70,316	42,673
WALES (66.7% poll)	869,135	472,711	397,064

European Parliament Election Results

	1979	1984	1989
Mid and West Wales	Labour	Labour	Labour
North Wales	Conservative	Conservative	Labour
South Wales	Labour	Labour	Labour
South East Wales	Labour	Labour	Labour

In 1994 Welsh representation in the European Parliament was increased to five MEPs and there were boundary changes.

	1994
Mid and West Wales	Labour
North Wales	Labour
South Wales Central	Labour
South Wales East	Labour
South Wales West	Labour

All five Welsh MEPs are members of the Socialist Group in the Parliament.

Polls in European Parliamentary Elections

(UK polls shown in brackets)

1979	34.1% (31.6%)	1989	40.7% (36.2%)
1984	39.3% (32.6%)	1994	42.8% (36.5%)

Welsh Euro-constituencies Ranked by Majorities (Election 9 June 1994)

1. Glenys Kinnock	(Labour)	South Wales East	120,247
2. Wayne David	(Labour)	South Wales Central	86,082
3. David Morris	(Labour)	South Wales West	84,970
4. Eluned Morgan	(Labour)	Mid and West Wales	29,234
5. Joe Wilson	(Labour)	North Wales	15,242

Welsh Euro-constituencies and Matching Westminster Constituencies

European Constituency	Westminster Constituencies
Mid and West Wales	Brecon and Radnor; Carmarthen; Ceredigion and Pembroke North; Llanelli; Meirionnydd Nant Conwy; Montgomery; Pembroke.

North Wales	Alyn and Deeside; Caernarfon; Clwyd North West; Clwyd South West; Conwy; Delyn; Wrexham; Ynys Môn/Anglesey.
South Wales Central	Cardiff Central; Cardiff North; Cardiff South and Penarth; Cardiff West; Cynon Valley; Pontypridd; Rhondda; Vale of Glamorgan.
South Wales East	Blaenau Gwent; Caerphilly; Islwyn; Merthyr Tydfil and Rhymney; Monmouth; Newport East; Newport West; Torfaen.
South Wales West	Aberavon; Bridgend; Gower; Neath; Ogmore; Swansea East; Swansea West.

Committee of the Regions

Wales has three representatives of the United Kingdom's 24 members of the Committee of the Regions which advises on the distribution of European Community funds. There is one representative each from the Conservative Party, the Labour Party and Plaid Cymru.

Office of the European Commission in Wales: 4 Cathedral Road, Cardiff CF1 9SG.

There is a Wales Europe Centre in Brussels, opened in 1992.

WELSH MEMBERS OF THE PRIVY COUNCIL

Lord Aberdare (1974)	Lord Griffiths (1980)	John Morris (1970)
Kenneth Baker (1984)	Michael Heseltine (1979)	Lord Rees (1983)
Lord Chalfont (1964)	Lord Howe (1972)	Sir Wyn Roberts (1991)
Lord Cledwyn (1966)	Lord Jenkins (1964)	Lord Thomas (1964)
Lord Crickhowell (1979)	Aubrey Jones (1955)	Viscount Tonypandy (1968)
Denzil Davies (1978)	Sir Edward Jones (1979)	Sir Tasker Watkins (1980)
Tristan Garel-Jones (1992)	Neil Kinnock (1983)	Alan Williams (1977)
Lord Gibson-Watt (1974)	Lord Merlyn-Rees (1974)	

WELSH LORD CHANCELLORS

Lord George Jeffreys:	1685–1688
Lord Elwyn-Jones:	1974–1979

WELSH PEERS ACTIVE IN THE HOUSE OF LORDS

Lord Aberdare	Cross-bencher	Succeeded to the title in 1957
Lord Brooks of Tremorfa	Labour	Life peerage 1978
Lord Callaghan of Cardiff	Labour	Life peerage 1987
Lord Chalfont	Cross-bencher	Life peerage 1964
Lord Cledwyn of Penrhos	Labour	Life peerage 1979
Lord Crickhowell	Conservative	Life peerage 1987
Lord Davies of Penrhys	Labour	Life peerage 1974
Lord Elis-Thomas of Conwy	Plaid Cymru/Cross-bencher	Life peerage 1992
Lord Elyston-Morgan	Labour	Life peerage 1981
Lord Evans of Claughton	Liberal Democrat	Life peerage 1992
Lord Geraint of Ponterwyd	Liberal Democrat	Life peerage 1992
Lord Gibson-Watt	Conservative	Life peerage 1979
Lord Griffiths of Fforestfach	Conservative	Life peerage 1991
Lord Hooson	Liberal Democrat	Life peerage 1979
Lord Howe of Aberavon	Conservative	Life peerage 1992
Lord Jenkins of Hillhead	Liberal Democrat	Life peerage 1987
Earl Lloyd-George of Dwyfor	Cross-bencher	Succeeded to the title in 1968
Lady McFarlane of Llandaff	Cross-bencher	Life peerage 1979
Lord Merlyn-Rees	Labour	Life peerage 1992
Lord Morris of Castle Morris	Labour	Life peerage 1990
Lord Mostyn	Conservative	Succeeded to the title in 1965
Lord Ogmore	Liberal Democrat	Succeeded to the title in 1976
Lord Parry	Labour	Life peerage 1975
Lord Prys-Davies	Labour	Life peerage 1982
Lord Richard	Labour	Life peerage 1990
Viscount St Davids	Conservative	Succeeded to the title in 1991
Lord Swansea	Conservative	Succeeded to the title in 1934
Lord Thomas of Gwydir	Conservative	Life peerage 1987
Viscount Tonypandy	Cross-bencher	Hereditary peerage 1983
Baroness White of Rhymney	Labour	Life peerage 1970
Lord Williams of Mostyn	Labour	Life peerage in 1992

COUNTY, DISTRICT AND COMMUNITY COUNCILS

County Councils

County council and address	Approximate population	Number of councillors (1993)
Clwyd		
Shire Hall, Mold, Clwyd, CH7 6NB.	402,000	64
Dyfed		
County Hall, Carmarthen, Dyfed, SH31 1JP.	342,00	70
Gwent		
County Hall, Cwmbran, Gwent, NP44 2XH.	432,000	63
Gwynedd		
County Offices, Caernarfon, Gwynedd, LL55 1SH.	239,000	62
Mid Glamorgan		
County Hall, Cathays Park, Cardiff, CF1 3NE.	527,000	74
Powys		
County Hall, Llandrindod Wells, Powys, LD1 5LG.	117,000	46
South Glamorgan		
County Hall, Atlantic Wharf, Cardiff, CF1 5VW.	383,000	62
West Glamorgan		
County Hall, Swansea, SA1 3SN.	358,000	61

For areas of counties see p.2.

District Councils

Address	Approx. population	No. of councillors (1991)
Aberconwy Borough		
Town Hall, Llandudno, Gwynedd, LL30 2UY.	54,000	41
Alyn and Deeside District		
Council Offices, Glynne Way, Hawarden, Clwyd, CH5 3NU.	72,000	43
Arfon Borough		
Town Hall, Bangor, Gwynedd, LL57 2RE	55,000	39
Blaenau Gwent Borough		
Municipal Offices, Ebbw Vale, Gwent, NP3 6XB.	75,000	44

Brecknock Borough
    Oxford House, 40 The Watton, Brecon, Powys, LD3 7HR.   41,000   44
Cardiff City
    City Hall, Cardiff, CF1 3ND.   273,000   65
Carmarthen District
    Council Offices, Spilman St., Carmarthen, Dyfed, SA31 1LE.   55,000   37
Ceredigion District
    Town Hall, Aberystwyth, Dyfed, SY23 2EB.   64,000   44
Colwyn Borough
    Civic Centre, Abergele Road, Colwyn Bay, Clwyd, LL29 8AR.   55,000   34
Cynon Valley Borough
    Rock Grounds, High St., Aberdare, Mid Glamorgan, CF44 7AE.   64,000   38
Delyn Borough
    Delyn House, Chapel Street, Flint, Clwyd, CH6 5BD.   66,000   42
Dinefwr Borough
    Municipal Offices, Crescent Road, Llandeilo, Dyfed, SA19 6HW.   38,000   32
Dwyfor Borough
    Council Offices, Pwllheli, Gwynedd, LL53 5AA.   28,000   29
Glyndŵr District
    Council Offices, Wynnstay Road, Rhuthun, Clwyd, LL15 1YN.   41,000   35
Islwyn Borough
    Civic Centre, Blackwood, Gwent, NP2 2YW.   65,000   35
Llanelli Borough
    Town Hall, Llanelli, Dyfed, SA15 3AN.   74,000   35
Lliw Valley Borough
    Civic Centre, Penllergaer, Swansea, West Glamorgan, SA4 1GM.   62,000   33
Meirionnydd District
    Council Offices, Cae Penarlag, Dolgellau, Gwynedd, LL40 2YB.   33,000   41
Merthyr Tydfil Borough
    Town Hall, Merthyr Tydfil, Mid Glamorgan, CF27 8AN.   59,000   33
Monmouth Borough
    Mamhilad House, Mamhilad Park Estate, Pontypool, Gwent, NP4 OYL.   75,000   40
Montgomery District
    Council Offices, Severn Road, Welshpool, Powys, SY21 7AS.   52,000   46
Neath Borough
    Civic Centre, Neath, West Glamorgan, SA11 3QZ.   64,000   34
Newport Borough
    Civic Centre, Newport, Gwent, NP9 4UR.   130,000   47
Ogwr Borough
    Civic Offices, Angel Street, Bridgend, Mid Glamorgan, CF31 1LX.   130,000   49

Port Talbot Borough		
Civic Centre, Port Talbot, West Glamorgan, SA13 1PJ.	50,000	31
Preseli-Pembrokeshire District		
Cambria House, PO Box 27, Haverfordwest, Dyfed, SA61 17P.	70,000	40
Radnor District		
Council Offices, Llandrindod Wells, Powys, LD1 6AN.	23,000	33
Rhondda Borough		
Municipal Offices, Pentre, Rhondda, Mid Glamorgan,CF41 7BT.	76,000	33
Rhuddlan Borough		
Council Offices, 34 Russell Street, Rhyl, Clwyd, LL18 3DD.	54,000	32
Rhymney Valley District		
Council Offices, Ystrad Mynach, Hengoed, Mid Glam., CF8 7SP.	101,000	46
South Pembrokeshire District		
District Offices, Llanion Park, Pembroke Dock, Dyfed, SA72 6DZ.	42,000	30
Swansea City		
The Guildhall, Swansea, West Glamorgan, SA1 4PA.	182,000	51
Taff Ely Borough		
Municipal Buildings, Pontypridd, Mid Glamorgan, CF37 2DP.	95,000	44
Torfaen Borough		
Gwent House, Gwent Square, Cwmbran, Gwent, NP44 1YP.	88,000	44
Vale of Glamorgan Borough		
Civic Centre, Holton Road, Barry, South Glamorgan, CF6 6RU.	119,000	46
Wrexham Maelor Borough		
Guildhall, Wrexham, Clwyd, LL11 1AY.	114,000	46
Ynys Môn/Anglesey Borough		
Borough Council Offices, Llangefni, Anglesey, Gwynedd.	68,000	39

Lists of elected members of county and district councils can be obtained from the offices of the chief executive for each authority.

Community Councils

There are almost 800 elected community councils and communities in Wales including 84 town councils. Only two of the 37 districts in Wales, Islwyn (Gwent) and Rhondda (Mid Glamorgan) do not have community councils. The number of community councils and communities is shown in the table.

Clwyd	122 (includes 12 town councils)
Dyfed	232 (includes 22 town councils)*
Gwent	57 (includes 8 town councils)
Gwynedd	122 (includes 19 town councils)†

Mid Glamorgan	50 (includes 6 town councils)
Powys	108 (includes 16 town councils)
South Glamorgan	53 (includes 4 town councils)
West Glamorgan	44 (includes 1 town council)

*This figure includes St David's City Council
†This figure includes Bangor City Council

Further information about community councils can be obtained from: the General Secretary, Welsh Association of Community and Town Councils, 11 Jellicoe Gardens, Roath, Cardiff, CF2 5QZ.

Note: St Asaph is the only one of the 30 ancient cathedral sites of England and Wales which does not have civic city status.

LOCAL GOVERNMENT COMMISSIONERS

Commissioner for Local Government in Wales
Derwen House, Court Road, Bridgend, Mid Glamorgan, CF31 1BN.

The Commissioner (Ombudsman) can investigate complaints from members of the public against Welsh local authorities – excluding community councils – police authorities, the Cardiff Bay Development Corporation and the Development Board for Rural Wales (town and country planning functions only of the last two).

Commercial transactions are excluded unless the purchase or sale of land is involved.

Complaints can be made directly or through a local councillor but the authority against whom the complaint is being made must have been approached first.

Local Government Boundary Commission for Wales
Caradog House, 1st Floor, 1–6 St Andrews Place, Cardiff, CF1 3BE.

The Commission reviews the areas and electoral arrangements of Welsh local authorities and reports to the Secretary of State for Wales.

RESPONSIBILITIES OF ELECTED COUNCILS IN WALES

County Councils

Caravan sites	Food and Drugs Acts
Education	Highways
Fire Service	Housing (reserve powers)

National Parks and Countryside
Police
Public libraries,* museums, art galleries
Social services

Strategic planning
Traffic and transportation functions
Weights and measures
Fire Service

* Five *district* councils in Wales have library powers – Cynon Valley, Llanelli, Merthyr Tydfil, Newport and Rhondda.

District Councils

Allotments Acts
Airports
Baths and pools
Car parks
Cemeteries and crematoria
Electoral registration
Environmental health

Housing
Markets and fairs
Museums and art galleries
Parks and open spaces
Planning
Public transport undertakings
Refuse collection and disposal

Also: Libraries, food and drugs, and Weights and Measures when so ordered by the Secretary of State for Wales.

Community Councils

Allotments
Baths, washhouses, watering places
Burial grounds
Car parks
Clocks
Green spaces and camping sites
Gymnasia

Playing fields
Public walks, footpaths, verges and churchyards
Shelters
Street lighting
Village halls
War memorials

All planning applications must be notified to community councils.

PARTY POLITICAL CONTROL OF COUNTY AND DISTRICT COUNCILS

(Positions in 1994)

County Councils

Labour   Clwyd, Gwent, Mid Glamorgan, South Glamorgan, West Glamorgan
Independent   Powys
No Overall Control Dyfed, Gwynedd.

District Councils

Labour   Alyn and Deeside, Blaenau Gwent, Cardiff, Cynon Valley, Dinefwr, Islwyn, Llanelli, Lliw Valley, Merthyr Tydfil, Neath, Newport, Ogwr, Port Talbot, Rhondda, Rhymney Valley, Swansea, Torfaen, Wrexham Maelor.

Conservative   Monmouth.

Independent   Brecknock, Carmarthen, Ceredigion, Colwyn, Delyn, Dwyfor, Glyndŵr, Meirionnydd, Montgomery, Preseli, Pembrokeshire, Radnor, Rhuddlan, South Pembrokeshire, Ynys Môn/Anglesey.

No Overall Control   Aberconwy, Arfon, Taff Ely, Vale of Glamorgan.

NEW WELSH COUNCILS FROM 1996

From 1996, the eight county councils and 37 district councils of Wales, established in 1974, will be replaced by 22 all-purpose unitary authorities with elections for them held in 1995. The number of councillors will be reduced from just over 2,000 to under 1,300. Community councils will remain.

Unitary authority	Estimated population	Unitary authority	Estimated population
Anglesey	69,000	Neath and Port Talbot	140,000
Caernarfonshire		Bridgend	130,000
and Merionethshire	116,000	Vale of Glamorgan	119,000
Aberconwy and Colwyn	109,000	Rhondda, Cynon, Taff	238,000
Denbighshire	91,000	Merthyr Tydfil	60,000
Flintshire	144,000	Caerphilly	171,000
Wrexham	123,000	Blaenau Gwent	73,000
Powys	121,000	Torfaen	91,000
Cardiganshire	68,000	Monmouthshire	81,000
Pembrokeshire	114,000	Newport	137,000
Carmarthenshire	169,000	Cardiff	302,000
Swansea	232,000		

WELSH TWINNING ARRANGEMENTS

(County, District and Community Councils)

Aberdare: Slagelse, Denmark

Abergavenny: Oestringen, Germany

Aberystwyth:	St Brieuc, France
Afan:	Bagneux, France
	Heilbron, Germany
Bangor:	Lannion, France
	Soest, Germany
Blaenafon:	Centras, France
Brecknock:	Blauberen, Germany
Brecon:	Saline, Michigan, USA
Bridgend:	Langenau, Germany
Caldicot:	Wagshausel, Germany
Cardiff:	Lugansk, (formerly called Voroshilovgrad), Ukraine
	Nantes, France
	Stuttgart, Germany
	Xiamen, China
Cardigan:	Briode, France
Carmarthen:	Lesneven, France
	Santa Marinella, Italy
Chepstow:	Cormelles, France
Colwyn:	Konstantz, Germany
	Roissy-en-Brie, France
Crymych:	Plumeun, France
Cwmbran:	Bruchsal, Germany
Delyn:	Menden, Germany
Dolgellau:	Gueande, France
Dyfed:	Vejle, Denmark
Govilon:	Misillac, France
Gwent:	Charante-Marihine, France
	Guangxi/Zhuang, China
	Karlsruhe, Germany
Hay-on-Wye:	Redu, Belgium
Llandeilo:	Le Conquet, France
Llandovery:	Pluguffan, France
Llantwit Major:	Le Pouliguen, France
Machynlleth:	Belleville, Michigan, USA
Manorbier:	Vernon-la-Garenne, France
Merthyr Tydfil:	Clichy-la-Garenne, France
Mid Glamorgan:	Alb-Donau Kreis, Germany
Milford Haven:	Romilly-sur-Seine, France
Monmouth:	Carbonne, France
	Waldbronn, Germany

Mumbles:	Kinsale, Irish Republic
Neath:	Esslingen, Germany
	Schiedam, Netherlands
	Udine, Italy
	Velenje, Slovenia
	Vienne, France
Newport:	Heidenheim, Germany
	Kutasisi, Georgia
	Wuzhou, China
Penarth:	St Pol-de-Leon, France
Pencoed:	Waldsassen, Germany
Pontypridd:	Nurtigen, Germany
Radnor:	Hochschwarzwald, Germany
Radyr and Morganstown:	St Philbert de Grand Lieu, France
Rhymney Valley:	Ludwigsburg, Germany
St David's:	Naas, Irish Republic
South Glamorgan:	Loire Atlantique, France
	Baltimore County, Maryland, USA
South Pembrokeshire:	Bergen, Germany
Swansea:	Cork, Irish Republic
	Ferrara, Italy
	Mannheim, Germany
	Nantong, China
	Pau, France
Torfaen:	Morioka, Japan
Tredegar:	Orvault, France
Usk:	Graben-Neudorf, Germany
Vale of Glamorgan:	Fecamp, France
	Muscron, Belgium
	Rheinfelden, Germany
Wrexham:	Markischer Kreis, Germany
	Xiang'fan, China
Ynys Môn/Anglesey:	Dun Laoghaire, Irish Republic
	Mafeteng, Lesotho
WALES:	LESOTHO

LAW COURTS

Crown Courts on the Wales and Chester Circuit

(Circuit Office, 3rd Floor, Churchill House, Churchill Way, Cardiff, CF1 4HH.)

1st tier: Caernarfon, Cardiff, Mold and Swansea
2nd tier: Carmarthen, Newport and Welshpool
3rd tier: Dolgellau, Haverfordwest and Merthyr Tydfil

(There are also Crown Courts on the Wales and Chester Circuit in Chester, Knutsford and Warrington.)

1st tier courts deal with High Court civil cases and criminal cases and are served by High Court and Circuit judges.

2nd tier courts deal with criminal cases only and are served by High Court and Circuit judges.

3rd tier courts deal with criminal cases only and are served by Circuit judges.

County Courts

There are 33 County Courts in Wales located at the places listed below.

County Courts are presided over by Circuit judges and recorders. They have general jurisdiction to determine all actions founded on tort and contract involving sums of not more than £5,000. The courts can also deal with certain other types of cases such as landlord and tenant.

Divorce proceedings must commence in County Courts and nearly all are subsequently determined in them. Some courts also have jurisdiction in other matrimonial matters as well as bankruptcy and race relations. See 'Additional Jurisdiction' key below.

Aberdare (B)	Cardiff (A, B, D, R)
Aberystwyth (A, B, D)	Cardigan
Ammanford	Carmarthen (A, B, D)
Bangor (A, B)	Chepstow
Bargoed	Conwy and Colwyn Bay
Barry	Haverfordwest (A, B, D)
Blackwood (B, D)	Holywell
Brecon	Llandrindod Wells
Bridgend (B, D)	Llanelli (D)
Caernarfon (A, B, D)	Llangefni (D)
Caerphilly	Merthyr Tydfil (B, D)

Mold   Porthmadog (B)
Monmouth   Rhyl (B, D)
Neath and Port Talbot (B, D)   Swansea (A, B, D)
Newport (A, B, D)   Welshpool and Newtown (B, D)
Pontypool   Wrexham (A, B, R)
Pontypridd (B, D)

Additional Jurisdiction
A – Admiralty   B – Bankruptcy   D – Divorce   R – Race Relations

Magistrates Courts

The 85 Magistrates Courts in Wales are listed by counties below. They have the power to pass sentences of up to six months imprisonment and fines of up to £2,000 for any one offence.

The courts are manned by over 1,000 lay magistrates (Justices of the Peace) and two stipendiary (paid) magistrates in Cardiff and Merthyr Tydfil.

Magistrates Courts also deal with preliminary hearings in cases which are subsequently tried at Crown Courts.

Clwyd
Abergele   Denbigh   Mold
Colwyn Bay   Flint   Prestatyn
Corwen   Llangollen   Wrexham

Dyfed
Aberaeron   Fishguard   Narberth
Aberystwyth   Haverfordwest   Newcastle Emlyn
Ammanford   Lampeter   Pembroke
Cardigan   Llandovery   St Clears/Whitland
Carmarthen   Llandeilo   Tenby
Crymych   Milford Haven

Gwent
Abergavenny   Cwmbran   Newport, Pentonville
Abertillery   Ebbw Vale   Pontypool
Blackwood   Monmouth   Tredegar
Chepstow   Newport, Civic Centre   Usk

Gwynedd

Amlwch	Caernarfon	Llanrwst
Bala	Dolgellau	Menai Bridge
Bangor	Holyhead	Porthmadog
Barmouth	Llandudno	Pwllheli
Beaumaris	Llangefni	Tywyn
Blaenau Ffestiniog		

Mid Glamorgan

Aberdare	Merthyr Tydfil	Porth
Bargoed	Pontlottyn	Talbot Green
Bridgend	Pontypridd	Ton Pentre
Caerphilly		

Powys

Brecon	Llanidloes	Rhayader
Builth Wells	Machynlleth	Talgarth
Crickhowell	Newtown	Welshpool
Llandrindod Wells	Presteigne	Ystradgynlais

South Glamorgan

Barry	Cardiff	Cowbridge

West Glamorgan

Gowerton	Pontardawe	Swansea, Dynevor Place
Neath	Port Talbot	Swansea, Grove Place

Coroners Courts

There are 17 coroners' districts in Wales listed by counties below.

Clwyd

East Clwyd:	23 Chester Street, Mold, CH7 1EG.
South Clwyd:	59 King Street, Wrexham, LL11 1HR.
West Clwyd:	16 St Peter's Square, Rhuthun, LL15 1AD.

Dyfed

Carmarthen:	Corner House, Llandeilo, SA19 6SG.
Ceredigion:	6 Upper Portland Street, Aberystwyth, SY23 2OU.
Pembroke:	17 Hamble Terrace, Milford Haven, SA73 3JA.

Gwent

Victoria Chambers, 11 Clytha Park Road, Newport, NP9 4TS.

Gwynedd

Eryri: 19 Bangor Street, Caernarfon, LL55 1AW.
Llŷn ac Eifionydd: 103 High Street, Porthmadog, LL49 9EY.
Meirionnydd: 5 Plasey Street, Bala, LL23 7SW.
Ynys Môn: 19 Bangor Street, Caernarfon, LL55 1AW.

Mid Glamorgan

Northern Coroner's District: 3 Victoria Square, Aberdare, CF44 7LA.
Southern Coroner's District: 51 The Parade, Cardiff, CF2 3AB.

Powys

Mid Wales House, Great Oak Street, Llanidloes, SY18 6BN.

South Glamorgan

Police Headquarters, Cathays Park, Cardiff, CF1 3NN.

West Glamorgan

Swansea and Gower Coroner's District: Calvert House, Calvert Terrace, Swansea, SA1 6AD.
West Glamorgan Coroner's District: Grasmere, Christopher Road, Skewen.

Coroners inquire into deaths if there is reason to believe that a person has died violently, unnaturally, unexpectedly or from unknown causes, by holding an inquest or by having a post-mortem examination made.

Inquests are also held by coroners when treasure trove is discovered.

Coroners must be either solicitors or doctors.

CROWN PROSECUTION SERVICE

The Crown Prosecution Service is responsible for all prosecutions following police investigations, except those for breaches of the Official Secrets Act, terrorism, race relations and minor traffic offences.

Offices in Wales

For North Wales and Dyfed-Powys: 491 Abergele Road, Old Colwyn, Colwyn Bay.
For South Wales and Gwent: 20th Floor, Pearl Assurance Building, Greyfriars Road, Cardiff.

POLICE FORCES

Distribution of Forces

Force	Headquarters	Strengths		
		1948	*1968*	*1992*
Dyfed-Powys (3 divisions)	Carmarthen	406	781	960
Gwent (3 divisions)	Cwmbran	480	768	1,000
North Wales (Clwyd and Gwynedd (4 divisions)	Colwyn Bay	433	914	1,356
South Wales (Mid, South and West Glamorgan) (8 divisions)	Bridgend	1,455	2,376	3,164
WALES		2,774	4,839	6,480

Notifiable Offences Recorded by the Police

	1990	*1992*
Dyfed-Powys	20,780	26,554
Gwent	31,653	39,994
North Wales	37,842	47,811
South Wales	138,973	163,270
WALES	229,248	277,629

PENAL INSTITUTIONS

HM Prison and Remand Centre, Knox Road, Cardiff.
HM Prison, Oystermouth Road, Swansea.
Young Offenders Institute (Closed), Usk, Gwent.
Young Offenders Institute (Open), Usk, Gwent.

In 1993 the Home Office announced that a private prison for 800 was to be opened at Coity, Bridgend, Mid Glamorgan, and that a secure unit for young offenders was to be opened at Neath.

FIRE SERVICES

The eight fire services in Wales are based on the 1974 counties but these are to be reduced to three with local government reorganization from 1996: North Wales, Mid Wales, South Wales.

	Number of fire stations	Full-time personnel	Part-time personnel	Control room staff	Civilian staff
1987	153	1,720	1,508	138	300
1991	151	1,703	1,326	144	274

Total call-outs in 1990–91: 51,421

4

THE WELSH LANGUAGE • NATIONAL AND URDD EISTEDDFODAU • WELSH-LANGUAGE ORGANIZATIONS • PLACE-NAMES

THE SMALLER LANGUAGES OF EUROPE – HOW WELSH COMPARES

Number of Welsh-speakers*

According to the Census of 1991, some 546,551 people in Wales are able either to speak, read or write Welsh. The Census records a total Welsh-speaking population of 508,098.

*See also 'Language Surveys' below.

More Speakers (approximate numbers)

Catalan	7.5 million	Latvian (Lettish)	1.5 million
Finnish	4.6 million	Occitan	1.5 million
Albanian	4.25 million	Macedonian	1.2 million
Lithuanian	2.4 million	Estonian	1.0 million
Galician	2.2 million	Sardinian (Sardu)	0.8 million
Slovenian	1.9 million		

About the Same Number of Speakers (500,000 – 800,000)

Rhaeto-Romansch/Ladin/Friulian (Northern Italy and Switzerland)	810,000
Basque	630,000
Breton	510,000

Fewer Speakers (approximate numbers)

Frisian	411,000
Maltese	400,000

Letzburgesch (Luxembourg)	355,000
Icelandic	250,000
Corsican	220,000
Kashubian (Caixubi)	100,000
(around Gdansk, Poland)	
Scots Gaelic	65,000
Sorb	50,000
(Cottbus and Bautzen areas of Upper Saxony, Germany)	
Faroese	48,000
Lapp (Northern Norway, Sweden, Finland)	20,000

Note: In the case of many of the languages above, there are no official statistics; the figures given are estimates from a number of sources.

DATES OF SIGNIFICANCE AND INTEREST

Language developments – stages

Mid-6th century – late 8th century:	Early Welsh
Late 8th century – mid-12th century:	Old Welsh
Mid-12th century – late 14th/early 15th centuries:	Middle Welsh
Late 14th/early 15th centuries – present:	Modern Welsh

Significant dates

c.600 AD The oldest extant poem in Welsh, *Y Gododdin* by Aneirin, was composed in Strathclyde, Scotland, and described the Battle of Catterick, Yorkshire.

C7th– The oldest inscription in Welsh dates from some time in these
C9th centuries and is on the seven-foot high St Cadfan's Stone at Tywyn.

c.1050 The stories now known as *The Mabinogion* were first written down.

1250 What is generally regarded as the oldest manuscript in Welsh, *Llyfr Du Caerfyrddin* (*The Black Book of Carmarthen*), is thought to date from not earlier than this year.

c.1300 At Strata Florida Abbey scriptorium, the collection of medieval Welsh court poetry, *Llawysgrif Hendregadredd*, was assembled.

c.1322– Einion the Priest (Einion Offeiriad) compiled an important Welsh poetic
1327 grammar.

1451 Codification of traditional strict poetry metres for the awdl (ode).

1536 The Act of Union disallowed the use of Welsh for official purposes.

1546 The first book was printed in Welsh (in London) – *Yn y lhyvyr hwnn* ('In this book') by Sir John Price.

1547   William Salesbury published his *Dictionary in Englyshe and Welshe.*

1549   The Act of Uniformity laid down that all acts of public worship had to be in English.

1556   William Salesbury published *A Brief and Playne Introduction Teaching How to Pronounce the Letters of the British Tong (Now Com'enly Called Welsh).*

1563   An Act of this year required all churches in Wales to have Welsh translations of the Book of Common Prayer and the Bible by 1567.

1567   The New Testament was translated into Welsh by William Salesbury.

1567   A book on Welsh grammar was published in Milan by Gruffydd Robert, a Catholic exile.

1588   Publication of Bishop William Morgan's translation of the Bible into Welsh.

c.1600   The first full-length play in Welsh, *Troelus a Chresyd*, was written by an anonymous author.

1621   Publication of a major Welsh grammar book by Dr John Davies and of *Salmau Cân* – the first Welsh book in which music appeared.

1630   The first cheap Welsh Bible was published – *Y Beibl Bach.*

1632   Publication of a major Welsh–Latin dictionary *Dictionarium Duplex*, by Dr John Davies.

1703   Publication of the Breton Abbé Pezron's book *L'Antiquité de la Nation et la langue des Celtes* stimulated studies into Welsh and other Celtic languages.

1707   Edward Lhuyd's *Archaeologica Britannica* was published and became the basis of future study of the Celtic languages.

1717   A new issue of the Welsh Bible was published.

1718   The first legal printing press in Wales was established at Adpar near Newcastle Emlyn. (It was moved to Carmarthen in 1725.) By this time over 300 books had been published in Welsh.

1719   The oldest extant book in Welsh was published – *Eglurhad o Gatechism Byrraf y Gamanfa.* The first book in Welsh known to have been published in America, at Philadelphia, was *Annerch i'r Cymru* by the Quaker Ellis Pugh.

1725   Publication of an important English–Welsh dictionary by John Rhydderch.

1731   Griffith Jones's Circulating Schools were introduced and eventually made a majority of Welsh-speakers literate for the first time.

1770   The first Welsh-language magazine was published – *Trysorfa Gwybodaeth.*

1793   The first Welsh-language political periodical was published – *Y Cylchgrawn Cymraeg.*

1814	The first Welsh-language newspaper, *Seren Gomer*, was published in Swansea.
1837	Welsh was allowed to be used in Church wedding services.
1839	A Welsh system of shorthand was invented by Thomas Roberts and published in his book *Stenographia*.
1854–79	Publication by Thomas Gee of the first Welsh-language encyclopaedia *Y Gwyddoniadur*.
1870	By this date some 30 Welsh-language periodicals were being published, mainly of a religious nature.
1877	Publication of Sir John Rhys's *Lectures on Welsh Philology* – the first attempt at a systematic and scientific study of the Welsh language by a Welshman since Edward Lhuyd (see 1707).
1880	First performance – in Llanberis – of a full-length play in Welsh, *Glyndŵr* by Beriah Gwynfe Evans.
1885	The Society for the Utilisation of the Welsh Language (Cymdeithas yr Iaith Gymraeg) was formed and was instrumental in making Welsh a subject in the school curriculum.
1891	The first language census showed the number of Welsh-speakers over the age of two in Wales was 898,914.
1892	*Cymru'r Plant* children's magazine founded. (Now called *CIP*.)
1911	The largest ever number of Welsh-speakers over the age of three in Wales was recorded – 977,366.
1913	Publication of Sir John Morris-Jones's very influential *Welsh Grammar – Historical and Comparative*.
1922	Urdd Gobaith Cymru (The Welsh League of Youth) was founded by Sir Ifan ab Owen Edwards.
1923	The first Welsh-language broadcasts were transmitted by Station 5WA from Cardiff.
1927	The official report *Welsh in Education* was published and led to the limited use of Welsh in teaching in primary schools in Welsh-speaking areas.
1928	The Board of Celtic Studies produced a report, *Orgraff yr Iaith Gymraeg*, which settled the controversy over the spelling of Welsh.
1929	The first Urdd Eisteddfod was held at Corwen.
1935	The first Welsh-language sound film, *Y Chwarelwr* ('The Quarryman') was made by Sir Ifan ab Owen Edwards.
1937	The first Welsh Books Campaign was launched by the Urdd.
1938	A Welsh-language petition, with 250,000 signatures, calling for the official recognition of Welsh in law courts, was presented to Parliament.
1939	At Aberystwyth, the first Welsh-language primary school was opened by the Urdd.

1942   The Welsh Courts Act allowed Welsh to be used in court proceedings.

1943   The Union of Welsh Publishers and Booksellers was formed.

1947   The first local authority Welsh-language primary school was opened in Llanelli.

Urdd Siarad Cymraeg (The League of Welsh Speaking) was founded.

1950   The first 'all Welsh' National Eisteddfod was held at Caerphilly.

The first part of *Geiriadur Prifysgol Cymru / A Dictionary of the Welsh Language* was published.

1952   Undeb Rhieni Ysgolion Cymraeg (The Union of Parents of Welsh Schools) was formed.

1956   A Welsh books grant was introduced by the government.

Bangor Normal College and Trinity College, Carmarthen, introduced courses for teaching through the medium of Welsh.

The first bilingual secondary school, Ysgol Glan Clwyd, Rhyl, was opened.

1959   Yr Academi Gymreig was founded.

1960   The first rate demand forms in Welsh anywhere in Wales were issued in Llanelli.

1961   Cyngor Llyfrau Cymraeg (The Welsh Books Council) was established.

1962   The first bilingual school in south Wales, Ysgol Rhydfelen, was opened.

Cymdeithas yr Iaith Gymraeg (The Welsh Language Society) was founded.

1963   The Welsh-language scientific journal, *Y Gwyddonydd*, was launched.

1964   The Elections (Welsh Forms) Act was passed allowing Welsh versions of official election forms.

1965   Undeb y Gymraeg Byw (The Union of Living Welsh) was founded.

1966   The Welsh Books Council took over responsibility for the annual Welsh Books Campaign from the Urdd.

1967   The Welsh Language Act allowed Welsh in legal proceedings and Welsh versions of official forms but this did not give Welsh official status.

Merched y Wawr, the Welsh-language women's movement, was founded.

1968   A Welsh Language Unit was established at Treforest to provide teaching materials.

The Gittins Report recommended that every child in primary schools in Wales should have the opportunity to learn Welsh.

The first bilingual postage stamp was issued.

1969   The registration of births and deaths in Welsh was introduced.

The first ever Welsh Office circular in Welsh, Circular 82/69, was issued.

1970   Adfer was founded to preserve Welsh-speaking communities.

1971   Registration of marriages in Welsh was introduced.

Mudiad Ysgolion Meithrin (Welsh Nursery Schools Movement) was founded.

Y Gymdeithas Wyddonol Genedlaethol (National Scientific Association) was formed for Welsh-speaking scientists.

1972   The Bowen Report recommending bilingual road signs was accepted by the government.

Sefydliad Cymru (The Institute of Wales) was founded.

Termau Cyfraith (legal terms in Welsh) was published.

1973   A Welsh Language Council was established to advise the government.

Translation facilities were introduced at the Crown Courts in Cardiff, Carmarthen and Mold. Swansea and Caernarfon followed later.

The first *papur bro* (local Welsh-language community newspaper) was published – *Y Dinesydd* of Cardiff.

Publication of *Geiriadur Termau: A Dictionary of Terms* for use in Welsh-language teaching.

The Wlpan method of intensive Welsh teaching was introduced.

1974   Welsh MPs were allowed to take the oath in Welsh as well as in English and 11 of 36 did so.

Neuadd Pantycelyn, Aberystwyth, became the first Welsh-language hall of residence in the University of Wales.

1976   Barddas, the society to encourage Welsh-language poetry was founded.

1978   The National Language Centre was established at Nant Gwrtheyrn, Llŷn.

The first film to be dubbed into Welsh was *Shane*.

1979   Radio Cymru was launched.

1981   The census showed Gwynedd to be the only county in Wales with a Welsh-speaking majority.

1982   S4C was launched making Welsh the first European minority language with its own television channel.

A Welsh-language Sunday newspaper, *Sulyn*, was launched but ceased publication after 14 issues.

1984   The Welsh Learners' Society (Cyngor y Dysgwyr) was formed.

1985   Cefn, the Welsh language civil rights movement, was established.

The centre for Advanced Welsh and Celtic Studies was established at University College of Wales, Aberystwyth.

1986   *Rhosyn a Rhith (Coming Up Roses)* became the first Welsh-language film to get a general release throughout Britain.

1987   Welsh was first used officially within the Vatican at a beatification ceremony for three sixteenth-century Welsh Catholic martyrs.

For the first time a planning application – for a housing development at Llanrhaedr, Clwyd – was turned down on the grounds that it might harm the Welsh language.

1988   An advisory Welsh Language Board was established.

Y Beibl Cymraeg Newydd, a new translation of the Bible, was published.

A School of Welsh Medium Studies was established at University College, Bangor.

S4C began providing a teletext service in Welsh.

The BBC introduced a page of Welsh on its Ceefax teletext service for the whole of Britain.

Blaenau Ffestiniog Magistrates' Court became the first in Wales to conduct all its proceedings in Welsh unless otherwise requested.

1989   The Open University offered its first course in Welsh and provided its first publications in Welsh.

The Hippocratic Oath was taken in Welsh for the first time by newly qualified doctors.

Welsh was used for the first time in the House of Lords ceremony for swearing in new Queen's Counsel.

Pont ('Bridge') society for newcomers to Wales was established.

Yr Atlas Cymraeg, the first fully bilingual atlas, was published.

The publication of the first new encyclopaedia in Welsh this century – *Chwilota*, in seven volumes – was completed.

1991   The Census showed that, for the first time since 1911, the decline in the number of Welsh-speakers had been halted.

1992   The Passport Office agreed to process applications in Welsh.

1993   A new Welsh Language Act improved the status of Welsh within public bodies and made the Welsh Language Board a statutory body.

1994   *Hedd Wyn* became the first Welsh-language film to be nominated for a Hollywood Oscar, in the 'Best Foreign Language Film' category.

WELSH-SPEAKERS IN WALES AGED THREE AND OVER

Census year	Number	% of the population of Wales
1891*	898,914(two and over)	54.4
1901	929,824	49.9
1911	977,366	43.5
1921	929,183	37.2

Census year	Number	% of the population of Wales
1931	909,261	36.8
1951	714,686	28.9
1961	656,002	26.0
1971	542,425	20.9
1981	503,559	18.9
1991	508,098	18.7

*The 1891 census figures are open to a number of criticisms so 1901 is usually regarded as the first acceptable language census.

The total number of people in Wales recorded as being able to speak, read or write Welsh in 1991 was 546,551. No official statistics are available on the use of Welsh in the rest of Great Britain.

WELSH-SPEAKERS BY COUNTY AND DISTRICT

	1981		1991	
	Number (thousands)	%	Number (thousands)	%
Clwyd	69.6	18.7	71.4	18.2
Alyn and Deeside	5.1	7.4	6.8	9.6
Colwyn	13.1	28.5	13.6	25.5
Delyn	11.5	18.4	11.6	17.8
Glyndŵr	16.3	43.3	16.1	39.9
Rhuddlan	8.3	16.6	8.5	16.2
Wrexham Maelor	15.2	14.3	14.9	13.4
Dyfed	146.2	47.0	145.0	43.7
Carmarthen	30.5	62.1	30.9	58.0
Ceredigion	34.8	65.1	36.0	59.1
Dinefwr	25.3	72.0	24.8	66.5
Llanelli	36.9	51.1	33.5	46.5
Preseli Pembrokeshire	16.1	24.8	16.5	24.4
South Pembrokeshire	2.6	7.1	3.3	8.2
Gwent	10.6	2.5	10.3	2.4
Blaenau Gwent	1.8	2.4	1.7	2.3
Islwyn	1.8	3.0	2.2	3.4
Monmouth	1.8	2.6	1.5	2.0
Newport	3.0	2.3	2.9	2.3
Torfaen	2.1	2.5	2.1	2.5

Gwynedd	135.1	63.0	138.4	61.0
Aberconwy	17.1	36.9	18.4	36.0
Arfon	37.1	76.6	38.1	74.6
Dwyfor	20.0	81.5	19.8	75.4
Meirionydd	20.9	71.2	20.8	65.4
Ynys Môn	39.3	61.6	41.2	62.0
Mid Glamorgan	42.7	8.3	43.3	8.5
Cynon Valley	7.1	11.1	5.9	9.5
Merthyr Tydfil	4.8	8.2	4.2	7.5
Ogwr	10.2	8.3	10.5	8.3
Rhondda	7.4	9.4	6.1	8.2
Rhymney Valley	6.6	6.6	7.5	7.6
Taff Ely	6.5	7.4	8.9	9.7
Powys	21.4	20.5	22.9	20.2
Brecknock	9.2	24.2	9.2	23.0
Montgomery	11.1	24.1	11.8	23.3
Radnorshire	1.0	5.1	1.9	8.3
South Glamorgan	20.7	5.7	24.5	6.5
Cardiff	14.7	5.7	17.2	6.4
Vale of Glamorgan	6.0	5.8	7.4	6.8
West Glamorgan	57.4	16.4	52.3	15.0
Lliw Valley	24.8	43.2	22.4	36.9
Neath	9.0	14.2	8.2	13.0
Port Talbot	5.1	9.8	3.2	8.6
Swansea	18.5	10.5	17.5	10.0

LANGUAGE SURVEYS

S4C Welsh Language Survey

According to a survey conducted by the London broadcasting research organization RSMB, which was published by S4C in March 1993, there are 750,000 Welsh-speakers in Wales with a total of 1.5 million able to understand some Welsh. In the rest of the UK, the RSMB figures showed 376,000 Welsh-speakers in England, 18,000 in Scotland and 1,000 in Northern Ireland.

Welsh Office Social Survey

A Welsh Office Social Survey carried out in 1992, the results of which were published in July 1993, indicated that 21.5 per cent of the population of Wales spoke Welsh, 16.9 per cent fluently or fairly well, while almost 34 per cent were able to speak at least some Welsh.

THE NATIONAL EISTEDDFOD AND THE GORSEDD – DATES OF SIGNIFICANCE AND INTEREST

1789   The first modern eisteddfod was held at Corwen.

1792   The first ever meeting of the Gorsedd of Bards was held on Primrose Hill, London.

1819   Start of the association between the Gorsedd and the Eisteddfod.

1819–   Provincial eisteddfodau were held.
1858

1832   First-known use of the title of 'Archdruid' was at the Beaumaris Eisteddfod.

1858   'The Great Eisteddfod' at Llangollen: Gorsedd ceremonies became a part of Eisteddfod pageantry.

1860   At Denbigh the decision was made that a single National Eisteddfod would be held alternately in north and south Wales. A 300-strong Eisteddfod Council was established to organize the festival and prepare subjects for competition.

1861   The first National Eisteddfod to be held was at Aberdare.

1866   The first National Eisteddfod to be held outside Wales was at Chester.

1867   A Crown was first presented for a *pryddest* – a poem in free verse.

1868   The Eisteddfod Council was disbanded.

1876   At Wrexham, the first official Archdruid, David Griffith ('Clwyd-fardd'), was appointed and the first known Recorder was also appointed.

1880   The National Eisteddfod Association, now the Court, was established to administer the National Eisteddfod.

1883   The National Eisteddfod compositions and adjudications began to be published regularly.

1894   The National Eisteddfod was first visited by a member of the Royal Family, the Prince of Wales.

1895   The first Herald Bard was appointed.

1899   A visit of Bretons to the Cardiff National Eisteddfod led to the formation of the Gorsedd of Brittany in 1900.

1912   The Chair and Crown were won for the first time by the same person, T. H. Parry-Williams.

1917   'The Black Eisteddfod' at Birkenhead: the Chair was won by Ellis Humphrey Evans ('Hedd Wyn') who had been killed in action in France.

1918   The first Eisteddfod offering a prize for the performance of a play.

     The National Eisteddfod Association decided that henceforth the Eisteddfod would always be held during the first week of August.

1924   At Pontypool in this year, the first radio broadcast was made from a national eisteddfod.

1928   At the Treorchy National Eisteddfod, eight Cornishmen were made members of the Gorsedd to create a Cornish Gorsedd.

1929   The last National Eisteddfod to be held outside Wales was at Liverpool.

1937   The National Eisteddfod Court and the Council were created by agreement between the National Eisteddfod Association and the Gorsedd.

     A Gold Prose Medal for Literature was introduced.

1938   The National Eisteddfod Office in London was closed.

1939   At the Denbigh National Eisteddfod both Chair and Crown were withheld for the first time.

1940   A 'Radio Eisteddfod' was held at Bangor because of the outbreak of war.

1946   The Queen, then Princess Elizabeth, was made a member of the Gorsedd at the Mountain Ash National Eisteddfod.

1947   The first Attendant Druid was appointed.

1948   The Local Government Act allowed local authorities to contribute to cultural and leisure events, including the Eisteddfod held within their areas.

     The number of times that a person could win the Chair or Crown was limited to two.

1949   The position of President of the Day was introduced, replacing the former three persons a day.

1950   Introduction of the 'all Welsh' rule and a purpose-built pavilion at the Caerphilly National Eisteddfod.

     At 15 the harpist Ann Griffiths became the youngest ever member of the Gorsedd.

1951   A Gold Medal for Art was introduced.

1952   The Court was established as the governing body and the Council, with specialist committees, became the executive body.

     The first National Eisteddfod events were shown, on film, on television.

1953   At the Rhyl National Eisteddfod, Dilys Cadwaladr became the first woman to win the Crown. (There had been a previous woman winner in 1883, but the winning poem then had been in English.)

1954   A Gold Medal for Architecture was introduced.

1955   The first Cymrawd (Fellow) of the National Eisteddfod was Canon Maurice Jones.

1959   The first two full-time organizers were appointed – one for north Wales and one for south Wales.

1960   The Cardiff National Eisteddfod was the first to benefit from the Eisteddfod Act of 1959 which allowed local authorities in Wales to make contributions to the event wherever it was being held in Wales.

1964   At Swansea, English translation facilities were made available for the first time.

1966   A Prose Medal ceremony was introduced at the Aberafan National Eisteddfod.
       A petition for royal patronage was granted so that the designation 'Royal' for the festival became permanent instead of having to be applied for annually, and it also applied to the Council and the central office.

1968   The first Drama Tent was introduced on the Eisteddfod field.

1971   The Archdruid of Wales was recognized as also being the head of the Gorseddau of Brittany and Cornwall.

1972   At the Haverfordwest National Eisteddfod, a Welsh learners' tent was provided for the first time.

1978   The first director was appointed, with offices in Cardiff.
       The European Community made its first grant – of £500 – to the Eisteddfod.

1983   A Welsh Learner of the Year competition was introduced.

1985   The Chair was won (at the Rhyl National Eisteddfod) for the first time by someone who had learned Welsh – Robat Powel of Ebbw Vale.

1988   The Newport National Eisteddfod was the first to be supported financially by all eight Welsh county councils.

1990   The amount of commercial sponsorship of the Eisteddfod exceeded £1 million for the first time.

1992   The Gorsedd assumed responsibility for the Prose Medal ceremony.
       A full-time officer for Welsh learners was appointed.

1993   The Drama Medal competition was withdrawn from the Eisteddfod.
       The first calendar of local eisteddfodau was published by the National Eisteddfod.

LOCATIONS OF THE NATIONAL EISTEDDFOD SINCE ITS INCEPTION

1861	Aberdare	1897	Newport	1932	Aberavon
1862	Caernarfon	1898	Blaenau Ffestiniog	1933	Wrexham
1863	Swansea	1899	Cardiff	1934	Neath
1864	Llandudno	1900	Liverpool	1935	Caernarfon
1865	Aberystwyth	1901	Merthyr Tydfil	1936	Fishguard
1866	Chester	1902	Bangor	1937	Machynlleth
1867	Carmarthen	1903	Llanelli	1938	Cardiff
1868	Rhuthun	1904	Rhyl	1939	Denbigh
1869*	Holywell	1905	Mountain Ash	1940	Radio Eisteddfod (Bangor)
1870	Rhyl	1906	Caernarfon	1941	Old Colwyn (*curtailed*)
1871	*no Eisteddfod held*	1907	Swansea	1942	Cardigan (*curtailed*)
1872	Tremadog	1908	Llangollen	1943	Bangor (*curtailed*)
1873	Mold	1909	London	1944	Llandybïe
1874	Bangor	1910	Colwyn Bay	1945	Rhosllanerchrugog
1875	Pwllheli	1911	Carmarthen	1946	Mountain Ash
1876	Wrexham	1912	Wrexham	1947	Colwyn Bay
1877	Caernarfon	1913	Abergavenny	1948	Bridgend
1879	Birkenhead	1914	*no Eisteddfod held*	1949	Dolgellau
1880*	Caernarfon	1915	Bangor (*curtailed*)	1950	Caerphilly
1881	Merthyr Tydfil	1916	Aberystwyth	1951	Llanrwst
1882	Denbigh	1917	Birkenhead	1952	Aberystwyth
1883	Cardiff	1918	Neath	1953	Rhyl
1884	Liverpool	1919	Corwen	1954	Ystradgynlais
1885	Aberdare	1920	Barry	1955	Pwllheli
1886	Caernarfon	1921	Caernarfon	1956	Aberdare
1887	London	1922	Ammanford	1957	Llangefni
1888	Wrexham	1923	Mold	1958	Ebbw Vale
1889	Brecon	1924	Pontypool	1959	Caernarfon
1890	Bangor	1925	Pwllheli	1960	Cardiff
1891	Swansea	1926	Swansea	1961	Rhosllanerchrugog
1892	Rhyl	1927	Holyhead	1962	Llanelli
1893	Pontypridd	1928	Treorchy	1963	Llandudno
1894	Caernarfon	1929	Liverpool	1964	Swansea
1895	Llanelli	1930	Llanelli	1965	Newtown
1896	Llandudno	1931	Bangor	1966	Aberavon

Note: the Eisteddfodau held between 1869 and 1880 were not held under the auspices of a national organization but were *ad hoc* arrangements.

1967	Bala	1978	Cardiff	1989	Llanrwst
1968	Barry	1979	Caernarfon	1990	Rhymney Valley
1969	Flint	1980	Gorseinon	1991	Mold
1970	Ammanford	1981	Machynlleth	1992	Aberystwyth
1971	Bangor	1982	Swansea	1993	Llanelwedd
1972	Haverfordwest	1983	Llangefni	1994	Neath
1973	Rhuthun	1984	Lampeter	1995	Colwyn Bay
1974	Carmarthen	1985	Rhyl	1996	Llandeilo
1975	Cricieth	1986	Fishguard	1997	Bala
1976	Cardigan	1987	Porthmadog	1998	Bridgend
1977	Wrexham	1988	Newport		

A National Eisteddfod is proclaimed a year and a day in advance by the Gorsedd of Bards inside a Gorsedd Circle of twelve stone pillars, the Archdruid officiating from the central Maen Llog (the Logan Stone).

A record attendance of 164,100 at a National Eisteddfod was set at Mold in 1991.

The Most Frequently Visited Venues

(Excluding the 1869–1880 period)

Caernarfon	8	Cardiff	5	Rhyl	4
Bangor	6	Aberystwyth	4	Wrexham	4
Swansea	6	Llanelli	4		

The National Eisteddfod has been held at venues in England on seven occasions.

WINNERS OF THE CHAIR AND CROWN AT THE NATIONAL EISTEDDFOD SINCE 1861

	Crown (For a *pryddest* in free verse)	Chair (For an *awdl* in strict metre)
1861		Morris Williams
1862		Rowland Williams*
1863		William Ambrose
1864		Richard Ffoulkes Edwards
1865		*withheld*
1866		Robert Thomas
1867	(1st year awarded) Rowland Williams	Richard Parry
1868	Lewis William Lewis	*withheld*

*Subsequently elected Archdruid

74

Between 1869 and 1880 there was no 'National' Eisteddfod under a central organization after the Eisteddfod Council was disbanded. A new central organization was introduced in 1880 with the establishment of the National Eisteddfod Association (now the Court).

	Crown (For a *pryddest* in free verse)	Chair (For an *awdl* in strict metre)
1881	Watkin Hezekiah Williams	Evan Rees*
1882	Dafydd Rees Williams	*withheld*
1883	Anna Walter Thomas	*withheld*
1884	Edward Foulkes	Evan Rees
1885	Griffith Tecwyn Parry	Watkin Hezekiah Williams
1886	John Cadfan Davies*	Richard Davies
1887	John Cadfan Davies	Robert Arthur Williams
1888	Howell Elvet Lewis*	Thomas Tudno Jones
1889	Howell Elvet Lewis	Evan Rees
1890	John John Roberts	Thomas Tudno Jones
1891	David Adams	John Owen Williams
1892	John John Roberts	Evan Jones
1893	Ben Davies	John Ceulanydd Williams
1894	Ben Davies	Howell Elvet Lewis
1895	Lewis William Lewis	John Owen Williams*
1896	*withheld*	Ben Davies
1897	Thomas Mafonwy Davies	John Thomas Job
1898	Richard Roberts	Robert Owen Hughes
1899	Richard Roberts	*withheld*
1900	John Thomas Job	John Owen williams
1901	John Gwili Jenkins*	Evan Rees
1902	Robert Silyn Roberts	T. Gwynn Jones
1903	John Evans Davies	John Thomas Job
1904	Richard Machno Humphreys	J. Machreth Rees
1905	Thomas Mathonwy Davies	*withheld*
1906	Hugh Emyr Davies	John James Williams*
1907	John Dyfnallt Owen*	Thomas Davies
1908	Hugh Emyr Davies	John James Williams
1909	W. J. Gruffydd	T. Gwynn Jones
1910	William Crwys Williams*	R. Williams Parry
1911	William Crwys Williams	William Roberts
1912	T. H. Parry-Williams	T. H. Parry-Williams

*Subsequently elected Archdruid.

	Crown (For a *pryddest* in free verse)	*Chair* (For an *awdl* in strict metre)
1913	William Evans*	Thomas Jacob Thomas
1914	*no Eisteddfod held*	*no Eisteddfod held*
1915	T. H. Parry-Williams	T. H. Parry-Williams
1916	*withheld*	J. Ellis Williams
1917	William Evans	Ellis Humphrey Evans
1918	D. Emrys Lewis	John Thomas Job
1919	William Crwys Williams	D. Cledlyn Davies
1920	James Evans	*withheld*
1921	Albert Evans Jones*	Robert John Rowlands
1922	Robert Beynon	J. Lloyd-Jones
1923	Albert Evans Jones*	D. Cledlyn Davies
1924	Edward Prosser Rhys	Albert Evans Jones
1925	William Evans	Dewi Morgan
1926	David Emrys Jones	David James Jones ('Gwenallt')
1927	Caradog Prichard	*withheld*
1928	Caradog Prichard	*withheld*
1929	Caradog Prichard	David Emrys Jones
1930	William Jones	David Emrys James
1931	Albert Evans Jones	David James Jones ('Gwenallt')
1932	Thomas Eurig Davies	D. J. Davies
1933	Simon B. Jones	Edgar Phillips*
1934	Thomas Eurig Davies	William Morris*
1935	Gwilym R. Jones	E. Gwyndaf Evans*
1936	David Jones	Simon B. Jones
1937	J. M. Edwards	T. Rowland Hughes
1938	Edgar H. Thomas	Gwilym R. Jones
1939	*withheld*	*withheld*
1940	T. Rowland Hughes	*withheld*
1941	J. M. Edwards	Roland Jones
1942	Herman Jones	*withheld*
1943	Dafydd Owen	David Emrys James
1944	J. M. Edwards	D. Lloyd Jenkins
1945	*withheld*	Tom Parri Jones
1946	Rhydwen Williams	Geraint Bowen*
1947	Griffith John Roberts	John Tudor James
1948	Euros Bowen	D. Emrys James

*Subsequently elected Archdruid.

	Crown (For a *pryddest* in free verse)	*Chair* (For an *awdl* in strict metre)
1949	John Tudor James	Roland Jones
1950	Euros Bowen	Gwilym Tilsley*
1951	T. Glynne Davies	Brinley Richards*
1952	*withheld*	John Evans
1953	Dilys Cadwaladr	E. Llwyd Williams
1954	E. Llwyd Williams	John Evans
1955	W. J. Gruffydd*	Gwilym Ceri Jones
1956	*withheld*	Mathonwy Hughes
1957	Dyfnallt Morgan	Gwilym Tilsley
1958	Llew Jones	T. Llew Jones
1959	Tom Huws	T. Llew Jones
1960	W. J. Gruffydd	*withheld*
1961	L. Haydn Lewis	Emrys Edwards
1962	D. Emlyn Lewis	Caradog Prichard
1963	Tom Parri Jones	*withheld*
1964	Rhydwen Williams	Bryn Williams*
1965	Tom Parri Jones	William David Williams
1966	Dafydd Jones	Dic Jones
1967	Eluned Phillips	Emrys Roberts*
1968	Haydn Lewis	Bryn Williams
1969	Dafydd Rowlands	James Nicholas
1970	Bryan Martin Davies	Tomi Evans
1971	Bryan Martin Davies	Emrys Roberts
1972	Dafydd Rowlands	Dafydd Owen
1973	Alan Lloyd Roberts (Alan Llwyd)	Alan Lloyd Roberts (Alan Llwyd)
1974	William George*	Moses Glyn Jones
1975	Elwyn Roberts	Gerallt Lloyd Owen
1976	Alan Lloyd Roberts (Alan Llwyd)	Alan Lloyd Roberts (Alan Llwyd)
1977	Donald Evans	Donald Evans
1978	Siôn Eirian	*withheld*
1979	Meirion Evans	*withheld*
1980	Donald Evans	Donald Evans
1981	Siôn Aled	John Gwilym Jones*
1982	Eirwyn George	Gerallt Lloyd Owen
1983	Eluned Phillips	Einion Evans
1984	John Roderick Rees	Aled Rhys William

*Subsequently elected Archdruid.

Crown	*Chair*
(For a *pryddest* in free verse)	(For an *awdl* in strict metre)
1985 John Roderick Rees	Robat Powell
1986 T. James Jones	Gwyn ap Gwilym
1987 John Griffith Jones	Ieuan Wyn
1988 T. James Jones	Elwyn Edwards
1989 Selwyn Griffiths	Idris Reynolds
1990 Iwan Llwyd	Myrddin ap Dafydd
1991 Einir Jones	Robin Llwyd ab Owain
1992 Cyril Jones	Idris Reynolds
1993 Eirwyn George	Meirion MacIntyre Huws
1994 Gerwyn Williams	Emyr Lewis

Note: Since 1948 no one may win either the Chair or the Crown on more than two occasions.

Women winners: The Chair has never been won by a woman but the Crown has been won by women on five occasions – in 1883 (for an ode in English), 1953, 1967, 1983 and 1991.

WINNERS OF THE PROSE MEDAL AT THE NATIONAL EISTEDDFOD SINCE 1937

1937	John Owen Jones (first award)	1959	William Owen
1938	Elena Puw Morgan	1960	Rhiannon Davies Jones
1939	John Gwilym Jones	1961	*withheld*
1940	Thomas Hughes Jones	1962	William Owen
1941	Gwilym Richard Jones	1963	William Llywelyn Jones
1942	*withheld*	1964	Rhiannon Davies Jones
1943	*withheld*	1965	Eigra Lewis Roberts
1944	*withheld*	1966	*withheld*
1945	*withheld*	1967	*withheld*
1946	Dafydd Jenkins	1968	Eigra Lewis Roberts
1947	*withheld*	1969	Emyr Jones
1948	Robert Ivor Parry	1970	*withheld*
1949	*withheld*	1971	Ifor Wyn Williams
1950	*withheld*	1972	Dafydd Rowlands
1951	Islwyn Ffowc Ellis	1973	Emyr Roberts
1952	Owen Elias Roberts	1974	Dafydd Ifans
1953	*withheld*	1975	*withheld*

1954	Owen Elias Roberts	1976	Marged Prichard
1955	Morris Selyf Roberts	1977	Robert Gerallt Jones
1956	William Thomas Gruffydd	1978	Harri Williams
1957	Tom Parri Jones	1979	Robyn Lewis
1958	Edward Cynolwyn Pugh	1980	R. Gerallt Jones
1981	John Griffith Jones	1988	*withheld*
1982	Gwilym M. Jones	1989	Irma Chilton
1983	Tudor Wilson Evans	1990	*withheld*
1984	John Idris Owen	1991	Angharad Tomos
1985	Margaret Dafydd	1992*	Robin Llywelyn
1986	Ray Evans (Mrs)	1993	Mihangel Morgan
1987	Margiad Williams	1994	Robin Llywelyn

*The first year that the Gorsedd became responsible for the Prose Medal ceremony.

OFFICIAL ARCHDRUIDS OF THE GORSEDD OF BARDS

Clwydfardd (David Griffiths)	1876–1894
Hwfa Môn (Rowland Williams)	1895–1905
Dyfed (Evan Rees)	1905–1923
Cadfan (John Cadfan Davies)	1923–1924
Elfed (Howell Elvet Lewis)	1924–1928
Pedrog (John Owen Williams)	1928–1932
Gwili (John Gwili Jenkins)	1932–1936
J. J. (John James Williams)	1936–1939
Crwys (William Crwys Williams)	1939–1947
Wil Ifan (William Evans)	1947–1950
Cynan (Sir Albert Evans-Jones)	1950–1954
Dyfnallt (John Dyfnallt Owen)	1954–1957
William Morris	1957–1960
Trefin (Edgar Phillips)	1960–1962
Cynan (Sir Albert Evans-Jones)	1963–1966
Gwyndaf (E. Gwyndaf Evans)	1966–1969
Tilsli (Gwilym Richard Tilsley)	1969–1972
Brinli (Brinley Richards)	1972–1975
Bryn (R. Bryn Williams)	1975–1978
Geraint (Geraint Bowen)	1978–1981
Jâms Nicholas (James Nicholas)	1981–1984
Elerydd (W. J. Gruffydd)	1984–1987
Emrys Deudraeth (Emrys Roberts)	1987–1990

Ap Llysor (William George)   1990–1993
John Gwilym (John Gwilym Jones)   1993–1996

Note: in 1923 tenure was limited to four years – suspended during the Second World War – and in 1947 it was limited to three years.
   Only Sir Albert Evans-Jones ('Cynan') has been elected Archdruid twice.
   Archdruids must have won the Chair, Crown or Prose Medal at a National Eisteddfod.

BARDIC ORDERS OF THE GORSEDD OF BARDS

Ovates (green robes)   Membership is obtained by passing the first two examinations of the Gorsedd or by recommend- ation for services to Wales.

Bards (blue robes)   Membership can only be obtained by passing the third and final examination of the Gorsedd.

Druidic Order (white robes) Membership is only obtained by recommendation.

In 1994 there was some 1,500 members of the Gorsedd.

URDD GOBAITH CYMRU – DATES OF SIGNIFICANCE AND INTEREST

1922   Urdd Gobaith Cymru was founded by Sir Ifan ab Owen Edwards.
1925   The first Peace Message from the Urdd to the world was broadcast by the BBC.
1928   The first summer camp was held at Llangrannog.
1929   The first Urdd National Eisteddfod was held (at Corwen).
1930   The first full-time organizer for north Wales was appointed.
1931   Welsh learners were invited to join the Urdd.
1932   The first Mabolgampau (Youth Games) were held (at Llanelli).
        The first full-time organizer for south Wales was appointed.
1933   The first Urdd summer cruise was organized.
        The first broadcast from the Urdd Eisteddfod took place.
1939   The first Welsh-language primary school in Wales was established by the Urdd in Aberystwyth.
1940   The Urdd modified its structure to include the 16–25 age group.
1946   The first county trophy was awarded (to Meirionnydd).
1947   Pantyfedwen near Borth was donated to the Urdd by Sir David James.
1948   The first international camp was held in Aberystwyth.
1950   The first summer camp was held at Glan Llyn.
1952   A Chair and Crown were first offered as prizes at the Urdd Eisteddfod.

1954   The last Mabolgampau were held (at Mountain Ash).
1960   The last international camp was held at Aberystwyth.
1968   Cefncwrt Farm, Llangrannog, was bought.
1974   The Eisteddfod was extended from three to four days.
1983   The Eisteddfod was extended from four to five days.
1984   Handicapped children from special schools competed at the Eisteddfod for the first time.
1989   The Eisteddfod was extended from five to six days.
1991   Translation facilities were made available at an Eisteddfod for the first time.

LOCATIONS OF THE URDD NATIONAL EISTEDDFOD

1929	Corwen	1955	Abertridwr	1977	Barry
1930	Caernarfon	1956	Caernarfon	1978	Llanelwedd
1931	Swansea	1957	Ammanford	1979	Maesteg
1932	Machynlleth	1958	Mold	1980	Abergele
1933	Caerphilly	1959	Lampeter	1981	Newcastle Emlyn
1934	Old Colwyn	1960	Dolgellau	1982	Pwllheli
1935	Carmarthen	1961	Aberdare	1983	Aberavon
1936	Blaenau Ffestiniog	1962	Rhuthun	1984	Mold
1937	Gwauncaegurwen	1963	Brynaman	1985	Cardiff
1938	Aberystwyth	1964	Porthmadog	1986	Bethesda
1939	Llanelli	1965	Cardiff	1987	Merthyr Tydfil
1940	Rhyl	1966	Holyhead	1988	Newtown
1941–45	*no eisteddfodau held*	1967	Carmarthen	1989	Cross Hands
1946	Corwen	1968	Llanrwst	1990	Caernarfon
1947	Treorchy	1969	Aberystwyth	1991	Tonyrefail
1948	Llangefni	1970	Llanidloes	1992	Rhuthun
1949	Pontarddulais	1971	Swansea	1993	Gorseinon
1950	Wrexham	1972	Bala	1994	Dolgellau
1951	Fishguard	1973	Pontypridd	1995	Crymych
1952	Machynlleth	1974	Rhyl	1996	Rhosllanerchrugog
1953	Maesteg	1975	Llanelli	1997	Islwyn
1954	Bala	1976	Menai Bridge		

Most Frequently Visited Venue
Caernarfon 3

WINNERS OF THE CHAIR AND CROWN AT THE URDD NATIONAL EISTEDDFOD

	Chair (Main poetry competition)	*Crown* (Main prose competition)
1952	*withheld*	Catrin Puw Morgan
1953	Desmond Healy	Brynmor Jones
1954	Dic Jones	Catrin Puw Morgan
1955	Dic Jones	*withheld*
1956	Dic Jones	Catrin Puw Morgan
1957	Dic Jones	Mairwen Lewis
1958	T. James Jones	Marian Rees
1959	Dic Jones	Catrin Lloyd Rowlands
1960	Dafydd Edwards	John Rowlands
1961	John Gwilym Jones	Eigra Lewis
1962	Gerallt Lloyd Jones	Enid Wyn Baines
1963	Donald Evans	David Wyn Davies
1964	Mary Hughes	Geraint Lloyd Owen
1965	Gerallt Lloyd Owen	Robin Gwyndaf Jones
1966	Peter Davies	Mair Gibbard
1967	Peter Davies	Dafydd Huw Williams
1968	John Hywen Edwards	John Clifford Jones
1969	Gerallt Lloyd Owen	Nan Lloyd Roberts
1970	*withheld*	Ieuan Wyn Gruffydd
1971	Arwel John	Siôn Eirian
1972	Arwel John	Delyth Beasley
1973	Islwyn Edwards	Eifion Glyn Roberts
1974	Myrddin ap Dafydd	Eirug Wyn
1975	Dilwyn Lewis	Tom Jones
1976	Aled Owen	Gwyneth Williams
1977	Esyllt Maelor	Janet Jones
1978	Robin Llwyd ab Owain	Catherine Gwynn
1979	Peredur Lynch	*withheld*
1980	Iwan Lloyd Williams	Gwenan Jones
1981	Meirion Morris	Ffion Eleri Edwards
1982	Lleucu Morgan	Gwawr Maelor
1983	Sioned Lewis Roberts	*withheld*
1984	*withheld*	Angharad Jones
1985	Meirion Davies	Bethan Evans

	Chair (Main poetry competition)	*Crown* (Main prose competition)
1986	Non Vaughan Evans	Mary Elizabeth Jones
1987	Sarah Ogwen Williams	Emyr Davies
1988	Tudur Dylan Jones	Karl Harrison
1989	Nia Owain Hughes	Mared Wyn Hughes
1990	Meirion Wyn Jones	Angharad Puw Davies
1991	Daniel Evans	Anwen James
1992	Ceri Wyn Jones	Siân Wyn Jones
1993	Damian Walford Davies	Eirian Edmund
1994	Mererid Puw Davies	Eurgain Evans

HEN WLAD FY NHADAU

Hen Wlad Fy Nhadau ('Land Of My Fathers') was composed by Evan James (words) and his son James James (music) during one weekend in January, 1856, in Pontypridd, Mid Glamorgan, and was originally called 'Glan Rhondda'.

It was first performed in public later in 1856 at Tabor Chapel, Maesteg, Mid Glamorgan, and the first printed version appeared in 1858, the year it won first prize at the Llangollen Eisteddfod.

It quickly became increasingly popular and was soon adopted as the Welsh National Anthem although no definite date can be given for this. However 1866, when the National Eisteddfod was held at Chester, is widely regarded as the year it was recognized as the anthem.

> Mae hen wlad fy nhadau yn annwyl i mi,
> Gwlad beirdd a chantorion enwogion o fri;
> Ei gwrol ryfelwyr, gwladgarwyr tra mad,
> Dros ryddid collasant eu gwaed.
>
> Gwlad, gwlad, pleidiol wyf i'm gwlad;
> Tra mor yn fur i'r bur hoff bau
> O bydded i'r hen iaith barhau.
>
> *Translation*:
> The old land of my fathers is dear to me,
> Land of poets and singers, famous men of renown;
> Its brave warriors, fine patriots,
> Gave their blood for freedom.

My country, my country, I am devoted to my country,
While the sea is a wall to the pure loved land
O may the old language endure.

ORGANIZATIONS CONCERNED WITH THE WELSH LANGUAGE

Adfer
(To preserve Welsh-speaking
local communities) — 26 Penrhosgarnedd, Bangor, Gwynedd.

Bwrdd yr Iaith Gymraeg
(Welsh Language Board) — Market Chambers, 5–7 St Mary Street, Cardiff, CF1 2RT

Canolfan Iaith Genedlaethol — Llithfaen, Pwllheli, Gwynedd, LL53 6PA.

Nant Gwrtheyrn
(National Welsh Language Centre)

Cefn
(Welsh-language civil rights movement) — 1 Stryd y Castell, Caernarfon, Gwynedd, LL55 1SE.

Cyngor Llyfrau Cymraeg
(Welsh Books Council) — Castell Brychan, Aberystwyth, Dyfed.

CYD (Cyngor y Dysgwyr)
(Welsh Learners Council) — Adran y Gymraeg, Yr Hen Goleg, Aberystwyth, Dyfed, SY23 2AX.

Cymdeithas yr Iaith Gymraeg
(Welsh Language Society) — Pen Roc, Rhodfa'r Môr, Aberystwyth, Dyfed, SY23 2AZ.

Eisteddfod Genedlaethol Cymru
(National Eisteddfod of Wales) — 40 Parc Tŷ Glas, Llanishen, Cardiff, CF4 5WU.

Merched y Wawr
(Welsh women's society) — Penlan-Merwyn, Aberporth, Dyfed, SY23 2DX

Mudiad Ysgolion Meithrin
(Welsh Nursery Schools Movement) — 145 Albany Road, Roath, Cardiff, CF2 3NT.

Pont ('Bridge' – Welsh society for
newcomers to Wales) — 17 Heol Urban, Llandaf, Cardiff, CF5 2QP.

Rhieni Dros Addysg Gymraeg
(Parents for Welsh Education) — Cartref, Trelawnyd, Rhyl, Clwyd.

S4C (Sianel Pedwar Cymru)
(Welsh-language television channel)   Parc Tŷ Glas, Llanishen, Cardiff, CF4 5DU.

Undeb Cenedlaethol Athrawon Cymru
(National Union of Welsh Teachers)   Pen Roc, Rhodfa'r Môr, Aberystwyth, Dyfed.

Uned Iaith Genedlaethol Cymru CBAC
(WJEC National Language Unit of Wales)   245 Western Avenue, Cardiff, CF5 2YX.

Urdd Gobaith Cymru   Swyddfa'r Urdd, Ffordd Llanbadarn,
(Welsh League of Youth)   Aberystwyth, Dyfed.

For Welsh-language schools see chapter 7.
For Welsh-language broadcasting and newspapers see chapter 9.

ENGLISH AND WELSH PLACE-NAMES IN WALES (INCLUDING SPELLING DIFFERENCES)

Aberavon	*Aberafan*	Bow Street	*Nant-y-Fallen*
Aberdare	*Aberdâr*	Brawdy	*Breudeth*
Abergavenny	*Y Fenni*	Brecon	*Aberhonddu*
Abermule	*Aber-miwl*	Brecon Beacons	*Bannau Brycheiniog*
Aberthaw	*Aberddawan*	Bridgend	*Pen-y-bont ar Ogwr*
Abertillery	*Abertyleri*	Bristol Channel	*Môr Hafren*
Acton	*Gwaunyterfyn*	Briton Ferry	*Llansawel*
Ambleston	*Treamlod*	Broadhaven	*Aber Llydan*
Ammanford	*Rhydaman*	Broughton	*Brychdwn*
Anglesey	*Môn*	Buckley	*Bwcle*
Bala Lake	*Llyn Tegid*	Builth Wells	*Llanfair-ym-Muallt*
Bangor-on-Dee	*Bangor Is-coed*	Burry Port	*Porth Tywyn*
Bardsey Island	*Ynys Enlli*	Bynea	*Y Bynie*
Barmouth	*Abermo*	Caerleon	*Caerllion*
Barry	*Y Barri*	Caerphilly	*Caerffili*
Beaumaris	*Biwmaris*	Caldey Island	*Ynys Bŷr*
Bedwellty	*Bedwellte*	Cardiff	*Caerdydd*
Berriew	*Aberriw*	Cardigan	*Aberteifi*
Bersham	*Y Bers*	Carew	*Caeriw*
Bishopston	*Llandeilo Ferwallt*	Carmarthen	*Caerfyrddin*
Bishton	*Trefesgob*	Carmel Head	*Trwyn Carmel*
Blackwood	*Coed-duon*	Carway	*Carwe*
Bonvilston	*Tresimwn*	Castleton	*Cas-bach*

Chepstow	*Cas-gwent*	Holywell	*Treffynnon*
Chirk	*Y Waun*	Hope	*Yr Hob*
Church Village	*Gartholwg*	Horseshoe Pass	*Yr Oernant*
Cilmery	*Cilmeri*	Kenfig	*Cynffig*
Clyro	*Cleirwy*	Kidwelly	*Cydweli*
Colwyn Bay	*Bae Colwyn*	Killay	*Cilâ*
Cowbridge	*Y Bont-faen*	Kinmel Bay	*Bae Cinmel*
Coychurch	*Llangrallo*	Knighton	*Trefyclo*
Criccieth	*Cricieth*	Knucklas	*Cnwclas*
Crickhowell	*Crucywel*	Lampeter	*Llanbedr Pont Steffan*
Crimea Pass	*Bwlch Gorddinan*	Lamphey	*Llandyfái*
Dee	*Dyfrdwy*	Landore	*Glandŵr*
Denbigh	*Dinbych*	Laugharne	*Lacharn*
Devil's Bridge	*Pontarfynach*	Letterston	*Treletert*
Dovey	*Dyfi*	Little Haven	*Aber Bach*
Ebbw Vale	*Glyn Ebwy*	Little Orme	*Trwyn-y-fuwch*
East Mouse	*Ynys Amlwch*	Llandough	*Llandochau*
Fairbourne	*Y Friog*	Llandovery	*Llanymddyfri*
Ferryside	*Glanyferi*	Llandudno Junction	*Cyffordd Llandudno*
Fishguard	*Abergwaun*	Llangibby	*Llangybi*
Flat Holm	*Ynys Hafren*	Llan-gors Lake	*Llyn Syfaddan*
Flint	*Y Fflint*	Llanthony	*Llanddewi Nant Hodni*
Glasbury	*Y Clas-ar-Wy*	Llantilio Crossenny	*Llandeilo Gresynni*
Glynneath	*Glyn Nedd*	Llantilio Pertholey	*Llandeilo Bertholau*
Goodwick	*Wdig*	Llantwit Major	*Llanilltud Fawr*
Goldcliff	*Allteurin*	Llanvapley	*Llanfable*
Gospel Pass	*Bwlch yr Efengyl*	Llawhaden	*Llanhuadain*
Gower	*Gŵyr*	Llay	*Llai*
Gowerton	*Tre-Gŵyr*	Lleyn	*Llŷn*
Grassholm	*Gwales*	Loughor	*Casllwchwr*
Great Orme	*Gogarth*	Magor	*Magwyr*
Greenfield	*Maes-glas*	Manorbier	*Maenorbŷr*
Gresford	*Gresffordd*	Mathry	*Mathri*
Grosmont	*Y Grysmwnt*	Menai Bridge	*Porthaethwy*
Halkyn	*Helygain*	Merthyr Vale	*Ynysowen*
Haverfordwest	*Hwlffordd*	Middle Mouse	*Ynys Badrig*
Hawarden	*Penarlâg*	Milford Haven	*Aberdaugleddyf*
Hay-on-Wye	*Y Gelli (Gandryll)*	Mold	*Yr Wyddgrug*
Hell's Mouth	*Porth Neigwl*	Monknash	*Yr As Fawr*
Holyhead	*Caergybi*	Monmouth	*Trefynwy*

Montgomery	*Trefaldwyn*	Portskewett	*Porth Sgiwed*
Morriston	*Treforys*	Presteigne	*Llanandras*
Mountain Ash	*Aberpennar*	Puffin Island	*Ynys Seiriol*
Mumbles	*Y Mwmbwls*	Pyle	*Y Pîl*
Narberth	*Arberth*	Quakers Yard	*Mynwent y Crynwyr*
Nash	*Yr As Fach*	Raglan	*Rhaglan*
Neath	*Castell-nedd*	Ramsey Island	*Ynys Dewi*
Nevern	*Nyfer/Nanhyfer*	Red Hill	*Bryn Goch*
Newborough	*Niwbwrch*	Rhayader	*Rhaeadr Gwy*
Newbridge (Gwent)	*Trecelyn*	Roch	*Y Garn*
Newbridge-on-Wye	*Y Bontnewydd-ar-Wysg*	Rogerstone	*Tŷ-du*
Newcastle Emlyn	*Castellnewydd Emlyn*	Rumney	*Tredelerch*
Newmarket	*Trelawnyd*	Ruthin	*Rhuthun*
New Moat	*Y Mot*	Salt Island	*Ynys Halen*
Newport (Dyfed)	*Trefdraeth*	Sennybridge	*Pontsenni*
Newport (Gwent)	*Casnewydd-ar-Wysg*	Seven Sisters	*Blaendulais*
New Quay	*Ceinewydd*	Severn	*Hafren*
New Radnor	*Maesyfed*	Skenfrith	*Ynysgynwraidd*
Newtown	*Y Drenewydd*	Skerries	*Ynysoedd y Moelrhoniaid*
Offa's Dyke	*Clawdd Offa*	Sketty	*Sgeti*
Ogmore-by-Sea	*Aberogwr*	Skewen	*Sgiwen*
Ogmore Vale	*Cwm Ogwr*	Skirrid	*Ysgyryd*
Old Radnor	*Pencraig*	Snowdon	*Yr Wyddfa*
Overton	*Owrtyn*	Snowdonia	*Eryri*
Oystermouth	*Ystumllwynarth*	Solva	*Solfach*
Painscastle	*Llanbedr Castell-paen*	South Bishop	*Em-Sger*
Pass of the Cross	*Bwlch-y-groes*	St Ann's Head	*Penrhos*
Paviland	*Pen-y-fai*	St Asaph	*Llanelwy*
Pembrey	*Pen-bre*	St Athan	*Sain Tathan*
Pembroke	*Penfro*	St Bride's Bay	*Bae Sain Ffraid*
Pembroke Dock	*Doc Penfro*	St Brides Wentloog	*Llansanffraidd Gwynllŵg*
Pendine	*Pentywyn*	St Clears	*Sanclêr*
Penmark	*Pen-marc*	St David's	*Tyddewi*
Peterston Wentloog	*Llanbedr Gwynllŵg*	St David's Head	*Penmaendewi*
Plynlimon	*Pumlumon*	St Dogmael's	*Llandudoch*
Point of Ayr	*Y Parlwr Du*	St Donat's	*Sain Dunwyd*
Pontypool	*Pont-y-pŵl*	St Fagans	*Sain Ffagan*
Port Dinorwic	*Y Felinheli*	St Lythan's	*Llwyneliddon*
Port Eynon	*Porth Einon*	Strata Florida	*Ystrad-fflur*
Port Penrhyn	*Abercegin*	Sully	*Sili*

Swansea	*Abertawe*	Usk	*Brynbuga*
Taffs Well	*Ffynnon Taf*	Usk (river)	*Wysg*
Talbot Green	*Tonysguboriau*	Vale of Glamorgan	*Bro Morgannwg*
Talley	*Talyllychau*	Valley	*Y Fali*
Tenby	*Dinbych-y-pysgod*	Velindre	*Felindre*
Three Cocks	*Aberllynfi*	Welshpool	*Y Trallwng*
Tintern	*Tyndyrn*	Wentloog	*Gwynllŵg*
Trecastle	*Trecastell*	Wenvoe	*Gwenfô*
Tredunnock	*Tredynog*	Whitland	*Hendy-gwyn*
Trelech	*Tryleg*	Wiston	*Cas-wis*
Tretower	*Tretŵr*	Wolf's Castle	*Cas-blaidd*
Tumble	*Y Tymbl*	Worm's Head	*Pen Pyrod*
Tusker Rock	*Craig y Sger*	Wrexham	*Wrecsam*
Undy	*Gwndy*	Wye	*Gwy*

WELSH NAMES FOR PLACES OUTSIDE WALES (INCLUDING SPELLING DIFFERENCES)

Adriatic Sea	*Môr Adria*	British Isles	*Ynysoedd Prydain*
Alps	*Yr Alpau*	Brittany	*Llydaw*
Antarctic	*Antarctig*	Bulgaria	*Bwlgaria*
Argentina	*Ariannin*	Burgundy	*Bwrgwyn*
Arctic	*Arctig*	Cambridge	*Caergrawnt*
Asia Minor	*Asia Lleiaf*	Canary Islands	*Yr Ynysoedd Dedwydd*
Atlantic Ocean	*Môr Iwerydd*	Caribbean Sea	*Y Môr Caribî*
Balearic Islands	*Ynysoedd Baleares*	Chad	*Tchad*
The Balkans	*Y Balcannau*	Channel Islands	*Ynysoedd Normandi*
Baltic Sea	*Môr Baltig* or *Môr Llychlyn*	Canterbury	*Caergaint*
		Cape Horn	*Yr Horn*
Basque Country	*Gwlad y Basg*	Cape of Good Hope	*Penrhyn Gobaith Da*
Bath	*Caerfaddon*	Cape Verde Islands	*Ynysoedd y Penrhyn Gwyrdd*
Bavaria	*Bafaria*		
Belgium	*Gwlad Belg*	Carlisle	*Caerliwelydd*
Birkenhead	*Penbedw*	Celtic Sea	*Y Môr Celtaidd*
The Black Country	*Y Wlad Ddu*	Cheshire	*Swydd Gaer*
Black Forest	*Fforest Ddu*	Chester	*Caer (Caerllion Fawr)*
Bristol	*Bryste*	China	*Tsieina*
Britain	*Prydain*	Chubut	*Camwy*

Cornwall	*Cernyw*	Jordan	*Gwlad Iorddonen*
Crete	*Creta*	Kent	*Caint*
Czechoslovakia	*Tsiecoslofacia*	Kington	*Ceintun*
Danube	*Donaw*	Lake District	*Bro'r Llynnoedd*
Dead Sea	*Y Môr Marw*	Lancashire	*Sir Gaerhirfryn*
Devon	*Dyfnaint*	Lebanon	*Libanus*
Dominican Republic	*Gweriniaeth Dominica*	Leicester	*Caerlŷr*
Dublin	*Dulyn*	Liverpool	*Lerpwl*
Edinburgh	*Caeredin*	London	*Llundain*
Egypt	*Yr Aifft*	Ludlow	*Llwydlo*
England	*Lloegr*	Luxembourg	*Lwcsembwrg*
English Channel	*Y Môr Udd*	Manchester	*Manceinion*
Europe	*Ewrop*	Mediterranean Sea	*Y Môr Canoldir*
Exeter	*Caer Wysg*	Mersey	*Merswy*
Far East	*Y Dwyrain Pell*	Midlands	*Canolbarth Lloegr*
Finland	*Y Ffindir*	Middle East	*Y Dwyrain Canol*
Firth of Forth	*Aber Gweryd/Moryd*	Nantwich	*Yr Heledd Wen*
	Forth	Northwich	*Yr Heledd Ddu*
Flanders	*Fflandrys*	Near East	*Y Dwyrain Agos*
Florence	*Fflorens*	Netherlands	*Yr Iseldiroedd*
Forth of Tay	*Moryd Tay*	New York	*Efrog Newydd*
Forest of Dean	*Fforest y Ddena*	New Zealand	*Seland Newydd*
France	*Ffrainc*	Nile	*Nîl*
Gascony	*Gwasgwyn*	North Sea	*Môr Tawch/Môr y*
Germany	*Yr Almaen*		*Gogledd*
Glastonbury	*Ynys Afallon*	Norway	*Norwy*
Gloucester	*Caerloyw*	Orkney Islands	*Ynysoedd Erch*
Greece	*Gwlad Groeg*	Oswestry	*Croesoswallt*
Hebrides	*Ynysoedd Heledd*	Oxford	*Rhydychen*
Hereford	*Henffordd*	Pacific Ocean	*Y Cefnfor Tawel*
Holland	*Yr Isalmaen*	Peru	*Periw*
Hungary	*Hwngari*	Phillipines	*Pilipinas*
Iceland	*Ynys yr Iâ/Gwlad yr Iâ*	Poland	*Gwlad Pwyl*
Ireland	*Iwerddon*	Portugal	*Portiwgal*
Irish Republic	*Gweriniaeth Iwerddon*	Pyrenees	*Pyrenau*
Irish Sea	*Môr Iwerddon*	Red Sea	*Y Môr Coch*
Isle of Man	*Ynys Manaw*	Rhineland	*Rheindir*
Isle of Wight	*Ynys Wyth*	Rome	*Rhufain*
Italy	*Yr Eidal*	Russia	*Rwsia*

Salisbury	*Caersallog*	Ukraine	*Wcrain*
Scandinavia	*Llychlyn*	United Arab Emirates	*Emiradau Arabaidd*
Scotland	*Yr Alban*		*Unedig*
Shrewsbury	*Amwythig*	United Kingdom	*Y Deyrnas Unedig*
Shropshire	*Swydd Amwythig*	United States of	*Unol Daleithiau*
Somerset	*Gwlad yr Haf*	America	*America*
South Africa	*De Affrica*	Urals	*Wralau*
Spain	*Sbaen*	Vatican City	*Dinas y Fatican*
St George's Channel	*Sianel San Sior*	Venice	*Fenis*
Stonehenge	*Côr y Cewri*	Vietnam	*Fietnam*
Strathclyde	*Ystrad Clud*	West Indies	*Ynysoedd India'r*
Swaziland	*Gwlad Swasi*		*Gorllewin*
Switzerland	*Y Swistir*	Western Samoa	*Gorllewin Samoa*
Thailand	*Gwlad Thai*	Wirral	*Cilgwri*
Thames	*Tafwys*	Worcester	*Caerwrangon*
Trent (river)	*Trannon*	York	*Caerefrog*
Tropic of Cancer	*Trofan Cancr*	Yugoslavia	*Iwgoslafia*
Tropic of Capricorn	*Trofan Capricorn*		
Turkey	*Twrci*		

SOME COMMON WELSH PLACE-NAME ELEMENTS

aber	estuary or confluence	*caer*	camp, fort, fortress, stronghold
allt	hillside, hill slope, wood	*carn*	cairn, mountain, prominence,
afon	river		rock
bach/fach	lesser, little, small	*carreg/cerrig*	rock/rocks, stone/stones
ban	bare hill, beacon, peak	*castell*	castle
bedd	grave	*cefn*	ridge
bedwen	birch	*clwyd*	gate
betws	house of prayer, chapel of ease	*coch*	red
blaen	end, head, head of a valley,	*coed*	forest, trees, wood
	source of a river, upland	*cors*	bog, marshy ground
borth/porth	gate, harbour, port	*craig*	rock
bro	region	*croes/groes*	cross, cross-roads
bron	hill-breast, hill-side, slope of a	*cwm*	coombe, valley
	hill	*cymer*	confluence, junction
bryn	hill	*dinas*	hill fort, town
bwlch	gap, pass	*dôl*	meadow
cae	enclosure, field (closed)	*du*	black

dŵr	water	*moel*	bare hill
dyffryn	vale	*mynydd*	moorland, mountain
efail	smithy	*nant*	brook
eglwys	church	*neuadd*	hall
esgair	long ridge	*newydd*	new
ffordd	road, way	*pandy*	fulling mill
ffynnon	spring, well	*pant*	a hollow, valley
gelli	grove	*pen*	end, head, top
glan	bank, hillock, river-bank	*pistyll*	spout, waterfall
glyn	deep valley, glen	*plas*	hall, mansion
gwaun	common, moor, mountain	*pont*	bridge
	pasture	*pwll*	pit, pool
gwern	bog, place where alders grow,	*rhaeadr*	waterfall
	swamp	*rhiw*	hill, slope
hafod	summer dwelling	*rhos*	moor, moorland
hendre	winter dwelling	*rhyd*	ford
hir	long	*sarn*	causeway
isaf	lower, lowest	*ton*	grassland, lea
llan	church, enclosure	*traeth*	beach, shore, strand
llwyn	bush, grove	*tref/tre*	hamlet, homestead, town
llyn	lake	*troed*	base, foot
llys	court, hall ,mansion	*tŷ*	house
maen	stone	*uchaf*	higher, highest, upper
maes	field (open), plain	*ynys*	holm, island, water meadow
mawr/fawr	big	*ystrad*	low flat land, strath, vale,
melin	mill		valley floor

5

RELIGION

DATES OF SIGNIFICANCE AND INTEREST

61AD   Destruction of the Druid strongholds on Anglesey by Suetonius Paulinus.

c.304   Martyrdoms of the Christian saints Aaron and Julius, reputedly at Caerleon.

c.384   The British monk Pelagius, who may have been a native of Usk, began preaching a system of free will which was denounced as heresy by Rome in 418 and a mission was sent under St Germanus to counter Pelagianism in Britain in 429.

546   Bangor Cathedral was founded by St Deiniol.

c.560   St Asaph Cathedral was founded by St Mungo (Kentigern).

589   Traditional date of the death of St David.

602/3   St Augustine and leaders of the Celtic Church in Wales met at Aust on the River Severn and at Bangor-on-Dee to discuss – unsuccessfully – merger with the Catholic Church, that is submission to Canterbury rather than direct allegiance to Rome.

615   A monastic community is thought to have been established on Bardsey in or about this year and three pilgrimages to it became regarded as equivalent to one to Rome.

768   The Welsh Church began to accept the date of the Roman Easter.

928   Hywel Dda made a pilgrimage to Rome.

1071   The first continental medieval monastic house in Wales was founded by the Benedictines at Chepstow.

1091   Hervé, a Breton, was made Bishop of Bangor – the first Norman church appointment in Wales.

1107   First recorded consecration of a Bishop of Llandaff – Urban. He was the first bishop of a Welsh diocese to profess obedience to Canterbury.

1115   First recorded consecration of a Norman Bishop of St David's – Bernard.

1120	The remains of St Dyfrig, regarded as the founder of Welsh monasticism, were brought from Bardsey to Llandaff by Bishop Urban to enhance the prestige of his diocese.
	St David's cult was approved by Pope Calixtus II and two pilgrimages to St David's became popularly regarded as equivalent to one to Rome.
1125	First recorded visit of a Papal Legate to Wales – Cardinal John of Crema to Llandaff.
1131	The first Cistercian houses in Wales were founded – Basingwerk Abbey and Tintern Abbey.
1150	By this year, four territorial dioceses existed in Wales with clearly defined boundaries – Bangor, Llandaff, St Asaph and St David's. The boundaries of archdeaconries, rural deaneries and parishes were still being fixed.
1188	Gerald of Wales accompanied Archbishop Baldwin of Canterbury on a tour of Wales preaching the Third Crusade.
c.1200	By the beginning of the thirteenth century, the Welsh monastic tradition came to an end as settlements of 'claswyr' (secular canons) were disbanded or converted to cathedral chapters.
1203	St David's case for metropolitan status independent of Canterbury – championed by Gerald of Wales – was abandoned.
1219	The first Papal nomination of a Welsh bishop occurred – William, Prior of Goldcliffe, to Llandaff.
1256	Richard of Carew became the first bishop of a Welsh diocese (St David's) to be consecrated in Rome.
1284	Archbishop Pecham of Canterbury toured Wales to assert his authority in the wake of the Edwardian Conquest.
1377	The last monastic house in Wales was founded, that of the Austin Friars at Newport, Gwent.
1398	The Archbishop of Canterbury, Roger Walden, decreed that henceforth the Feast of St David would be celebrated on 1 March.
1423	Philip Morgan from the St David's diocese was the first Welshman to be designated Archbishop of York (by Henry V). However, the nomination was rejected by Pope Martin.
1536–1540	Some 47 religious houses in Wales were dissolved by Henry VIII affecting about 250 monks, friars and nuns.
1539–1679	Welsh religious martyrs – some 25 Protestants and Catholics – were executed. Sixteen of the executions took place in England (See Chapter 14).

1549	The Act of Uniformity laid down that all acts of public worship were to be in English.
1561	Thomas Young of Hodgeston, Pembrokeshire, became the first Welsh Archbishop of York.
1567	The Prayer Book and the New Testament were translated into Welsh.
1568	The first Catholic book printed in Welsh, *Athravaeth Gristnogawl*, was published by Morys Clynnog.
1588	The Bible was translated into Welsh by Bishop William Morgan.
1621	Edmwnd Prys's metrical translation of the Psalms was published.
1630	The first cheap Welsh Bible was published.
1639	The first Independent (Puritan) Church in Wales was at Llanfaches, Gwent, established by William Wroth, and marked the beginning of Nonconformity in Wales.
1641	Dr John Williams of Conwy was consecrated Archbishop of York.
1649	The first Baptist Church in Wales was at Ilston, Gower.
1653	The first Quaker meeting in Wales was held at Rhiwabon, Clwyd.
1657	George Fox, the Quaker leader, toured Wales to a mixed reception.
1676	Statistics collected now indicated fewer than 5 per cent of the Welsh were Dissenters.
1682	Beginning of the migration to America of some 2,000 Quakers, mainly from Montgomeryshire, Merionethshire and Radnorshire, during the 'Great Persecution'.
1686	The last royal pilgrimage ever to take place in the British Isles was by James II to Holywell.
1696	The oldest existing chapel in Wales, Maesyronnen, Glasbury, Powys, dates from this year.
1700	The Welsh Baptist Association was formed.
1726	The first Arminian church in Wales was founded at Llanrhydowen, Cardiganshire.
1730	The oldest known Jewish community in Wales, at Swansea, was certainly in existence by this time.
1735	'The Great Awakening' – the start of the Methodist Revival with the conversion of Howell Harris.
1737– 1761	Griffith Jones's 'circulating schools' succeeded in making about half the population of Wales literate.
1742	The first Welsh Association (Sasiwn) of Methodists was held at Deugoedydd near Llandovery and the first Methodist meeting house was acquired at Groeswen near Caerphilly.
	William Seward was stoned to death while preaching at Hay-on-Wye, Powys, so becoming the first 'Methodist martyr'.

1743	The first meeting of the United Association of Methodists in Wales, at Plas-y-Watford near Caerphilly, adopted Calvinism.
1755	The first and only Moravian Society chapel in Wales was founded at Haverfordwest.
1762	The second Methodist Revival began.
1770	The first Welsh Bible to be printed in Wales was produced at Carmarthen.
1785	The first Welsh chapel in London was founded in Wilderness Row.
1789	The first successful Sunday School movement in Wales was started by Thomas Charles.
1807	The first Baptist College was founded at Abergavenny – later moved to Pontypool.
1811	The Methodists broke with the Anglican Church to form their own church.
1823	The Methodist 'Confession of Faith' was formulated at Aberystwyth.
1827	St David's Theological College for Anglicans was founded at Lampeter.
1832	The first temperance society in Wales was founded in Holyhead.
1837	The first Methodist College in Wales was founded in Bala.
1839	A Baptist College was founded at Haverfordwest – later moved to Aberystwyth – and a Congregational College at Brecon.
1840	Dom Thomas Joseph Brown was consecrated Vicar Apostolic of the Welsh District – the first time since the Reformation that a Catholic Bishop had responsibility for the whole of Wales. (Catholicism was outlawed from 1584 to 1679.)
	Monmouth was transferred from the Anglican diocese of Hereford to Llandaff.
1841	A Congregational College was founded at Bala, later moved to Bangor.
1846	At Merthyr Tydfil the first Mormon missionaries in Wales became active.
1850	The hierarchy of the Catholic Church was restored with a suffrage see for Newport and Menevia.
1851	The first and only religious census to be conducted in Britain showed 2,769 Nonconformist and 1,180 Anglican places of worship in Wales with 75 per cent of the population Nonconformist.
1859	A major revival began at Tre'r-ddôl, Dyfed, led by John Rowland, and this resulted in a great increase in chapel building.
1862	The North Wales Baptist College was founded at Llangollen.
1864	A General Assembly for Wales was established by the Calvinistic Methodists (Presbyterians).

1866	The Baptist Union of Wales was formed with two assemblies – one Welsh and one English.
1871	The Welsh Congregational Union was formed.
1872	Wales's largest chapel, Tabernacl, Morriston, was opened.
1874	The first Salvation Army mission in Wales was opened in Cardiff.
1881	The Sunday Closing Act was passed with Monmouthshire excluded.
1887	The Disestablishment of the Anglican Church in Wales became official Liberal Party policy.
	The first Boys' Brigade company in Wales was formed in Newport, Gwent.
1889	The Society of St Teilo was founded by Catholics in Wales.
1892	St Michael's and All Saints Theological College (Anglican) was established at Aberdare but later moved to Llandaff.
1896	The Roman Catholic diocese of Cardiff was created.
1904	The last major revival in Wales began, led by Evan Roberts. In its wake the Pentecostal Apostolic Church (headquarters near Llanelli) was founded.
1906	The Presbyterian Church in Wales established the United Theological College at Aberystwyth.
	A monastic settlement was re-established on Caldey Island – first by Anglican Benedictines and later by the Trappist Cistercian order.
1910	A Royal Commission on Religion in Wales – established in 1906 – reported.
1916	Cardiff became a Roman Catholic archdiocese.
1917	A Representative and Governing Body of the Anglican Church in Wales was established.
1920	The Church in Wales was disestablished and the first Archbishop of Wales was elected.
	The new Anglican diocese of Monmouth was created.
1921	The Sunday Closing Act was extended to Monmouthshire (Gwent).
1922–1924	*Y Geiriadur Beiblaidd* ('The Bible Dictionary') was published, a major work of scholarship.
1923	The new Anglican diocese of Swansea and Brecon was created.
1929	Eight Welsh Catholic martyrs were beatified in Rome.
1932	A Welsh Religious Advisory Council was set up by the BBC.
1940	Disbursement of Church funds, under the Disestablishment Act, to the University of Wales and the (then) 13 county councils.
1947	The first purpose-built mosque in Wales, Noor-el-Islam, opened in Cardiff.

1948	Britain's first ever Muslim conference was held in Cardiff.
1970	Six Welsh Catholic martyrs were canonized in Rome.
1980	The Representative Body of the Church in Wales voted for the ordination of women deacons.
1982	The first ever Papal visit to Wales was made by Pope John Paul II.
1987	Re-organization of the Catholic Church in Wales – a new diocese of Menevia was created at Swansea together with a new diocese at Wrexham (formerly Menevia) and a further three Welsh Catholic martyrs were beatified.
1989	The first purpose-built Sikh gurdwara in Wales was opened in Cardiff.
1990	Cytûn – Churches Together in Wales – was established.
1992	The Representative Body of the Church of Wales decided that Llandaff was to become the premier diocese in Wales and permanent seat of the Archbishop of Wales.
1993	In Cardiff the first ever visit to Wales was made by the Dalai Lama.

MEMBERSHIP OF CHRISTIAN DENOMINATIONS AND OTHER RELIGIONS

There have been no entirely reliable statistics for membership of churches since the 1851 census, the only religious census ever undertaken in Britain, and even then religious questions on the census form were not compulsory.

The 1851 census showed that there were 2,769 Nonconformist and 1,180 places of worship in Wales with some 75 per cent of the population stated to be Nonconformist.

The findings of the Royal Commission on Religion in Wales, which reported in 1910, showed that the Anglican Church then had the support of one in three Christians in Wales compared with only one in four in 1851.

Currently, there are about 5,000 places of Christian worship in Wales including some 1,450 Church in Wales churches, about 1,200 Presbyterian Church in Wales churches, some 600 Baptist churches together with some 670 congregations of the Union of Welsh Independents (Congregationalists).

In 1990, with five per cent of the UK population, Wales had 10 per cent of its churches, six per cent of its claimed members and five per cent of its ministers.

In common with the rest of the UK, church membership and attendance has been in decline in Wales for many years, the exception to this trend being among some of the smaller evangelical churches.

Approximate Membership of the Main Christian Churches

Church in Wales	108,000	Wesleyan Methodists	16,000
Presbyterian Church of Wales		English Baptists	13,000
(Calvinistic Methodists)	70,000	United Reformed Church	7,500
Union of Welsh Independents		Christian Bretheren	4,700
(Congregationalists)	67,000	Salvation Army	2,300
Catholic Church	60,000	Unitarians	1,100
Baptist Union of Wales	41,000		

Denominational Journals

Y Goleuad	Presbyterian Church of Wales	*Seren Cymry*	Welsh Baptists
Gwyliedydd	Wesleyan Methodists	*Y Tyst*	Independents
Y Llan	Church in Wales	*Yr Ymofynydd*	Unitarians

Non-Christian Faiths

There are sizeable minorities in Wales who are members of non-Christian faiths and these are found mainly in Cardiff, Newport and Swansea.

All the world's major religions are represented in Wales – Buddhism, Hinduism, Islam, Judaism and Sikhism. Islam has the greatest number of adherents and there appear to be over 10,000 Muslims in Wales, mainly Sunni.

In 1993 Cardiff had eight mosques, three Sikh gurdwaras (temples), two Hindu mandirs (temples) and two synagogues (one orthodox, one new), while there were seven mosques and a synagogue in Newport, two mosques in Swansea and one at Haverfordwest.

There are 17 Buddhist Meditation Centres – at Aberystwyth, Bangor, Builth Wells, Cardiff (5), Colwyn Bay, Llangynllo (Powys), Cwmbrân, Machynlleth, Pwllheli, Raglan and Swansea (3). The Baha'i faith has nine local spiritual assemblies – at Cardiff (Whitchurch), Glan Conwy, Llanberis, Llanwrtyd Wells, Newport, Old Colwyn, Penarth, Swansea and Tonyrefail (Mid Glamorgan).

The oldest established non-Christian faith in Wales is Judaism, present since about 1730 in Swansea with other communities formed later in Cardiff in 1840, Merthyr Tydfil in 1848, Pontypridd in 1867 and Tredegar in 1873. The total number of Jews in Wales never seems to have exceeded 4,000–5,000 while the present total is less than 2,000.

The oldest Muslim community in Britain, dating to the second half of the nineteenth century, is that of Yemenis in Cardiff.

ORGANIZATION AND HIERARCHY OF CHRISTIAN DENOMINATIONS

Church in Wales Dioceses

Bangor: All of Gwynedd except those areas under St Asaph.
Cathedral Church – St Deiniol.

Llandaff (Premier diocese): All of Mid Glamorgan, South Glamorgan except Cardiff east of the River Rumney, and Port Talbot and Neath in West Glamorgan.
Cathedral Church – St Peter and St Paul.

Monmouth: All of Gwent and Cardiff east of the Rumney River.
Cathedral Church – St Woolos, Newport.

St Asaph: All of Clwyd and parts of Gwynedd and Powys.
Cathedral Church – St Asaph.

St David's: Dyfed and parts of Powys.
Cathedral Church – St David and St Andrew.

Swansea and Brecon: West Glamorgan except Port Talbot and Neath, and parts of Powys.
Cathedral Church – St John the Evangelist, Brecon.

There are 18 border parishes which opted to remain within the Church of England at disestablishment in 1920.

Archbishops of the Church in Wales

Alfred George Edwards	1920–1934	(and Bishop of St Asaph)
Charles Alfred Howell Green	1934–1944	(and Bishop of Bangor)
David Lewis Prosser	1944–1949	(and Bishop of St David's)
John Morgan	1949–1957	(and Bishop of Llandaff)
Alfred Edwin Morris	1957–1967	(and Bishop of Monmouth)
William Glyn Hughes Simon	1968–1971	(and Bishop of Llandaff)
Gwilym Owen Williams	1971–1982	(and Bishop of Bangor)
Derrick Greenslade Childs	1983–1986	(and Bishop of Monmouth)
George Noakes	1987–1991	(and Bishop of St David's)
Alwyn Rice Jones	1991–	(and Bishop of St Asaph)

Roman Catholic Dioceses

Cardiff (Archdiocese): Mid Glamorgan, South Glamorgan, Gwent, Hereford. Cathedral Church – St David.

Menevia (Swansea): Dyfed, West Glamorgan, Powys except for Montgomery. Cathedral Church – St Joseph.

Wrexham: Gwynedd, Clwyd and Montgomery. Cathedral Church – St Mary.

Roman Catholic Archbishops of Cardiff

James R. Bilsborrow	1916–1920	John A. Murphy	1961–1983
Francis Mostyn	1920–1939	John Aloysius Ward	1983–
Michael McGrath	1940–1961		

Presbyterian Church of Wales (Eglwys Bresbyteraidd Cymru) – Presbytery Boundaries

1. Aberteifi – De
2. Aberteifi – Gogledd
3. Arfon
4. Brecon, Radnor, Hereford
5. Caerfyrddin – De
6. Caerfyrddin – Gogledd
7. Chester, Flint, Denbigh
8. Dwyrain Dinbych
9. Dyffryn Clwyd
10. Dyffryn Conwy
11. Fflint
12. Glamorgan – East
13. Glamorgan – West
14. Lancashire and Cheshire
15. Liverpool
16. Llŷn and Eifionydd
17. Llundain
18. Manchester
19. Dwyrain Meirionnydd
20. Gorllewin Meirionnydd
21. Môn
22. Montgomery and Shropshire
23. Morgannwg – Dwyrain
24. Morgannwg – Gorllewin
25. Gwent
26. South Pembrokeshire
27. Penfro – Gogledd
28. Trefaldwyn Isaf
29. Trefaldwyn Uchaf
30. North West Coast

Union of Welsh Independents (Undeb yr Annibynwyr Cymraeg) – Association Boundaries

1. Cyfundeb Llŷn ac Eifionydd
2. Gogledd Arfon
3. Dwyrain Dinbych a Fflint
4. Gorllewin Dinbych a Fflint

5. Maldwyn	12. Gogledd Morgannwg a Mynwy
6. Meirionnydd	13. Cynffig/Nedd
7. Môn	14. Dwyrain Morgannwg
8. Aberteifi	15. Gorllewin Morgannwg
9. Brycheiniog	16. Penfro
10. Gorllewin Caerfyrddin	17. Lerpwl a'r Cylch
11. Dwyrain Caerfyrddin	18. Llundain

Baptist Union of Wales (Undeb Bedyddwyr Cymraeg) – Boundaries

1. Môn	6. Dwyrain Morgannwg
2. Sir Caernarfon	7. Gorllewin Morgannwg
3. Brycheiniog	8. Gwent
4. Caerfyrddin a Cheredigion	9. Penfro
5. Dinbych, Fflint a Meirion	10. Maesyfed a Maldwyn

Methodist District Boundaries

South Wales Area: South Dyfed, South Powys, Mid Glamorgan, South Glamorgan, West Glamorgan, Gwent

Cymru: Gwynedd, Clwyd, North Dyfed, North Powys

Baptist Association Boundaries

South Wales Area: (a) East Glamorgan, including some parts of South Powys
(b) Gwent
(c) West Wales, including some parts of South Dyfed

North Wales English-speaking churches come under the Lancashire and Cheshire Association.

United Reformed Church

Wales comprises one Province divided into six districts:

1. North Wales	4. West Wales
2. East Wales	5. Pembrokeshire
3. South Wales	6. Mid Wales

Salvation Army

1. South Wales Division
2. Liverpool and North Wales Division

CYTÛN (CHURCHES TOGETHER IN WALES)

Full Members

Baptist Union of Great Britain
Baptist Union of Wales
Church in Wales
Congregational Federation
Presbyterian Church of Wales
Roman Catholic Church

Salvation Army
Society of Friends
Union of Welsh Independents
United Reformed Church
Wesleyan Methodists

Observers

Lutheran Church
Orthodox Church

Seventh Day Adventists

The objects of Cytûn are the advancement of the Christian religion and of any other purposes which are charitable according to the law of England and Wales.

WELSH SAINTS

The most commonly accepted feast days are listed.

13 January	Elian (Eilian) (6th century)
15 January	Lleudadd (6th century)
25 January	Dwynwen (*c*.460)
29 January	Gildas (Badonicus) (*c*.500–*c*.570)
31 January	Melangell (died *c*.590)
1 February	Brigid (Ffraid) (*c*.450–*c*.525)
3 February	Seiriol (6th century)
9 February	Teilo (6th century)
13 February	Dyfnog (7th century)
1 March	David (Dewi) (*c*.520–*c*.589)
3 March	Non (late 5th century) – the mother of David
29 March	Gwynllyw (Woolos) (died *c*.500)
5 April	Derfel (6th century)

7 April	Brynach (5th/6th century)
15 April	Padarn (Paternus) (5th or 6th century)
20 April	Beuno (died c.640)
27 April	Cynidir (Enoder) (6th century)
6 May	Asaph (flor. c.600)
16 May	Carannog (5th century)
21 May	Gollen (7th century)
16 June	Curig (6th century)
20 June	Govan (6th century) and Julius and Aaron (died c.304)
2 July	Euddogwy (Oudoceus) (died c.615)
3 July	Peblig (Publicius) (5th century)
28 July	Samson (c.490–c.565)
23 August	Tydfil (died c.480)
11 September	Deiniol (6th century)
21 September	Mabon (6th century)
25 September	Cadog (early 6th century)
1 November	Cadfan (died early 6th century)
3 November	Winefride (Gwenfrewi) (7th century)
5 November	Cybi (6th century)
6 November	Illtud (died c.505)
12 November	Tysilio (7th century)
14 November	Dyfrig (Dubricius) (flor. c.475)
15 November	Malo (died c.640)
22 November	Paulinus (died c.505)
5 December	Justinian (Stinan) (6th century) also 23 August
30 December	Tathan (Tatheus) (early 6th century)

SUNDAY OPENING OF PUBLIC HOUSES

The Sunday Closing Act, 1881, effective from Feburary 1882, led to the closing of public houses on Sundays in all parts of Wales excluding Monmouthshire (Gwent) to which Sunday closing was not extended until 1921.

Referenda on the continued closing of public houses have been held every seven years since 1961.

Referendum Results

8 November 1961
Voting to stay dry: the counties of Anglesey, Cardigan, Caernarfon, Carmarthen, Denbigh, Merioneth, Montgomery and Pembroke.

Voting for Sunday opening: the counties of Brecon, Flint, Glamorgan, Monmouth and Radnor and the county boroughs of Cardiff, Merthyr Tydfil, Newport and Swansea.

6 November 1968
Voting to stay dry: the counties of Anglesey, Caernarfon, Cardigan, Carmarthen and Merioneth.

Voting for Sunday opening: as for 1961 with the addition of the counties of Denbigh, Montgomery and Pembroke.

5 November 1975
Voting to stay dry: the districts of Ynys Môn/Anglesey, Arfon, Carmarthen, Ceredigion, Dwyfor and Meirionydd.

Voting for Sunday opening: all other 12 districts where polls were held. No polls were held in 19 districts which were already wet.

3 November 1982
Voting to stay dry: the districts of Ceredigion and Dwyfor.

Voting for Sunday opening: all other districts where polls were held while those not polling remained wet.

8 November 1989 (detailed results)

District	For	Against	Percentage poll
Aberconwy	7,233	2,260	22.3
Arfon	8,245	4,861	31.0
Cardiff	14,890	3,910	8.8
Carmarthen	7,782	5,715	31.5
Ceredigion	10,961	10,133	41.0
Colwyn	6,982	2,365	21.8
Dinefwr	4,919	2,952	26.1
Dwyfor	*4,563*	*5,951*	*40.0*
Llanelli	7,815	3,316	18.9
Meirionnydd	7,219	4,637	48.0
Newport	18,964	4,442	24.7
Preseli	9,760	2,632	23.3
Taff Ely	6,573	1,648	11.9
Ynys Môn/Anglesey	12,141	6,770	35.0

Polls were not requisitioned in the other 23 Welsh districts which thus remained wet. Only Dwyfor voted for continued Sunday closing.

6

EDUCATION

DATES OF SIGNIFICANCE AND INTEREST

1407   A free grammar school was founded at Oswestry, a largely Welsh town at that time.

1541   Between this year and 1632, numerous grammar schools were founded or re-founded in Wales including those at Abergavenny, Bangor, Beaumaris, Botwnnog, Brecon, Caerleon, Caernarfon, Carmarthen, Chepstow, Cowbridge, Harlech, Haverfordwest, Hawarden, Llanrwst, Monmouth, Northop, Trelech, Presteigne, Rhiwabon, Rhuthun, Swansea, Usk and Wrexham.

1571   Jesus College, Oxford, was founded by Dr Hugh Price of Brecon for Welsh undergraduates.

1650   The Act for the Propagation and Preaching of the Gospel in Wales led to the foundation of some 63 schools in Wales – the first state schools in Britain. (The Act lapsed in 1653.)

1672   The first Welsh Dissenting Academy, providing higher education for non-Anglicans, was founded at Brynllywarch, Mid Glamorgan, by Samuel Jones, a former Fellow of Jesus College.

1674   The 'Welsh Trust' was founded by Thomas Gouge. Many schools were founded in Wales but instruction was in English only.

1682   Swansea Grammar School was founded by Bishop Gore.

1699   The Society for the Promotion of Christian Knowledge was founded. By 1727 the society had founded 96 schools in Wales with English generally used as the language of instruction, although Welsh was used in north-west Wales.

1700   The first works' charity school in Wales was founded by Sir Humphrey Mackworth at Esgair-hir lead mines in North Cardiganshire.

1731   The start of Griffith Jones's 'Circulating Schools' in which Welsh was used for teaching adults and children. The movement lapsed in 1779.

1737   The first issue of *Welch Piety* containing reports on the Circulating Schools movement.

1773   The peak year for Circulating Schools with 13,205 pupils in 243 schools.

1789   Thomas Charles started the first successful Sunday School movement in Wales.

1806   The first British (Nonconformist) school in Wales was opened in Swansea.

1812   The first National (Anglican) school in Wales was opened at Penley, Flintshire.

1826   The first Mechanics' Institute in Wales was opened in Swansea.

1827   St David's College, Lampeter, was founded by the Anglican Church.

1834   The first Treasury grant – of £84 – to a school in Wales was for a National school at Abergwili, Dyfed.

1847   The *Report of the Inquiry into the State of Education in Wales* was published – the controversial 'Blue Books'.

1848   Llandovery School was opened.
Trinity College, Carmarthen, was founded for Anglican teachers.

1852   St David's College, Lampeter, became a degree-awarding institution – the first in Wales.

1853   The first art schools in Wales were opened in Caernarfon and Swansea.

1856   St Mary's teacher training college was opened in Caernarfon.

1858   Bangor Normal College for Nonconformists was opened by Hugh Owen.

1870–74 Some 200 board schools were opened in Wales.

1872   The first teacher training college for women in Wales was opened in Swansea by the British and Foreign Schools Society.
University College of Wales, Aberystwyth, opened.

1878   Dr Williams School for Girls was founded at Dolgellau.

1881   The Aberdare Report recommended a network of intermediate schools for Wales and two new university colleges, one in the north and one in the south.

1883   University College, Cardiff, was founded and became the first to admit women undergraduates. (Women were admitted to Aberystwyth in 1884.)

1884   University College of North Wales, Bangor, was founded.

1888   The Cross Commission recommended bilingual teaching in Welsh schools.

1889   The Welsh Intermediate and Technical Education Act allowed intermediate (secondary) education to be paid for from local rates 13 years before this was possible in England.

1891   The South Wales and Monmouthshire School of Cookery was opened in Cardiff.

1893   A Royal Charter was granted for the establishment of the University of Wales with some 1,000 undergraduates in the three constituent colleges of Aberystwyth, Bangor and Cardiff.

1894   The first purpose-built county school in Wales – now the Sir Hugh Owen School – was opened in Caernarfon.

1896   The Central Welsh Board was established to administer the 1889 Act – an inspectorate and examining body for intermediate schools.

1906   The first Workers' Educational Association (WEA) branch in Wales was established in Barry. (The first in north Wales was in Wrexham in 1908.)

1907   The Welsh Department of the Board of Education was established to administer elementary and secondary education in Wales.

1913   Carmarthen Farm Institute – the first such institute in Wales – was founded.

1914   Teacher training colleges were opened by local education authorities at Barry (for women) and at Caerleon (for men).

        By this date there were some 100 intermediate schools in Wales established under the 1889 Act.

1920   University College, Swansea, was founded.

1927   Coleg Harlech was founded – the first residential college for adults in Wales.

1929   The University of Wales began awarding teacher training certificates for colleges of education in Wales.

1931   The Welsh National School of Medicine was founded in Cardiff.

1934   The post of special advisor in Welsh to the Chief Inspector of Schools in Wales was created.

1939   The first Welsh-medium primary school was established (in Aberystwyth) by Urdd Gobaith Cymru.

1940   Undeb Cenedlaethol Athrawon Cymru (National Union of Teachers in Wales) was founded.

1945   Emergency teacher training colleges were established at Cardiff and Wrexham to meet the post-war demand for teachers.

1947   The first local authority Welsh-medium primary school was established, in Llanelli.

1948   The Welsh Joint Education Committee took over the functions of the CWB (see 1896).

1949   The first comprehensive school in England and Wales was established at Holyhead.

The Cardiff College (later the Welsh College) of Music and Drama was established.

1956   Bangor Normal College and Trinity College, Carmarthen, introduced courses on teaching through the medium of Welsh.

The first bilingual secondary school in Wales – Ysgol Glan Clwyd, Rhyl – was opened.

1961   Atlantic College, St Donat's, South Glamorgan, was established.

1962   The first bilingual secondary school in south Wales was opened in Pontypridd – Ysgol Rhydfelen.

1964   The Welsh College of Librarianship was established at Aberystwyth. (Absorbed into the University College in 1989.)

Gregynog, near Newtown, was given to the University of Wales by the Davies family of Llandinam.

1967   The University of Wales Institute of Science and Technology (UWIST) became a constituent college of the university.

1969   The Welsh National College of Agriculture was opened in Aberystwyth.

1970   The Polytechnic of Wales was established at Treforest, Mid Glamorgan.

The Open University appointed a Regional Director for Wales.

The Welsh Office took over responsibility for primary and secondary education.

1971   Mudiad Ysgolion Meithrin (The Welsh Nursery Schools Movement) was founded in Aberystwyth.

1972   St David's University College, Lampeter, became a constituent college of the University of Wales.

Publication of *Geiriadur Termau: A Dictionary of Terms* for use in Welsh-language teaching.

1975   Gwent College of Higher Education and North East Wales Institute of Higher Education founded.

1976   South Glamorgan Institute of Higher Education and West Glamorgan Institute of Higher Education founded.

1978   The Welsh Office took over responsibility for further and higher education in Wales.

1987   The University of Wales Institute of Science and Technology (UWIST) and University College, Cardiff, merged to form the University of Wales College of Cardiff.

1988   The Curriculum Council for Wales was established.

1989   The last grammar school in Wales, Whitland Grammar School, was closed.

1990   The National Curriculum began to be implemented with Welsh becoming a core subject in designated Welsh-medium schools and a foundation subject elsewhere.

1991   The first secondary school in Wales to opt out of local education authority control was Cwmcarn School, Gwent.

1992   The Polytechnic of Wales became the University of Glamorgan after deciding not to become a constituent college of the University of Wales.

Higher education and further education in Wales were taken out of local authority control and the Higher Education Funding Council for Wales and the Further Education Funding Council for Wales were established.

1993   The first primary school in Wales to opt out of local education authority control was Ysgol Caergeiliog, Anglesey.

The Community University of the Valleys was launched by the University College Swansea and the Open University for part-time undergraduate degree study from home.

1994   The Curriculum Council for Wales took over the functions of PDAG (the Welsh-language education development committee) to become the Curriculum and Assessment Authority for Wales.

SCHOOLS PUPILS, 1992–1993

	Nursery*	Primary	Secondary	Special	Total in maintained schools	Pupils in independent schools
Clwyd	173	35,448	27,269	832	63,549	2,140
Dyfed	222	31,035	24,289	230	55,685	919
Gwent	913	41,291	29,440	415	71,248	1,885
Gwynedd	–	19,187	15,445	280	34,912	1,157
Mid Glamorgan	1,209	55,205	37,743	765	94,481	694
Powys	–	10,580	7,885	138	18,603	576
South Glamorgan	803	36,905	27,229	691	64,853	3,073
West Glamorgan	236	32,616	23,263	225	56,104	720
WALES	3,556	262,267	192,563	3,576	459,436	11,164

*Nursery school figures are for full-time and part-time pupils.

GCSE AND A LEVEL RESULTS, 1993

GCSE

Candidates	Subjects entered	Grade A passes	Grade C or better passes	Grade E or better passes	Grade G or better passes
59,384	246,942	25,507	117,741	204,962	239,404

A level

Candidates	Subjects entered	Subjects passed				
		0	1	2	3	4 or more
6,086	1	1,796	4,290			
3,947	2	476	983	2,488		
4,710	3	97	302	828	3,483	
323	4 or more	6	6	15	86	210
15,066		2,375	5,581	3,331	3,569	210

SCHOOLS IN WALES 1992–1993

		Maintained			Independent
	Nursery	Primary	Secondary	Special	
Clwyd	3	245	33	11	12
Dyfed	3	313	31	5	6
Gwent	11	213	33	6	7
Gwynedd	–	191	23	5	9
Mid Glamorgan	23	304	42	10	7
Powys	–	109	13	4	5
South Glamorgan	10	158	27	15	13
West Glamorgan	2	164	27	5	6
WALES	52	1,697	229	61	65

Welsh-Speaking Schools, 1992–1993

Primary
Number of schools where Welsh is main or sole medium of instruction:

	Clwyd	Dyfed	Gwent	Gwynedd	Mid.Glam.	Powys	S.Glam.	W.Glam.
No. schools	39	176	6	158	29	21	11	17
No. pupils	4,772	11,841	987	14,937	6,651	1,222	2,355	3,323

Secondary

Number of schools where Welsh is taught as first language:

	Clwyd	Dyfed	Gwent	Gwynedd	Mid.Glam.	Powys.	S.Glam.	W.Glam.
No. schools	4	10	1	19	4	4	1	2
No. pupils	2,852	6,731	366	11,784	3,511	2,126	1,102	29,791

The Education Reform Act, 1988, defines Welsh-speaking secondary schools as those where more than half of the subjects – including religious education and subjects other than English and Welsh and which are also foundation subjects – are taught wholly or partly in Welsh.

Secondary schools in 1992–1993 where Welsh was taught

As both a first and second language	59 (25.8%)
As a first language only	13 (5.7%)
As a second language only	140 (61.1%)
Not at all	17 (7.4%)

LEADING INDEPENDENT SCHOOLS

(Year of foundation shown in brackets after school names. The number of pupils shown for each school is approximate.)

Members of the Headmasters' Conference

Christ College, Brecon (1541)	Co-educational (360 pupils)
Llandovery College (1847)	Co-educational (240 pupils)
Monmouth School (1614)	Boys (540 pupils)
Rydal School, Colwyn Bay (1885)	Co-educational (330 pupils)

Society of Headmasters and Headmistresses of Independent Schools

Rougemont School, Gwent (1919)	Co-educational (230 pupils)
Ruthin School (1574)	Co-educational (170 pupils)
St David's College, Llandudno (1965)	Boys (230 pupils)

Girls' School Association

Haberdashers' Monmouth School (1872)	(630 pupils)
Howell's School, Llandaff (1860)	(570 pupils)
Howell's School, Denbigh (1860)	(300 pupils)
Penrhos College, Colwyn Bay (1880)	(240 pupils)

SCHOOLS WHICH HAVE OPTED OUT OF LOCAL EDUCATION AUTHORITY CONTROL

Cwmcarn Comprehensive School, Gwent (1991)
Bishop Vaughan Roman Catholic Comprehensive School, Swansea (1992)
Brynmawr Comprehensive School, Gwent (1992)
Ysgol Emrys ab Iwan, Abergele, Clwyd (1993)
Ysgol Caergeiliog, Anglesey (1993)
Ysgol Maelor, Penley, near Wrexham (1993)
Stanwell Comprehensive School, Penarth, South Glamorgan (1993)
Llanerfel Church in Wales Primary School, Llanerfel, Welshpool (1993)
Derwen Primary School, Higher Kinnerton, Clwyd (1993)
Eirias Comprehensive School, Colwyn Bay (1993)
Pen-y-Bryn Primary School, Colwyn Bay (1993)
St Alban's Roman Catholic Comprehensive School, Pontypool (1994)
St Cyres Comprehensive School, Dinas Powys (1994)
Bryn Elian Comprehensive School, Colwyn Bay (1994)
Our Lady and St Michael Roman Catholic School, Abergavenny (1994)
Mary Immaculate Roman Catholic School, Cardiff (1994)

FURTHER AND HIGHER EDUCATION, 1992–1993

	Further Education		Higher Education	
	Enrolments	Full-time equivalents	Enrolments	Full-time equivalents
Clwyd				
Deeside College	4,720	1,700	67	19
Llandrillo Technical College	8,210	2,871	234	135
Llysfasi College of Agriculture	1,151	213		
North East Wales Institute	2,953	1,687	3,399	2,552
Welsh College of Horticulture	537	259		
Dyfed				
Carmarthenshire College of Technology and Art	4,422	1,924	329	325
Ceredigion College of Further Education	1,535	744		
Pembrokeshire College	2,095	1,352		
Trinity College, Carmarthen			1,251	1,251
Welsh Agricultural College	81	61		

Gwent

Gwent College of Higher Education	531,	240	4,927	3,182
Gwent Tertiary College	15,372	6,719	63	24

Gwynedd

Coleg Harlech	148	142		
Coleg Meirionnydd–Glynllifon	1,294	576		
Coleg Normal			1,031	984
Coleg Pencraig	1,176	524	32	13
Gwynedd Technical College	3,272	1,553		

Mid Glamorgan

Aberdare College	1,704	592		
Bridgend College	4,422	1,608		
Merthyr Tydfil College	2,532	851	17	7
Pencoed College	650	263	19	8
Pontypridd College	4,013	1,841	42	15
Rhondda College	1,803	487		
Ystrad Mynach College	2,812	1,185	40	10

Powys

Coleg Powys	3,919	1,185		

South Glamorgan

Barry College	3,378	1,512		
Cardiff Institute of Higher Education	1,271	668	5,520	4,491
Coleg Glan Hafren	5,142	2,358	83	48
Welsh College of Music and Drama	275	24	416	416

West Glamorgan

Afan College	2,507	1,057		
Gorseinon College	2,432	1,342		
Neath College	4,666	2,061		
Swansea College	6,212	2,425		
Swansea Institute of Higher Education	789	327	3,762	2,878

WALES	95,934	40,523	33,085	25,713

UNIVERSITY EDUCATION

University of Wales

	1988–90	1990–91	1991–92	1992–93
Full-time undergraduates	18,492	19,858	22,331	25,171
Full-time postgraduates	3,808	3,844	4,479	4,953

Full-Time Equivalent Students at University of Wales Constituent Colleges

	1990–91	1991–92	1992–93
Aberystwyth	3,801	4,276	4,662
Bangor	3,616	4,105	4,547
Cardiff	9,169	10,296	11,010
Swansea	5,693	6,460	7,160
St David's, Lampeter	974	1,091	1,223
College of Medicine, Cardiff	1,098	1,127	1,522
TOTAL	24,351	27,355	30,124

University of Wales Students, 1992–93
from Wales   31%
from rest of the UK 56%
from abroad   13%

Open University in Wales

	1990	1991	1992	1993
Undergraduates	3,030	3,157	3,301	3,359
Postgraduates	132	159	211	229

University of Glamorgan

	Enrolments	Full-time equivalents
Students in 1992–93	11,529	9,063

7

HEALTH SERVICES

DATES OF SIGNIFICANCE AND INTEREST

*c.*945 The Laws of Hywel Dda specified payment for medical treatment and placed mediciners (doctors) twelfth in order of precedence at court.
1349 The Black Death first appeared in Wales and killed up to 100,000 by 1420.
1352 The oldest record of lay medical practitioners in Wales comes from Newborough, Anglesey.
1354 Henry, first Duke of Lancaster, born at Grosmont Castle, Gwent, wrote *Le Livre des Seintes Medicines* ('The Book of Sacred Medicines/ Remedies').
*c.*1470– Birth in the Vale of Clwyd of Bened ap Rhys (Bened Feddyg – Bened 1480 the Doctor), compiler of the earliest surviving medical manuscript in Welsh.
1490s Lewis of Caerleon, who flourished at this time, was physician to Henry VII (Henry Tudor) and his mother, and possibly Catherine of Aragon also.
1544, Thomas Phaer (or Phayer), a lawyer and physician and resident of 1553 Cilgerran, Pembrokeshire, published the first medical books written in English for the intelligent layperson – *The Regiment of Life* and *The Book of Children*.
1593 Plague killed 35 people in Presteigne, Radnorshire.
1638 In Bedwellty, Monmouthshire, 82 people died of plague.
1652 In the last outbreak of plague to occur in Wales, about 400 died in Haverfordwest.
1705–6 A smallpox outbreak killed 60 people in Penmachno, Gwynedd.
1722–3 A smallpox outbreak killed over 70 people in Carmarthen.
1726–31 Hundreds died throughout Wales in a typhus outbreak.
1739 Death of John Jones, reputed to have been the last of the famous Meddygon Myddfai (Physicians of Myddfai).

1762	Smallpox killed 20 people in Holyhead.
1774	Cardiff became the first town in Wales to obtain an Improvement Act for paving, lighting, cleaning streets, lanes and passages and removing public nuisances.
1817	The first hospital was established in Swansea, later Swansea General.
1832	The first cholera epidemic killed about 500 people throughout Wales.
1834	Poor Law Amendment Act brought the treatment of the poor under the control of orthodox medicine for the first time.
1837	First public hospital in Cardiff opened – Cardiff (later Royal) Infirmary.
1848	A community health hospital was opened at Blaenau Ffestiniog.
1849	A second cholera epidemic killed over 3,000 people in Wales.
1851	The first medical officer of health in Wales was appointed at Towyn, Denbighshire.
1854	The third cholera epidemic killed about 1,000 people in Wales.
1865	In Swansea 15 people died of yellow fever in the only outbreak of the disease ever to occur in Britain.
1866	The fourth and last cholera epidemic killed about 2,000 people in Wales.
1870	Cardiff Medical Society, the oldest in Wales, was formed.
1884	Flat Holm began to be used to isolate suspected cholera patients.
1885	The first woman doctor in Wales, Frances Hoggan, was registered.
1887	The first hospital was opened in the Rhondda Valleys.
1906	The first purpose-built sanatorium in Wales opened at Allt-yr-Yn, Newport.
1910	The King Edward VII National Memorial Association was formed to campaign to stamp out tuberculosis in Wales.
1912	The Welsh Health Service Insurance Commission was established.
1914	By now the South Wales Miners Medical Scheme had the best developed medical facilities in the UK for ordinary people.
1915	The first pit-head baths in Wales were opened at Deep Navigation Colliery, Treharris, Gwent.
1918	The Prince of Wales Orthopaedic Hospital was opened in Cardiff – 'the Welsh Roehampton'.
1918–19	A 'Spanish flu' epidemic killed about 10,000 people throughout Wales.
1919	The Welsh Board of Health was established.
1920	The South Wales Sanatorium opened at Talgarth, Powys, was the largest in the UK with 304 beds.
1939	The South Wales Coal Dust Research Committee was established.
	A report showed that seven of the thirteen Welsh counties had the highest incidence of tuberculosis in England and Wales.

1943   Tenovus, the medical charity and research organization, was founded in Cardiff.

1944   The first mass radiography unit for chest X-rays in the UK was established by the Welsh National Memorial Association.

1946   A Pneumoconiosis Research Unit was established at Llandough Hospital near Cardiff.

1948   The Welsh Regional Hospital Board was established as hospitals were nationalized under the National Health Service Act.

1960   The world's first fully equipped spina bifida unit was opened in Cardiff by Tenovus.

1962   A smallpox outbreak in south Wales killed 17 people.

1967   The Tenovus Cancer Research Centre in Cardiff was opened.

1971   The University Hospital of Wales, Cardiff, was opened.

1977   The Welsh Health Common Services Authority was established.

1982   BUPA private hospital was opened in Cardiff.

1985   The Heartbeat Wales campaign was launched to tackle the heart disease problem in Wales.

1986   *Termau Meddygol* ('Medical Terms') was published by the Board of Celtic Studies.

1987   The Welsh Health Promotion Authority was established.

1989   Newly qualified doctors were allowed to take the Hippocratic Oath in Welsh for the first time.

1992   The first NHS Trust (Pembrokeshire) and the first fund-holding general practices in Wales were established.

DISTRICT HEALTH AUTHORITIES

District Health Authorities either provide health services through directly managed units or by obtaining the services from National Health Service Trusts which began to be introduced in Wales in 1992.

Clwyd	Preswylfa, Hendy Road, Mold, Clwyd, CH7 1PZ.
East Dyfed	Starling Park House, Johnstown, Carmarthen, Dyfed, SA31 3HU.
Gwent	Brecon House, Mamhilad Park Estate, Pontypool, Gwent, NP4 0YB.
Gwynedd	Coed Mawr, Bangor, Gwynedd, LL57 4TP.
Mid Glamorgan	Albert Road, Pontypridd, Mid Glamorgan, CF37 1LA.
Pembrokeshire	Meyler House, St Thomas Green, Haverfordwest, Dyfed, SA61 1QP.
Powys	Mansion House, Bronllys, Brecon, Powys, LD3 0LS.
South Glamorgan	The Temple of Peace, Cathays Park, Cardiff, CF1 3NW.
West Glamorgan	36 Orchard Street, Swansea, SA1 5AQ.

FAMILY HEALTH SERVICE AUTHORITIES

Family Health Service Authorities administer the provision of general medical and pharmaceutical services, general dental services and general ophthalmic services for their locality.

Under the National Health Service and Community Care Act 1990, Family Health Service Authorities replaced Family Practitioner Committees.

Clwyd	Trinity House, Trinity Street, Wrexham, Clwyd, LL11 1NW.
East Dyfed	Francis Well, Carmarthen, Dyfed, SA31 2AB.
Gwent	Brecon House, Mamhilad Park Estate, Pontypool, Gwent, NP4 DYB.
Gwynedd	Erlydon, Campbell Road, Caernarfon, Gwynedd, LL55 1WU.
Mid Glamorgan	Churchill House (5th Floor), Churchill Way, Cardiff, CF1 4TW.
Pembrokeshire	As for East Dyfed.
Powys	N Block, Bronllys Hospital, Bronllys, Brecon, Powys, LD3 0LS.
South Glamorgan	Churchill House (6th Floor), Churchill Way, Cardiff, CF1 4TW.
West Glamorgan	Trinity Buildings, 21 Orchard Street, Swansea, SA1 5BE.

PERSONNEL IN THE NHS (At September, 1992)

Staff employed by the NHS, excluding family practitioners

Medical and dental	2,848
Nurses and midwives	27,347
Professional and technical	5,796
Administrative and clerical	8,315
Ambulances, ancillary and maintenance	10,802

Medical practitioners	1,835
Dental practitioners	831

NATIONAL HEALTH SERVICE HOSPITALS IN WALES, 1992–1993

Name	Staffed beds	Type
Clwyd		
Abergele	65	Acute
Broughton	24	Mental handicap
Chirk	31	Acute

Name	Staffed beds	Type
Coed Du	14	Mental handicap
Colwyn Bay Community	42	Acute
Deeside Community	31	Acute
Denbigh Infirmary	52	Acute
Dobshill	61	Geriatric
Flint Cottage	18	Acute
Gwynfa	18	Mental illness
HM Stanley	102	Long stay
Holywell Cottage	19	Acute
Llangollen	18	Acute
Lluesty	64	Geriatric
Meadowslea	54	Geriatric
Mold	40	Acute
North Wales	328	Long stay
Penley	32	Geriatric
Prestatyn	12	Acute
Royal Alexandra	69	Mainly long stay
Rhuthun	48	Acute
Trevalyn	31	Geriatric
Ysbyty Glan Clwyd	480	Acute
Ysbyty Maelor	616	Mainly acute

East Dyfed

Aberaeron	14	Geriatric
Amman Valley	28	Partly acute
Bronglais General	247	Mainly acute
Bryntirion	59	Long stay
Ceredigion and District	30	Acute
Cartrefle	7	Mental handicap
Llandovery Cottage	18	Acute
Mynydd Mawr	50	Geriatric
Prince Phillip, Llanelli	208	Mainly acute
Saint David's, Carmarthen	322	Mental illness
Tregaron	30	Geriatric
West Wales General	474	Mainly acute

Gwent

Abertillery and District	69	Partly acute
Allt-yr-Yn	74	General
Blaenavon Health Care Unit	10	Acute

121

Name	Staffed beds	Type
Blaina and District	47	Mainly long stay
County Hospital, Griffithstown	54	Partly acute
Ebbw Vale	40	Mainly long stay
Llanfrechfa Grange	145	Mental handicap
Monmouth General	25	Acute
Mount Pleasant, Chepstow	86	Mainly long stay
Nevill Hall	443	Acute
Oakdale	20	Geriatric
Pen-y-Fal	274	Mental illness
Pontypool and District	44	Mainly long stay
Royal Gwent	650	Acute
Saint Cadoc's	214	Mental illness
Saint Lawrence	132	Plastic surgery, burns
Saint Woolos	364	Mainly long stay
Tredegar General	58	Mainly long stay

Gwynedd

Bodfaen	6	Mental illness
Bronygarth	31	Mainly long stay
Bryn Beryl	40	Partly acute
Brynseiont	43	Mainly long stay
Bryn-y-Neuadd	224	Long stay
Cefni	43	Geriatric
Conwy	67	Geriatric
Dolgellau and District	32	Mainly acute
Druid	35	Geriatric
Eryri	36	Geriatric
Ffestiniog Memorial	17	Acute
Garth Angharad	7	Mental handicap
Llandudno General	162	Mainly acute
Llwyn View	10	Mental handicap
Minffordd	22	Mental illness
St David's, Bangor	109	Acute
Stanley Sailors	23	Acute
Towyn and District	21	Partly acute
Valley	28	Long stay
Ysbyty Gwynedd	503	Mainly acute

Mid Glamorgan

Aberbargoed and District	36	Partly acute

Name	Staffed beds	Type
Aberdare General	132	Partly acute
Bridgend General	167	Partly acute
Caerphilly Miners	174	Mainly acute
Dewi Sant	120	Geriatric
East Glamorgan	522	Mainly acute
Energlyn	15	Geriatric
Fedw Hir	42	Geriatric
Glanrhyd	191	Mental illness
Hensol	282	Mental handicap
Llwynypia	160	Mainly long stay
Llynfi	20	Mental illness
Maesgwyn	60	Geriatric
Maesteg General	51	Acute
Mardy	85	Mainly long stay
Mountain Ash	44	Mainly long stay
Park	139	Mental illness
Penyfai	154	Mental illness
Porth	25	Acute
Prince Charles	470	Acute
Princess of Wales	367	Acute
Redwood Memorial	21	Partly acute
Saint Tydfil's	140	Long Stay
Tonteg	22	Long stay
Treherbert	33	Acute
Ysbyty George Thomas	100	Mainly long stay
Ystrad Mynach	115	Long stay
Pembrokeshire (NHS Trust)		
South Pembrokeshire	67	Mainly long stay
Tenby Cottage	16	Acute
Withybush	359	Mainly acute
Powys		
Brecon War Memorial (including St David's, Brecon)	66	Mainly acute
Broddyfi Community	49	Partly acute
Bronllys	84	Long stay
Brynhyfryd	55	Mental handicap
Builth Cottage	23	Acute

Name	Staffed beds	Type
Knighton	20	Mainly long stay
Llandrindod War Memorial	66	Partly acute
Llandrindod and District	38	Partly acute
Llys Maldwyn	57	Mental handicap
Mid Wales	243	Mental illness
Montgomery County Infirmary	48	Partly acute
Victoria War Memorial, Welshpool	53	Partly acute
Ystradgynlais Community	52	Mainly long stay

South Glamorgan

Barry Community	26	Acute
Cardiff Royal Infirmary	378	Mainly acute
Ely	297	Mental handicap
Lansdowne	126	Long stay
Llandough	379	Acute
Prince of Wales, Rhydlafar	124	Mainly acute
Rookwood	84	Mainly acute
Royal Hamadryad	50	Mental illness
Sully	132	Long stay
University Hospital of Wales	840	Mainly acute
Velindre	99	Radiotherapy
Whitchurch	371	Mental illness

West Glamorgan

Cefn Coed	339	Mental illness
Clydach	22	Acute
Cymla	60	Geriatric
Fairwood	21	Acute
Garngoch	40	Mental illness
Gorseinon	70	Long stay
Groeswen	50	Geriatric
Hill House	80	Partly acute
Llwyneryr	23	Mental handicap
Morriston	582	Mainly acute
Mount Pleasant, Swansea	62	Geriatric
Neath General	326	Acute
Port Talbot	27	Acute
Singleton	521	Acute
Tonna	80	Mental illness

Hospital In-patients, 1992–1993

Staffed beds (average available daily)	18,070
Occupied beds (average occupied daily)	13,789
Discharges and deaths	503,657

Hospital Out-patients, 1992–1993

New cases	716,078
Total attendances	3,369,403

Amenity Beds in National Health Service Hospitals, 1991–1992

Clwyd	10	Pembrokeshire	5
East Dyfed	17	Powys	4
Gwent	0	South Glamorgan	3
Gwynedd	16	West Glamorgan	17
Mid Glamorgan	0	WALES	72

Patients may be charged for the hotel part of the cost of amenity beds in order to be in a single room or small ward. No charge is made for medical treatment.

COMMUNITY HEALTH COUNCILS

Community Health Councils put the views of the public to local health authorities, investigate National Health Service standards and suggest improvements, and help with complaints.

The councils are statutory bodies and are not part of the National Health Service management.

The 22 Community Health Councils are listed below.

Clwyd
Clwyd North: HM Stanley Hospital, St Asaph.
Clwyd South: 9 Park Grove Road, Wrexham.

East Dyfed
Carmarthen: 12a Lammas Street, Carmarthen.
Ceredigion: 5 Chalybeate Street, Aberystwyth.
Llanelli–Dinefwr: c/o The Town Hall, Llanelli.

Gwent

North Gwent:	St Michael's House, St Michael's Road, Abergavenny.
South Gwent:	2 Emlyn Walk, Newport.

Gwynedd

Aberconwy:	3 Trinity Square, Llandudno.
Anglesey:	8a High Street, Llangefni.
Arfon–Dwyfor:	Bodfan Eryri Hospital, Bangor.
Meirionnydd:	Beechwood House, Dolgellau.

Mid Glamorgan

East Glamorgan:	13 Gelliwastad Road, Pontypridd.
Merthyr Tydfil–	
Cynon Valley:	2nd Floor, Hollies Health Centre, Swan Street, Merthyr Tydfil.
Ogwr:	c/o District Health Offices, Maesteg Road, Tondu.
Rhymney Valley:	Pierhead Buildings, Bedwelyn Road, Ystrad Mynach, Hengoed.

Pembrokeshire

Pembrokeshire:	2 Picton Place, Haverfordwest.

Powys

Brecon and Radnor:	11 The Bulwarks, Brecon.
Montgomery:	Ladywell House, Newtown.

South Glamorgan

Cardiff:	15 St David's House, Wood Street, Cardiff.
Vale of Glamorgan:	24 Broad Street Parade, Barry.

West Glamorgan

Neath–Afan:	67 Margam Road, Port Talbot.
Swansea and	
Lliw Valley:	42 High Street, Swansea.

ALL-WALES BODIES

The National Health Service Commissioner for Wales

Pearl Assurance Building, Greyfriars Road, Cardiff, CF1 3AG.

The Commissioner (Ombudsman) investigates complaints by individuals or organizations that they have suffered injustice or hardship as a consequence of a failure to provide required services.

Clinical judgements and activities taken in the provision of general practitioner services are excluded from investigation by the Commissioner.

The Welsh Health Promotion Authority

Brunel House, 2 Fitzalan Road, Cardiff, CF2 1EB.

Established in 1987, the function of the Welsh Health Promotion Authority is to provide leadership, support and news for the promotion of health and the prevention of disease in Wales. It is a statutory health authority.

NATIONAL HEALTH SERVICE TRUSTS

NHS Trusts assume responsibility for the ownership and management of hospitals and other establishments and facilities previously managed by a district health authority.

Trusts are corporate bodies with a board of directors and a chairman appointed by the Secretary of State for Wales. There are executive and non-executive directors.

Growth of NHS Trusts

From 1992, one Trust:
Pembrokeshire NHS Trust, Withybush General Hospital, Fishguard Road, Haverfordwest, Dyfed, SA61 2P2.

From 1993, 13 more Trusts:
Glan Clwyd District General Hospital NHS Trust, Glan Clwyd Hospital, Bodelwyddan, Nr Rhyl, Clwyd, LL18 5UJ.
Wrexham Maelor Hospital NHS Trust, Wrexham Maelor Hospital, Croesnewydd Road, Wrexham, Clwyd, LL13 7TD.
Gofal Cymuned Clwydian Community Care NHS Trust, Catherine Gladstone House, Hawarden Way, Deeside, Clwyd, CH5 2EP.
Powys Health Care NHS Trust, Felindre, Bronllys Hospital, Bronllys, Brecon, Powys, LD3 0LS.
Glan Hafren NHS Trust, Royal Gwent Hospital, Cardiff Road, Newport, Gwent, NP9 2UB.
Gwent Community Health NHS Trust, Grange House, Llanfrechfa Grange Hospital, Cwmbran, Gwent, NP44 8YN.
Llandough Hospital NHS Trust, Llandough Hospital, Llandough, Penarth, South Glamorgan, CF6 1XX.
Bridgend and District NHS Trust, Quarella Road, Bridgend, Mid Glamorgan, CF31 IYE.
Swansea NHS Trust, Singleton Hospital, Sketty, Swansea, SA2 8QA.
Llanelli–Dinefwr NHS Trust, Prince Philip Hospital, Bryngwynmawr, Dafen, Llanelli, SA14 8QF.

Carmarthen and District NHS Trust, West Wales General Hospital, Glangwili, Carmarthen, Dyfed, SA31 2AF.
Ceredigion and Mid Wales NHS Trust, Bronglais General Hospital, Aberystwyth, Dyfed, SY23 1ER.
South and East Wales Ambulance NHS Trust, South Glamorgan Ambulance Headquarters, Ty Bronna, St Fagans Road, Fairwater, Cardiff, CF5 3XP.

From 1994, 8 more Trusts
Rhondda Health Care NHS Trust, Llwynypia Hospital, Llwynypia, Tonypandy, Rhondda, Mid Glamorgan, CF40 2LX.
Velindre NHS Trust, Velindre Road, Whitchurch, Cardiff, CF4 7XL.
Derwen NHS Trust West Wales, St David's Hospital, Job's Well Road, Carmarthen, Dyfed, SA31 3HB.
North Wales Ambulance Service NHS Trust, Delfryn, HM Stanley Hospital, St Asaph, Clwyd.
Mid Glamorgan Ambulance Service NHS Trust, Ambulance Headquarters, Church Village, Pontypridd, Mid Glamorgan, CF38 1BS.
Gwynedd Hospitals NHS Trust, Ysbyty Gwynedd, Penrhosgarnedd, Bangor, Gwynedd, LL57 2PW.
Gwynedd Community Health NHS Trust, Bryn y Neuadd Hospital, Llanfairfechan, Gwynedd, LL33 0HA.
Nevill Hall and District NHS Trust, Nevill Hall Hospital, Brecon Road, Abergavenny, Gwent, NP7 7EC.

FUND-HOLDING PRACTICES

General practitioners with 7,000 or more patients (originally 9,000 or more) can apply for fund-holding status. They then become responsible for their own NHS budgets and can negotiate directly with hospitals in any region, public or private. Their allocations also cover community health services, medicine and staff costs.

Growth of fund-holding practices in Wales
From 1991:   7
From 1992:   26
From 1993:   71
From 1994   119

PRIVATE HEALTH CARE, 1993

Private Hospitals

Clwyd:	Yale Hospital, Wrexham	19 beds
Dyfed:	Werndale Hospital, Carmarthen	28 beds
Gwent:	St Joseph's Hospital, Newport	63 beds
Gwynedd:	North Wales Centre, Llandudno	52 beds
South Glamorgan:	BUPA Hospital, Cardiff	74 beds
West Glamorgan:	Sancta Maria Hospital, Swansea	33 beds
WALES		269 beds

Private Registered Nursing Homes and Beds, 1993

Clwyd:	100 (2,786 beds)	Pembrokeshire:	13 (435 beds)
East Dyfed:	21 (846 beds)	Powys:	7 (265 beds)
Gwent:	69 (2,311 beds)	South Glamorgan:	29 (1,191 beds)
Gwynedd:	34 (927 beds)	West Glamorgan:	85 (2,417 beds)
Mid Glamorgan:	22 (944 beds)	WALES:	380 (12,122 beds)

Registered Private Homes and Voluntary Homes, 1992

County	Private homes	Voluntary homes
Clwyd	17	15
Dyfed	55	8
Gwent	17	3
Gwynedd	66	1
Mid Glamorgan	35	4
Powys	16	0
South Glamorgan	81	8
West Glamorgan	21	6

8

THE MEDIA

DATES OF SIGNIFICANCE AND INTEREST

1586–87 A secret Catholic printing press is thought to have been in use illegally in a cave at Llandudno. There may also have been secret Catholic presses in Brecon and Flintshire.

1679   The first patent was granted for printing and publishing an annual Welsh almanac (at Shrewsbury).

1718   The first legal printing press in Wales was established by Isaac Carter at Adpar near Newcastle Emlyn. (It was moved to Carmarthen in 1725.)

1770   The first Welsh-language magazine appeared – *Trysorfa Gwybodaeth*.

1793   The first Welsh-language political periodical, *Y Cylch-grawn Cymraeg*, appeared.

1804   The first issue of the weekly *Cambrian* of Swansea appeared – the first English-language newspaper in Wales.

1807   The *North Wales Chronicle* of Bangor was launched.

1810   The oldest surviving newspaper in Wales, the *Carmarthen Journal*, was launched.

1814   *Seren Gomer*, the first Welsh-language newspaper, was started in Swansea.

1829   *The Monmouthshire Merlin* first appeared.

1832   *The Welshman* and the *Caernarfon and Denbigh Herald* first appeared.

1843   *Yr Amserau* first appeared.

1854   The *Telegraphic Despatch* of Swansea first appeared – the first newspaper in Wales to be published more frequently than once a week.

1857   *Baner Cymru* was launched by Thomas Gee.

1859   *Yr Amserau* and *Baner Cymru* merged as *Baner ac Amserau Cymru*.

1860   The *Cambrian News* first appeared.

1861   The *Cambria Daily Leader* of Swansea was launched – the first daily newspaper in Wales.

1866   The *Merthyr Express* was launched.

1869   The *Western Mail* of Cardiff, the oldest surviving daily newspaper in Wales, first appeared.

1872   The *South Wales Daily News* was launched in Cardiff.

1875   *Tarian y Gweithwyr* ('The Workers' Shield') was published in Aberdare. (Its last issue was in 1934.)

1884   The *South Wales Echo* first appeared.

1890   *Y Cymro* was first published.

1892   The *South Wales Argus* of Newport first appeared.

1896   The first news film ever shot in Britain showed the Prince and Princess of Wales visiting the Cardiff Exhibition.

1898   *Llais Llafur* ('Labour Voice') – the first Welsh-language socialist newspaper – was launched in Ystalyfera. (Its last issue was in 1971.)

1908   Frank Mason, owner of the *Tenby Observer*, won a High Court case which established the right of the press in Britain to be admitted to local council meetings.

1911   The *Merthyr Pioneer* socialist newspaper first appeared.

1923   Station 5WA began broadcasting from Cardiff. This was followed by BBC studios in Swansea in 1924 and Bangor in 1935.

1930   The *South Wales Daily Post* of Swansea was launched.

1937   The BBC Welsh Home Service was established.

1952   BBC television service began in Wales and the Broadcasting Council for Wales was created. The first governor representing Wales was appointed to the BBC's Board of Governors.

1954   Launch of the first Sunday newspaper to be printed and published in Wales – the *Empire News*. (Production ceased in 1957.)

1958   Commercial television provided by TWW (Television Wales and the West) began in Wales.

1962   WWN (Wales West and the North – Teledu Cymru) commercial television company began broadcasting.

1963   The Thomson Foundation for Third World news media training was established in Cardiff.

         WWN was taken over by TWW after running into financial difficulties.

1964   BBC Wales television was established.

1968   HTV (Harlech Television) took over the commercial television franchise in Wales from TWW.

1969   Colour television became available in Wales.

1973   The first of some 50 *papurau bro*, local Welsh-language community newspapers, appeared – *Y Dinesydd* of Cardiff.

1974	Swansea Sound was launched – the first commercial radio station in Wales.
	The *Wrexham Evening Leader* was founded.
1978	BBC Wales was established.
1979	BBC Radio Cymru was launched.
1980	The Cardiff Broadcasting Company commercial radio station went on the air.
1981	The *South Wales Argus*, the last independent evening newspaper in Wales, was taken over by Express Newspapers.
1982	S4C (Sianel Pedwar Cymru) was launched.
	BBC television studios in Bangor were opened.
	A Welsh-language Sunday newspaper, *Sulyn,* was launched but ceased publication after 14 issues.
1983	Marcher Sound, Wrexham, and Gwent Broadcasting, Newport, commercial radio stations were launched.
	BBC Radio Clwyd and BBC Radio Gwent began broadcasting.
1985	Cardiff Broadcasting and Gwent Braodcasting were taken over by Red Dragon Radio after running into financial difficulties.
1988	The weekly Welsh-language magazine *Golwg* was launched.
1989	*Wales on Sunday* newspaper was launched.
1990	Red Dragon Radio split into Touch AM and Red Dragon FM.
	The first cable television service in Wales began operating in West Glamorgan.
1991	BBC Radio Gwent was closed.
1992	The first community radio stations in Wales, Radio Ceredigion at Aberystwyth and Radio Maldwyn at Newtown, were approved by the Radio Authority.
1992	*Y Faner* (formerly *Baner ac Amserau Cymru*) ceased publication.
1993	Marcher Coast, Commercial Radio Station of Colwyn Bay, began broadcasting.

ENGLISH-LANGUAGE NEWSPAPERS PUBLISHED IN WALES

(Note: circulation figures fluctuate)
*Indicates the circulation of group or series of which this title is part.

Title	*Approximate Circulation (1993)*
Daily – morning	
Western Mail (Cardiff)	72,000

Title	Approximate Circulation (1993)
Daily – evening	
South Wales Argus (Newport)	40,000
South Wales Echo (Cardiff)	78,000
South Wales Evening Post (Swansea)	68,000
Wrexham Evening Leader	33,000
Weekly – Sunday	
Wales on Sunday (Cardiff)	62,000
Weekly – Wednesday–Saturday	
Abergavenny Chronicle (Friday)	10,000
Abergele Visitor (Wednesday)	5,300
Barry and District News (Thursday)	7,000
Brecon Express (Wednesday)	n/a
Burry Port Star (Thursday)	18,000*
Caernarfon and Denbigh Herald (Friday)	15,000
Cambrian News (Aberystwyth) (Friday)	24,000
Caridgan and Tivyside Advertiser (Friday)	8,500*
Carmarthen Journal (Wednesday)	21,000
Carmarthen Times and Citizen (Friday)	18,000
Chronicle (Clwyd Edition) (Friday)	44,000*
Corwen Times (Friday)	11,000
County Echo (Fishguard) (Friday)	4,000
County Times and Express (Newtown) (Saturday)	18,000
Cynon Valley Leader (Thursday)	71,000*
Fishguard and Tivyside Advertiser (Friday)	8,500*
Glamorgan Gazette (Thursday)	16,000
Gwent Gazette (Thursday)	16,000
Gwent Gazette (Thursday)	9,000
Holyhead and Anglesey Mail (Wednesday)	11,000
Llanelli Star (Thursday)	18,000*
Llantrisant Observer (Thursday)	71,000*
Merioneth Express (Friday)	n/a
Merthyr Express (Thursday)	12,000
Monmouthshire Beacon (Thursday)	6,000
Narbeth and Whitland Observer (Friday)	7,500*
North Wales Weekly News (Thursday)	26,000
Pembroke County and West Wales Guardian (Friday)	15,000

Title	*Approximate Circulation (1993)*
Penarth Times (Friday)	6,000
Pontypridd Observer (Thursday)	71,000*
Radnor Express (Wednesday)	n/a
Rhondda Leader (Thursday)	71,000*
South Wales Guardian (Haverfordwest) (Thursday)	13,000
Tenby Observer (Friday)	7,500*
Weekly Argus (Newport) (Friday)	122,000
Western Telegraph and Cymric Times (Haverfordwest) (Wednesday)	29,000
Wrexham Leader (Friday)	15,000

FREE NEWSPAPERS PUBLISHED IN WALES (Weekly publication)

(Note: circulation figures fluctuate)
* Indicates the circulation of group or series of which this title is part.

Title	*Approximate circulation (1993)*
Aberdare Herald and Post (Thursday)	23,000
Abergavenny and Monmouth News (Thursday)	8,000*
Bangor and Anglesey Chronicle (Thursday)	56,000*
Bangor and Anglesey Mail (Wednesday)	44,000*
Barry Gem (Friday)	19,000*
Blackwood and Risca News (Thursday)	104,000*
Bridgend and District Recorder (Friday)	45,000
Bridgend and Ogwr Herald and Post (Thursday)	49,000*
Caernarfon and Lleyn Chronicle (Thursday)	57,000
Caerphilly and Blackwood Chronicle (Thursday)	19,000*
Caerphilly Challenger (Friday)	53,000*
Campaign – Blackwood (Thursday)	38,000
Campaign – Caerphilly and Rhymney Valley (Thursday)	52,000
Campaign – Ebbw Vale (Thursday)	28,000
Campaign – Merthyr Tydfil and Cynon Valley (Thursday)	42,000
Campaign – Pontypridd and Llantrisant (Thursday)	61,000
Campaign – Rhondda (Thursday)	28,000
Cardiff Independent (Wednesday)	112,000
Cardiff Post (Thursday)	100,000
Chepstow Free Press (Friday)	4,500

Title	Approximate Circulation (1993)
Chepstow and Caldicot News (Thursday)	104,000*
Clwyd Herald and Post (Wednesday)	39,000
Cwmbran and Pontypool News (Thursday)	104,000*
Cwmbran Star (Friday)	14,000
Cynon Valley Special (Thursday)	10,000
Denbigh Free Press (Friday)	11,000
Free Press of Monmouthshire	13,000
Holyhead and Anglesey Chronicle (Thursday)	n/a
Llandudno Advertiser (Friday)	7,000
Merthyr Herald and Post (Thursday)	22,000*
Mold and Deeside Midweek Leader (Thursday)	33,000
Monmouth and Abergavenny News (Thursday)	104,000
Neath Guardian (Thursday)	28,000*
Neath Herald of Wales (Thursday)	20,000
Newport and Cwmbran Herald and Post (Thursday)	68,000
Newport News (Thursday)	104,000*
Newport Free Press (Thursday)	37,000
North Wales Pioneer (Thursday)	31,000
Port Talbot Guardian (Thursday)	22,000
Rhyl, Prestatyn and Abergele Journal (Wednesday)	33,000
Rhyl and Prestatyn Visitor (Wednesday)	24,000
Swansea Herald of Wales (Thursday)	84,000
Vale Advertiser (Llandudno Junction) (Friday)	12,000*
Vale Post (Wednesday)	39,000*
Vale of Glamorgan Gem (Friday)	15,000
Wrexham Midweek Leader (Friday)	34,000
Wrexham and Mold Mail (Friday)	39,000*

WELSH-LANGUAGE NEWSPAPERS

Weekly

Title	Approximate average circulation
Y Cymro (Oswestry)	4,300
Y Dydd (Dolgellau) Bilingual	2,500
Herald Cymraeg, Herald Môn (Caernarfon)	1,500

Monthly (*papurau bro*)

The approximate combined circulation of these local Welsh-language community newspapers is 70,000.

Title	Area served
Yr Angor	Aberystwyth, Llanbadarn Fawr and Penparcau
Yr Angor	Merseyside Welsh
Yr Arwydd	Mynydd Bodafon and district, Anglesey
Y Barcud	Tregaron and district, Dyfed
Y Bedol	Rhuthun and district
Y Bigwn	Denbigh
Blewyn Glas	Bro Dyfi (Dovey), Gwynedd
Y Cardi Bach	Whitland and St Clears
Y Clawdd	Wrexham and district
Clebran	Crymych, Maenclochog and district, Dyfed
Clecs y Cwm a'r Dref	Neath and district
Clochdar	Cynon Valley, Aberdare
Clonc	Lampeter and district
Cwlwm	Carmarthen
Dail Dysynni	Dysynni Valley, Gwynedd
Y Dinesydd	Cardiff and district
Y Ddolen	Ystwyth Valley, Dyfed
Eco'r Wyddfa	Llanberis, Llanddeiniolen and Llanrug.
Y Ffynnon	Eifionydd, Llŷn, Gwynedd
Y Gadlas	Conwy–Clwyd district
Y Gambo	South-west Ceredigion, Dyfed
Y Garthen	Teifi Valley
Y Glannau	St Asaph area
Glo Man	Amman Valley
Y Gloran	Upper Rhondda Fawr
Y Glorian	Llangefni and district, Anglesey
Goriad	Bangor and Y Felinheli
Yr Hogwr	Bridgend and district
Llafur Bro	Ffestiniog and district
Llais	Tawe Valley
Llais Aeron	Aeron Valley, Dyfed
Llais Ardudwy	Ardudwy, Gwynedd
Llais Ogwen	Ogwen Valley, Gwynedd
Llanw Llŷn	Abersoch area, Llŷn, Gwynedd

Lleu	Nantlle Valley, Gwynedd
Y Llien Gwyn	Fishguard and district
Y Llofwr	Dinefwr area, Dyfed
Y Mandral	Rhondda Fach area
Nene	Johnstown, Penycae and Rhosllannerchrugog area
Yr Odyn	Llanrwst and district
Papur Fama	Mold and district
Papur Menai	Menai Strait area, Anglesey
Papur Pawb	Talybont, Tre'r-ddôl and district, Dyfed
Papur y Cwm	Gwendraeth Valley, Dyfed
Y Pentan	Conwy and district
Pethe Penllyn	Bala, Llanuwchllyn and district
Plu'r Gweunydd	Welshpool and district
Y Rhwyd	North-west Anglesey
Seren Hafren	Severn Valley and Newtown, Powys
Tafod Elái	Taff-Ely, Mid Glamorgan
Y Tincer	Borth, Genau'r-glyn and district, Dyfed
Wilia	Swansea and district
Yr Wylan	Beddgelert, Penrhyndeudraeth, Porthmadog and district
Yr Ysgub	Ceiriog Valleys, Powys

BROADCASTING

Television

BBC Wales:	Studios at Aberystwyth, Bangor, Cardiff and Swansea.
HTV Wales:	Studios at Cardiff and Mold.
S4C:	Studios at Cardiff. (Welsh Fourth Channel Authority/Awdurdod Sianel Pedwar Cymru: Parc Tŷ Glas, Llanishen, Cardiff.)

Cable Television

Three licences for the provision of cable television in Wales had been granted by the end of 1993. Only one company (Starvision) was operating at the end of 1994:

Cabletel (UK)	Cardiff and Penarth (103,000 homes)
Starvision Network	West Glamorgan (122,000 homes)
Newport Cablevision	Newport, Cwmbran and Pontypool (85,000 homes)

Radio

BBC

Radio Wales:	882 kHz and 340 metres
Radio Cymru:	92.95 and 96.8 MHz
Radio Clwyd:	657 metres

Independent

Marcher Gold and MFM:	Wrexham, 1260 kHz, 103.4 and 97.1 MHz
Red Dragon FM and Touch AM:	Cardiff and Newport, 103.2 MHz, 1359 kHz; 97.4 MHz, 1305 kHz
Swansea Sound:	Swansea, 96.4 MHz, 1170 metres.

Community radio

Radio Ceredigion:	Aberystwyth, 103.3 and 96.6 MHz
Radio Maldwyn:	Newtown, 756 kHz
Marcher Coast:	Colwyn Bay, 96.3 MHz

Community radio stations are also to be established for the Heads of the Valleys of south Wales and for Pembrokeshire.

Regional radio

Galaxy Radio:	Bristol (from 1994), 97.2 MHz – to cover south Wales from Chepstow to Barry and inland.

BROADCASTING IN WELSH

S4C

First transmissions in Welsh (1992–93):	524 hours BBC
	901 hours HTV and independent producers
Repeat transmissions in Welsh (1992–93):	25 hours BBC
	205 hours HTV and independent producers
	1,655 hours

BBC Radio Cymru

There are 90 hours of broadcasting in Welsh per week giving an average figure of 4,680 hours a year.

Marcher Gold (Sain-y-Gororau)

There is one hour a night on weekdays giving an average of 5 hours a week of Welsh-language broadcasting.

Swansea Sound (Sain Abertawe)
There is an average of 20 hours of Welsh-language broadcasting a week.

Touch AM
There is one hour per week of bilingual broadcasting.

Radio Ceredigion
There are 42 hours of Welsh-language broadcasting a week.

9

TRANSPORT

DATES OF SIGNIFICANCE AND INTEREST

1280s   The River Clwyd was diverted in a 2½ mile-long (4 km.) canal – a task that took three years to complete – so that Rhuddlan Castle could be supplied by sea.

1599   Holyhead was designated a posting station for Royal Mail to Ireland.

1661   The first temporary lighthouse on the Welsh coast was at St Ann's Head, Milford Haven. (Made permanent in 1714.)

1697   The first known tramway in Wales was constructed by Sir Humphrey Mackworth in Neath.

1752   The first turnpike road in Wales linked Wrexham and Shrewsbury.

1755   William Edwards built a bridge over the River Taff at Pontypridd with an arch spanning 40 ft. – the longest arch in Britain at the time.

1765   The Chester to Holyhead road was completely turnpiked.

1766   The first Welsh Canal Act was passed – for a canal from Kidwelly to Carway, Gwendraeth Fawr Valley.

1767   A Cardiff to Merthyr Tydfil road via Caerphilly was opened.

1768   The first modern north Wales canal linked Hawarden to the River Dee.

1778   The first lighthouse on the Smalls, Pembrokeshire, was built – at that time the most remote lighthouse in the British Isles.

1785   The first mail coach ran between London and Milford Haven.

1792   Llansamlet Canal was opened.

1793   Amlwch port was built.

1794   The Glamorganshire Canal was opened between Cardiff and Merthyr Tydfil.

1795   The Carmarthen Dock, Llanelli, was opened.
        The Neath Canal was opened between Neath and Glynneath.

1796   The Monmouthshire Canal between Newport and Pontnewynydd was opened.

1797	The Montgomery Canal was completed to Garthmyl via Welshpool from Frankton Junction.
1798	The Swansea Canal was opened between Swansea and Ystradgynlais.
1799	The Crumlin branch of the Monmouthshire Canal was opened.
1800	The Brecon Canal from Brecon to Tal-y-bont was opened.
1801	The 600 ft. (182.9 m.) long Chirk Aqueduct was opened. The first railway of any sort in north Wales was built by Lord Penrhyn between Penrhyn Quarries, Bethesda and Port Penrhyn.
1804	The world's first steam locomotive ran the 9¾ miles between Penydarren and Abercynon.
1805	Pontcysyllte Aqueduct opened – the longest aqueduct in Britain at 1,007 ft. (307 m.). The Llangollen branch of the Ellesmere Canal was opened.
1807	The world's first fare-paying passenger railway opened – the horse-drawn Oystermouth to Mumbles Railway.
1812	The Brecon and Monmouthshire Canal was opened from Newport to Brecon. The Aberdare branch of the Glamorganshire Canal was opened.
1816	The Irish Sea was first crossed by balloon, by Windham Sadler.
1821	The Montgomery Canal was extended to Newtown. The port at Porthmadog was opened.
1824	The Port Tennant (Neath and Swansea Junction) Canal was opened and was linked to the Neath Canal.
1826	The Menai suspension bridge was opened – the longest iron bridge in the world at the time with a 579 ft. (176.5 m.) span.
1828	Porthcawl Dock was opened and was linked to the Llynfi Valley by tramway.
1829	The Holyhead turnpike road was completed after 20 years' work.
1832	Burry Port harbour was opened.
1835	Llanelli New Dock was opened.
1836	The Ffestiniog Railway between Ffestiniog and Porthmadog was completed – the first narrow-gauge railway in the world.
1838	Port Talbot Dock was opened.
1839	Cardiff West Bute Dock was opened.
1840	The Taff Vale Railway was opened between Cardiff and Abercynon.
1841	The Taff Vale Railway was extended from Abercynon to Merthyr Tydfil.
1842	Town Dock, Newport, was opened.
1844	County road boards were established for six south Wales counties

following the attacks on turnpike roads during the Rebecca Riots – these were the first county road boards in Britain.

1846   The Taff Vale Railway was extended into the Cynon Valley.

1848   The Conwy railway bridge and the Chirk viaduct were opened.

1850   The South Wales Railway was opened from Chepstow to Neath and Swansea.

    Landore viaduct was completed and Aberystwyth harbour opened.

    The Britannia rail bridge across the Menai Strait was opened – the world's first tubular bridge and the world's longest span bridge at the time.

1851   The railway extension to Admiralty Pier, Holyhead, was opened.

    The Vale of Neath Railway reached Neath and Swansea.

1852   The Chepstow rail bridge was opened linking the South Wales Railway with the Great Western Railway.

    The South Wales Railway reached Carmarthen.

1853   The Vale of Neath Railway was extended from Aberdare to Merthyr Tydfil.

1854   The South Wales Railway reached Haverfordwest.

1856   The South Wales Railway reached Neyland (New Milford) and the Neyland to Waterford ferry service began.

    The Taff Vale Railway was extended into the Rhondda Valley.

1857   The Crumlin Viaduct was opened – at 200 ft. (61 m.) the highest railway viaduct in Britain.

1858   The Rhymney Railway from Cardiff to Rhymney was opened.

1859   Bute East Dock, Cardiff, was opened.

    South Dock, Swansea, was opened.

    Corris narrow-gauge railway was opened.

1861   Briton Ferry Dock was opened.

1862   The Vale of Llangollen Railway was opened from Rhiwabon to Llangollen.

    The broad-gauge Ely Valley Railway was opened to Penygraig in the Rhondda.

1863   Torpantau Tunnel on the Merthyr Tydfil to Brecon rail line was opened – the highest railway tunnel to be built in Britain, at 1,313 ft. (400 m.).

1864   The railway reached Aberystwyth.

1865   The Ffestiniog Railway became the first narrow-gauge railway in the world to carry passengers.

    The Central Wales Railway reached Llandrindod, Llangammarch and Llanwrtyd Wells.

The Ogmore Valley Railway was opened from Tondu to Nantymoel.

The Tal-y-llyn narrow-gauge railway was opened.

Penarth Dock was opened.

1866   The Aberystwyth to Shrewsbury rail link was completed.

1867   Barmouth viaduct was opened – at 800 ft. (243.8 m.) the longest timber estuarine bridge in the world.

The Cambrian Railway reached Pwllheli.

1872   The last broad-gauge rail lines in Wales were converted to standard gauge.

The Garw Valley was linked by rail to Porthcawl.

1873   The Holyhead breakwater was completed – at nearly 1½ miles the longest breakwater in Britain.

The Glyn Valley narrow-gauge railway was opened.

1874   Roath Basin, Cardiff, was opened.

1875   Alexandra Dock, Newport, was opened.

1879   The London and North Western Railway reached Blaenau Ffestiniog.

1880   Holyhead Inner Harbour was opened.

1881   The Prince of Wales Dock, Swansea, was opened.

1885   At Neath the first electric tram service in Wales began operating.

1886   The Severn Tunnel was opened.

1887   Cardiff Roath Dock was opened.

1888   Milford Dock was opened.

Barry Railway was completed.

1889   Barry Dock was opened – the largest dock in Britain, covering 73 acres (29.5 hectares).

Hawarden rail bridge was opened.

1894   South Dock, Newport, was opened.

1895   On Anglesey, the last turnpike-road toll gates in Britain were removed.

1896   The Snowdon Mountain Railway was opened – the highest railway in Britain at 3,493 ft. (1,064.7 m.) and the only rack-and-pinion railway in the British Isles.

Aberystwyth Cliff Railway was opened.

1897   Tal-y-cafn bridge across the River Conwy was opened.

1898   Barry New Dock was opened.

Port Talbot New Dock was opened.

The first motor buses in Wales came into service in Llandudno.

The Abercynon to Merthyr Tydfil length of the Glamorganshire Canal was closed.

1900   The Aberdare Canal was closed.

1902   The Vale of Rheidol Line was opened.

1904   Llanelli North Dock was opened.
        The Tanat Valley standard-gauge light railway was opened.

1906   Newport Transporter Bridge was opened.
        The Great Western Railway reached Fishguard Harbour and the Fishguard to Rosslare ferry service began.

1907   The Queen Alexandra Dock, Cardiff, was opened – the largest masonry dock in the world when built.

1909   King's Dock, Swansea, was opened.

1910   The first airship crossing of the Bristol Channel was made from Cardiff to Minehead by E. T. Willows of Cardiff.

1912   The first flight across the Irish Sea was by Denys Corbett Wilson from Goodwick, Pembrokeshire, to Enniscorthy in 1 hour 40 minutes.

1914   The first trolley buses in Wales began operating in Aberdare.

1915   The Abercynon to Pontypridd length of the Glamorganshire Canal was closed.

1920   Queen's Dock, Swansea, was opened.

1923   Britain's longest narrow-gauge railway was completed – the 21¼ mile long Welsh Highland Railway.

1924   The last horse-drawn tram service on the British mainland – between Pwllheli and Llanbedrog – ceased operating.

1929   The number of motor vehicles registered in Wales exceeded 100,000.

1930–33 Some 20 passenger lines in Wales were closed.

1930   The Crumlin branch of the Monmouthshire Canal was closed.

1931   Cardiff Airport, Pengam Moors, was opened.

1934   The last toll was taken on the Neath Canal.

1935   Penmaenmawr viaduct and Penmaenbach tunnel were completed.

1942   The last length of the Glamorganshire Canal was closed.

1950   The world's first scheduled helicopter service began operating – between Cardiff, Wrexham and Liverpool.

1952   The first international flights from Wales began, operated by Aer Lingus using RAF Rhoose.

1954   Cardiff-Wales Airport opened at Rhoose.

1956   The Llandudno to Colwyn Bay tramway closed.

1958   A new road bridge over the River Conwy at Conwy was opened.

1960   The Mumbles Railway, the only electrified railway in Wales, closed.

1962   The world's first hovercraft service began between Rhyl and Wallasey.
        Queensferry road bridge was opened.

1966   The Port Talbot by-pass was opened – the first length of urban motorway in Britain.

The Severn Bridge was opened.

The Heads of the Valleys Road was completed.

1967   The first Royal Mail Postbus in Britain ran between Llanidloes and Llangurig, Powys.

Brynglas tunnels on the M4 in Newport opened – the first motorway tunnels in Britain.

1969   The Swansea to Cork ferry service started.

The Llandudno cabin lift opened – the longest cable-car system in Britain.

1970   Port Talbot ore terminal was opened.

In Cardiff the last trolley bus service in Wales ceased operating.

1973   There was a record number of 424 road deaths in Wales.

1975   The Cleddau Bridge, Milford Haven, was opened.

1976   The InterCity 125 train was introduced on the London to south Wales line.

1980   Britannia road bridge over the Menai Strait was opened.

1984   The number of road vehicles registered in Wales exceeded one million.

1987   The number of passengers using Cardiff-Wales Airport exceeded 500,000 for the first time.

1988   The last British Rail steam train in regular service anywhere in Britain ran on the Vale of Rheidol Line.

1991   The Conwy road tunnel on the A55 North Wales Expressway was opened – Britain's first immersed tube tunnel.

1992   Construction of the Second Severn Bridge began.

1994   The number of passengers using Cardiff-Wales Airport exceeded one million for the first time.

1995   The M4 and the A55 North Wales Expressway scheduled for completion.

1996   The Second Severn Bridge scheduled for completion.

BRITISH RAIL STATIONS

South Wales Main Line

Severn Tunnel Junction, Newport, Cardiff Central, Pontyclun, Pencoed, Bridgend, Port Talbot Parkway, Neath, Swansea High Street. (See also under Swansea and West Wales.) Also Caldicot, Chepstow, Cwmbran, Pontypool Road and Abergavenny to the Midlands and the North.

Valley Lines

Cynon Aberdare, Cwmbach, Fernhill, Mountain Ash, Penrhiwceiber, Abercynon North.

Rhondda Treherbert, Ynyswen, Treorchy, Ton Pentre, Ystrad Rhondda, Llwynypia, Tonypandy, Dinas, Porth, Trehafod.

Rhymney Rhymney, Pontlottyn, Tir-Phil, Brithdir, Bargoed, Gilfach Fargoed, Pengam, Hengoed, Ystrad Mynach, Llanbradach, Aber, Caerphilly. (See also under Cardiff and South Glamorgan.)

Taff Merthyr Tydfil, Pentre-bach, Troedyrhiw, Merthyr Vale, Quaker's Yard, Abercynon South, Pontypridd, Treforest, Treforest Estate, Taffs Well (See also under Cardiff and South Glamorgan.)

Maesteg Line Wildmill, Sarn, Tondu, Garth (Mid Glamorgan), Maesteg, (Ewenny Road), Maesteg.

Cardiff and South Glamorgan

Radyr, Llandaf, Cathays, Cardiff Queen Street, Cardiff Bay.

Ninian Park, Waun-Gron Park, Fairwater, Danescourt, Coryton, Whitchurch, Rhiwbina, Birchgrove, Tŷ Glas, Heath Low Level.

Lisvane and Thornhill, Llanishen, Heath High Level.

Grangetown, Cogan, Eastbrook, Dinas Powys, Cadoxton, Barry Docks, Barry, Barry Island.

Dingle Road, Penarth.

Swansea and West Wales

Swansea High Street, Gowerton, Llanelli, Pembrey and Burry Port, Kidwelly, Ferryside, Carmarthen, Whitland, Narberth, Kilgetty, Saundersfoot, Tenby, Penally, Manorbier, Lamphey, Pembroke, Pembroke Dock, Clunderwen, Clarbeston Road, Haverfordwest, Johnston, Milford Haven, Fishguard Harbour.

Swan Line

Llansamlet, Skewen, Briton Ferry, Pyle.

South-Central Wales (Heart of Wales Line)

Llanelli, Bynea, Llangennech, Pontarddulais, Pantyffynnon, Ammanford, Llandybïe, Fairfach, Llandeilo, Llangadog, Llanwrda, Llandovery, Cynghordy, Llanwrtyd, Llangammarch, Garth, Cilmeri, Builth Road, Llandrindod Wells, Pen-y-Bont, Dolau, Llanbister Road, Llangynllo, Knucklas, Knighton.

Mid-Wales and Cardigan Bay Coast

Welshpool, Newtown, Caersws, Machynlleth, Dovey Junction, Borth, Aberystwyth.

Pwllheli, Abererch, Penychain, Cricieth, Porthmadog, Minffordd, Penrhyndeudraeth, Llandecwyn, Talsarnau, Tygwyn, Harlech, Llandanwg, Pensarn, Llanbedr, Dyffryn Ardudwy, Tal-y-bont, Llanaber, Barmouth, Morfa Mawddach, Fairbourne, Llwyngwril, Llangelynin, Tonfannau, Tywyn, Aberdyfi, Penhelig.

North Wales

Shotton (High and Low Level), Flint, Prestatyn, Rhyl, Abergele and Pensarn, Colwyn Bay, Llandudno Junction, Deganwy, Llandudno, Conwy, Penmaenmawr, Llanfairfechan, Bangor, Llanfairpwll, Bodorgan, Ty Croes, Rhosneigr, Valley, Holyhead.

Glan Conwy, Tal-y-cafn, Dolgarrog, North Llanrwst, Llanrwst, Betws-y-coed, Pont-y-pant, Dolwyddelan, Roman Bridge, Blaenau Ffestiniog.

Wrexham Central and Wrexham General, Gwersyllt, Cefn-y-bedd, Caergwrle, Hope, Penyffordd, Buckley, Hawarden, Hawarden Bridge, Rhiwabon, Chirk, Gobowen.

Number of Railway Stations

	1961	1992
Clwyd	67	17
Dyfed	86	34
Gwent	52	7
Gwynedd	80	49
Mid Glamorgan	101	48
Powys	74	16
South Glamorgan	40	29
West Glamorgan	38	5
TOTAL	538	205

LENGTHS OF RAILWAY

	1961	1992
Clwyd	214 miles (344 km.)	72 miles (116 km.)

	1961	*1992*
Dyfed	340 miles (547 km.)	137 miles (220 km.)
Gwent	198.5 miles (319.5 km.)	56 miles (90 km.)
Gwynedd	303 miles (488 km.)	147.5 miles (238 km.)
Mid Glamorgan	320 miles (516 km.)	78 miles (125.5 km.)
Powys	248 miles (399 km.)	93 miles (150 km.)
South Glamorgan	94.5 miles (152 km.)	61 miles (98 km.)
West Glamorgan	170.5 miles (274 km.)	69 miles (110 km.)
Total	1,889 miles (3,034 km.) Passenger and freight line lengths	713 miles (1,147 km.) passenger line lengths only. 935 miles (1,504 km.) passenger and freight line lengths.

Maximum Rail Lengths Achieved in Wales

1927	London and North Western Railway (LNWR)	13,795 miles (22,200 km.)
	Great Western Railway (GWR)	6,460 miles (10,396 km.)
Total		20,195 miles (32,594 km.)
		(Passenger and freight line lengths)

Longest Railway Tunnels Wholly in Wales

Blaenau Ffestiniog Tunnel (1879)	2 miles 341 yards (3.533 km.)
Rhondda Tunnel (1890–1968)	1 mile 1,724 yards (3.186 km.)
Merthyr Tunnel (1853–1967)	1 mile 753 yards (2.298 km.)
Caerphilly Tunnel (1871)	1 mile 173 yards (1.767 km.)

Longest Rail Tunnel Partly in Wales

Severn Tunnel (1886)	4 miles 626 yards (7 km.)

NARROW-GAUGE RAILWAYS

Name	Gauge	Length	Locomotives
Bala Lake (Rheilffordd Llyn Tegid)*(6)†	1 ft. 11½ ins. (0.600m.)	4.5 miles (7.2km.)	3 steam, 2 diesel
Brecon Mountain*(2)	1 ft. 11½ ins. (0.600m.)	2.0 miles (3.2km.) (to be extended)	9 steam, 3 diesel
Fairbourne(3)	1 ft. 3 ins. (0.311m.)	2.17 miles (3.5km.)	4 steam, 1 diesel, 1 battery electric car
Ffestiniog*(12)	1 ft. 11½ ins. (0.600m.)	13.5 miles (21.7km.)	9 steam, 9 diesel
Great Orme (3)	3 ft. 6 ins. (1.067m.)	1 mile (1.6km.)	cable cars
Llanberis Lake (Rheilffordd Llyn Padarn)*(2)	1 ft. 11½ ins. (0.600m.)	2 miles (3.2km.)	4 steam, 6 diesel
Snowdon Mountain(5)	2 ft. 7½ ins. (0.800m.)	4.7 miles (7.6km.)	7 steam, 2 diesel
Tal-y-llyn*(12)	2 ft. 3 ins. (0.686m.)	7.25 miles (11.7km.)	6 steam, 3 diesel
Teifi Valley Railway (3)	1 ft. 11½ ins. (0.600m.)	2 miles (3.2km.)	1 steam, 3 diesel
Vale of Rheidol*(8)	1 ft. 11½ ins. (0.600m.)	11.45 miles (18.4km.)	1 steam, 3 diesel
Welsh Highland*(2)	1 ft. 11½ ins. (0.600m.)	¾ mile (1.2km.) (to be extended)	5 steam, 7 diesel
Welshpool and Llanfair*(6)	2 ft. 6 ins. (0.762m)	8 miles (12.9km.)	8 steam, 2 diesel

*These eight railways are marketed as 'The Great Little Trains of Wales'.
†Figures in brackets after railway names indicate the number of stations and halts on the line.

STANDARD-GAUGE PRIVATELY PRESERVED RAILWAYS

Gwili Railway (2)†	1.6 miles (2.6km.) long (to be extended)	5 steam and 5 diesel locomotives
Llangollen Railway (Cymdeithas Rheilffordd Llangollen) (4)	5.5 miles (8.85 km.) (to be extended to 10 miles/16km)	7 steam and 6 diesel locomotives

† Figures in brackets after railway names indicate the number of stations and halts on the line.

LIGHTHOUSE CONSTRUCTION AROUND THE WELSH COAST

St Ann's Head, Milford Haven	1714	Point Lynas, Anglesey	1837
The Skerries	1717	Trwyn Du, Anglesey	1837
Flat Holm	1737	South Bishop	1839
Point of Ayr	1777	Llanddwyn Island, Anglesey	1846
The Smalls	1778	Saundersfoot	1848
The Mumbles	1793	Great Orme's Head	1862
Swansea	1803	Whitford Point, Gower	1865
South Stack, Holyhead	1809	St Tudwal's Island	1877
Admiralty Pier, Holyhead	1821	Strumble Head	1908
Bardsey	1821	Skokholm	1916
Caldey	1828	Watwick Point, Milford Haven	1970
Nash Point, South Glamorgan	1832		

LIFEBOAT STATIONS AROUND THE WELSH COAST

(Listed anti-clockwise)

Flint* – Rhyl† – Llandudno* – Conwy*– Beaumaris* – Moelfre† – Holyhead† – Treaddur Bay† – Porthdinllaen – Abersoch* – Pwllheli† – Cricieth* – Barmouth† – Aberdyfi* – Borth† – Aberystwyth* – New Quay† – Cardigan† – Fishguard – St Davids – Little and Broadhaven* – Angle–Tenby* – Burry Port† – Horton and Port Eynon† – Mumbles† – Port Talbot* – Porthcawl* – Atlantic College, St Donat's* – Barry Dock – Penarth*

*Indicates inshore lifeboat stations (all year)
†Indicates inshore lifeboat stations (summer only)

COASTGUARD MARINE RESCUE CENTRES

There are three coastguard rescue centres around the Welsh coast:

Anglesey: Holyhead
Haverfordwest: Castle Way, Dale
Swansea: Mumbles

WALES–IRELAND FERRY SERVICES

Crossing	Duration	Frequency
Holyhead – Dun Laoghaire*	1 hr. 50 mins.	4 sailings daily (summer only)
Holyhead – Dun Laoghaire	3½ hours	2–4 sailings daily
Holyhead – Dublin	3½ hours	2 sailings daily
Fishguard – Rosslare	3½ hours	2 sailings daily
Fishguard – Rosslare*	1 hr. 40 mins.	5 sailings daily (summer)
		2 sailings daily (winter)
Pembroke Dock – Rosslare	4¼ hours	2 sailings daily (summer)
		1 sailing daily (winter)
Swansea – Cork	10 hours	Daily – March to October only

*By catamaran

PORTS

Location	Operator
Barry	Associated British Ports
Caernarfon	Caernarfon Harbour Trust
Cardiff	Associated British Ports
Fishguard	Sealink Harbours Ltd.
Holyhead	Sealink Harbours Ltd.
Milford Haven/Pembroke Dock	Milford Haven Port Authority
Mostyn	Mostyn Dock Company
Neath/Briton Ferry	Neath Harbour Commissioners
Newport	Associated British Ports
Port Talbot	Associated British Ports
Port Penrhyn	Anglesey Shipping Company
Porthmadog	Dwyfor District Council
Shotton	Welsh Water
Swansea	Associated British Ports

Yacht Berths and Moorings

There are about 7,000 berths and moorings for yachts and pleasure craft around the Welsh coast in over 30 locations.

AIRFIELDS AVAILABLE FOR CIVIL USE

Location	Operator
Aberporth, Dyfed	Ministry of Defence
Caernarfon, Gwynedd	Snowdon Mountain Aviation
Cardiff–Wales, South Glamorgan*	Cardiff–Wales Airport Ltd.
Hawarden, Clwyd	British Aerospace
Mona, Gwynedd	Ministry of Defence weekdays, Mona Flying Club weekends
Montgomeryshire, Welshpool	Pool Aviation Ltd.
St Athan, South Glamorgan	Ministry of Defence
Swansea, West Glamorgan	Swansea Aviation Ltd.
Valley, Gwynedd	Ministry of Defence

*Only Cardiff–Wales has Customs facilities

Passengers Handled at Cardiff–Wales Airport in Selected Years

	1966	1976	1986	1991
Scheduled	106,496	111,898	66,187	118,291
Charter	48,340	105,531	440,461	422,585

(Terminal flights and transit flights are included in the above figures)

ROADS

Stages in the Construction of the M4

Section	Length	Completion
Port Talbot by-pass	4.4 miles (7.1 km.)	July, 1966
Severn Bridge	3,240 feet (928 m.)	September, 1966
Newhouse–Coldra (Newport)	11.9 miles (19.25 km.)	March, 1967
Newport by-pass	6.7 miles (10.8 km.)	May, 1967
Morriston by-pass	4.0 miles (6.4 km.)	September, 1972
Pontarddulais by-pass	8.4 miles (13.5 km.)	April, 1977
Tredegar Park–St Mellons	5.0 miles (8.0 km.)	October, 1977
Pyle by-pass	5.3 miles (8.5 km.)	November, 1977
Coryton–Pencoed	12.2 miles (19.6 km.)	December, 1977
Castleton–Coryton	7.5 miles (12.0 km.)	July, 1980
Bridgend by-pass	8.3 miles (13.35 km.)	September, 1981
Lonlas–Earlswood	3 miles (4.8 km.)	February, 1993
Earlswood–Baglan	3.1 miles (5.0 km.)	Due for completion 1995

Road Lengths

	1975	*1992*
Motorway	28 miles (45 km.)	75 miles (120 km.)
Trunk	1,017 miles (1,637 km.)	981 miles (1,590 km.)
Principal	1,480 miles (2,383 km.)	1,630 miles (2,642 km.)
Other classified	7,643 miles (12,302 km.)	7,770 miles (12,562 km.)
Unclassified	8,954 miles (14,412 km.)	10,245 miles (16,618 km.)
Total	19,122 miles (30,777 km.)	20,689 miles (33,531 km.)

Last Two Letters Identifying Vehicle Registration Offices in Wales

Bangor:	CC, EY, FF, JC
Cardiff:	AX, BO, DW, HB, KG, NY, TG, TX, WO
Haverfordwest:	DE, EJ
Swansea:	CY, EP, TH, WN

Longest Road Bridges Wholly in Wales

Menai Bridge, main span: 579 ft. (175 m.) Eighth longest road bridge in UK.
George Street Bridge, Newport, main span: 500 feet (152 m.) Joint tenth longest
road bridge in UK.

DEATHS AND INJURIES IN ROAD ACCIDENTS (1992)

	Serious injuries	*Pedestrian deaths*	*Pedal cyclist deaths*	*Two-wheeled motor vehicles deaths*	*Car users deaths*	*Goods/ PSV deaths*	*Total road deaths*
Clwyd	341	9	3	6	12	-	30
Dyfed	530	8	1	3	22	2	36
Gwent	297	8	2	4	16	1	31
Gwynedd	244	6	-	2	7	-	15
Mid Glamorgan	261	18	-	7	12	4	41
Powys	198	2	-	3	13	1	19
South Glamorgan	240	11	2	3	14	1	31
West Glamorgan	263	6	1	2	7	1	17
WALES	2,314	68	9	30	103	10	220

The worst year for road deaths in Wales was 1973 when 424 people were killed.

United Kingdom Comparisons (1991)

	Road deaths per 100,000 population	Road deaths per 10,000 vehicles	Motor vehicles per 1,000 population	Pedestrian deaths per 100,000 population	Total deaths
England	8.0	1.8	446	2.6	3,854
WALES	7.9	1.9	419	2.5	227
Scotland	9.5	2.6	362	3.4	487
Great Britain	8.1	1.9	437	2.7	4,468
Northern Ireland	12.0	3.3	355	2.9	185
United Kingdom	8.2	1.9	435	2.7	4,753

ROAD VEHICLE LICENCES ISSUED

(In selected years)

1926	83,302	*1950*	212,800	*1990*	1,222,000
1930	103,522	*1960*	450,600	*1991*	1,208,600
1938	133,542	*1970*	728,600	*1992*	1,229,200
1946	145,196	*1980*	934,700		

CANALS

Brecon and Monmouthshire Canal	34½ miles (55.5 km.)
Llangollen Canal	11 miles (17.7 km.)
Montgomery Canal	7 miles (11.3 km.)*
Neath Canal	4 miles (6.4 km.)

*To be extended to 11.8 miles (19 km.) by 1995.

Longest Canal Tunnels

Chirk	459 yards (420 metres) Llangollen Canal
Ashford	375 yards (343 metres) Monmouthshire Canal
Whitehouses	191 yards (175 metres) Llangollen Canal

Maximum Canal Lengths Achieved

1820: South Wales – 154 miles (248 km.)
North Wales – 61 miles (98 km.)

10

THE WELSH ECONOMY

DATES OF SIGNIFICANCE AND INTEREST

1300s   From this century the woollen industry of the Vale of Ceiriog made north-east Wales the most economically advanced area in Wales for centuries.

1536,   The 'Acts of Union' stimulated economic activity as stable
1543   political conditions were created in Wales encouraging investment.

1570   A brass and wire foundry was established in Tintern.

1584   Dutch and German smelters helped establish the copper industry in the Vale of Neath.

1666   Irish cattle imports were banned, stimulating the increased droving of Welsh cattle into England.

1704   A lead and silver smelter was opened at Gadlys, Bagillt.

1717   At Pontypool the 'Japanning' of tinplate was developed.

1750   By this year 50 per cent of British copper was coming from the Swansea area.

1757   The first ironworks were established along the heads of the Valleys in south Wales.

1815   By this date one-third of British iron was produced in south Wales.

1830   By this date 40 per cent of British iron was produced in south Wales.

1831   The repeal of the slate tax stimulated the north Wales slate industry.

1834   The abolition of duty on coal exports from Welsh ports in British ships stimulated the coal export trade.

1855   The first coal train from the Rhondda arrived in Cardiff docks.

1859   This was the peak year for copper production in Wales.

1861   At Landore, William Siemens developed the open-hearth method of steel production.

1862   This was the peak year for lead production in Wales.

1869   This was the peak year for silver production in Wales.

1878   The open-hearth method of steel production with phosphoric ores was developed at Blaenafon by Sidney Gilchrist Thomas and Percy Gilchrist.

1883   This was the peak year for zinc production in Wales.

1885   The Admiralty decided to use south Wales coal exclusively on Royal Navy ships.
        The Brymbo steelworks were opened.

1891   The United States McKinley Tariff seriously affected Welsh tinplate exports.

1896   Shotton steelworks were opened.

1898   This was the peak year for slate production in Wales.

1902   The world's biggest nickel smelter was opened by Ludwig Mond at Clydach, Swansea Valley.

1904   This was the peak year for gold production in Wales.

1908   The man-made fibre industry was established in Wales with the opening of an artificial silk factory at Greenfield, Clwyd, by a German company.

1913   This was the peak year for coal production in Wales.

1920   This was the peak year for employment in the coal industry in Wales.

1921   Britain's first major oil refinery, Llandarcy, was opened near Skewen, West Glamorgan.

1932   This was the peak year for unemployment in Wales – 36.8 per cent of the working population.

1933   The Milk Marketing Scheme introduced guaranteed prices for farmers.

1934   The Special Areas Act was passed to help 'distressed' areas like the south Wales valleys.
        Courtaulds established a viscose rayon factory at Greenfield.
        This was the peak year for anthracite production in south Wales.

1936   The first industrial estate in Wales was opened at Treforest.

1938   The Ebbw Vale steelworks opened, the first continuous strip plant in Britain.

1939   De Havilland opened an aircraft factory at Broughton, Clwyd.

1942   Open-cast coal-mining began in Wales.

1945   The Distribution of Industry Act gave the government powers to direct businesses to areas of high unemployment.

1946   This was the peak year for fish landings in Wales.

1947   The Agriculture Act guaranteed prices for other agricultural products in addition to milk.

1948   Hoover opened a washing-machine factory at Merthyr Tydfil and nylon manufacturing began at Pontypool.

1951   The Abbey steelworks at Port Talbot were opened.

1954	The first *Digest of Welsh Statistics* was published.
1955	The Farmers' Union of Wales was founded.
	A record low of 13,400 unemployed was recorded in Wales in July.
1960	The first refinery on Milford Haven was opened by Esso.
1962	Llanwern steelworks, Newport, were opened.
1963	Baglan Bay petro-chemicals plant was opened.
1964	The Ford Company opened a plant in Swansea.
	The last coal was exported from Cardiff.
1967	This was the peak year for housebuilding in Wales with 20,158 completions.
1968	Trawsfynydd nuclear power station was opened.
1971	The Rio Tinto zinc smelter was opened at Holyhead.
1972	Wylfa nuclear power station was opened.
1973	Sony's television factory, Bridgend, was the first major Japanese investment in Wales.
	The Wales TUC was formed.
	Drilling for oil and gas began off the Welsh coast.
1975	The Land Authority for Wales was created.
	The European Regional Development Fund was introduced.
1976	The Welsh Development Agency was established.
1978	The Confederation of British Industry (CBI) Wales was formed.
	Steelmaking ended at East Moors, Cardiff, and at Ebbw Vale.
1980	Shotton steelworks closed.
	Ford opened an engine plant at Bridgend.
1988	*The Welsh Economic Review* began publication.
1991	Bosch opened a major car component factory near Cardiff.
	The first commercial gas find was made off the north Wales coast.
1992	The Wales Tourist Board was given overseas marketing powers.
	The Toyota engine plant on Deeside began production.
1993	The main British Airways maintenance base was opened at Cardiff–Wales Airport.

STAGES OF WELSH ECONOMIC DEVELOPMENT

To the late eighteenth/early nineteenth centuries
Agriculture dominated the economy of Wales although there were some small-scale industrial enterprises from the sixteenth century. Cattle-droving played a major role in the Welsh economy from the Middle Ages. The first turnpike roads and canals were built at the end of this period.

From the early nineteenth century to the 1920s
The basis of the Welsh economy became the heavy industries: iron and steel, non-ferrous metals, slate quarrying and coal-mining, although agriculture remained important. A dense railway network was constructed and many docks were built, but canals declined. From 1860 to 1913, south Wales was the most dynamic part of the British economy, growing faster than any part of England or Scotland.

Since the 1920s
Coal-mining, slate quarrying, iron, steel and non-ferrous metal manufacture declined, together with employment in agriculture. A diversified manufacturing sector developed after the Second World War and, together with an expanding service sector – banking, insurance, tourism, etc. – came to provide the majority of jobs. Steel-making remained important but comparatively little coal-mining was to continue. There was a considerable expansion in female employment, particularly that on a part-time basis. Trade-union membership declined sharply. Road transport became increasingly important and the railway network shrank dramatically. Many basic industries, nationalized between 1945 and 1951, were privatized in the 1980s and 1990s.

WELSH PRODUCTION FIGURES

Steel

(*in thousands of tonnes*)
1980	2,951
1985	4,731
1991	5,695
1992	5,744

Coal

(*in millions of tonnes*)
1970	16.10	deep mined	1991	3.05	deep mined
	2.34	open cast		2.14	open cast
1980	8.75	deep mined	1992	2.60	deep mined
	2.31	open cast		2.28	open cast

Number of Welsh Coal Mines

(*In selected years*)

1950 (calendar year)	British Coal	127
	Other mines	157
1964–65	British Coal	105
	Other mines	105
1980–81	British Coal	36
	Other mines	86
1991–92	British Coal	4
	Other mines	69

Total Electricity Generated

(*in millions of KWh a year*)

1980	23,381	1989	22,587
1985	28,253	1991	23,058

Crude Oil Distillation Capacity

(*in thousands of tonnes*)

1960	7,875	1980	24,123
1970	24,640	1992	19,851

Water
(*average daily output in megalitres*)

	Total	Supplied to England
1958	1,192	561
1968	1,529	637
1978	1,711	627
1989	2,269	1,070
1991	2,441	1,168

Gas Availability

(*from British Gas operations in Wales in millions of therms*)

1970–71	19,447	1985–86	342,650	1991–92	1.085,700
1980–81	172,604	1990–91	1,053,400		

Area under Crops and Grass

(*in thousands of hectares*)

| 1961 | 1,054.9 | 1981 | 1,102.2 | 1992 | 1,129.0 |
| 1971 | 1,037.2 | 1991 | 1,123.7 | | |

Total Cattle

(*in thousands*)

| 1961 | 1,171.2 | 1981 | 1,413.7 | 1992 | 1,334.0 |
| 1971 | 1,368.3 | 1991 | 1,348.4 | | |

Total Sheep and Lambs

(*in thousands*)

| 1961 | 5,526.0 | 1981 | 8,201.5 | 1992 | 11,123.8 |
| 1971 | 6,052.9 | 1991 | 10,850.8 | | |

Total Pigs

(*in thousands*)

| 1961 | 216.3 | 1981 | 131.1 | 1992 | 104.4 |
| 1971 | 253.2 | 1991 | 103.1 | | |

Total Poultry

(*in thousands*)

| 1961 | 4,442.4 | 1981 | 7,482.7 | 1992 | 5,749.2 |
| 1971 | 5,741.6 | 1991 | 7,246.5 | | |

Wheat

(*in thousands of tonnes*)

| 1961 | 21 | 1981 | 50 | 1992 | 80 |
| 1971 | 33 | 1990 | 70 | | |

Winter and Summer Barley

(*in thousands of tonnes*)

| 1961 | 64 | 1981 | 230 | 1992 | 180 |
| 1971 | 193 | 1990 | 170 | | |

Oats

(in thousands of tonnes)

1961	115	1981	25	1992	20
1971	67	1990	20		

Potatoes

(early and main crops in thousands of tonnes)

1961	137	1981	150	1992	114
1971	168	1990	132		

Timber Felled

(in cubic metres)

1960	Forestry Commission	135
	Private	nil
1970	Forestry Commission	236
	Private	70
1980	Forestry Commission	480
	Private	90
1991	Forestry Commission	797
	Private	175
1992	Forestry Commission	858
	Private	165

Landings in Wales of Fish Taken by British Vessels

(in tonnes)

1961	12,367	1981	21,789	1992	7,230
1971	9,444	1991	9,629		

THE CIVILIAN WORKFORCE

	Workforce	Employed	Male	Female	Part-time female (of female total)
1971	1,120,000	962,000	629,000	333,000	104,000
1981	1,193,000	939,000	551,000	389,000	159,000
1990	1,284,000	993,000	525,000	467,000	213,000
1991	1,290,000	985,000	509,000	475,000	218,000
1992	1,257,000	942,000	478,000	464,000	219,000

Changes in the Employment of the Civilian Workforce

	Agriculture, forestry, fishing	Manufacturing	Construction	Services
1971	28,000	324,000	64,000	472,000
1981	23,000	240,000	54,000	562,000
1990	20,000	238,000	48,000	661,000
1992	19,000	209,000	42,000	650,000

Unemployment

	January	July
1985	185,852	176,477
1987	176,866	152,129
1990	90,349	83,202
1991	101,452	115,993
1992	128,755	125,156

Industrial Stoppages

	Working days lost (thousands)	No. of workers involved (thousands)
1980	2,918	143.9
1981	292	124.9
1982	283	134.0
1983	353	42.1
1984	3,527	84.1
1985	940	62.0
1986	78	36.0
1987	203	58.0
1988	116	26.0
1989	307	59.0
1990	84	13.0
1991	20	4.0
1992	10	6.0

EMPLOYMENT OPPORTUNITIES

Movement of Government Offices to Wales

1967   Passport Office, Newport.
1967   Land Registry, Swansea (sub-office to 1974 then district registry).
1968   Royal Mint, Llantrisant.
1969   Business Statistics Office, Newport (now the Central Statistical Office).
1969   Driver and Vehicle Licensing Centre, Swansea (now Driving and Vehicle Licensing Agency).
1976   Companies House, Cardiff.
1991   Patent Office, Newport.

Enterprise Zones

1981   Swansea Enterprise Zone (the first in Britain). Wound up in 1991.
1983   Delyn Enterprise Zone. Wound up in 1993.
1984   Milford Haven Enterprise Zone.

EZs were created to stimulate industrial and commercial activity. Businesses set up in Enterprise Zones enjoy numerous advantages for a ten year-period including freedom from planning restrictions, from payment of local rates and from contributing to industrial training levies, as well as tax concessions.

Business Parks, Enterprise Parks, Industrial Estates, Trading Estates and Science Parks

(Numbers in each county)

Clwyd	79	Mid Glamorgan	116
Dyfed	54	Powys	43
Gwent	69	South Glamorgan	31
Gwynedd	29	West Glamorgan	33

GOVERNMENT AGENCIES

The Land Authority for Wales (*1975*)

Custom House, Custom House Street, Cardiff, CF1 5AP.
The Land Authority for Wales is responsible for acquiring and disposing of land for private development where the private sector would find this difficult or impossible.

The Welsh Development Agency (*1976*)
Pearl House, Greyfriars Road, Cardiff, CF1 3XV.
The WDA promotes industrial development in Wales by encouraging overseas investment. Equity and loan capital is made available for capital projects. The agency also provides government factories, can assist small firms and has powers to undertake land reclamation and urban renewal.

The Development Board for Rural Wales (*1977*)
Ladywell House, Newtown, Powys, SY16 1JB.
The board provides factories, key workers' housing and advice for small businesses. It has a general responsibility to promote the economic and social well-being of mid-Wales – that is, the districts of Brecknock, Ceredigion, Merionnydd and Montgomery – and particular responsibility for the new town of Newtown.

Cardiff Bay Development Corporation (*1987*)
Baltic House, Mount Stuart Square, Cardiff, CF1 6DH.
The CBDC has the responsibility of developing some 2,700 acres in the run-down docklands area of Cardiff.

PRIVATIZATION OF NATIONALIZED INDUSTRIES

1986	Wales Gas
1989	Welsh Water
1990	South Wales Electricity Board (SWEB) and Merseyside and North Wales Electricity Board (MANWEB)

TRAINING AND ENTERPRISE COUNCILS

The purpose of training and enterprise councils (TECs) is to provide effective training to meet the current and future requirements of the local labour market, and to stimulate business enterprise with particular support for new and expanding small firms.

TECs are employer-led groups and have management boards consisting of representatives of local industry and commerce, trade unions, the public sector and voluntary organizations.

The Seven TECs in Wales

TECs	*Boundaries*
Gwent TEC, Glyndwr House, Unit B2 Cleppa Park, Newport, Gwent, NP9 1YE.	Gwent County
Mid Glamorgan TEC, 17–20 Centre Court, Main Avenue, Treforest Industrial Estate, Pontypridd, Mid Glamorgan, CF37 5YL.	Mid Glamorgan County
North East Wales TEC, Wynnstay Buildings, Hightown Barracks, Kingsmill Road, Wrexham, Clwyd, LL13 8BH.	Wrexham Maelor and Delyn Boroughs, Glyndŵr and Alyn and Deeside Districts.
North West Wales TEC (Targed), 1st Floor, Bron Castell, High Street, Bangor, Gwynedd, LL57 7YS.	Gwynedd County, Colwyn and Rhuddlan Boroughs.
Powys TEC, 1st Floor, St David's House, Newtown, Powys, SY16 1RB.	Powys County
South Glamorgan TEC, 3–7 Drake's Walk, Atlantic Wharf, Cardiff, CF4 5PJ.	South Glamorgan County
West Wales TEC, 3rd Floor, Orchard House, Orchard Street, Swansea, SA1 5DJ.	West Glamorgan and Dyfed Counties

Persons Training in TECs, 1992

Gwent	5,260	Powys	1,328
Mid Glamorgan	6,449	South Glamorgan	3,150
North East Wales	2,336	West Glamorgan	7,793
North West Wales	3,433		

ASSISTED AREAS

(*Designated from 1 August 1993*)

Businesses in assisted areas can qualify for government help such as low factory rentals and low-interest-rate loans and can also obtain European Community grants. Development areas attract more help than intermediate areas.

Development Areas

Fishguard	Holyhead	South Pembrokeshire
Haverfordwest	Merthyr Tydfil and Rumney	Wrexham (western part)

Intermediate Areas

Aberdare

Bangor and Caernarfon

Blaenau Gwent and Abergavenny

Bridgend

Cardigan

Llanelli

Neath and Port Talbot

Newport (western part)

Pontypool and Cwmbran

Pontypridd and Rhondda

Porthmadog and Ffestiniog

Pwllheli

Shotton, Flint and Rhyl (eastern part)

Swansea

Wrexham (eastern part)

Areas Not Assisted

Aberystwyth

Brecon

Cardiff

Carmarthen

Conwy and Colwyn

Denbigh

Dolgellau and Barmouth

Lampeter and Aberaeron

Llandeilo

Llandrindod Wells

Machynlleth

Monmouth

Newport (eastern part)

Newtown

Shotton, Flint and Rhyl (western part)

Welshpool

The 34 areas listed above are the same as the Department of Employment's 'Travel to Work' areas in Wales, the smallest areas for which unemployment rates are used. They are approximately self-contained labour markets.

Just over 70 per cent of the workforce in Wales live in assisted areas compared with just under 61 per cent in Scotland and just under 29 per cent in England.

ORGANIZATIONS CONCERNED WITH EMPLOYMENT

Advisory, Conciliation and Arbitration Service (ACAS) Wales: Tŷ Glas Road, Llanishen, Cardiff, CF4 5PH.

Confederation of British Industry (CBI) Wales: Pearl Assurance Building, Greyfriars Road, Cardiff, CF1 3AG.

Department of Employment, Office for Wales: Companies House, Crown Way, Cardiff, CF4 3UU.

Health and Safety Executive: Brunel House, 2 Fitzalan Road, Cardiff, CF2 1SA.

The Regional Office of Industrial Tribunals: Caradog House, St Andrews Place, Cardiff, CF1 3BE.

Wales Trade Union Council (TUC): Transport House, 1 Cathedral Road, Cardiff, CF1 9HA.

CHAMBERS OF COMMERCE

Cardiff Chamber of Commerce and Industry: 101–8 The Exchange, Mount Stuart Square, Cardiff, CF1 6RD

Chester and North Wales Chamber of Commerce: 1st Floor, Reliance House, Waterloo Road, Chester, CH2 4AG.

Federation of Welsh Chambers of Commerce: 101–8 The Exchange, Mount Stuart Square, Cardiff, CF1 6RD.

Newport and Gwent Chamber of Commerce: Caradog House, Cleppa Park, Newport, NP1 9UG.

West Wales Chamber of Commerce and Shipping: Burrow Chambers, East Burrow Road, Swansea, SA1 1RF.

UNIONS AFFILIATED TO THE WALES TUC, 1993–1994

		Membership
1.	UNISON*	98,673
2.	Amalgamated Engineering and Electrical Union*	84,033
3.	Transport and General Workers' Union*	64,986
4.	General, Municipal and Boilermakers' and Allied Trade Unions*	58,500
5.	Manufacturing, Science, Finance*	33,375
6.	Union of Shop, Distributive and Allied Workers*	20,500
7.	Iron and Steel Trades Confederation*	14,000
8.	National Union of Teachers	13,906
9.	National Union of Mineworkers*	12,500
10.	National Association of Schoolmasters and Union of Women Teachers	10,628
11.	Graphical, Paper and Media Union*	9,518
12.	Civil and Public Services Association	9,015
13.	Union of Communication Workers*	8,995
14.	Union of Construction, Allied Trades and Technicians*	8,000
15.	National Union of Civil and Public Servants	7,200
16.	Banking, Insurance and Finance Union	6,849
17.	National Communications Union*	5,001
18.	Inland Revenue Staff Federation	4,585

19.	Rail, Maritime and Transport Workers*	4,416
20.	National Association of Teachers in Further and Higher Education	3,700
21.	Bakers, Food and Allied Workers*	3,645
22.	Fire Brigades Union*	3,000
23.	Institution of Professional Managers and Specialists	2,700
24.	Broadcasting, Entertainment, Cinematography and Theatre Union*	2,003
25.	Association of University Teachers	1,975
26.	British Actors Equity Association	1,800
27.	National Union of Knitwear, Footwear and Apparel Trades*	1,423
28.	Society of Communications Executives	1,321
29.	Engineers' and Managers' Association	1,224
30.	Musicians Union	1,138
31.	Transport and Salaried Staffs Association*	1,086
32.	National Union of Insurance Workers	993
34.	Chartered Society of Physiotherapists	918
35.	Society of Radiographers	885
36.	Associated Society of Locomotive Engineers and Firemen*	828
37.	National Union of Marine, Aviation and Shipping Transport Officers	823
38.	National Union of Journalists	702
39.	United Road Transport Union	520
40.	Communication Management Association	507
41.	Electrical and Plumbing Industries Union*	500
42.	Prison Officers Association	422
43.	National Association of Licensed House Managers	394
44.	Association of First Division Civil Servants	392
45.	National Association of Probation Officers	370
46.	National Association of Colliery Overmen, Deputies and Shotfirers*	310
47.	Union of Textile Workers*	200
48.	National League of Blind and Disabled*	150
49.	Writers' Guild of Great Britain	84

* Trade unions affiliated to the Labour Party

TRADES COUNCILS AFFILIATED TO THE WALES TUC

Clwyd	Buckley; Colwyn Bay; Deeside; Flint; Vale of Clwyd; Wrexham.
Dyfed	Aberystwyth; Ammanford; Carmarthen; Gwendraeth; Llanelli; Preseli.
Gwent	Abercarn; Blackwood; Brynmawr; Ebbw Vale; Nantyglo; Newport; Risca; Torfaen; Tredegar.

Gwynedd	Bangor; Caernarfon; Holyhead; Merioneth.
Mid Glamorgan	Llantrisant; Merthyr Tydfil; Mid Glamorgan (Ogwr); Pontypridd; Rhondda; Rhymney Valley.
Powys	Llanidloes; Montgomeryshire.
South Glamorgan	Cardiff; Vale of Glamorgan.
West Glamorgan	Neath; Port Talbot; Swansea.

Eight county associations are also affiliated to the Wales TUC.

HOUSING

Welsh Building Societies

Name	Founded in	Full-time branches	Estate agency branches
Principality (Cardiff)	1860	49	20
Swansea	1869	7	none
Monmouthshire (Newport)	1923	Head office only	none

Building Societies Association – Committee for Wales Member Building Societies

Alliance and Leicester
Birmingham Midshires
Bradford and Bingley
Bristol and West
Cheltenham and Gloucester
Halifax
Leeds and Holbech
Leeds Permanent

Monmouthshire
National and Provincial
Nationwide
Principality
Swansea
Woolwich
Yorkshire
Other member: Abbey National plc.

Housing Associations

Adamsdown	15–17 Moira Terrace, Adamsdown, Cardiff, CF2 1EJ.
Cadwyn	266–8 Whitchurch Road, Cardiff, CF4 3ND.
Clwyd Alyn	46–54 Water Street, Rhyl, Clwyd, LL18 1SS.
Cynon-Taf	Britannia Building, 17–19 Cardiff St, Aberdare, Mid Glamorgan, CF44 7DP.
Gwalia	125 Walter Road, Swansea, SA1 5RG.

Hafod	25 Cathedral Road, Cardiff, CF1 9HD.
Merthyr Tydfil	Glebeland Street, Merthyr Tydfil, Mid Glamorgan, CF47 8AS.
Mid Wales	Ty Castell, Park Street, Newtown, Powys.
Monmouth and Llandaff	22a Gold Tops, Newport, NP9 4PG.
Newydd	121 Broad Street, Barry, South Glamorgan.
North Wales	1 Penrhyn Street, Colwyn Bay, Clwyd.
Swansea	61–3 Mansel Street, Swansea, SA1 5TN.
Wales and West	3 Alexandra Gate, Ffordd Pengam, Tremorfa, Cardiff, CF2 2UD.
Welsh Federation of Housing Associations:	Norbury House, Norbury Road, Fairwater, Cardiff, CF5 3AS.

Shelter Cymru

25 Walter Road, Swansea, SA1 5NN.

Shelter Cymru has two Housing Rights Centres:

93 Tylycelyn Road, Penygraig, Rhondda, CF40 11A.
23 Abbatt Street, Wrexham, Clwyd.

Housing Completions, 1960–1992

	1960	1970	1980	1992
Private sector	6,078	8,684	5,932	7,104
Housing associations	4	73	917	2.497
Local authorities	5,434	6,686	3,702	133

Housing Tenure (1992)

	Number	Percentage
Owner-occupied	857,000	71
Local authority or housing corporation rented	217,000	18
Privately rented	95,000	8
Housing associations	32,000	3

Age of Housing Stock

	Number	Percentage
Pre-1918	442,000	36.8
1919–1944	154,000	12.8
1945–1991	604,000	50.3

BANKS

(Branches in 1992)

Lloyds	295	Trustee Savings Bank	70
Midland	186	Abbey National Bank	33
National Westminster	125	Co-operative Bank	14
Barclays	87	Bank of Wales	4

11

THE ARMED FORCES AND WALES

THE WELSH REGIMENTS

Formation

South Wales Borderers (24th Regiment of Foot):	8 March 1689
*Royal Welch Fusiliers (23rd Regiment of Foot):	16 March 1689
Welch Regiment (41st Regiment of Foot):	11 March 1719
†Welsh Guards:	26 February 1915
‡1st The Queen's Dragoon Guards:	1 January 1959
('The Cavalry Regiment of Wales') – from the merger of the King's Dragoon Guards and the Queen's Bays, 2nd Dragoon Guards)	
*Royal Regiment of Wales:	11 June 1969
(From the merger of the South Wales Borderers and the Welch Regiment)	

*These two regiments are part of the Prince of Wales Division.
†This regiment is part of the Guards Division.
‡This regiment is part of the Royal Armoured Corps.

Royal Regiment of Wales

Honours

Blenheim, Ramillies, Oudenarde, Malplaquet, Belleisle, Martinique 1762, St Vincent 1797, Cape of Good Hope 1806, India, Talavera, Bourbon, Busaco, Fuentes d'Onor, Java, Salamanca, Detroit, Queenstown, Miami, Vittoria, Pyrenees, Nivelle, Niagara, Orthes, Peninsula, Waterloo, Ava, Candahor 1842, Ghuznee 1842, Cabool 1842, Chillianwallah, Gujerat, Punjab, Alma, Inkerman, Savastopol, South Africa 1877–79, Burma 1885–87, Relief of Kimberley, Paardeberg, South Africa 1899–1902.

Mons, Marne 1914, Aisne 1914, 1918, Ypres 1914, 1915, 1917, 1918, Gheluvelt, Loos, Somme, Cambrai 1917, 1918, Pilckem, Doiran 1917, 1918, Macedonia 1915–18, Landing at Helles, Gallipoli 1915–16, Gaza, Baghdad, Tsingtao.

Norway 1940, Normandy Landing, Sully, Caen, Falaise, Le Havre, Lower Maas, Reichswald, North-West Europe 1944–45, North Africa 1940–42, Croce, Italy 1943–45, Crete, Canea, Mayu Tunnels, Pinwe, Kyaukmyaung Bridgehead, Sittang 1945.

Korea 1951–52.

Marches
'March of the Men of Harlech' (Quick)
'Scipio' (Slow)
Also 'God Bless the Prince of Wales', 'Ap Shenkin', 'The 'Warwickshire Lad' and 'The Lincolnshire Poacher'.

Motto
'Gwell Angau Na Chywilydd' ('Better Death Than Dishonour').

Mascot
Regimental goat – all officially named 'Gwilym Jones' but called 'Taffy'.

Nicknames
'The Old Agamemnons', 'The Swabs', 'The Bengal Tigers', 'Howard Greens', 'The Invalids', 'The Ups and Downs'.

Affiliations
The Ontario Regiment (Canada), The Royal New South Wales Regiment (Australia).

Regimental museums
Brecon (South Wales Borderers) and Cardiff Castle (Welch Regiment).

Regimental headquarters
Maindy Barracks, Cardiff.

Colonel-in-Chief
The Prince of Wales.

Royal Welch Fusiliers

Honours
Namur 1695, Blenheim, Ramillies, Oudenarde, Malplaquet, Dettingen, Minden, Coruna, Martinique 1809, Albuhera, Badajoz, Salamanca, Vittoria, Pyrenees, Nivelle, Orthes, Toulouse, Peninsula, Waterloo, Alma, Inkerman, Sevastopol,

Lucknow, Ashantee 1873–74, Burma 1885–87, Relief of Ladysmith, South Africa 1899–1902, Pekin 1900.

Marne 1914, Ypres 1914, 1917, 1918, Somme 1916, 1918, Hindenburg Line, Vittoria Venato, Doiran 1917, 1918, Gallipoli 1917, 1918, Egypt 1915–17, Gaza, Baghdad.

St Omer, La Bassem, Caen, Lower Maas, Reichswald, Weege, Rhines, Madagascar, Donbaik, North Arakan, Kohima.

Marches
'British Grenadier' (Quick)
'War March of the Men of Glamorgan' (Slow)
Also John Philip Sousa's last march, 'The Royal Welch Fusiliers', was presented to the regiment by the United States Marine Corps in 1930 to mark the friendship between the two units dating from the 1900 Siege of Peking (Beijing) during the Boxer Rising.

Mottoes
'Ich Dien' ('I Serve') and 'Nil Aspera Terrent' ('Nor Do Difficulties Deter').

Mascot
Regimental goat. (This is the oldest known use of a mascot in the British Army.)

Nicknames
'The Nanny Goats', 'The Royal Goats'.

Affiliations
Royal 22e Regiment (Canada); 3rd Battalion, The Frontier Force (Pakistan); 4th Battalion, The Royal Malay Regiment.

Regimental museum
The Queen's Tower, Caernarfon Castle.

Regimental headquarters
Hightown Barracks, Wrexham.

Colonel-in-Chief
The Queen.

The Welsh Guards

Honours
Loos, Givenchy, Flers-Courcelette, Morval, Pilckem, Poelcappelle, Cambrai 1917, 1918, Canal du Nord, Sambre, Defence of Arras, Boulogne, Mont Pincon,

Brussels, Hechtell, Fondouk, Hamman Lif, Monte Ornito, Monte Piccolo, Battaglia.
Northern Ireland 1982.
Falklands 1982.

Marches
'The Rising of the Lark' (Quick).
'Men of Harlech' (Slow).

Motto
'Cymru Am Byth' ('Wales For Ever').

Nicknames
'The Daffy Taffs', 'The Foreign Legion', 'The Jam Boys'.

Affiliations
5th/7th Battalion, Royal Australian Regiment.

Regimental museum
Wellington Barracks, Birdcage Walk, London.

Regimental headquarters
Wellington Barracks, Birdcage Walk, London.

Colonel-in-Chief
The Queen Mother.

1st the Queen's Dragoon Guards ('The Cavalry Regiment of Wales')

Honours
Ramillies, Oudenarde, Malplaquet, Dettingen, Warburg, Beaumont, Willems, Waterloo, Sevastopol, Lucknow, Taku Fort, Pekin 1860, South Africa 1879, South Africa 1901–2.

Mons, Le Cateau, Marne 1914, Messines 1914, Ypres 1914–15, Somme 1916–18, Morval, Scarpe 1917, Cambrai 1917–18, Amiens, Pursuit to Mons, France and Flanders 1914–18.

Afghanistan 1919.

Somme 1940, Beda Fomm, Defence of Tobruk, Gazala, Defence of Alamein Line, El Alamein, Advance to Tripoli, Tebega Gap, El Hamra, North Africa 1914–43, Monte Camino, Gothic Line, Corlano, Lamone Crossing, Rimini Line, Agenta Gap, Italy 1943–5.

Marches
'The Radetsky March' (Quick).
'The Rusty Buckle' and 'The Queen's Dragoon Guards' (Slow).

Motto
'Pro Rege Et Patria' ('For King and Country').

Nicknames
'The Bays', 'The Rusty Buckles'.

Affiliations
The Governor General's Bodyguard (Canada), 7th Light Horse (Australia).

Regimental museum
Cardiff Castle (formerly at Shrewsbury).

Regimental headquarters
Maindy Barracks, Cardiff.

Colonel-in-Chief
The Queen Mother.

HOLDERS OF THE VICTORIA CROSS FROM WALES

Since the Victoria Cross was instituted during the Crimean War as the highest award for gallantry, 1,351 awards have been made – 42 of them to the servicemen listed below who were born in or were domiciled in Wales.

VCs were awarded posthumously to those whose names are shown in italic.

Crimean War

Captain Hugh Rowland, Llanrug, Gwynedd.
  41st Regiment, Inkerman, 5 November 1854.
Corporal Robert Shields, Cardiff.
  Royal Welch Fusiliers, Sebastopol, 8 September 1856.

Indian Mutiny

Second Lieutenant James Hills, Dolaucothi, Dyfed.
  Bengal Horse Artillery, Siege of Delhi, 9 July 1857.
Captain Hon. Augustus Anson, Slebech Hall, Dyfed.
  2nd/8th Regiment, Bolandshapur, 22 September 1857.
Bombardier Jacob Thomas, Llanwenio, Dyfed.
  Bengal Artillery, Lucknow, 27 September 1857.

Trumpeter Thomas Monaghan, Abertillery, Gwent.
   2nd Dragoon Guards (Queen's Bays), Jamo, 8 October 1858.

Zulu Wars

Private John Roberts, Raglan, Gwent.
   South Wales Borderers, Rorke's Drift, 23 January 1879.
Private John Williams, Abergavenny, Gwent.
   South Wales Borderers, Rorke's Drift, 23 January 1879.

Sudan

Private Samuel Vickery, Cardiff.
   1st Dorset Regiment, Tirah, 11 November 1897.

First World War

Lance Corporal William Fuller, Laugharne, Dyfed.
   Royal Welch Fusiliers, Chivy, France, 14 September 1914.
Able Seaman William Williams, Chepstow, Gwent.
   HMS *River Clyde*, Gallipoli, Turkey, 25 April 1915.
Second Lieutenant Rupert Hallowes, Port Talbot, West Glamorgan.
   4th Middlesex Regiment, Hooge, Belgium, 1 October 1915.
Private James Finn, Abertillery, Gwent.
   South Wales Borderers, Sann-i-Yat, Mesopotamia (Iraq), 25 April 1916.
Major Lionel Rees, Caernarfon, Gwynedd.
   Royal Flying Corps, Somme, 1 July 1916.
Private William Lewis, Milford Haven, Dyfed.
   Welch Regiment, Salonika, Greece, 23 October 1916.
Company Sergeant Major Frederick Barter, Cardiff.
   Royal Welch Fusiliers, Festubert, France, 16 May 1917.
Seaman William Williams, Amlwch, Gwynedd.
   HMS *Pargust*, North Atlantic, 7 June 1917.
Sergeant Robert Bye, Pontypridd, Mid Glamorgan.
   Welch Guards, Pilckem, Belgium, 31 July 1917.
Corporal James Davies, Wyndham, Ogmore Vale.
   Royal Welch Fusiliers, Pilckem, Belgium, 31 July 1917.
Sergeant Ifor Rees, Felinfoel, Llanelli, Dyfed.
   South Wales Borderers, Pilckem, Belgium, 31 July 1917.
Second Lieutenant Frederick Birks, Buckley, Clwyd.
   6th Australian Imperial Force, Ypres, 20 September 1917.

Lieutenant Colonel Lewis Pugh Evans, Aberystwyth.
  Royal Highlanders, Zonnebeke, Belgium, 4 October 1917.
Corporal John Collins, Penydarren, Merthyr Tydfil, Mid Glamorgan.
  Royal Welch Fusiliers, Wadi Saba, Palestine, 31 October 1917.
Captain John Russell, Holyhead, Gwynedd.
  Royal Army Medical Corps, Tel-el-Khuweilfeh, Palestine, 6 November 1917.
Captain Richard Wain, Llandaff, South Glamorgan.
  Tank Corps, Cambrai, France, 20 November 1917.
Captain Arthur Lascelles, Dyfi, Gwynedd.
  Durham Light Infantry, Masinières, France, 3 December 1917.
Captain Thomas Pryce, Llandysilio, Powys.
  Grenadier Guards, Vieux Berquin, France, 13 April 1918.
Lance Corporal George Onions, Pontypool, Gwent.
  Devonshire Regiment, Achiet-le-Petit, France, 22 August 1918.
Lance Corporal Henry Weale, Shotton, Clwyd.
  Royal Welch Fusiliers, Bazentin-le-Grand, France, 26 August 1918.
Lance Sergeant William Waring, Welshpool, Powys.
  Royal Welch Fusiliers, Ronssoy, France, 18 September 1918.
Lance Corporal Allan Lewis, Neath, West Glamorgan.
  6th Northamptonshire Regiment, Ronssoy, France, 21 September 1918.
Company Sergeant Major John Williams, Nantyglo, Gwent.
  South Wales Borderers, Villiers Outreaux, France, 8 October 1918.
Chief Petty Officer George Prowse, Landore, West Glamorgan.
  Royal Naval Volunteer Reserve, Pronville, France, 30 October 1918.

Russia

Sergeant Samuel Pearse, Penarth, South Glamorgan
  45th Royal Fusiliers, Yemstva, North Russia, 29 August 1919.

Second World War

Captain Bernard Warburton-Lee, Maelor, Clwyd.
  HMS *Hardy*, Narvik, Norway, 10 April 1940.
Lieutenant Commander Stephen Beattie, Leighton, Powys.
  HMS *Cambletown*, St Nazaire, France, 27 March 1942.
Commander John Linton, Malpas, Newport, Gwent.
  HM Submarine *Turbulent* off Corsica, 25 May 1943.
Lieutenant Tasker Watkins, Nelson, Mid Glamorgan.
  Welch Regiment, Normandy, 16 August 1944.

Flight Lieutenant David Lord, Wrexham, Clwyd.
  RAF Transport Command, Arnhem, Holland, 19 September 1944.
Corporal Edward Thomas Chapman, Pontlottyn, Gwent.
  Monmouthshire Regiment, Teutoberger Forest, Germany, 2 April 1945.
Captain Ian Liddell, Chepstow, Gwent.
  Coldstream Guards, Lingen, Germany, 3 April 1945.

Falklands War

Lieutenant Colonel Herbert Jones, Newry Fawr, Anglesey.
  Parachute Regiment, Goose Green, 28 May 1982.

THE ROYAL NAVY AND WALES

Royal Naval Dockyard, Pembroke Dock

During its 112-year existence from 1814 to 1926, over 250 ships were built at Pembroke Dock which at the height of its activity during the First World War (1914–18) employed 4,000 people, 500 of them women. Some of the important launchings at Pembroke are listed below:

1816   The first two ships were launched – the frigates HMS *Ariadne* and HMS *Valorous*.
1833   HMS *Royal William* was launched – the first ship built there with over 100 guns.
1834   Britain's first steam-powered warship, the paddle-driven HMS *Tartarus* was launched.
1843   The first royal steam yacht, the *Victoria and Albert*, was launched.
1846   The first Royal Navy ship to be driven by a screw propellor, HMS *Conflict*, was launched.
1852   The largest three-decked ship in the world, HMS *Duke of Wellington*, was launched.
1860   HMS *Prince Consort* was the first ironclad to be built at the dock.
1865   HMS *Lord Warden* was launched – the biggest (7,800 tons) and the fastest (13½ knots) wooden armoured vessel ever built for the Royal Navy.
1917   The first submarine to be built at Pembroke was launched.
1922   The last ship was launched – the fleet oiler *Oleander*.

Vessels with Welsh affiliations currently commissioned

HMS *Anglesey*: Offshore patrol vessel
HMS *Brecon*:   Minesweeper, Hunt class
HMS *Cardiff*: Guided-missile destroyer Type 42

ROYAL AIR FORCE FLYING STATIONS

Station	Date opened	Function
St Athan, South Glamorgan	1938	Major aircraft engineering base
Valley, Anglesey	1941	Flying training using Hawk aircraft; search and rescue.

AREAS OWNED BY THE MINISTRY OF DEFENCE (1993)

	hectares		*hectares*
Clwyd	466	Mid Glamorgan	7
Dyfed	6,718	Powys	12,591
Gwent	662	South Glamorgan	397
Gwynedd	793	West Glamorgan	nil

THE TERRITORIAL ARMY IN WALES

Reorganization of the Territorial Army in Wales in the early 1990s reduced its strength from 4,500 to approximately 3,800.

Royal Regiment of Wales
2nd Battalion Headquarters at Cardiff with companies at Abertillery, Pontypridd and Swansea.

Royal Welch Fusiliers
3rd Battalion Headquarters at Wrexham with companies at Caernarfon, Colwyn Bay and Queensferry.

104 Air Defence Regiment Royal Artillery
Newport – part of the Allied Rapid Reaction Corps.

Royal Monmouthshire Royal Engineers (Militia)
Headquarters at Monmouth with squadrons at Cwmbran and Swansea.

Royal Signals
A squadron at Cardiff and a troop at Brecon.

In addition, there is a Royal Electrical and Mechanical Engineers (REME) company at Prestatyn, a Royal Military Police detachment at Cardiff, and the (Welsh) General Hospital of the Royal Army Medical Corps and a detachment of the 144 Field Ambulance at Cardiff.

157 (Wales and Midlands) Transport Regiment, Royal Corps of Transport
Headquarters at Cardiff with squadrons at Carmarthen, Cefn Forest and Swansea and troops at Haverfordwest and Lampeter.

12

THE ARTS

DATES OF SIGNIFICANCE AND INTEREST FOR MAJOR ORGANIZATIONS AND VENUES

1835   Swansea Museum and Art Gallery was opened.
1853   The first art schools in Wales were opened in Caernarfon and Swansea.
1872   The South Wales Choral Union was formed in Aberdare.
1881   The Royal Cambrian Academy was founded in Conwy.
1906   The Welsh Folk Song Society was founded in Llangollen.
1911   The Glynn Vivian Art Gallery, Swansea, opened.
1918   The Welsh National Council of Music was established.
1927   The opening of the National Museum, Cardiff, gave Wales its first major art gallery.
1928   A BBC Welsh orchestra was formed.
1930   The Three Valleys Festival was inaugurated.
        The first Welsh Books Festival was held in Cardiff.
1934   The Welsh Folk Dance Society was formed in Bala.
1937   The Contemporary Art Society of Wales was established.
1945   The National Youth Orchestra of Wales was founded.
1946   Welsh National Opera was founded.
        The Welsh Committee of the Arts Council of Great Britain was formed.
1949   The Welsh (originally the Cardiff) College of Music and Drama was opened.
1950   The first Welsh Drama Festival was held.
1954   The Guild for the Promotion of Welsh Music was established.
1958   Yr Academi Gymreig was founded.
1960   The Watercolour Society of Wales was founded.
1961   The Welsh Books Council was founded.
1962   The Welsh Theatre Company was established. (Dissolved in 1978.)

1967   The Welsh Arts Council came into existence. (Independent of the Arts Council of Great Britain from 1993).

1968   The professional chorus of Welsh National Opera was formed. Cwmni Theatr Cymru was formed in Bangor.

1969   The Welsh Arts Council introduced annual awards to writers.

1970   Saunders Lewis was nominated for the Nobel Prize for Literature. The Welsh Film Board was founded.

1973   The Welsh Philharmonia, the orchestra of Welsh National Opera, was founded.

1974   The BBC Welsh Orchestra achieved full symphony status. The Welsh Jazz Society was formed.

1981   Theatre Wales was established.

1982   The Union of Welsh Writers was founded. St David's Hall was opened in Cardiff.

1983   The Cardiff Singer of the World competition was inaugurated. The BBC Welsh Chorus was formed.

1984   The first Brecon Jazz Festival was held.

1988   BAFTA (British Association of Film and Television Arts) Cymru was founded in Cardiff. Hay-on-Wye Festival of Literature was founded. Ffilm Cymru, the Film Foundation for Wales, was founded.

1989   The first Welsh International Film Festival was held in Aberystwyth. A National Film Archive was established in Aberystwyth.

1991   The Association of Publishers in Wales was founded.

1992   The Welsh Film Board was founded.

1993   The BBC Welsh Symphony Orchestra was renamed BBC National Orchestra of Wales. Cardiff International Arena was opened. The Welsh National Opera became the holders of the first opera 'Oscar' in the International Classical Music Awards, for the Peter Stein production of Debussy's *Pelléas and Mélisande*.

1994   *Hedd Wyn* became the first Welsh-language film to be nominated for a Hollywood Oscar.

1995   Swansea the British City of Literature with a Welsh National Centre for Literature opened.

2000   Cardiff Opera House scheduled to open on 1 March.

WELSH PERIODICALS CONCERNED WITH THE ARTS

Barddas (founded 1976)
Barn (founded 1962)
Golwg (founded 1988)
Llên Cymru (founded 1950)
New Welsh Review (founded 1988)

Planet (founded 1970)
Poetry Wales (founded 1965)
Taliesin (founded 1961)
Y Traethodydd (founded 1845)

THEATRES AND CONCERT HALLS
(Maximum seating capacity shown in brackets)

Abercrave	Madam Patti Theatre (150)
Aberdare	Coliseum Theatre (621)
Abergavenny	The Town Hall (335)
Aberystwyth	Arts Centre: Great Hall(936),
	Theatr y Werin (327)
	Theatr y Castell (120)
Ammanford	Aman Centre (200)
Barmouth	Dragon Theatre (237)
Barry	The Memorial Hall (1,116)
Bangor	Theatr Gwynedd (343)
	John Phillips Hall (400)
	Pritchard Jones Hall (674)
Blackwood	Miners' Institute (430)
Blaenafon	Workmen's Hall (350)
Blaengarw	Workmen's Hall (268)
Builth Wells	Market Theatre (200)
	Strand Theatre (400)
	Wyeside Arts Centre (200)
Burry Port	The Memorial Hall (400)
Caernarfon	Theatr Seilo (297)
Cardiff	Cardiff International Arena (5,000)
	Chapter (108)
	City Hall Assembly Room (800)
	Howardian Centre (360)
	Llanover Hall Arts Centre (120)
	New Theatre (1,157)
	Reardon Smith Theatre (445)
	Sherman Theatre: Main (472), Arena (240)

	St David's Hall (1,956)
	University Concert Hall (300)
	Welsh College of Music and Drama:
	Bute Theatre (245), Caird Theatre (50)
Cardigan	Theatr Mwldan (145)
Carmarthen	Lyric Theatre (669)
	St Peter's Civic Hall (500)
	Trinity College: Theatr Haliwell (375), Theatr Parry (300)
Chepstow	The Drill Hall (200)
Colwyn Bay	Prince of Wales Theatre (440)
Connah's Quay	Civic Theatre (500)
Conwy	Civic Theatre (240)
Corwen	The Pavilion (1,250)
Cowbridge	St Donat's Arts Centre: Bradenstoke Hall (300), Tythe Barn (158)
Cwmbran	Congress Theatre (300)
	Llantarnam Hall Arts Centre (150)
Denbigh	Theatr Twm o'r Nant (152)
Ebbw Vale	Beaufort Theatre (391)
Felinfach	Theatr Felinfach (263)
Ferndale	Workmen's Hall (750)
Ffestiniog	Village Hall (240)
Harlech	Theatr Ardudwy (296)
Holyhead	Concert Hall (425)
	Ucheldre Centre (200)
Holywell	Leisure Centre (150)
	Sports Hall (450)
Knighton	Community Centre (500)
Lampeter	Lampeter Arts Hall (400)
Llandegla	Theatr Llandegla (65)
Llandrindod Wells	Albert Hall Theatre (460)
	Grand Pavilion (600)
Llandudno	Arcadia Theatre (1,137)
	Canolfan Aberconwy (970)
	North Wales Arts Theatre (1,500)
Llanelli	Theatr Elli (493)
Llangefni	Theatr Fach (117)
Llangollen	Royal International Pavilion: Arena (6,000), Main Hall (400), Gallery (150)
Llantrisant	Leisure Centre (1,000)
Maesteg	Town Hall (752)

Merthyr Tydfil	Rhydycar Leisure Centre (1,800)
Milford Haven	Torch Theatre (297)
Mold	Theatre Clwyd: Main Hall (600), Emlyn Williams Room (300), Clwyd Room (250)
Nantymoel	Berwyn Arts Centre (296)
Neath	Gwyn Hall: Main Hall (850), D. J. Williams Room (300)
Newport	Dolman Theatre (400)
	Newport Centre: Main Hall (2,024), Riverside Room (400), Kingsway Room (150)
Newtown	Theatr Hafren (568)
Pembroke Dock	Pater Hall (300)
Penarth	Paget Rooms (398)
Pontardawe	Theatr Cwmtawe (400)
Pontypridd	Municipal Hall (400)
	Hawthorn Leisure Centre: Sports Hall (900), Concert Hall (350)
Porthcawl	Pavilion (698)
Port Talbot	Afan Lido (2,500)
	Princess Royal Theatre (850)
Prestatyn	Nova Centre (350)
Rhayader	Community Centre (500)
Rhyl	Coliseum (660)
	Gaiety (700)
	Library, Museum and Arts Centre (80)
	Little Theatre (196)
	New Pavilion (1,032)
Swansea	Brangwyn Hall (1,200)
	Dylan Thomas Theatre (200)
	Grand Theatre (1,050)
	Patti Pavilion (524)
	Swansea Leisure Centre: Main Hall (900), Amphitheatre (400)
	Taliesin Arts Centre (365)
Tenby	De Valence Centre (600)
Tredegar	Leisure Centre (600)
Treorchy	Parc and Dare Theatre (800)
Wrexham	Library and Arts Centre (170)
Ystradgynlais	Miners' Welfare Hall (367)

Note: Some of these halls are also used as cinemas.

SYMPHONY ORCHESTRAS

BBC National Orchestra of Wales: Broadcasting House, Llandaff, Cardiff.
The Orchestra of Welsh National Opera: John Street, Cardiff.

CINEMAS

Abertillery	The Metropole
Aberystwyth	The Commodore
Ammanford	The Welfare Cinema
Bala	Neuadd Buddug
Bangor	The Plaza
Bargoed	The Cameo
Barry	Theatre Royal
Blaina	The Gaiety
Brecon	The Coliseum (two screens)
Brynmawr	The Market Hall
Cardiff	Capitol Odeon (five screens)
	Chapter (two screens)
	MGM (three screens)
	Monico (two screens)
	Monroe
	Odeon Queen Street (three screens)
Colwyn Bay	Princess Theatre
Cwmbran	Scene (three screens)
Denbigh	The Futura
Fishguard	The Studio
Haverfordwest	The Palace
Holyhead	The Empire
Holywell	Focus Cinemas
Llandudno	The Palladium
Llanelli	The Entertainments Centre (two screens)
Merthyr Tydfil	Cefn Community Centre
	The Flicks
Monmouth	The Magic Lantern
Neath	The Windsor
Newbridge	The Memorial Hall
Newport	MGM (three screens)
New Quay	The Memorial Hall

Newtown	The Regent
Pontypool	The Scala
Porthcawl	The Regent
Porthmadog	The Coliseum
Port Talbot	The Plaza (four screens)
Prestatyn	The Scala
Pwllheli	The Town Hall Cinema
Rhyl	The Apollo
St Athan	The Astra
Swansea	UCI (United Cinemas International) (ten screens)
	Odeon (three screens)
	The Studio
Tenby	The Royal Playhouse
Tredegar	The Palace
Treharris	The Palace
Tywyn	The Tywyn Cinema
Welshpool	The Pola
Wrexham	The Hippodrome
Ystradgynlais	The Super Cinema

MUSEUMS

Clwyd

Denbigh	Library, Museum and Art Gallery
	Classic Car Museum
Holywell	Grange Cavern Military Museum
	Greenfield Valley Heritage Park
Llangollen	Chwarel Wynne Slate and Mine Museum
	Llangollen Motor Museum
	Plas Newydd Museum
Mold	Daniel Owen Museum
Wrexham	Bersham Heritage Centre and Ironworks
	Geological and Folk Museum of North Wales

Dyfed

Aberystwyth	Ceredigion Museum
	Llywernog Silver–Lead Mine Museum
	Yr Hen Gapel, Tre'r Ddôl
Cardigan	Geler Jones Museum
Carmarthen	The Carmarthen Museum, Abergwili

Dre-Fach	Museum of the Welsh Woollen Industry
Haverfordwest	Castle Museum and Art Gallery
	Scolton Manor Museum
Kidwelly	Kidwelly Heritage and Tinplate Museum
Llanelli	Parc Howard Museum and Art Gallery
Pembroke	National Museum of Gypsy Caravans, Romany Crafts and Lore
Tenby	Tenby Museum and Art Gallery

Gwent

Abergavenny	Abergavenny and District Museum
Blaenafon	Big Pit Mining Museum
Caerleon	Roman Legionary Museum
Caldicot	Caldicot Castle Museum
Chepstow	Chepstow Museum
Monmouth	Monmouth Museum
Newport	Newport Museum and Art Gallery
Pontypool	Valleys Inheritance Museum
Usk	Gwent Rural Life Museum

Gwynedd

Bangor	Bangor Museum and Art Gallery
	Doll Museum
	Museum of Welsh Antiquities
Barmouth	Lifeboat Museum
	Old Country Life Museum
Beaumaris	Museum of Childhood
Betws-y-coed	Conwy Valley Railway Museum
Caernarfon	Caernarfon Air Museum
	Maritime Museum
	Royal Welch Fusiliers Museum, Caernarfon Castle
	Segontium Roman Fort Museum
Cricieth	New Lloyd George Museum
Holyhead	Holyhead Maritime Museum
Llanberis	Museum of the North
	Welsh Slate Museum
Llandudno	Llandudno Museum and Art Gallery
Nefyn	Library, Historical and Maritime Museum
Porthmadog	Ffestiniog Railway Museum
	Maritime Museum
Tywyn	Narrow Gauge Railway Museum

Mid Glamorgan

Bridgend	South Wales Police Museum
Butetown,	
Rhymney Valley	Butetown Museum
Merthyr Tydfil	Cyfarthfa Castle Museum and Art Gallery
	Joseph Parry Museum
Nelson	Llancaiach Fawr Living History Museum
Porthcawl	Porthcawl Museum
Trehafod	Rhondda Heritage Park

Powys

Brecon	Brecknock Museum
	Museum of the South Wales Borderers and Monmouthshire Regiment
Llanidloes	Llanidloes Museum
Llandrindod Wells	Museum of Local History and Industry
Newtown	Robert Owen Museum
	W. H. Smith Museum
Rhayader	Rhayader Museum
Talgarth	Howell Harris Museum
Welshpool	Powysland Museum and Montgomery Canal Centre
	Clive Museum, Powis Castle

South Glamorgan

Cardiff	1st The Queen's Dragoon Guards Museum, Cardiff Castle
	National Museum of Wales
	Welch Regiment Museum, Cardiff Castle
	Welsh Folk Museum, St Fagans
	Welsh Industrial and Maritime Museum
Rhoose	Welsh Aircraft Museum

West Glamorgan

Afan Argoed	Welsh Miners' Museum
Crynant	Cefn Coed Colliery Museum
Margam	Margam Museum
	Neath Museum
Swansea	Royal Institution of South Wales Museum
	Swansea Maritime and Industrial Museum
	Swansea Museum

ART GALLERIES

(See also under *Museums*. This list does not include small artist-run galleries or exhibition spaces in libraries.)

Clwyd
Llangollen	European Centre for Traditional and Regional Cultures
Mold	Oriel, Theatr Clwyd
St Asaph	National Portrait Gallery, Bodelwyddan Castle
Wrexham	Wrexham Library Arts Centre

Dyfed
Aberystwyth	Aberystwyth Arts Centre
	National Library of Wales
Carmarthen	Henry Thomas Gallery
Fishguard	West Wales Arts Centre
	Workshop Wales Gallery
Haverfordwest	Graham Sutherland Gallery, Picton Castle
Lampeter	Y Galeri
Llanelli	Nevill Gallery
Milford Haven	Dockside Gallery

Gwent
Chepstow	5D Fine Art
	Workshop Gallery
Cwmbran	Llantarnam Grange Arts Centre

Gwynedd
Beaumaris	Oriel Fach
Blaenau Ffestiniog	Oriel y Ddraig
Bodorgan	Michael Webb Fine Art
Caernarfon	Arfon Gallery
	The Richard Wilson Centre
	Parc Glynllifon (sculpture park)
Conwy	Plas Mawr, Royal Cambrian Academy
Llanbedrog	Oriel Plas Glyn-y-Weddw
Llandudno	Oriel Mostyn
Llangefni	Oriel Môn
	Oriel Ynys Môn
Menai Bridge	Tegfryn Art Gallery

Mid Glamorgan
Bridgend	Nolton Gallery

Pontypridd	The Circle Gallery, Muni Arts Centre
	Pontypridd Historical and Cultural Centre
Treforest	Y Bont Gallery, University of Glamorgan

Powys

Bleddfa	The Old School Gallery
Brecon	Sable and Hogg Gallery
Builth Wells	Wyeside Arts Centre
Clyro	Kilvert Gallery
Crickhowell	Riverside Gallery
Machynlleth	The Tabernacle Cultural Centre
Newtown	Davies Memorial Gallery
Welshpool	Oriel 31

South Glamorgan

Cardiff	Albany Gallery
	Chapter Arts Centre
	Ffotogallery
	The Gallery, Richard Beere Interiors
	Howard Gardens Gallery
	Manor House Fine Arts
	Martin Tinney Gallery
	The Old Library Gallery
	Oriel Gallery
	St David's Hall
	Third Wave Gallery
Cowbridge	Old Hall Gallery
	John Owen Gallery
Penarth	Turner House Gallery

West Glamorgan

Pontardawe	The Cross Gallery
Port Talbot	Sculpture at Margam (sculpture park)
Swansea	Attic Gallery
	Café Gallery
	The Craftsman Gallery
	Ceri Richards Gallery
	Glynn Vivian Art Gallery

FESTIVALS

Aberystwyth Musical Festival	July/August
Abergavenny Festival	June
Barmouth Arts festival	September
Beaumaris Festival	May/June
Builth Wells Kidfest	August
Brecon Jazz Festival	August
Caernarfon Folk Festival	October
Cardiff Butetown Carnival	August
Cardiff Festival	September/October
Cardiff Singer of the World Competition	June (biennially)
Cardiff Summer Festival	August
Carmarthen Gŵyl Myrddin Festival	October
Chepstow Festival	July
Cilgerran Coracle Festival	August
Conwy Festival	July
Cricieth Festival of Music and Arts	June
Deeside Festival	June
Dolgellau Folk Festival	July
Dyffryn (South Glamorgan) Festival of Music and Drama	July/August
Ely (Cardiff) Festival	July
Ffostrasol (Dyfed) Gŵyl Werin y Cnapan	July
Fishguard Music Festival	July
Gower Festival	July
Gregynog Festival	June/July
Hay-on-Wye Literature Festival	May
Holyhead Arts Festival	April/May
Llandeilo – Gŵyl Dinefwr	June
Llandovery Theatre and Arts Festival	June/September
Llandrindod Wells Victorian Festival	September
Llandudno Festival	October
Llandudno Organ Festival	July
Llanelli Festival	November
Llanfyllin Festival	July
Llangollen International Jazz Festival	May
Llangollen International Musical Eisteddfod	July
Llantilio Crosseny Festival of Music and Drama	April/May

Llantrisant Festival	April/May
Llantrisant Folk Festival	April
Lower Machen Festival	June
Margam Festival	June/July
Mold Festival	June/July
Machynlleth Festival	August
Narberth Children's Festival	August
Newport International Competition for young pianists	October (triennially)
Newport International Festival of Musical Theatre	May
Newtown Mayfest	May
Newtown – Mid Wales Opera Festival	September
Penarth Jazz Festival	July
Pontrhydfendigaid Eisteddfod	May
Pontardawe Music Festival	August
Presteigne Festival of Music and the Arts	August/September
Rhymney Valley Festival	July
Royal National Eisteddfod of Wales	July/August
St Asaph – North Wales Musical Festival	September/October
St David's Cathedral Festival	May/June
Swansea Festival	September/October
Swansea Fringe Festival	September/October
Tenby Arts Festival	September
Urdd Gobaith Cymru National Eisteddfod	May/June
Usk Festival	July
Vale of Glamorgan Festival	August
Welsh Proms, St David's Hall, Cardiff	July
Wrexham Maelor Arts Festival	May

In addition to the eisteddfodau listed above, about 80 local eisteddfodau are held throughout Wales every year. A calendar listing these can be obtained from Eisteddfod Genedlaethol Cymru, 40 Parc Tŷ Glas,Llanishen, Cardiff, CF4 5WY.

THE ARTS COUNCIL OF WALES

Holst House, 9 Museum Place, Cardiff CF1 3NX.
The Welsh Arts Council changed its title in 1994 after becoming independent of the Arts Council of Great Britain.

WELSH ARTS COUNCIL EXPENDITURE ON THE ARTS

(£thousands)

	1986-87	1987-88	1988-89	1989-90	1990-91	1992-93
Art	524.8	515.3	624.1	623.7	708.3	860.8
Drama	1,808.4	1,841.8	1,983.0	2,045.9	2,227.1	2,726.5
Literature	572.7	605.9	664.3	685.0	768.0	948.7
Music	2,523.3	2, 585.1	2,762.6	2,785.8	3,879.3	3,838.0
Dance, Film, Craft, etc.	1,822.1	1,840.2	1,952.5	2,157.0	2,369.3	3,408.6
Total	7,251.3	7,388.3	7,983.8	8,297.4	9,952.0	11,782.6

WINNERS OF WELSH ARTS COUNCIL PRIZES FOR BOOKS IN ENGLISH AND WELSH

1969
Pennar Davies	*Meibion Darogan*
Raymond Garlick	*A Sense of Europe*
Glyn Jones	*The Dragon Has Two Tongues*
Gwilym R. Jones	*Cerddi*

1970
Marion Eames	*Y Stafell Ddirgel*
T. Wilson Evans	*Iwan Tudur*
J. Gwyn Griffiths	*Cerddi Cairo*
Sally Roberts Jones	*Turning Away*
John Ormond	*Requiem and Celebration*
Harri Webb	*The Green Desert*
Gwynne Williams	*Rhwng Gewyn ac Asgwrn*

1971
Dannie Abse	*Selected Poems*
Euros Bowen	*Achlysuron*
Joseph Clancy	*The Earliest Welsh Poetry*
David Tecwyn Lloyd	*Safle'r Gerbydres*
Derec Llwyd Morgan	*Pryderi*
John Stuart Williams	*Dic Penderyn*

1972
Pennar Davies	*Y Tlws yn y Lotws*

Emyr Humphreys	*National Winner*
Bobi Jones	*Allor Wydn*
Richard Jones	*The Tower is Everywhere*
David Tecwyn Lloyd	*Lady Gwladys a Phobl Eraill*
Roland Mathias	*Absalom in the Tree*

1973

Raymond Garlick	*A Sense of Time*
Harri Pritchard Jones	*Dychwelyd*
Alison Morgan	*Pete*
Gerallt Lloyd Owen	*Cerddi'r Cywilydd*
Iorwerth Peate	*Tradition and Folk Life*
Kate Roberts	*Gobaith*
Gwyn Thomas	*Enw'r Gair*
R. S. Thomas	*H'm*
R. Bryn Williams	*O'r Tir Pell*

1974

David Jenkins	*T. Gwynn Jones: Cofiant*
John Ormond	*Definition of a Waterfall*
Alun Richards	*Dai Country*

1975

J. Eirian Davies	*Cân Galed*
T. Glynne Davies	*Marged*
Jeremy Hooker	*Soliloquies of a Chalk Giant*
Emyr Humphries	*Flesh and Blood*
Leslie Norris	*Mountains, Polecats, Pheasants and Other Elegies*
Peter Tinniswood	*Except You're a Bird*
John G. Williams	*Maes Mihangel*

1976

Ruth Bidgood	*Not Without Homage*
J. M. Edwards	*Cerddi Ddoe a Heddiw*
Gwilym R. Jones	*Y Syrcas a Cherddi Eraill*
Alan Llwyd	*Edrych Trwy Wydrau Lledrith*
Alun Llywelyn-Williams	*Gwanwyn yn y Ddinas*
Kenneth Morgan	*Keir Hardie*
Marged Pritchard	*Gwylanod ar y Mynydd*
Bernice Rubens	*I sent a letter to my love*

1977

Jane Edwards	*Dros Fryniau Bro Afallon*
Donald Evans	*Egin*
Raymond Garlick	*Incense*
Owain Owain	*Mical*
R. J. Rowlands	*Cerddi R. J. Rowlands y Bala*
Gwyn Thomas	*Cadwynau yn y Meddwl*
Gwyn A. Williams	*Goya and the Impossible Revolution*

1978

Aled Islwyn	*Lleuwen*
Jane Edwards	*Miriam*
Alice Thomas Ellis	*The Sin Eater*
Dyfed Evans	*Bywyd Bob Owen*
Stuart Evans	*The Caves of Alienation*
Paul Ferris	*Dylan Thomas*
Rhiannon Davies Jones	*Llys Aberffraw*
Gwyn Thomas	*Y Traddodiad Barddol*

1979

Gillian Clarke	*The Sundial*
Marion Eames	*I Hela Cnau*
James Hanley	*A Kingdom*
Emyr Humphreys	*The Best of Friends*
Dic Jones	*Storom Awst*
Tristan Jones	*The Incredible Voyage*
Leslie Norris	*Sliding*
John Rowlands	*Tician, Tician*
Gwyn A. Williams	*The Merthyr Rising*
J. G. Williams	*Betws Hirfaen*

1980

Dannie Abse	*Pythagoras*
Siôn Eirian	*Bob yn y Ddinas*
Geraint Vaughan Jones	*Y Ffoaduriaid*
Alun Llywelyn-Williams	*Golau yn y Gwyll*
Roland Mathias	*Snipe's Castle*
Robert Minhinnick	*Native Ground*
Philip Owens	*Look, Christ*
Caradog Prichard	*Cerddi Caradog Prichard*
Raymond Williams	*The Fight for Manod*

1981

Jean Earle	*A Trial of Strength*
Hywel Teifi Edwards	*Gŵyl Gwalia*
Alan Llwyd	*Cerddi'r Cyfannu*
David Smith and	
Gareth Williams	*Fields of Praise*
Nigel Wells	*Winter Festivals*

1982

Alun Jones	*Pan Ddaw'r Machlud*
R. Merfyn Jones	*The North Wales Quarrymen 1874–1922*
Rhiannon Davies Jones	*Eryr Pengwern*
Kenneth O. Morgan	*Rebirth of a Nation: Wales 1880–1980*

1983

Rachel Bromwich	*Dafydd ap Gwilym: Poems*
Marion Eames	*Y Gaeaf Sydd Unig*
Alice Ellis Thomas	*The 27th Kingdom*
R. Tudur Jones	*Ffydd ac Argyfwng Cenedl*
Alan Llwyd	*Yn Nydd yr Anghenfil*

1984

Duncan Bush	*Aquarium*
Donald Evans	*Machlud Canrif*
Gwynn ap Gwilym	*Gwales*
Emyr Humphreys	*The Taliesin Tradition*
Siân James	*Dragons and Roses*
Geraint H. Jenkins	*Hanes Cymru yn y Cyfnod Modern Cynnar: 1530–1760*
Mike Jenkins	*Empire of a Smoke*
Alun Jones	*Oed Rhyw Addewid*
Robert Minhinnick	*Life Sentences*

1985

Geraint Bowen	*Cerddi*
Bryan Martin Davies	*Lleoedd*
David Hughes	*The Pork Butcher*
Christopher Meredith	*This*
J. P. Ward	*The Clearing*
Glanmor Williams	*Grym Tafodau Tân*
Ivor Wilks	*South Wales and the Rising of 1839*

1986

Duncan Bush	*Salt*
J. Eirian Davies	*Cerddi*
Mary Jones	*Resistance*
Rhiannon Davies Jones	*Dyddiadur Mary Gwyn*
Elyn L. Jones	*Cyfrinach Hannah*
Christopher Norris	*Contest of Faculties*
Oliver Reynolds	*Skevington's Daughter*
Angharad Tomos	*Yma o Hyd*
Gwyn A. Williams	*When Was Wales?*
Raymond Williams	*Loyalties*

1987

Dannie Abse	*Ask the Bloody Horse*
Stephen Gregory	*The Cormorant*
Douglas Houston	*With the Offal Eaters*
Nesta Wyn Jones	*Rhwng Chwerthin a Chrio*
Alan Llwyd	*Barddoniaeth y Chwedegau*
Gwylon Phillips	*Llofruddiaeth Shadrach Lewis*
J. Beverley Smith	*Llywelyn ap Gruffudd*
Frances Thomas	*Seeing Things*
Peter Thomas	*Strangers from a Secret Land*
Rhydwen Williams	*Amser i Wylo*

1988

T. Glynne Davies	*Cerddi*
Bobi Jones	*Llenyddiaeth Gymraeg 1902-36*
Rhiannon Davies Jones	*Cribau Eryri*
Hilary Llywelyn-Williams	*The Tree Calendar*
Sheenagh Pugh	*Beware Falling Tortoises*
Oliver Reynolds	*The Player Queen's Wife*
William Owen Roberts	*Y Pla*
Bernice Rubens	*Our Father*
Huw Walters	*Canu'r Pwll a'r Pulpud*
Glanmor Williams	*Recovery, Reorientation and Reformation*

1989

Tony Conran	*Blodeuwedd*
Donald Evans	*Iasau*
Catherine Fisher	*Immrana*
Alan Llwyd	*Yn y Dirfawr Wag*

D. Tecwyn Lloyd   *John Saunders Lewis*
Christopher Meredith   *Shifts*
Prys Morgan   *Beibl i Gymru*
Leslie Norris   *The Girl from Cardigan*
Nigel Wells   *Wilderness/Just Bounce*
Rhydwen Williams   *Liwsi Regina*

1990

John Barnie   *The King of Ashes*
Carol-Ann Courtney   *Morphine and Dolly Mixtures*
Sioned Davies   *Pedeir Keinc y Mabinogi*
Hywel Teifi Edwards   *Codi'r Hen Wlad yn ei Hôl*
Christine Evans   *Cometary Phases*
Alun Jones   *Plentyn y Bwtias*
David Jones   *Rebecca's Children*
Dic Jones   *Os Hoffech Wybod*
R. Gerallt Jones   *Cerddi 1955–1989*
Selyf Roberts   *Gorwel Agos*

1991

John Davies   *Hanes Cymru*
Menna Elfyn   *Aderyn Bach Mewn Llaw*
Geraint H. Jenkins   *Cadw Tŷ Mewn Cwmwl Tystion*
Bobi Jones   *Crio Chwerthin*
Alan Llwyd   *Cerddi 1968–90*
Russell Celyn Jones   *Soldiers and Innocents*
Moelwyn Merchant   *Fragments of Life*
Sheenagh Pugh   *Selected Poems*
Bernice Rubens   *Kingdom Come*
Gwyn Thomas   *Gwelaf Afon*
Robert Watson   *Whilom*

1992

Emyr Humphreys   *Bonds of Attachment* (English Book of the Year Award)
Christopher Meredith   *Griffri*
Catherine Merriman   *Silly Mothers*
Gerallt Lloyd Owen   *Cilmeri* (Welsh Book of the Year Award)
M. Wynn Thomas   *Morgan Llwyd, Ei Gyfeillion a'i Gyfnod*
Angharad Tomos   *Si Hei Lwli*

1993

Ruth Bidgood   *Selected Poems*

Andrew Davies	*B. Monkey*
Robin Llywelyn	*Seren Wen ar Gefndir Gwyn* (Welsh Book of the Year Award)
Robert Minhinnick	*Watching the Fire Eater* (English Book of the Year Award)
Mihangel Morgan	*Hen Lwybr a Storïau Eraill*
John Rowlands	*Ysgrifau ar y Nofel*

1994

Robin Chapman	*W. J. Gruffydd* (Welsh Book of the Year Award)
Gillian Clarke	*The King of Britain's Daughter*
Christopher Evans	*Aztec Century*
Paul Ferris	*Caitlin* (English Book of the Year Award)
Mihangel Morgan	*Saith Pechod Marwol*
Gwyn Thomas and Ted Breeze Jones	*Anifeiliaid y Maes Hefyd*

The winners of the Book of the Year Award receive £3,000 each and the runners-up £1,000 each.

AMERICAN LITERARY AWARDS WON BY WRITERS FROM WALES

Loines Award for Poetry (American National Institute of Arts and Letters):	1954	David Jones
Poetry magazine Oscar Bleumenthal Prize:	1938	Dylan Thomas
Poetry magazine Levinson Prize:	1945	Dylan Thomas
	1953	Vernon Watkins
	1961	David Jones

MAJOR BRITISH LITERARY AWARDS WON BY WRITERS FROM WALES

Arvon Foundation Poetry Competition:	1985	Oliver Reynolds *Rorschach Writing*
Booker McConnell Prize (National Book League):	1970	Bernice Rubens *The Elected Member*
Cholmondley Award for Poetry (Society of Authors):	1975	John Ormond
	1978	Leslie Norris
		R. S. Thomas
Evening Standard Drama Award:	1961	Gwyn Thomas (Most Promising Playwright)

Hawthornden Prize (Society of Authors):	1938	David Jones *In Parenthesis*
	1959	Emyr Humphreys *A Toy Epic*
Heinemann Award (Royal Literary Society):	1955	R. S. Thomas *Song at the World's Turning*
	1961	Jan Morris *World of Venice*
John Llewelyn Rhys Memorial Award (National Book League):	1944	Alun Lewis *The Last Inspection*
	1965	Julian Mitchell *The White Father*
	1968	Peter King (runner-up for *Seven Foot With a Wooden Leg*)
Queen's Gold Medal for Poetry:	1964	R. S. Thomas
Somerset Maugham Award (Society of Authors):	1955	Emyr Humphreys *Hear and Forgive*
	1966	Julian Mitchell *The White Father*
	1982	Adam Mars-Jones *Lantern Lectures*
UK National Poetry Prize	1984	Tony Curtis
W. H. Smith Literary Award:	1984	David Hughes *The Pork Butcher*
Yorkshire Post Best First Book:	1976	Siân James *One Afternoon* (runner-up)
Yorkshire Post Book of the Year:	1979	Siân James *Yesterday*

FELLOWS OF YR ACADEMI GYMREIG/THE WELSH ACADEMY

(Yr Academi Gymreig/The Welsh Academy, Mount Stuart House, Mount Stuart Square, Cardiff, CF1 6DQ.)

English Section

Dr Dannie Abse
Emyr Humphreys
Dr Glyn Jones
Professor Gwyn Jones

Roland Mathias
Elaine Morgan
Leslie Norris
Bernice Rubens

Welsh Section

Pennar Davies
J. Gwyn Griffiths
Gwilym R. Jones
R. S. Thomas

Gwilym R. Tilsley
John Roberts Williams
Rhydwen Williams

13

SPORT

ANGLING

World Fresh Water Championships

1987	Individual champion	Clive Branson
1989	Team champions	Wales

ASSOCIATION FOOTBALL

The World Cup

Wales reached the quarter-finals in Sweden in 1958 losing 1–0 to Brazil.

European Cup-Winners Cup

Cardiff City lost 4–3 on aggregate to HSV Hamburg in the 1968 semi-finals.

Home International Championship wins by Wales

1907	1937	
1920	1939	(shared with England and Scotland)
1924	1952	(shared with England)
1928	1956	(four-way tie)
1933	1960	(shared with England and Scotland)
1934	1970	(shared with England and Scotland)

The home championship competition was discontinued in 1984.

FA Cup

Cardiff City beat Arsenal 1–0 in the final in 1927.
Cardiff City lost to Sheffield United 1–0 in the final in 1925.
Cardiff City lost to Wolverhampton Wanderers 3–1 in the semi-finals in 1921.
Swansea City lost to Bolton Wanderers 3–0 in the semi-finals in 1926.
Swansea City lost to Preston North End 2–1 in the semi-finals in 1964.

Charity Shield

Cardiff City beat Corinthians 2–1 in the final in 1927.

FA Youth Cup

Cardiff City lost 2–0 to Arsenal in the final in 1971.

Autoglass Trophy

Swansea City beat Huddersfield Town 3–1 in a penalty shoot-out in the final in 1994.

Football League Champions

Swansea City	Division Three (South), 1924–5
Newport County	Division Three (South), 1938–9
Cardiff City	Division Three (South), 1946–7
Swansea City	Division Three (South), 1948–9
Cardiff City	Division Three, 1992–3

League of Wales Champions

Cwmbran Town	1992–3 (Inaugural season)
Bangor City	1993–4

Welsh Record in Senior International Matches
(To October, 1994)

Opponents	Played	Won	Drawn	Lost
Albania	1	1	0	0
Argentina	1	0	0	1
Austria	5	1	1	3

Opponents	Played	Won	Drawn	Lost
Belgium	6	3	1	2
Bulgaria	2	1	0	1
Brazil	7	1	1	5
Canada	2	1	0	1
Chile	1	0	0	1
Costa Rica	1	1	0	0
Cyprus	2	2	0	0
Czechoslovakia (including combined Czech and Slovak side)	12	4	2	6
Denmark	3	1	0	2
England	97	14	21	62
Estonia	1	1	0	0
Faeroe Islands	2	2	0	0
Finland	6	3	2	1
France	4	1	1	2
Germany (East)	4	1	0	3
Germany (West)	8	0	4	4
Germany	2	1	0	1
Greece	2	1	0	1
Holland	4	0	0	4
Hungary	8	3	2	3
Iceland	5	3	1	1
Iran	1	1	0	0
Irish Republic	8	5	0	3
Israel	4	2	2	0
Italy	4	1	0	3
Japan	1	1	0	0
Kuwait	2	0	2	0
Luxembourg	3	3	0	0
Malta	3	3	0	0
Mexico	2	0	1	1
Moldova	1	0	0	1
Northern Ireland (includes results against Ireland to 1922)	90	42	21	27
Norway	6	1	2	3
Poland	2	1	0	1
Portugal	2	1	0	1
Romania	5	1	1	3
Saudi Arabia	1	1	0	0

Scotland	101	18	23	60
Spain	5	1	2	2
Sweden	5	0	1	4
Switzerland	2	1	0	1
Turkey	4	2	0	2
Uruguay	1	0	1	0
USSR	5	1	2	2
Yugoslavia	7	0	2	5

Welsh Cup Winners

1878	Wrexham
1879	Newtown
1880	Druids (Rhiwabon)
1881	Druids
1882	Druids
1883	Wrexham
1884	Oswestry
1885	Druids
1886	Druids
1887	Chirk
1888	Chirk
1889	Bangor
1890	Chirk
1891	Shrewsbury Town
1892	Chirk
1893	Wrexham
1894	Chirk
1895	Newtown
1896	Bangor
1897	Wrexham
1898	Druids
1899	Druids
1900	Aberystwyth
1901	Shrewsbury Town
1902	Wellington Town (now Telford United)
1903	Wrexham
1904	Druids
1905	Wrexham

1906	Wellington Town (see 1902)
1907	Oswestry
1908	Chester
1909	Wrexham
1910	Wrexham
1911	Wrexham
1912	Cardiff City (in the first 'all South Wales' final v. Pontypridd)
1913	Swansea City
1914	Wrexham
1915	Wrexham
1916–1919	No competition
1920	Cardiff City
1921	Wrexham
1922	Cardiff City
1923	Cardiff City
1924	Wrexham
1925	Wrexham
1926	Ebbw Vale
1927	Cardiff City
1928	Cardiff City
1929	Connah's Quay
1930	Cardiff City
1931	Wrexham
1932	Swansea City
1933	Chester
1934	Bristol City (an 'all English' final v. Tranmere Rovers)

1935	Tranmere Rovers (an 'all English' final v. Chester)	1970	Cardiff City
1936	Crewe Alexandra (an 'all English' final v. Chester)	1971	Cardiff City
1937	Crewe Alexandra	1972	Wrexham
1938	Shrewsbury Town	1973	Cardiff City
1939	South Liverpool	1974	Cardiff City
1940	Wellington Town (see 1902)	1975	Wrexham
1941–1946	No competition	1976	Cardiff City
1947	Chester	1977	Shrewsbury Town† (Cardiff City played in Europe)
1948	Lovell's Athletic	1978	Wrexham
1949	Merthyr Tydfil	1979	Shrewsbury Town† (Wrexham played in Europe)
1950	Swansea City	1980	Newport City
1951	Merthyr Tydfil	1981	Swansea City
1952	Rhyl	1982	Swansea City
1953	Rhyl	1983	Swansea City
1954	Flint Town United	1984	Shrewsbury Town† (Wrexham played in Europe)
1955	Barry Town	1985	Shrewsbury Town† (Bangor City played in Europe)
1956	Cardiff City		
1957	Wrexham		
1958	Wrexham	1986	Wrexham
1959	Cardiff City	1987	Merthyr Tydfil
1960	Wrexham	1988	Cardiff City
1961	Swansea City*	1989	Swansea City
1962	Bangor City	1990‡	Hereford United† (Wrexham played in Europe)
1963	Borough United (Llandudno)		
1964	Cardiff City	1991	Swansea City
1965	Cardiff City	1992	Cardiff City
1966	Swansea City	1993	Cardiff City
1967	Cardiff City	1994	Barry Town
1968	Cardiff City		
1969	Cardiff City		

*Since 1961 Welsh Cup winners have qualified to play in the European Cup-Winners Competition.
†English clubs winning the Welsh Cup cannot qualify and the losing Welsh club in the final that year represents Wales in Europe. If no Welsh club reaches the final, Wales will not have a representative side in the Cup-Winners Competition that year.
‡Since 1990 the Welsh Cup Final has been played at the National Stadium, Cardiff Arms Park.

Most frequent winners of the Welsh Cup

Cardiff City	22
Wrexham	22
Swansea City	10
Shrewsbury Town	7

League of Wales and Europe

From the 1993–94 season, the League of Wales champions have competed in the UEFA Cup following the establishment of the League from the 1992–93 season. However Cwmbran Town, League winners in 1992–93 were allowed to compete in the European Cup while the runners-up in 1993–94, Inter Cardiff, were allowed to compete in the UEFA Cup together with Bangor City the League Champions.

Welsh Clubs in the English Football League

Aberdare Athletic	1921–1927
Cardiff City	1920–present
Merthyr Town	1920–1930
Newport County	1920–1988 (except for 1930–31 season)
Swansea City	1920–present
Wrexham	1921–present

Most Capped Welsh Players

(To September, 1994)

Neville Southall	76 caps	Ivor Allchurch	68 caps
Peter Nicholas	73 caps	Ian Rush	67 caps
Joey Jones	72 caps	Brian Flynn	66 caps

Most capped player in the British Championship – Billy Meredith, 48 caps.

Leading Goal Scorers

(To September, 1994)

Ian Rush	28	Ivor Allchurch	23
Trevor Ford	23		

European Golden Boot Award

In 1984, Ian Rush became the first Welshman to win the European Golden Boot Award on scoring 32 goals in the 1983–84 season.

ATHLETICS

British Athletics League Championship

Cardiff Athletic Club: 1972, 1973, 1974

British Athletics Cup (Men)

Cardiff Athletic Club: 1974

UK Records Held by Athletes Representing Wales

Lynn Davies, long jump: 8.23 m. 1968
Kirsty Wade, 800m.: 1 min. 57.42 s. 1985
Colin Jackson, 110m. hurdles: 13min.04 s. 1992

Marathons

London Marathon
1985   Won by Steve Jones in a record time of 2hrs.8min.16s.

Kathmandu Marathon
1993   First ever winner was Ieuan Ellis in 2hrs.24min.10s.

New York Marathon
1988   Steve Jones became the first Briton to win the event.

Long Jump Champion

Lynn Davies was the first person to hold the Olympic, Commonwealth and European long jump titles at the same time: Olympic Games 1964, and the Commonwealth and European Games both in 1966.

World Athletics Records

Colin Jackson: 110m. hurdles, 12.91 secs., Stuttgart, 20 August 1993

Colin Jackson: 60m. hurdles (indoors), 7.30secs., Sindelfingen, 6 March 1994

See also Olympic Games, Paralympics and Commonwealth Games.

BASEBALL

Wales v. England Internationals (1908–1994)

Played 69   Wales won 49   England won 19   Drawn 1

Most-capped Welsh Players (*To 1994*)

John Smith (Llanrumney)	16 caps	Ivor Hughes (Llanrumney)	13 caps
Steve Haines (Llanrumney)	13 caps	Tom Denning (Splott US)	12 caps

BILLIARDS

1937   World Amateur Billiards Championship was won by Horace Coles of Wales.

BOWLS

International Championship (British Isles Countries)

Wales   1920, 1925, 1930, 1931, 1933, 1934, 1937, 1938, 1946, 1948, 1957, 1978, 1982

British Isles Indoor Championship

Wales   1967 (Inaugural year)

Women's World Championship Triples

Wales   1977

World Singles Champions

1972	Maldwyn Evans, Rhondda:	world singles outdoor title, Worthing
1985	Terry Sullivan, Swansea:	world singles indoor title, Coatbridge, Scotland
1988	Janet Ackand, Penarth:	world women's singles outdoor title, Auckland, New Zealand
1990	John Price, Port Talbot:	world singles indoor title, Preston

BOXING

The Queensberry Rules governing boxing were revised in 1867 by John Graham Chambers from Llanelli.

World Champions from Wales

Percy Jones, Porthcawl
  Featherweight title, London, 26 January 1914. (The title was not recognized in the USA and was lost later in 1914.)
Freddie Welsh (Frederick Hall Thomas), Pontypridd
  Lightweight title, London, 7 July 1914. (Held to 1917.)
Jimmy Wilde, Tylorstown, Rhondda
  Flyweight title, Liverpool, 24 April 1916. (Wilde was the first holder of this world title and held it until 1923 – longer than anyone since.)
Howard Winstone, Merthyr Tydfil
  Featherweight title, London, 23 January 1968. (Title lost later in 1968.)
Steve Robinson, Cardiff
  Featherweight title (World Boxing Organization). Washington, County Durham, 17 April 1993.
Colin Jones, Gorseinon
  Drew the welterweight title fight in Reno, Nevada, 19 March 1983.

British, European and Commonwealth Title Holders from Wales

(Commonwealth titles were formerly known as British Empire titles.)

Tom Thomas, Penygraig:	British middleweight title, London, 23 May 1906.
Jim Driscoll, Cardiff:	British featherweight title, London, 1 June 1907.
Joe White, Cardiff:	British welterweight title, Cardiff, 8 August 1907. (Title disputed.)
Jim Driscoll, Cardiff:	Commonwealth featherweight title, London, 24 February 1908. (This was the first ever Commonwealth title to be won by anyone at any weight.)
Freddie Welsh, Pontypridd:	European lightweight title, Mountain Ash, 23 August 1909.
Freddie Welsh, Pontypridd:	British lightweight title, London, 8 November 1909.
Jim Driscoll, Cardiff:	European featherweight title, London, 3 June 1912.
Freddie Welsh, Pontypridd:	Commonwealth lightweight title, London, 16 December 1912.
Bill Beynon, Taibach:	British bantamweight title, London, 2 June 1913.

Percy Jones, Porthcawl:	British and European featherweight titles and disputed world title, London, 26 January 1914.
Jimmy Wilde, Tylorstown:	European flyweight title, London, 30 March 1914.
Johnny Basham, Newport:	British welterweight title, London, 14 December 1914.
Llew Edwards, Porth:	British featherweight title, London, 31 May 1915.
Llew Edwards, Porth:	Commonwealth featherweight title, Sydney, 18 December 1915.
Jimmy Wilde, Tylorstown:	British flyweight title, Liverpool, 14 February 1916.
Johnny Basham, Newport:	Commonwealth welterweight title, London, 13 November 1919.
Johnny Basham, Newport:	British and European middleweight titles, London, 31 May 1921.
Frank Moody, Pontypridd:	British middleweight title, London, 16 February 1927.
Billy 'Gypsy' Daniels, Newport:	British and Commonwealth light heavyweight titles, London, 25 April 1927.
Frank Moody, Pontypridd:	British light heavyweight title, London, 27 November 1927.
Jack Petersen, Cardiff:	British light heavyweight title, London, 23 May 1932.
Jack Petersen, Cardiff:	British heavyweight title, London, 12 July 1932.
Jack Petersen, Cardiff:	Commonwealth heavyweight title, London, 4 June 1934.
Tommy Farr, Penygraig:	British and Commonwealth heavyweight titles, London, 15 March 1937.
Ronnie James, Pontardawe:	British lightweight title, Cardiff, 12 August 1944.
Eddie Thomas, Merthyr Tydfil:	British welterweight title, London, 15 November 1949.
Eddie Thomas, Merthyr Tydfil:	Commonwealth welterweight title, Johannesburg, 27 January 1951.
Eddie Thomas, Merthyr Tydfil:	European welterweight title, Carmarthen, 19 February 1951.
Johnny Williams, Barmouth and Rugby:	British and Commonwealth heavyweight titles, London, 11 March 1952.
Cliff Curvis, Swansea:	British and Commonwealth welterweight titles, Liverpool, 24 July 1952.
Dennis Powell, Four Crosses, Powys:	British light heavyweight title, Liverpool, 26 March 1953.
Dai Dower, Abercynon:	Commonwealth flyweight title, London, 19 October 1954.
Dai Dower, Abercynon:	British flyweight title, London, 7 February 1953.
Dai Dower, Abercynon:	European flyweight title, London, 8 March 1955.
Joe Erskine, Cardiff:	British heavyweight title, Cardiff, 27 August 1956.
Joe Erskine, Cardiff:	Commonwealth heavyweight title, Leicester, 25 November 1957.

Dick Richardson, Newport: European heavyweight title, Dortmund, 27 March 1960.
Brian Curvis, Swansea: Commonwealth welterweight title, Swansea, 9 May 1960.
Brian Curvis, Swansea: British welterweight title, Nottingham, 21 November 1960.
Howard Winstone,
Merthyr Tydfil: British featherweight title, London, 2 May 1961.
Howard Winstone,
Merthyr Tydfil: European featherweight title, Cardiff, 9 July 19963.
Eddie Avoth, Cardiff: British light heavyweight title, London, 13 January 1969.
Eddie Avoth, Cardiff: Commonwealth lightweight title, Brisbane, 23 October 1970.
Pat Thomas, Cardiff: British welterweight title, London, 15 December 1975.
Johnny Owen,
Merthyr Tydfil: British bantamweight title, London, 29 November 1977.
Johnny Owen,
Merthyr Tydfil: Commonwealth bantamweight title, Ebbw Vale,
2 November 1978.
Pat Thomas, Cardiff: British light middleweight title, London, 11 September
1979.
Johnny Owen,
Merthyr Tydfil: European bantamweight title, Ebbw Vale, 28 February
1980.
Colin Jones, Gorseinon: British welterweight title, London, 1 April 1980.
Colin Jones, Gorseinon: Commonwealth welterweight title, London, 3 March 1981.
Colin Jones, Gorseinon: European welterweight title, Copenhagen, 5 November 1982
Neville Meade, Swansea: British heavyweight title, Birmingham, 12 October 1981.
David Pearce, Newport: British heavyweight title, Cardiff, 22 September 1983.
Robert Dickie, Carmarthen: British featherweight title, London, 9 April 1986.
Peter Harris, Swansea British featherweight title, Aberavon, 24 February 1988.
Floyd Havard, Clydach: British super featherweight title, Aberavon, 18 May 1988.
Robert Dickie, Carmarthen: British super featherweight title, Cardiff, 3 March 1991.
Robbie Regan, Blackwood: British flyweight title, Cardiff, 28 May 1991.
Neil Haddock, Llanelli: British super featherweight title, Bury, 13 October 1992.
Robbie Regan, Blackwood: European flyweight title, Cardiff, 14 November 1992.

Welsh Boxers Losing World Title Fights

Freddie Welsh: lost his world lightweight title in New York, 28 May 1917.
Jimmy Wilde: lost his world flyweight title in New York, 18 June 1923.
Tommy Farr: lost the world heavyweight title fight in New York, 30 August 1937.
Ronnie James: lost the world lightweight title fight in Cardiff, 4 September 1945.
Dai Dower: lost the world flyweight title fight in Buenos Aires, 30 March 1957.

Brian Curvis: lost the world welterweight title fight in London, 22 September 1964.
Howard Winstone: lost the world featherweight title fight in London, 7 September 1965.
Howard Winstone: lost the world featherweight title fight in Cardiff, 15 June 1967.
Howard Winstone: lost the world featherweight title fight in Mexico City, 14 October 1967.
Howard Winstone: lost his world featherweight title in Porthcawl, 24 July 1968.
Johnny Owen: lost the world bantamweight title fight in Los Angeles, 19 September, 1980.
Colin Jones: lost the world bantamweight title fight in Las Vegas, 13 August 1983.
Colin Jones: lost the world welterweight title fight in Birmingham, 19 January 1985.
Nicky Piper: lost the world super middleweight (World Boxing Council) title fight in London, 12 December 1992.
Floyd Havard: lost the world super featherweight (International Boxing Federation) title fight in Cardiff, 22 January 1994.
Nicky Piper: lost the light heavyweight (World Boxing Organization) title fight in Cardiff, 29 January 1994.

Lonsdale Belts

The first Lonsdale Belt ever awarded at any weight was to Freddie Welsh on winning the European lightweight title in 1909.

Other Lonsdale Belt holders from Wales have been: Jimmy Wilde, Jim Driscoll, Johnny Basham, Jack Petersen, Brian Curvis, Colin Jones, Johnny Owen, Pat Thomas, Robert Dickie and Robbie Regan.

COMMONWEALTH GAMES

Welsh Medal Table

		Gold	Silver	Bronze	Total
1930	Hamilton, Canada	–	2	1	3
1934	London	–	3	3	6
1938	Sydney, Australia	2	1	–	3
1950	Auckland, New Zealand	–	1	–	1
1954	Vancouver, Canada	1	1	5	7
1958	Cardiff	1	3	7	11
1962	Perth, Australia	–	2	4	6
1966	Kingston, Jamaica	3	2	2	7
1970	Edinburgh	2	6	4	12
1974	Christchurch, New Zealand	1	5	4	10

		Gold	Silver	Bronze	Total
1978	Edmonton, Canada	2	1	5	8
1982	Brisbane, Australia	4	4	1	9
1986	Edinburgh	6	5	12	23
1990	Auckland, New Zealand	10	3	12	25
1994	Victoria, Canada	5	6	6	17

The Top Ten Medal-Winning Countries in the 1994 Commonwealth Games

		Gold	Silver	Bronze	Total
1.	Australia	84	53	41	178
2.	Canada	38	41	49	128
3.	England	31	41	47	119
4.	Nigeria	12	13	13	38
5.	Kenya	7	4	8	19
6.	India	6	11	6	23
7.	Wales	5	6	6	17
8.	Scotland	5	3	10	18
9.	Northern Ireland	5	2	3	10
10.	New Zealand	4	16	17	37

CRICKET

County Cricket Championship

Glamorgan won in 1948 and 1969

2nd XI County Cricket Championship

Glamorgan won in 1965 and 1980

Gillete (now NatWest) Cup Final

Glamorgan lost to Middlesex at Lords in 1977

Sunday League Championship

Glamorgan won in 1993

Glamorgan Players Capped for England

Maurice Turnbull:	9 caps, 1930–31	Jeff Jones:	15 caps, 1963–67
J. C. Clay:	1 cap in 1935	Tony Lewis:*	9 caps, 1972–73
A. D. G. Matthews:	1 cap in 1937	Greg Thomas:	5 caps in 1986
Allan Watkins:	15 caps, 1948–52	Matthew Maynard:	first cap in 1988
Jim McConnon:	2 caps in 1954	Steve Watkin:	first cap in 1991
Gilbert Parkhouse:	9 caps, 1956–59	Hugh Morris:	first cap in 1991
Peter Walker:	3 caps in 1960		

*Captained England

Cyril Frederick Walters from Bedlinog was capped 11 times for England between 1933 and 1935 while playing for Worcestershire and captained England in one Test Match in 1934 – v. Australia at Trent Bridge.

Village Championship Trophy (played at Lords)

Gowerton won in 1975.
Marchwiel, Clwyd, won in 1980 and 1984.
St Fagans won in 1981, 1982 and 1991.

CYCLING

Sally McKenzie (née Hodge), Cardiff, won a gold medal at the world track cycling championships at Ghent, Belgium, in 1988.

DARTS

World Cup

1977   Won by Wales (Inaugural year of the competition)

Individual world title

1977   Leighton Rees (First holder of the title)

World Masters

1965   Alan Evans (First holder of the title)

Home International Series

1975, 1977   Won by Wales

British Open Championship

1975   Alan Evans
1989   Brian Cairns

Women's World Masters

1982   Ann-Marie Davies
1987   Ann Thomas

Women's British Open Championship

1981   Ann-Marie Davies
1984   Ann-Marie Davies

FENCING

1977   Wales won the Quadrangular Tournament
1980   Wales won the Winton Cup

FIGURE SKATING

British Championship – Men's Figure Skating

1989, 1990, 1991, 1992, 1993   Won by Steven Cousins

GOLF

World Match-Play Title

1987 and 1990   Ian Woosnam

US Masters

1991   Ian Woosnam

World Cup (formerly the Canada Cup

1987   Won by Wales (Ian Woosnam and David Llywelyn) in Hawaii.
1991   Wales (Ian Woosnam and Phillip Price) finished second to Sweden in Rome.

European Open Championship

1988   Ian Woosnam

British Masters

1994   Ian Woosnam

British Open Championship

1953   Dai Rees finished second to Ben Hogan
1954   Dai Rees finished second to Peter Thomson
1961   Dai Rees finished joint second behind Arnold Palmer

Ryder Cup

1957   Dai Rees captained the winning British Ryder Cup team

European Amateur Championship

1993   Wales won the Men's Team Championship in the Czech Republic

British Amateur Championship

1980   Duncan Evans (First ever Welsh winner)
1983   Philip Parker
1987   Paul Mayo
1989   Stephen Dodd

GREYHOUND RACING

The only Welsh 'Classic' was the Welsh Greyhound Derby. This was run at the Cardiff 'White City', Sloper Road, from 1928 to 1944 and from 1945 to 1977 at Cardiff Arms Park.

GYMNASTICS

British Champions from Wales (Men)

1922, 1923, 1924:	Stanley Leigh, Swansea YMCA
1928, 1929, 1930, 1931, 1932,	
1933, 1934, 1935, 1936, 1939:	Arthur Whitford, Swansea and Sketty Olympic
1947, 1948:	Jack Whitford, Sketty Olympic
1967:	Bobby Williams, Swansea YMCA
1983, 1984, 1986, 1987:	Andrew Morris, Swansea YMCA

British Champions from Wales (Women)

1951:	Cissie Davies, Swansea YWCA
1957, 1958:	Margaret Neale, Cardiff Olympic
1965:	Denise Goddard, Cardiff Olympic
1971:	Pam Hopkins, Penarth

HORSE RACING

Welsh Winning Jockeys in the Grand National

1911	Jack Anthony, Kidwelly, on 'Glenside'
1915	Jack Anthony, Kidwelly, on 'Ally Sloper'
1920	Jack Anthony, Kidwelly, on 'Troytown'
1921	Brychan Rees, Tenby, on 'Shaun Spadah'
1922	Lewis Rees, Tenby, on 'Music Hall'
1933	Dudley Williams, Nantgaredig, on 'Kellsboro Jack'
1936	Fulke Walwyn, Monmouth, on 'Reynoldstown'
1937	Evans Williams, Cowbridge, on 'Royal Mail' (This was the hundredth Grand National and the horse was also Welsh-owned and Welsh-trained.)
1940	Mervyn Jones, Carmarthen, on 'Bogskar'
1984	Neil Doughty, Kenfig Hill, on 'Hallo Dandy'
1985	Hywel Davies, Cardigan, on 'Last Suspect'
1992	Carl Llewellyn, Pembroke, on 'Party Politics'

The 1919 winner, 'Poethlyn', was Welsh-owned and Welsh-trained.

Welsh Winning Jockeys in the Derby, Oaks, 1,000 Guineas and 2,000 Guineas

1969	Geoff Lewis, Talgarth, on 'Right Track' (2,000 Guineas)
1971	Geoff Lewis, Talgarth, on 'Mill Reef' (Derby)
1971	Geoff Lewis, Talgarth, on 'Altesse Royal' (Oaks)
1973	Geoff Lewis, Talgarth, on 'Mysterious' (Oaks)
1973	Geoff Lewis, Talgarth, on 'Mysterious' (1,000 Guineas)
1994	Jason Weaver, Portskewett, on 'Mister Baileys' (2,000 Guineas)

The only Welsh horse to have won the Derby was 'George Frederick' in 1874, owned by William Sheward Cartwright of Cardiff.

ICE HOCKEY

Premier Division Championship

| 1989–90 | Cardiff Devils | 1993–94 | Cardiff Devils |
| 1992–93 | Cardiff Devils | | |

Champions Cup

| 1989–90 | Cardiff Devils | 1993–94 | Cardiff Devils |
| 1992–93 | Cardiff Devils | | |

Benson and Hedges Cup

(Formerly the Autumn Cup)

| 1992 | Cardiff Devils |
| 1993 | Cardiff Devils |

OLYMPIC GAMES – MEDAL WINNERS FROM WALES

Individual Medals

Lynn Davies	Long jump gold, 1964 (Tokyo)
Richard Meade	Equestrian gold, 1972 (Munich)
Tom Richards	Marathon silver, 1948 (London)
Martin Woodroffe	200 m. butterfly silver, 1968 (Mexico City)

Colin Jackson	110 m. hurdles silver, 1988 (Seoul)
John Disley	Steeplechase bronze, 1952 (Helsinki)
David Broome	Equestrian bronze, 1952 (Helsinki)
David Broome	Equestrian bronze, 1960 (Rome)

Team Medals

Paul Radmilovic	Water polo gold 1908 (London), 1912 (Stockholm), 1920 (Antwerp) 4 x 200 m. freestyle gold, 1908 (London)
David Jacobs	4 x 100 m. relay gold, 1912 (Stockholm)
Irene Steer	4 x 100 m. freestyle gold, 1912 (Stockholm)
John Ainsworth-Davis	4 x 100 m. relay gold, 1920 (Antwerp)
Christopher Jones	Water polo gold, 1920 (Antwerp)
Sir Harry Llewellyn	Equestrian gold, 1952 (Helsinki)
Richard Meade	Equestrian gold, 1968 (Mexico City)
Richard Meade	Equestrian gold, 1972 (Munich)
Robert Clift	Hockey gold, 1988 (Seoul)
Valerie Davies	4 x 100 m. freestyle bronze, 1932 (Los Angeles)
Sir Harry Llewellyn	Equestrian bronze, 1948 (London)
Graham Dadds	Hockey bronze, 1952 (Helsinki)
Nick Whitehead	4 x 100 m. relay bronze, 1960 (Rome)
Michelle Probert	4 x 100 m. relay bronze, 1980 (Moscow)
Robert Cottrell	Hockey bronze, 1984 (Los Angeles)
Helen Morgan	Hockey bronze, 1992 (Barcelona)

Paul Radmilovic competed in six Olympics between 1906 and 1928 including the intermediate Olympics of 1906. David Broome competed in five Olympics between 1960 and 1988 – he did not compete in 1992 because of injury, although selected.

Ron Jones was the British Olympic Athletics team captain in 1968.

PARALYMPICS 1992 (BARCELONA): MEDAL WINNERS FROM WALES

Gold Medals

Women's 100 metres	Tanni Grey	Women's 500 metres	Tanni Grey
Women's 200 metres	Tanni Grey	Men's 1,500 metres	John Nethercott
Women's 400 metres	Tanni Grey		

Silver Medals

Women's 200 metres Tracey Hinton   Men's Individual Table Tennis   Neil Robinson
Women's 400 metres Tracey Hinton

Bronze Medals

Men's 100 metres   Chris Hallam   Women's 100 metres   Tracey Hinton
Men's 800 metres   John Nethercott

POWERBOAT RACING

World Formula One Championship

Jonathan Jones   1968, 1989, 1991

ROWING

World Championships

Tonia Williams   Crew member, lightweight women's coxless fours,   Gold 1993
                                                                      Silver 1992

RUGBY LEAGUE

Welsh Record in International Matches, 1908–1994

Opponents	Played	Won	Lost	Drawn
England	59	15	42	2
France	31	13	18	0
Australia	9	0	9	0
New Zealand	7	3	4	0
Other Nationalities	5	1	4	0
Papua New Guinea	1	1	0	0

In beating Papua New Guinea 68–0 at Swansea in November, 1991, Wales established a world record victory in a Rugby League international.

World Cup

In 1975, in their only World Cup appearance, Wales finished third of the five competing nations.

European Championship
(England, France, Wales and Other Nationalities competing)
(22 seasons between 1935 and 1981 for the Jean Galia Trophy)

Wales won in 1936, 1937 and 1938.

Most Capped Welsh Rugby League International

Jim Sullivan (Wigan), 60 caps: for Wales 26, and for Great Britain 34, 1921–1946

Fastest 1,000 Points Scorer

Jonathan Davies (Widnes) 1989–1991

RUGBY UNION

World Cup

1987:   Wales finished third in the inaugural event in New Zealand.

Five Nations Championship

Grand Slam wins

1907–1908	1951–1952	No. of wins:	England	10
1908–1909	1970–1971		Wales	8
1910–1911	1975–1976		France	4
1949–1950	1977–1978		Scotland	3
			Ireland	1

Triple Crown wins

1892–1893	1910–1911	1975–1976	No. of wins:	England	17
1899–1900	1949–1950	1976–1977		Wales	17
1901–1902	1951–1952	1977–1978		Scotland	10
1904–1905	1964–1965	1978–1979		Ireland	6
1907–1908	1968–1969	1987–1988			
1908–1909	1970–1971				

Championship wins
1892–1893
1899–1900
1901–1902
1904–1905
1905–1906 (shared with Ireland)
1907–1908
1908–1909
1910–1911
1919–1920 (shared with England and Scotland)
1921–1922
1930–1931
1931–1932 (shared with England and Ireland)
1935–1936
1938–1939 (shared with England and Ireland)
1946–1947 (shared with England)
1949–1950
1951–1952
1953–1954 (shared with England and France)
1954–1955 (shared with France)
1955–1956
1963–1964 (shared with Scotland)
1964–1965
1965–1966
1968–1969
1969–1970 (shared with France)
1970–1971
1972–1973 (five-way tie)
1974–1975
1975–1976
1977–1978
1978–1979
1987–1988 (shared with France)
1993–1994

Five Nations Championship Outright Winners

Wales	22	France	10
England	20	Ireland	10
Scotland	13		

Welsh Record Against International Board Sides
(Results to March 1994)

Opponents	Played	Won	Lost	Drawn
England	100	48	40	12
Scotland	98	54	42	2
Ireland	97	58	33	6
France	68	37	28	3
Australia	16	8	8	0
New Zealand	15	3	12	0
South Africa	7	0	6	1

Welsh Record Against Non-International Board Sides When Caps were Awarded
(Results to October 1994)

Opponents	Played	Won	Lost	Drawn
Argentina	1	1	0	0
Canada	3	2	1	0
Fiji	3	3	0	0
Italy	1	1	0	0
Japan	1	1	0	0
Namibia	3	3	0	0
Portugal	1	1	0	0
Romania	3	1	2	0
Spain	1	1	0	0
Tonga	3	3	0	0
Western Samoa	4	2	2	0
Zimbabwe	2	2	0	0

Welsh Rugby Union Cup Winners

1972	Neath (Inaugural year)	1980	Bridgend	1988	Llanelli
1973	Llanelli	1981	Cardiff	1989	Neath
1974	Llanelli	1982	Cardiff	1990	Neath
1975	Llanelli	1983	Pontypool	1991	Llanelli
1976	Llanelli	1984	Cardiff	1992	Llanelli
1977	Newport	1985	Llanelli	1993	Llanelli
1978	Swansea	1986	Cardiff	1994	Cardiff
1979	Bridgend	1987	Cardiff		

Most frequent winners

Llanelli	9	Neath	3
Cardiff	6		

Welsh Rugby Union League Champions

1990–1991 (Inaugural year)

Premier Division	Neath
Division One	Newport
Division Two	Dunvant
Division Three	Llandovery

1991–1992

Division One	Swansea
Division Two	South Wales Police
Division Three	Tenby United
Division Four	Tumble

1992–1993

Division One	Llanelli
Division Two	Dunvant
Division Three	Treorchy Rhondda
Division Four	Tondu

1993–1994

Division One	Swansea
Division Two	Treorchy Rhondda
Division Three	Abercynon
Division Four	Builth Wells

Most-capped Welsh Players

(to September 1994)

J. P. R. Williams	55 caps (plus 8 British Lions caps)	1969–81
Gareth Edwards	53 caps (plus 10 British Lions caps)	1967–78
Gerald Davies	46 caps (plus 5 British lions caps)	1966–78
Phil Davies	44 caps	1985–
Ken Jones	44 caps	1947–57
Graham Price	41 caps (plus 12 British Lions caps)	1975–83

Leading Try Scorers in International Matches

(to September 1994)

Ieuan Evans	21	Gareth Edwards	20
Gerald Davies	20		

SHOWJUMPING

World Showjumping Champion

1961   David Broome, Crick, on 'Sunsalve'
1967   David Broome, Crick, on 'Mister Softee'
1969   David Broome, Crick, on 'Mister Softee'

SNOOKER

World Professional Champion

1970, 1973, 1974, 1975, 1976, 1978	Ray Reardon
1979	Terry Griffiths

World Amateur Champion

1976   Doug Mountjoy (Johannesburg)
1978   Cliff Wilson (Malta)
1982   Terry Parsons (Calgary)
1987   Darren Morgan (New Delhi)

World Cup

Wales won in 1979 and 1980

UK Open Championship

1978	Doug Mountjoy	1988	Doug Mountjoy
1982	Terry Griffiths		

British Open Championship

1983   Doug Mountjoy

Benson and Hedges Masters

1976   Ray Reardon   1980   Terry Griffiths
1977   Doug Mountjoy

Mercantile Classic

1982   Terry Griffiths   1989   Doug Mountjoy

SPEEDWAY

World Championship

1950 and 1953   Freddie Williams

SQUASH

British Squash League Championship

1990, 1992, 1994   Leekes Welsh Wizards

TENNIS

1960   British hard-court champion, Mike Davies, Swansea. (The first Welsh holder of the title.)
1964   British junior champion, British covered-court champion and French junior champion, Gerald Battrik, Bridgend.
1966   British junior Wimbledon champion, J. P. R. Williams, Bridgend.
1967   British under-21 champion, Gerald Battrick, Bridgend.
1988   Prudential Great Britain Senior National Championship, Sarah Loosemore, Dinas Powys.

FORMATION OF WELSH SPORTING BODIES AND
DEVELOPMENTS IN WELSH SPORT

1802	Royal Anglesey Yacht Club (Beaumaris)
1847	Royal Welsh Yacht Club (Caernarfon)
1876	Football Association of Wales (Wrexham)
1878	Football Association of Wales Welsh Cup
1881	Welsh Rugby Union (Neath)
1890	Welsh Hockey Association
1893	First Welsh athletics championships (men only)
1895	Welsh Golfing Union
1895	Welsh amateur golf championship
1895	Welsh Grand National
1897	Welsh amateur Swimming Association
1897	First Welsh swimming championships (men only)
1898	Welsh Women's Hockey Association
1902	Welsh Amateur gymnastics association
1904	Welsh professional golf championship
1904	Welsh Ladies Golf Union
1904	Welsh Bowling Association
1907	Welsh open bowls championship
1910	Welsh Amateur Boxing Association
1921	Glamorgan admitted to County Cricket Championship
1921	Table Tennis Association of Wales
1925	Welsh Lawn Tennis Association
1926	South Wales and Monmouthshire Cricket Association
1927	Welsh Baseball Union
1927	Welsh Amateur Weight-Lifting Association
1928	Welsh Badminton Union
1928	Welsh Greyhound Derby
1929	Football Association of Wales's first overseas tour (Canada)
1930	Welsh Ladies Lacrosse Association
1932	Welsh Women's Bowling Association
1934	Welsh Indoor Bowls Association
1938	Welsh Squash Racquets Association
1944	British Mountaineering Council (Welsh Committee)
1945	Welsh Netball Association
1947	British Horse Society (Welsh Committee)
1947	Welsh Amateur Fencing Union
1948	Welsh Amateur Athletics Association

1949	Welsh Youth Rugby Union
1949	Welsh Rugby League
1951	Cambrian Association of Welsh Motor Cycle Clubs
1952	First Welsh athletics championships for women
1952	Welsh Ladies Indoor Bowls Association
1953	Welsh Salmon and Trout Angling Association
1955	Basketball Association of Wales
1959	First Welsh Games
1963	Welsh Water Ski Association
1964	Welsh Yachting Association
1964	Welsh Rugby Union's first overseas tour (South Africa)
1966	Welsh Trampolining Association
1967	Welsh Tug-of-War Association
1967	Welsh Orienteering Association
1968	Welsh Cricket Association
1969	Cambrian Caving Council
1969	Welsh Small Bore Union
1970	Welsh Anglers Council
1971	Ski Council for Wales
1971	Welsh Association of Sub-Aqua Clubs
1971	Welsh Surfing Federation
1972	Welsh Rugby Union Cup
1971	Welsh Judo Association
1972	Sports Council for Wales
1972	Welsh Sports Association
1972	National Sports Centre (Cardiff)
1973	Welsh Cycling Union
1974	Welsh Curling Association
1975	Welsh Archery Federation
1976	Welsh Canoeing Association
1977	Welsh Hang Gliding Association
1977	Welsh Federation of Coarse Anglers
1979	Welsh Quoiting Board
1979	National Lawn Tennis Centre (Cardiff)
1980	Welsh Karate Federation
1980	National Outdoor Pursuits Centre (Plas-y-Deri, Menai Strait)
1981	Welsh Volleyball Association
1984	National Stadium, Cardiff Arms Park, completed
1984	Welsh Triathlon
1985	Welsh Amateur Rowing Association

1985   Welsh Ice Skating Association
1986   Wales National Ice Rink (Cardiff)
1989   Welsh Sports Hall of Fame opened (Cardiff)
1990   Federation of Sports Associations for the Disabled (Wales)
1990   Athletics Association of Wales
1990   Welsh Rugby Union National League introduced
1992   Football Association of Wales League of Wales introduced
1992   Sports Science and Sports Medicine Centre (Cardiff)
1992   Welsh Institute of Sports (Cardiff) – formerly the National Sports Centre

WELSH SPORTING HONOURS

BBC Wales/'Western Mail' Welsh Sports Personality of the Year

(Inaugurated in 1954)

1954	Ken Jones (athletics, rugby)	1974	Gareth Edwards (rugby)
1955	John Disley (athletics)	1975	Arfon Griffiths (football)
1956	Joe Erskine (boxing)	1976	Mervyn Davies (rugby)
1957	Dai Rees (golf)	1977	Phil Bennett (rugby)
1958	Howard Winstone (boxing)	1978	Johnny Owen (boxing)
1959	Graham Moore (football)	1979	Terry Griffiths (snooker)
1960	Brian Curvis (boxing)	1980	Duncan Evans (golf)
1961	Bryn Meredith (rugby)	1981	John Toshack (football)
1962	Ivor Allchurch (football)	1982	Steve Barry (athletics)
1963	Howard Winstone (boxing)	1983	Colin Jones (boxing)
1964	Lynn Davies (athletics)	1984	Ian Rush (football)
1965	Clive Rowlands (rugby)	1985	Steve Jones (athletics)
1966	Lynn Davies (athletics)	1986	Kirsty Wade (athletics)
1967	Howard Winstone (boxing)	1987	Ian Woosnam (golf)
1968	Martyn Woodroffe (swimming)	1988	Colin Jackson (athletics)
1969	Tony Lewis (cricket)	1989	Stephen Dodd (golf)
1970	David Broome (equestrianism)	1990	Ian Woosnam (golf)
1971	John Dawes (rugby)	1991	Ian Woosnam (golf)
1972	Richard Meade (equestrianism)	1992	Tanni Grey (paraplegic athletics)
1973	Berwyn Price (athletics)	1993	Colin Jackson (athletics)

Welsh Sports Hall of Fame – Roll of Honour

(At the Welsh Folk Museum, St Fagans, Cardiff)

Jack Anthony (horse racing)
Billy Boston (rugby league)
David Broome (equestrianism)
John Charles (football)
Gerald Davies (rugby union)
Lynn Davies (athletics)
Jim Driscoll (boxing)
Tanni Grey (paraplegic athletics)
Cliff Jones (rugby union)
Ken Jones (rugby union and athletics)
George Latham (football)
Valerie Latham (née Davies) (swimming)
Sir Harry Llewellyn (equestrianism)
Billy Meredith (football)

Cliff Morgan (rugby union)
Sheila Morrow (hockey)
Jack Petersen (boxing)
Paul Radmilovic (swimming)
Ray Reardon (snooker)
Dai Rees (golf)
Irene Steer (swimming)
Jim Sullivan (rugby league)
Eddie Thomas (boxing)
Maurice Turnbull (cricket)
Kirsty Wade (athletics)
Freddie Welsh (boxing)
Jimmy Wilde (boxing)
J. P. R. Williams (rugby union)

14

DISASTERS, BATTLES, DEATHS AND DISTURBANCES

COAL MINING ACCIDENTS (WITH FIVE OR MORE DEATHS)

(Caused by explosions unless otherwise stated and listed by the number of fatalities)

Date	Mine/Location	Deaths
1913, 14 October	Universal Colliery, Senghenydd, Mid Glamorgan	439
1894, 23 June	Albion Colliery, Cilfynydd, Mid Glamorgan	290
1878, 11 September	Prince of Wales Colliery, Abercarn, Gwent	268
1934, 22 September	Gresford Colliery, Wrexham	265
1867, 8 November	Ferndale Colliery, Rhondda	178
1890, 6 February	Llanerch Colliery, Pontypool	176
1860, 1 December	Risca Colliery, Gwent	142
1880, 15 July	New Risca Colliery, Gwent	120
1905, 11 July	National Colliery, Wattstown, Rhondda	119
1856, 15 July	New Cymmer Pit, Porth, Rhondda	114
1892, 26 August	Park Slip colliery, Tondu, Mid Glamorgan	112
1880, 10 December	Penygraig Colliery, Rhondda	101
1890, 10 March	Morfa Colliery, Taibach, Port Talbot	86
1879, 22 September	Waunllwyd, Ebbw Vale	84
1885, 24 December	Maerdy, Rhondda	81
1901, 24 May	Universal Colliery, Senghenydd, Mid Glamorgan	81
1852, 10 May	Middle Duffryn Colliery, Mountain Ash	65
1893, 11 April	Great Western Colliery, Pontypridd (Deaths caused by an underground fire)	63
1879, 13 January	Dinas Colliery, Rhondda	63
1878, 1 September	Abercarn, Gwent	62
1896, 28 January	Tylorstown Colliery, Rhondda	57
1869, 10 June	Ferndale Colliery, Rhondda	53
1849, 11 August	Lletty Shenkin Colliery, Aberdare	52

1927, 1 March	Marine Colliery, Cwm, Ebbw Vale	52
1862, 19 February	Gethin Colliery, Merthyr Tydfil	47
1960, 28 June	Six Bells Colliery, Aberbeeg, Gwent	45
1844, 14 February	Landshipping, Pembrokeshire	40
	(Deaths caused by flooding)	
1863, 17 October	Morfa Colliery, Taibach, Port Talbot	39
1887, 18 February	National Colliery, Wattstown, Rhondda	39
1871, 24 February	Pentre Colliery, Rhondda	38
1865, 16 June	New Bedwellty Colliery, Tredegar	36
1846, 14 January	Risca, Gwent	35
1865, 20 December	Upper Gethin Colliery, Merthyr Tydfil	34
1905, 10 March	Cambrian Colliery, Clydach Vale, Rhondda	33
1965, 17 May	Cambrian Colliery, Clydach Vale, Rhondda	31
1870, 10 February	Morfa Colliery, Taibach, Port Talbot	30
1852, 10 May	Gwendraeth Colliery, Pontyberem, Dyfed	27
	(Deaths caused by an inundation of quicksand)	
1859, 5 April	Neath Chain Colliery	26
	(Deaths caused by flooding)	
1909, 29 October	Darren Colliery, New Tredegar	26
1845, 2 August	Cwmbach, Aberdare	26
1875, 4 December	Old Pit, New Tredegar	22
1836, 10 May	Plas-yr-Argoed, Mold	21
1837, 17 June	Henwain Colliery, Blaina, Gwent	21
1858, 13 October	Lower Duffryn Colliery, Mountain Ash	20
1889, 13 March	Brynally Colliery, Pentre Broughton, Clwyd	20
1876, 18 December	South Wales Pit, Abertillery, Gwent	20
1872, 2 March	Victoria Colliery, Ebbw Vale	19
1874, 24 July	Charles Colliery, Llansamlet, West Glamorgan	19
1899, 18 August	Llest Colliery, Garw Valley	19
1877, 8 March	Worcester Pit, Swansea	17
1902, 3 September	McLaren Colliery, Swansea	16
1941, 11 July	Rhigos, Mid Glamorgan	16
1851, 4 September	Werfa Colliery, Aberdare	14
	(Shaft accident)	
1858, 13 October	Primrose Colliery, Ystalyfera	14
	(Suffocation by gas)	
1863, 26 December	Gin Pit, Maesteg	14
1884, 27 January	Naval Steam Colliery, Penygraig, Rhondda	14
1884, 8 November	Pochin Colliery, Tredegar	14
1850, 14 December	New Duffryn Colliery, Mountain Ash	13

1856, 20 September	Brynally Colliery, Pentre Broughton, Clwyd	13
	(Deaths caused by flooding)	
1861, 3 March	Blaengwawr Colliery, Aberdare	13
1844, 1 January	Dinas Middle Colliery, Rhondda	12
1863, 11 December	Green Pit, Rhiwabon, Clwyd	12
1875, 5 December	Llan Colliery, Pentyrch, Mid Glamorgan	12
1901, 10 September	Llanbradach, Mid Glamorgan	12
1856, 3 July	Old Coal Pit, Coalbrookvale, Nantyglo, Gwent	11
1872, 11 January	Oakwood No.1 Colliery, Maesteg	11
1848, 21 June	Victoria Colliery, Ebbw Vale	11
1905, 21 January	Elba Colliery, Gowerton	11
1932, 25 January	Glamorgan Colliery, Llwynypia, Rhondda	11
1853, 12 March	Risca Vale, Gwent	10
1884, 16 January	Garnant Colliery, Cwmaman	10
	(Shaft accident)	
1879, 11 June	Garth Colliery, Llynfi Valley	9
	(Shaft accident)	
1880, 3 August	Bersham Colliery, Clwyd	9
1923, 26 April	Trimsaran, Dyfed	9
1929, 10 July	Milfraen, Blaenafon, Gwent	9
1960, 12 April	Tower Colliery, Hirwaun	9
1844, 13 May	Broadmoor, Loveston, Dyfed	8
	(Shaft accident)	
1902, 4 June	Fochriw, Mid Glamorgan	8
1902, 1 October	Tirpentwys Colliery, Gwent	8
1869, 23 May	Llanerch Colliery, Pontypool	7
1873, 24 April	Wynnstay Colliery, Wrexham	7
1896, 4 August	Bryncoed Colliery, Neath	7
1907, 11 December	Dinas Main Colliery, Gilfach Goch, Mid Glamorgan	7
1929, 28 November	Wernbwll Colliery, Penclawdd	7
1936, 26 May	Loveston Colliery near Haverfordwest	7
	(Deaths caused by flooding)	
1956, 22 November	Lewis Merthyr Colliery, Trehafod, Rhondda	7
1844, 3 December	Fforest Level, Dinas, Rhondda	6
1863, 26 June	Park Colliery near Neath	6
1874, 5 April	Tillery Colliery, Abertillery	6
1879, 24 June	Meadow Pit, Cwmavon	6
1883, 11 February	Coedcae Colliery, Trehafod, Rhondda	6
1892, 24 August	Ynyscedwyn Colliery, Swansea Valley	6
	(Underground tramway accident)	

1895, 9 September	Tynybedw Colliery, Pentre, Rhondda	6
	Dowlais Cardiff Colliery, Aberdare	6
	(Both shaft accidents)	
1896, 9 December	River Level Pit, Abernant, Aberdare	6
	(Deaths caused by flooding)	
1902, 3 June	Gerwen Colliery, Llanelli	6
1907, March 5	Windsor Colliery, Abertridwr	6
	(shaft accident)	
1952, 5 July	Point of Ayr Colliery, Clwyd	6
1955, 6 September	Blaenhirwaun Colliery, Cross Hands	6
1971, 6 April	Cynheidre Colliery, Llanelli	6
1754, October	Llangyfelach, West Glamorgan	5
1786, 15 August	Engine Pit, Llantwit, Neath	5
1872, 25 January	Blackwood Colliery, Gwent	5
1873, 2 December	Hafod Colliery, Rhiwabon	5
1877, 11 April	Tynewydd Colliery, Porth, Rhondda	5
	(Deaths caused by flooding)	
1888, 14 May	Aber Colliery, Porth, Rhondda	5
1890, 20 January	Glyn Pits, Pontypool	5
1902, 4 March	Milfraen Colliery, Blaenafon	5
1902, 11 November	Deep Navigation Colliery, Mountain Ash	5
	(shaft accident)	
1907, 10 November	Seven Sisters Colliery, West Glamorgan	5
1941, 25 November	Abergorki Colliery, Treherbert, Rhondda	5

A half of all British mining disasters claiming over 100 lives occurred in Wales. Most of the worst explosions took place in the steam-coal area of east Glamorgan and west Monmouthshire (Gwent).

Annual reports by Her Majesty's Inspectors of Mines began in 1852.

MARITIME TRAGEDIES

Ship losses (with 10 or more deaths)

(Listed by number of fatalities)

A complete list of all ship losses on or near the Welsh coast is not possible and the details that follow are as accurate as records allow. All vessels are British unless otherwise stated.

| 1859, 26 October | The iron clipper *Royal Charter* was wrecked off the Anglesey coast in a ferocious gale, drowning 483 people. |

1848, 24 August	The American sailing vessel *Ocean Monarch* caught fire off Colwyn Bay killing 178 people.
1841, 20 February	The American emigrant ship *Governor Fenner* sank off Holyhead drowning 123 people.
1791, 18 December	The packet *Clermont* was wrecked off Holyhead drowning 110 people.
1915, 28 March	The liner *Falaba* was torpedoed off the Dyfed coast killing 104 people.
1823, 26 March	The packet *Alert* sank off the Skerries, Anglesey, drowning 100 people.
1939, 1 June	The submarine HMS *Thetis* sank during trials in Red Wharf Bay, Anglesey, with the loss of 99 lives.
1831, 17 August	The *Rothsay Castle* was wrecked in Conwy Bay drowning 93 people.
1917, 30 November	The liner *Apapa* was torpedoed by a German U-boat near South Stack, Anglesey, killing 77 people.
1793, late in year	The clipper *Pennsylvania* was wrecked on the Smalls drowning 75 people.
1753, 15 November	The *William and Mary* was wrecked on Pembrey Sands, Dyfed, drowning 69 people.
1760, 28 November	The Admiralty tender *Caesar* was wrecked off Pwll Du head, Gower, with the loss of at least 68 lives and possibly as many as 97.
1773, 8 January	The *Phoebe and Peggy* was wrecked off Solva, Dyfed, drowning over 60 people.
1736, late in year	In a shipwreck on Flat Holm 60 soldiers were drowned.
1817, 23 October	The *William and Mary* was wrecked on the Wolves Rock near Flat Holm drowning 54 people.
1831, 17 March	The paddle steamer *Frolic* was wrecked near Nash Point, South Glamorgan, with the loss of 51 lives.
1860, 27 February	The paddle steamer *Nimrod* was wrecked on St David's Head, Dyfed, with the loss of 45 lives.
1883, 27 January	The *James Gray* was wrecked on Tusker Rocks, Porthcawl, drowning 25 people and the *Agnes Jack* was wrecked off Port Eynon, Gower, drowning 18. (See also lifeboat losses.)
1947, 23 April	The steamship *Samtampa* was wrecked on Sker Point, Porthcawl, with the loss of its entire crew of 41. (See also lifeboat losses.)
1918, 24 February	The steamship *Renfrew* was torpedoed by a German

	U-boat off St Ann's Head, Dyfed, killing its entire crew of 40.
1941, 26 January	The Dutch vessel *Beemsterdijk* struck a mine off the Smalls, Dyfed, killing 39 of its 42 crew.
1673, 25 March	The first royal yacht, the *Mary*, was wrecked on the Skerries drowning 35 people.
1900, 28 December	The barque *Primrose Hill* was wrecked on South Stack, Holyhead, drowning 33 people.
1918, 4 February	The steamer *Treveal* was torpedoed by a German U-boat off the Skerries, Anglesey, drowning 33 people.
1882, 20 October	The steamship *Clan MacDuff* sank in a gale off Holyhead drowning 32 people.
1868, 22 January	In the Burry Estuary, 16 coastal vessels were lost in a gale with some 30 seamen drowned.
1941, 13 June	The ferry *St Patrick* was sunk by German aircraft off Strumble Head, Dyfed, with the loss of 30 lives.
1918, 5 February	The steamship *Mexico City* was torpedoed by a German U-boat off South Stack, Holyhead, killing 29 of the crew.
1918, 2 March	The steamship *Kenmare* was torpedoed by a German U-boat off the Skerries, Anglesey, with the loss of 29 crewmen.
1944, 10 December	The American Liberty ship *Dan Beard* was torpedoed by a German U-boat off Strumble Head, Dyfed, killing 29 of the crew.
1856, 6 February	The sailing ship *Great Duke* was wrecked near St Govan's Head, Dyfed, with the loss of 29 lives.
1918, 22 August	The steamship *Palmelia* was torpedoed by a German U-boat off South Stack, Holyhead, with the loss of 28 lives.
1894, 20 December	The barque *Osseo* was wrecked off Holyhead drowning its entire crew of 26.
1918, 29 January	The steamship *Ethelinda* was torpedoed by a German U-boat off the Skerries, Anglesey, killing 26 of the crew.
1921, 23 December	*The Maid of Delos* sank off the Dyfed coast drowning 26 people.
1830, 16 April	The Irish emigrant ship *Newry* was wrecked off Anglesey drowning 25 people.
1899, 29 March	The French barque *Le Marechal Lannes* was wrecked off Grassholm, Dyfed, drowning her entire crew of 25.
1941, 11 June	The cargo ship *Baron Carnegie* was sunk by German aircraft off Strumble Head, Pembrokeshire, killing 25 of the crew.

1873, 1 March	The iron sailing ship *Chacabuco* sank after a collision off the Great Orme drowning 24 of the crew.
1917, 27 December	The steamship *Adela* was torpedoed by a German U-boat off the Skerries, Anglesey, killing 24 of the crew.
1918, 15 April	The steamship *Cyrene* was torpedoed by a German U-boat off Bardsey killing 24 of the crew.
1918, 8 May	The steamer *Princess Dagmar* was torpedoed in the Bristol Channel by a German U-boat drowning 24 crewmen.
1840, 18 November	The paddle steamer *City of Bristol* was wrecked on Llangennith Sands, Gower, drowning about 22 people.
1855, 25 February	The steamer *Morna* was wrecked off North Bishop Rock, Pembrokeshire, drowning 21 people.
1894, 30 October	The Spanish steamship *Tormes* sank off Crow Rock near Pembroke drowning 21 of the crew.
1918, 21 April	The steamship *Landonia* was torpedoed by a German U-boat off Strumble Head, Pembrokeshire, drowning 21 of the crew.
1918, 15 June	The steamship *Strathnairn* was torpedoed by a German U-boat off the Bishops and Clerks, Pembrokeshire, drowning 21 crewmen.
1918, 14 October	The steamship *Dundalk* was torpedoed by a German U-boat off the Skerries, Anglesey, drowning 21 of the crew.
1926, 17 March	The Italian steamship *Fagarnes* sank after a collision off Swansea with the loss of 21 lives.
1929, 9 July	The Royal Navy Submarine *H47* sank after a collision off the Pembrokeshire coast with the loss of 21 lives.
1843, 7 January	The paddle steamer *Monk* was wrecked near Caernarfon drowning 20 people.
1886, 15 October	The iron sailing ship *Malleny* was wrecked on Tusker Rocks, Porthcawl, drowning 20 of the crew.
1900, 10 September	The German steamship *Stormarn* collided with the *Gordon Castle* in fog in Cardigan Bay killing 20 crew members.
1900, 8 October	The steamer *City of Vienna* sank following a collision off Swansea drowning 20 of the 21 crew.
1917, 28 October	The steamer *Eskmere* was torpedoed by a German U-boat in St Bride's Bay, Pembrokeshire, killing 20 of the crew.
1881, 13 October	The *Cyprian* was wrecked off Porthdinllaen, Llŷn, drowning 19 crewmen.

1918, 20 April	The steamer *Florrieston* was torpedoed by a German U-boat off South Stack, Holyhead, drowning 19 crewmen.
1945, 11 January	The steamer *Normandy Coast* was torpedoed by a German U-boat off Anglesey killing 19 of the crew.
1883, 31 October	The German barque *Alhambra* sank after a collision off Holyhead drowning 18 people.
1886, 15 October	The sailing ship *Teviotdale* was wrecked on Cefn Sidan Sands, Carmarthenshire, drowning 18 people.
1865, 14 January	The American Confederate paddle-steamer *Lelia* sank off the Clwyd coast drowning 18 people.
1908, 1 September	The barque *Amazon* sank in a gale on Margam Sands drowning 18 of the crew.
1917, 7 December	The steamer *Earl of Elgin* was torpedoed by a German U-boat in Caernarfon Bay drowning 18 of the crew.
1918, 7 April	The steamer *Boscastle* was torpedoed by a German U-boat off Strumble Head, Pembrokeshire, killing 18 of the crew.
1918, 16 September	The steamship *Serula* was torpedoed by a German U-boat off Strumble Head, Pembrokeshire, killing 17 of the crew.
1940, 22 November	The steamer *Pikepool* struck a mine off Linney Head, Pembrokeshire, killing 17 of the crew.
1892, 15 May	The steamer *Earl of Aberdeen* struck the Hats and Barrels reef off the Dyfed coast drowning 16 crewmen.
1941, 27 March	The cable-laying ship *Michael Faraday* was sunk by German aircraft off St Ann's Head, Pembrokeshire, killing 16 crewmen.
1917, 15 December	The steamer *Formby* was torpedoed in Caernarfon Bay killing 15 of the crew.
1824, 1 January	The brig *Hornby* was wrecked on the Great Orme drowning 14 crewmen.
1867, 27 October	The sailing ship *Earl of Chester* was wrecked off Rhosneigr, Anglesey, drowning at least 14 people.
1907, 17 February	The cargo ship *Orianda* sank following a collision off Barry which killed 14 of her crew.
1918, 9 May	The steamships *Baron Ailsa* and the *Wileysike* were both torpedoed by a German U-boat off the Pembrokeshire coast killing 14 members of the crews.
1828, 11 November	The French vessel *La Jeune Emma* was wrecked on Cefn Sidan Sands, Carmarthenshire, drowning 13 people.
1940, 3 March	The steamer *Cato* struck a mine off Nash point, Glamorgan, killing 13 of the crew.

1925, 25 November	The steamship *Sutton* sank in Cardigan Bay drowning all 12 of her crew.
1918, 26 January	The Irish steamer *Cork* was torpedoed by a German U-boat off Point Lynas, Anglesey, drowning 12 crewmen.
1812, 30 December	The brig *Fortune* was wrecked on the Smalls, Pembrokeshire, drowning all 11 of her crew.
1863, 20 January	The American vessel *Pamelia Flood* was wrecked off Aberffraw, Anglesey, drowning 11 people.
1879, 12 February	The *Mary Stenhouse* was wrecked near Rhosili, Gower, drowning 11 of the crew.
1882, 1 November	The Austrian barque *Petroslava* was wrecked on Skokholm drowning 10 of her 11 crew.
1898, 14 May	The steamer *Benholm* sank after a collision off Point Lynas, Anglesey, drowning 10 of the crew.
1917, 25 August	The steamer *Cymrian* was torpedoed by a German U-boat off Tusker Rocks, Porthcawl, killing 10 of the crew.
1936, 5 January	The Lowestoft drifter *Shore Breeze* was wrecked on St Ann's Head, Pembrokeshire, drowning her crew of 10.
1940, 22 August	The steamer *Thorold* was sunk by German aircraft off the Skerries, Anglesey, killing 10 of the crew.
1941, 21 March	The coaster *Millisle* was sunk by German aircraft off Caldey Island killing 10 crewmen.
1991, 6 January	The Maltese tanker *Kimya* capsized in a gale off Anglesey drowning 10 of her 12 crew.

No official statistics on wrecks around the British Isles were kept until the 1850s.

Landing Craft, Lifeboats, and Leave Boats

(Listed by the number of fatalities)

1943, 25 April	Landing craft *LGC 15* and *LGC 16* sank off Milford Haven drowning 78 men.
1739, 20 June	Thirteen men were drowned when their boat was swamped after taking coal to the Skerries beacon off Anglesey.
1847, 14 January	The Point of Ayr lifeboat capsized off Rhyl drowning its entire crew of 13.
1947, 23 April	The Mumbles lifeboat was wrecked off Sker Point, Porthcawl, drowning its crew of eight. (See also ship losses).

1822, 30 November	The Bardsey Light Tender sank between Aberdaron and Bardsey drowning all six people abroad.
1874, 24 January	In an accident off Llanddwyn, Anglesey, four pilots and two apprentices were drowned.
1903, 1 February	The Mumbles lifeboat lost six crewmen off Aberavon.
1919, 20 December	Six seamen were drowned returning to their ship by boat at Milford Haven.
1853, 23 January	Five members of the Rhyl lifeboat were drowned.
1883, 27 January	Five members of the Mumbles lifeboat crew were drowned. (See also ship losses.)
1888, 5 October	Five seamen were drowned off Colwyn Bay when their boat capsized while returning to their ship.
1920, 3 December	The Rhoscolyn lifeboat lost five of its crew off Llanddwyn, Anglesey.
1910, 12 October	Three members of St David's lifeboat were drowned in Ramsey Sound.
1916, 1 January	The Port Eynon lifeboat capsized drowning three of the crew.
1918, 10 October	Three seamen were drowned returning to their ship by boat at Milford Haven.

Ferries

(Listed by the number of fatalities)

1664, 10 December	The Abermenai ferry capsized in the Menai Strait drowning 79 people.
1645, 24 July	About 60 Parliamentary soldiers were reputed to have drowned crossing the Severn at New Passage in pursuit of Royalists after the Battle of Naseby.
1785, 5 December	The Abermenai ferry sank near Caernarfon drowning 56 people.
1723, 13 April	The Tal-y-foel ferry sank near Caernarfon drowning 30 people.
1820, 5 August	The Tal-y-foel ferry sank in the Menai Strait drowning 25 people.
1834, 27 December	A boat crossing from Penally to Caldey was swamped and 15 people were drowned.
1806, 25 December	The Conwy ferry capsized drowning about 14 passengers.
1889, 8 February	A ferry was swamped in Pembroke Dock and nine people were drowned.

1838, 1 September	The Aust–Beachley ferry sank drowning 14 people.
1855, 30 March	The Severn Ferry from Chepstow sank drowning seven people.
1777, 2 August	The Aust–Beachley ferry sank drowning five people.

Pleasure Boats

(Listed by the number of fatalities)

1893, 7 August	Off Aberavon beach, 22 members of a Sunday School party from Ystrad Rhondda were drowned.
1966, July 22	At Penmaenpool in the Mawddach estuary, 15 people were drowned.
1894, 1 August	Off Barmouth 10 people were drowned.
1951, 6 September	Five schoolboys were drowned off Cricieth.
1957, 16 July	Five people were drowned in a boating accident at Barmouth.
1992, 26 August	In a speedboat accident off Llandudno, five people were drowned.
1952, 19 August	Four members of one family were drowned when their cabin cruiser was wrecked near St Govan's Head, Dyfed.
1967, 7 August	Two men and a boy were drowned in the Dovey estuary when their raft overturned.

Launching Accident

1825, 2 May	Eight people were drowned at Monmouth during the launching of a brig.

Canal Boat Accident

1875, 19 June	Three people were drowned following a boat accident on the Glamorganshire Canal in Cardiff.

German Submarines Sunk off the Welsh Coast

1918, 19 May	U-B 119 off Bardsey.
1945, 7 March	U-1302 off St David's Head.
1945, 30 April	U-242 and U-325 north of the Skerries.

RAILWAY AND RAILWAY ENGINEERING ACCIDENTS

(Listed by number of fatalities)

1868, 20 August	At Abergele, Clwyd, 33 people were killed in a fire following a collision.
1921, 26 January	In a collision at Abermule, Powys, 17 people were killed.
1876, 21 April	An explosion during the construction of the Cymmer–Caerau rail tunnel, West Glamorgan, killed 13 workers.
1878, 19 October	In a collision at Pontypridd, Mid Glamorgan, 13 people were killed.
1893, 12 August	In a derailment near Llantrisant, Mid Glamorgan, 13 people were killed.
1911, 23 January	In a crash at Hopkinstown, Pontypridd, 12 people were killed.
1889, 22 January	During the construction of the Rhondda Tunnel at Abergwynfi, West Glamorgan, seven workers were killed in a roof collapse.
1866, 6 September	In a derailment at Bryncir near Cricieth, six people were killed.
1950, 27 August	In a collision at Penmaenmawr, Gwynedd, six people were killed.
1904, 3 October	In a collision near Lougher, five people were killed.
1857, 14 October	In a collision between Pyle and Port Talbot, four people were killed.
1878, 2 December	A runaway train killed four people at Tal-y-bont, Powys.
1987, 19 October	The Glanrhyd rail bridge in Dyfed collapsed into the River Tywi during floods as a train was crossing and four people were drowned.
1869, 10 June	A derailment at Maesycwmmer, Mid Glamorgan, killed three people.
1872, 19 March	In a collision at Dowlais, Mid Glamorgan, three people were killed.
1877, 20 November	Three people died following the collapse of a railway bridge into the River Alaw near Llannerch-y-medd, Anglesey.
1885, 25 August	A derailment on the Cardigan Bay–Whitland line killed three people.
1909, 21 April	In a boiler explosion at the Rhymney Railway locomotive sheds, Cardiff, three men were killed.

1865, 29 November	A coal train fell into North Dock, Swansea killing the driver and fireman.
1883, 1 January ⎫ 1933, 4 March ⎬	Landslides on the railway line at Friog near Barmouth, Gwynedd, killed a driver and a fireman on both
	occasions.
1925, 4 January	A driver and fireman were killed in a derailment at Tirphil near Bargoed.
1932, 23 August	An accident on the Great Orme tramway killed two passengers.
1960, 20 November	Two people were killed in a collision at Pontrhydyfen, West Glamorgan.
1965, 17 December	A landslide on the main line at Bridgend, Mid Glamorgan, killed a driver and co-driver.

Major Non-Fatal Accident

1991, 7 December	In the first major accident in its 110-year history, nearly 100 people were injured, several seriously, when two trains collided near the Welsh end of the Severn Tunnel.

AIRCRAFT ACCIDENTS (WITH SIX OR MORE DEATHS)

(Listed by the number of fatalities)

1950, 12 March	An Avro Tudor V aircraft returning from an Ireland–Wales rugby international, crashed at Llandow, South Glamorgan, killing 75 of the 78 passengers and the crew of five. This was the world's worst air disaster at the time.
1952, 10 January	A Dakota of Aer Lingus crashed into Moel Siabod, Gwynedd, killing all 20 passengers and the crew of three.
1943, 29 December	An American Flying Fortress crashed into Cwm Mountain, Clwyd, killing all 18 people aboard.
1941, 10 October	Two planes collided at RAF Llandwrog, Gwynedd, killing all 17 occupants.
1941, 28 August	During an attempt to save an RAF Blackburn Botha which crashed into the sea off Rhosneigr, Anglesey, 14 people were drowned including the plane's Polish crew of three.
1942, 20 July	An RAF Lockheed Hudson crashed near Llanfair Dyffryn Clwyd, killing all 13 aboard.

1942, 11 August	An American Flying Fortress crashed on Cadair Fronwen, Berwyn Mountains, Clwyd, killing its crew of 11.
1942, 23 August	An American Dakota crashed near Rhewl, Clwyd, killing 10 of the 12 people aboard.
1943, 16 September	An American Flying Fortress crashed in the Black Mountains, killing all 10 people aboard while another Flying Fortress crashed near Rhayader, Powys, also killing all 10 aboard.
1953, 8 January	An RAF Boeing B29 crashed near Llandegla, Clwyd, killing all 10 aboard.
1944, 23 January	An RAF Halifax crashed near Nant yr Haidd, Elan Valley, killing its crew of nine.
1943, 4 August	An American Flying Fortress crashed near Arenig Fawr, Gwynedd, killing its crew of eight.
1944, 11 April	An RAF Lancaster crashed near Llanwrtyd Wells killing its crew of eight.
1944, 20 December	An American Liberator crashed into the sea off Anglesey killing eight of its crew.
1942, 8 April	An RAF Wellington crashed near Llangammarch, Powys, killing its seven crew.
1942, 31 October	Two RAF planes, a Wellington and a Beaufort, collided in mid-air near Bangor killing the seven airmen aboard.
1942, 16 November	An RAF Lancaster crashed at Dolwen Hill near Llanerfyl, Powys, killing its seven crew.
1943, 26 January	An RAF Wellington crashed near Llansilin, Clwyd, killing its crew of five and two people on the ground.
1944, 4 January	An RAF Halifax crashed near Carreg-y-blaidd, Ysbyty Ifan, Gwynedd, killing its seven crew.
1944, 6 February	An RAF Lancaster broke up over the Rhinogs near Harlech killing its seven crew.
1944, 3 September	An RAF Halifax crashed on Yr Eifl, Llŷn, killing its seven crew.
1954, 4 March	An RAF Sunderland flying boat crashed in Milford Haven killing seven of its crew.
1941, 28 July	An RAF Wellington crashed into Garn Fadryn, Llŷn, killing its six crew.
1941, 17 August	An RAF Wellington crashed into Rhosfach Mountain in the Berwyn range, Clwyd, killing its crew of six.
1942, 16 April	An RAF Wellington crashed near Dyrysgol, Gwynedd, killing its six Czechoslovakian crew.

1942, 19 July	An RAF Wellington crashed in Milford Dock killing its six crew.
1942, 29 July	An RAF Wellington crashed into the Ysgolion Duon (Black Ladders), Snowdonia, killing its crew of six.
1942, 11 August	An RAF Wellington crashed in the sea at St Brides Bay, killing its six Polish crew and an American Flying Fortress crashed in the Berwyn Mountains killing its crew of six.
1942, 22 December	An RAF Wellington crashed near Bethesda, Gwynedd, killing its six crew.
1943, 13 February	An RAF Wellington crashed on Foel Grach, Snowdonia, killing its six crew.
1943, 15 May	An RAF Wellington crashed near Lake Vyrnwy killing its six crew.
1943, 28 May	An RAF Wellington crashed into Cadair Idris killing its six crew.
1943, 6 July	An RAF Lancaster crashed near Llangernyw, Clwyd, killing its six crew.
1944, 16 May	An RAF Wellington crashed near Llangernyw, Clwyd, killing its six crew.
1944, 19 September	An RAF Liberator crashed into Preseli Mountain killing its six crew.
1946, 18 January	An RAF Wellington crashed near Llandrillo, Gwynedd, killing its six crew.
1950, 15 March	An RAF Lincoln crashed into Carnedd Llywelyn, Snowdonia, killing its six crew.
1979, 8 June	A Cessna Skymaster crashed into Moel Siabod, Snowdonia, killing all six aboard.

GERMAN AIRCRAFT BROUGHT DOWN OVER WALES OR OFF THE WELSH COAST DURING THE SECOND WORLD WAR

(Shot down by RAF fighters except where otherwise shown; listed in chronological order.)

1940, 14 August	Three Heinkel 111s were shot down during a raid on Cardiff. Two crash-landed in Somerset and their eight crew were captured, and the third crashed in Bridgewater Bay killing its four crew. Another Heinkel 111 was shot

	down over north Wales after attacking RAF Hawarden and crashed just over the English border at Pulford, Cheshire. All four of the crew were captured.
1940, 7 September	A Junkers 88 crashed at Mallwyd near Machynlleth and its four crew and a Gestapo officer were captured.
1940, 13 September	*A Heinkel 111 crashed into a house at Newport, Gwent. Three of the crew were killed and one captured.
1940, 21 September	A Dornier 215 crashed near Dolgellau. One crew member was killed and three captured.
1940, 11 October	A Dornier 17 crashed into the sea off Bardsey with two crew members killed and two captured. Another Dornier 17 crashed into the sea north of the Llŷn peninsula killing its four crew.
1940, 16 October	†A Dornier 17 crashed near Nantglyn, Denbighshire, killing all its four crew.
1941, 14 April	†A Heinkel 111 crashed in the Carneddau range, Snowdonia. One crew member was killed and three captured.
1941, 8 May	A Heinkel 111 crashed near Wrexham killing its four crew. A Heinkel 111 crashed near Malpas, Denbighshire. Two of the crew were killed and two captured. A Heinkel 111 crashed near Bagillt, Flint, with three of the crew killed and two captured.
1941, 29 May	A Heinkel 111 crashed near Buckley, Flint, and its four crew were captured.
1941, 1 June	A Junkers 88 was shot down off Llandudno killing its four crew.
1941, 8 August	A Junkers 88 was badly damaged over north Wales and crash-landed in Ireland where its four crew were interned.
1941, 12 October	A Heinkel 111 was shot down off Holyhead killing its four crew.
1941, 22 October	A Heinkel 111 was shot down off Nefyn, Llŷn, killing its four crew.
1941, 1 November	A Heinkel 111 crashed near Gwalchmai, Anglesey, killing its four crew. †A Junkers 88 was shot down over north Wales and crashed near Pulford, Cheshire, killing its four crew.

* Brought down by hitting a barrage balloon – the first occasion this had happened in Britain.
† Brought down by anti-aircraft fire.

1942, 25 April	A Junkers 88 crashed into Gwaunceste Hill near Builth Wells after a raid on Bath. Two of the crew were killed and two captured.
1942, 18 May	A Junkers 88 was shot down over Cardigan Bay. Two of the crew were killed and two captured.
1942, 30 July	A Heinkel 111 crashed on Pwllheli beach. Three of the crew were killed and one captured.
1942, 5 August	A Junkers 88 crashed into the sea off the Carmarthenshire coast killing its four crew.
1942, 23 August	A Junkers 88 was badly damaged over north Wales and crash-landed in Ireland. One of the crew was killed and three were interned.
1943, 16 February	A Dornier 217 crashed into the sea off Mumbles killing its four crew.
1943, 18 May	Two Dornier 217s and one Junkers 88 were shot down during a raid on Cardiff. One crashed in the Bristol Channel and two in Somerset. Nine of the crews were killed and three captured.

FATALITIES IN GERMAN AIR RAIDS ON WALES

(In chronological order)

Date	Location	Deaths
1940, 9 July	RAF Penrhos, Gwynedd	2
1940, 9 July	Cardiff Docks	7
1940, 10 July	Swansea Docks	12
1940, 11 August	Manselton, Swansea	17
1940, 14 August	RAF Sealand, Clwyd	1
1940, 14 August	Pembroke Dock	5
1940, 18 August	Swansea	1
1940, 30 August	Gresford, Clwyd	8
1940, 31 August	Caergwrle, Clwyd	7
1940, 31 August	Rhos and Penycae, Clwyd	10
1940, 2 September	Swansea	33
1940, 3 September	Abergele, Clwyd	2
1940, 3 September	Cardiff	11
1940, 13 September	Newport	2
1940, 15 September	Cardiff	5

Date	Location	Deaths
1941, 2 January	Cardiff	165
1941, 17 January	Swansea	58
1941, 14 February	Sandfields, Port Talbot	6
1941, 19–21 February	Swansea	240
1941, 26 February	Cardiff	4
1941, 3 March	Cardiff and Penarth	51
1941, 11 March	Swansea	3
1941, 31 March	Swansea	3
1941, 12 April	Swansea	3
1941, 15 April	RAF Carew Cheriton, Dyfed	12
1941, 29 April	Cardiff	7
1941, 29 April	Cwmparc, Rhondda	26
1941, 11 May	RAF St Athan, South Glamorgan	3
1941, 12 May	Pembroke Dock	32
1941, 12 May	Pontrhydyfen, West Glamorgan	4
1941, 29 May	Groes, Clwyd	5
1941, 1 July	Newport	37
1941, 3 October	Rogerstone, Gwent	8
1941, 9 October	Newport	3
1941, 12 October	Tenby	1
1941, 20 October	Pentre, Queensferry, Clwyd	3
1941, 28 November	Swansea	1
1943, 16 February	Swansea	34
1943, 16 February	RAF Fairwood Common, Gower	3
1943, 18 May	Cardiff and Dinas Powys	43
1944, 28 March	Cardiff	9

A total of almost 1,000 civilians were killed in these air raids. (In the whole of the UK some 60,000 people died in air raids.)

NATURAL AND MAN-MADE DISASTERS AND EPIDEMICS

(In chronological order)

1349   The first visit of the Black Death ('Y Farwolaeth Fawr') to Wales, followed by reappearances in 1361 and 1369 with a further seven visits before 1420. In these years as many as 100,000 people may have died from the disease.

1573	A great storm carried a line of sand dunes almost two miles inland at Kenfig, Mid Glamorgan.
1607	Over 500 people and possibly as many as 2,000 were drowned along the south Wales coast in 'the Great Flood'. Gwent was particularly badly affected and in Carmarthenshire the village of Alkenchurch (or Hawton), at the mouth of the River Tywi, was washed away. There was also extensive flooding around Abergele on the north Wales coast.
1636–1637	Hundreds of people died of plague in the Presteigne area of Radnorshire.
1652	In Haverfordwest some 400 deaths were caused by an outbreak of plague, the last to occur in Wales.
1703	A great storm in November wrecked hundreds of vessels around the Welsh coast.
1705–1706	In Penmachno, Gwynedd, smallpox killed 60 people.
1722–1723	In Carmarthen smallpox killed 71 people.
1727–1731	Hundreds of people throughout Wales died in a typhus outbreak.
1762	In Holyhead smallpox killed about 50 people.
1832	A cholera outbreak this year followed by three others in 1849, 1856 and 1866 killed at least 5,000 people throughout Wales.
1865	In Swansea the only outbreak of yellow fever ever to occur in Britain killed 15 people.
1869	Nitro-glycerine being taken to a slate quarry detonated on the road to Cwm-y-glo near Caernarfon and killed nine people.
1875	The collapse of a reservoir dam for the Monmouthshire Canal at Cwmcarn, Gwent, killed at least 12 people.
1877	Serious flooding occurred in south Wales, with Bridgend very badly affected.
1881	Blizzards and exceptionally low temperatures in mid-January throughout Wales seriously disrupted rail services: five people in south Wales were frozen to death.
1885	A major fire at Aberystwyth University College killed three people.
1886	During three days of gales and heavy rain in mid-November, 200 houses at Aberystwyth were flooded, two bridges on the River Rheidol in the town were washed away; the keeper of the Mumbles lighthouse was swept out to sea and drowned and there was widespread flooding all over Wales from the valleys of the Mawddach and Dee to the Taff. (See also 'Ship Losses'.)
1890–1891	Snow and sub-zero temperatures from 21 December caused serious disruption in many parts of Wales for three weeks.

1909	The collapse of a trench during extension work on Alexandra Dock, Newport, killed 36 workmen.
1910	The collapse of a colliery dam at Clydach Vale, Rhondda, killed six people.
1918–1919	An influenza epidemic (Spanish 'flu) killed about 10,000 people throughout Wales.
1925	The collapse of Llyn Eigiau Dam, Dolgarrog, Gwynedd, killed 16 people.
1927	A great storm in late February caused the destruction of coastal cottages at Cricieth, broke the harbour wall at Porthmadog and washed away railway lines near Pwllheli, while an exceptionally high tide drowned cattle as far inland as Aberglaslyn.
1929	Some 400 people were made homeless in the Rhondda in November by devastating floods which also caused serious damage and destruction in many other parts of south Wales, including the blocking by a landslide of the newly opened Rhigos Mountain road.
1936	Gales and flooding in early January damaged Menai Bridge, Penarth Pier and the sea walls at Aberystwyth and Porthcawl.
1938	In severe gales in mid-January and early February affecting all Wales, serious damage was caused to Aberystwyth sea wall, the end of the town's pier was destroyed, a boy was drowned in the Rhymney River, Bardsey Island was cut in two and there was serious flooding at Barmouth, Corwen, Porthmadog, Rhyl, Towyn and Welshpool.
1940	A freak 'ice storm' on 27/8 January caused the collapse of electricity cables and telephone lines in many parts of Wales.
1947	From 19 January to 8 March almost all of Wales was affected by blizzards and continuous sub-zero temperatures.
1950	The collapse of three houses in Swansea killed seven people.
1952	Bala Lake (Llyn Tegid) burst its banks causing extensive flooding in the Vale of Edeyrnion.
1960	In disastrous floods in many parts of Wales in December, a boy was drowned at Cwmbach, Aberdare, 6,000 homes in Cardiff were affected, 3,000 people in Newtown, Powys, were cut off, 1,000 people were evacuated in the Rhondda, 62 factories were flooded on the Treforest Industrial Estate, and Cardiff Arms Park was left under four feet of water.
1962	A smallpox epidemic in south Wales killed 17 people.
1965	Many areas in Wales were affected by severe flooding in December: two men were drowned in the River Dee, a landslide on

the main railway line at Bridgend, Mid Glamorgan, caused the deaths of two railwaymen, and a boy was drowned in the River Usk at Caerleon.

1963–1964 From late December to February heavy snowfalls caused severe disruption throughout Wales.

1966 The Aberfan tip collapsed on Pantglas Junior School on 21 October after continuous heavy rain, killing 116 children and 28 adults.

1969 A blizzard on 19 February caused serious disruption for three days in south Wales.

1975 An oil leak from the tanker *Esso Tenby* off the Dyfed coast in May killed 1,300 sea-birds.

1978 A blizzard in mid-February caused serious disruption all over Wales for four days.

In October the tanker *Christos Bitas* was holed off the Pembrokeshire coast causing major oil pollution and the deaths of over 2,200 sea birds.

1979 Severe flooding in south and central Wales in late December particularly affected Cardiff, the South Wales valleys, Brecon, Builth and Carmarthen. Three people were drowned – two in Merthyr Tydfil and one in Monmouth.

1980 Severe flooding in north Wales in October forced 300 people to be evacuated from their homes in Blaenau Ffestiniog.

1982 Blizzards and continuous sub-zero temperatures in January caused massive disruption throughout Wales for 10 days.

1985 The tanker *Bridgeness* was holed off the Pembrokeshire coast in June causing major oil pollution and the deaths of over 2,000 sea-birds.

1987 Many parts of Wales were affected by severe flooding in October and four people were drowned when their train plunged into the swollen River Tywi at Glanrhyd Bridge.

1990 The breaching of the sea wall at Towyn and Kinmel Bay, Clwyd, during gales in late February, led to the evacuation of some 5,000 people as 2,800 homes were damaged.

1992 Much of south Wales was affected by flooding in early December and there was serious dislocation of road and rail services. Later in the month both north and south Wales were affected by further flooding and a man was drowned in the River Ogwen near Bethesda.

1993 Flash floods on 10/11 June caused considerable damage to some 500 homes in Llandudno and over 2,500 people had to be evacuated while there was also extensive flooding in Cardigan as the River Mwldan overflowed causing damage to 50 homes.

WELSH BATTLES, SKIRMISHES AND ENGAGEMENTS

51AD *Cefn Carnedd*: Between Caersws and Llanidloes, Powys, is the traditional site of a battle between the Deceangli supported by other Celtic tribesmen led by Caratacus (Caradoc), and a Roman army under Ostorius Scapula. Caratacus was decisively beaten, fled to the Brigantes (another Celtic tribe) but their Queen, Cartimandua, handed him over in chains to the Romans.

52 or 53 *Somewhere in south Wales*: The Celtic tribe of the Silures defeated the Second Augusta Legion in a pitched battle.

61 *Anglesey*: The island was conquered by Suetonius Paulinus with the Fourteenth and the Twentieth Legions. Druid strongholds were obliterated by this veteran of engagements in the Atlas Mountains of North Africa.

430 *Maes Garmon*: According to the Venerable Bede, in this battle near Mold, the Christian Welsh reputedly defeated the pagan Picts and Saxons with the cry of 'Alleluia!'

500 *Mount Badon*: In this battle, the exact location of which is not known, the Saxons were defeated by Britons reputedly led by Arthur.

577 *Dyrham*: A Saxon victory which separated, by land, the Welsh of Wales from those of the west of England. The exact site of the battle is uncertain but may have been near Bath.

598 *Catraeth (Catterick)*: This battle in Yorkshire, commemorated by Aneirin in his poem *Y Gododdin*, saw a force of some 300 mounted Britons from the Edinburgh area virtually annihilated by thousands of Saxon foot soldiers.

615 *Chester*: This was a Saxon victory which separated the Welsh of Wales by land from those of 'the Old North'. King Aethelfrith of Northumbria defeated Selyg ap Cynan Garwyn, King of Powys. Bede claimed that the battle was preceeded by the Saxon massacre of some 1,200 monks at Bangor Is-Coed.

654 *Winwaed Field*: This further Saxon victory near Leeds led to the final separation of Wales from 'the Old North'. The Bernicians under Oswy killed a number of British princes and King Penda of Mercia who was fighting with them.

796 *Morfa Rhuddlan*: According to tradition, Offa of Mercia killed Caradog, King of Gwynedd.

856 *Llandudno*: Rhodri Mawr defeated and killed the Viking leader Horm – hence the name of the landmark Great Orme's Head.

872	*Parciau Plateau*: In Anglesey a Danish Viking force was defeated by the Welsh.
878	Rhodri the Great was killed in a battle with the Mercians at an unknown site.
881	*Conwy*: Anarawd ap Rhodri of Gwynedd, in alliance with Danish Vikings, defeated a Mercian army.
893	*Buttington, (Powys)*: A combined Welsh and Mercian army defeated a Danish host which had marched across England from Essex.
950	*Nant Carno*: In this battle near Arwystli, Powys, following the death of Hywel Dda, the unification he had brought to much of Wales was shattered by the ensuing power struggle.
987	*Anglesey*: In a powerful Viking attack on the island, 1,000 Welsh were reported killed and another 2,000 taken as slaves.
1022	*Abergwili, Tywi Valley*: Llywelyn ap Seisyll of Gwynedd defeated Rhain, an Irish pretender to the thrones of Deheubarth and Gwynedd.
1039	*Rhyd-y-groes*: At an unidentified site on the River Severn, Leofric of Mercia was defeated by Gruffudd ap Llywelyn, ruler of Gwynedd and Powys.
1041	*Pencader*: Near Ystrad Tywi, Gruffudd ap Llywelyn defeated Hywel ab Edwin, ruler of Deheubarth, and his Irish allies.
1042	*Pwlldyfach*: In Dyfed, Hywel ab Edwin defeated a Viking army.
1044	*Aber Towy* (Dyfed): Hywel ab Edwin was killed by Gruffudd ap Llywelyn in a struggle for control of Deheubarth.
1052	*Llanllieni (Leominster)*: Gruffydd ap Llywelyn defeated an English force which included Norman mercenaries. This was the first time Welsh and Normans had met in battle.
1070	*Mechain*: A victory for Bleddyn ap Cynfyn, ruler of Gwynedd and Powys, in defence of his position and for control of Deheubarth.
1071	*Rhymney River*: In this battle near Cardiff, Caradog ap Gruffudd of Gwynllwg, with Norman assistance, defeated and killed Maredudd ab Owain of Deheubarth over the control of Glamorgan.
1074	*Glyn Cyfing*: In Merioneth Gruffudd ap Cynan defeated Trahaearn ap Caradog in a struggle for the control of Gwynedd.
1075	*Bron yr Erw*: In this battle near Clynnog Fawr, Llŷn, Trahaearn ap Caradog defeated Dublin-born Gruffudd ap Cynan and his Irish allies.
1081	*Mynydd Carn*: This major dynastic battle near St David's ended the political confusion in the wake of the death of the powerful

Gruffudd ap Llywelyn in 1063. It led to the establishment of the two great dynasties of Deheubarth under Rhys ap Tewdwr and Gwynedd under Gruffudd ap Cynan.

1087   *Llechryd Bridge*: Rhys ap Tewdwr, with Irish and Norse assistance, defeated Bleddyn ap Cynan, ruler of Deheubarth.

1088   At an unidentified site, Rhys ap Tewdwr returned from an enforced exile in Ireland and, with the help of a Danish fleet, defeated and killed Madog ap Bleddyn and his brother Rhiryd.

1091   *Llandudoch*: Near the mouth of the River Teifi, Rhys ap Tewdwr killed Gruffudd ap Maredudd, claimant to the throne of Deheubarth.

1094   *Coed Ysbwys*: The site of this battle has not been identified but it ended in a victory for the Welsh under Cadwgan ap Bleddyn against the Normans who were forced to abandon temporarily large parts of west and north Wales except for Pembroke Castle.

1096   *Gelli Carnant*: A Welsh victory over the Normans in Gwent.

1096   *Aber Llech*: Near Ystradgynlais the Welsh of Brycheiniog under Gruffudd ab Iorwerth defeated invading Normans.

1098   *Anglesey Sound*: A Norman–Danish force under the Earls of Chester and Shrewsbury, which had defeated the Welsh, was itself attacked by a Viking fleet under Magnus Barefoot, King of Norway. The Norwegians won and killed Earl Hugh of Shrewsbury.

1118   *Maes Maen Cymro*: Near Rhuthun, a ferocious battle for the control of territory in the area took place between Powys and Gwynedd with the latter prevailing.

1132   *Nanheudwy*: Near Llangollen, Powys gained revenge for the defeat of 1118 as Cadwallon, one of the sons of Gruffudd ap Cynan, ruler of Gwynedd, was killed in this encounter.

1136   *Between Loughor and Swansea*: In January the Welsh gained a victory over a Norman and English force, about 500 of whose number were said to have been killed. At about the same time, Gwenllian, wife of Gruffudd ap Rhys, ruler of Deheubarth, was killed leading an assault on Kidwelly Castle.

        Crug Mawr: Later in the same year, near Cardigan, Anglo-Normans and Flemings were defeated by the Welsh under Gruffudd ap Rhys. But the Welsh failed to capture Cardigan Castle from the Normans.

1146   *Wich*: The site of this battle in Maelor Saesneg is uncertain but it resulted in a defeat of the Welsh of Powys by Robert of Mold 'with much slaughter'.

1157   *Coleshill* and *Tal Moelfre*: Leading an expedition into Wales,

Henry II narrowly escaped death in an engagement at Coleshill near Basingwerk. At Tal Moelfre, Henry's illegitimate son was killed and his half-brother badly injured. Owain Gwynedd, however, was obliged to come to terms with the king.

1165 *Dyffryn Ceiriog*: A Welsh victory against Henry II.

1170 *Pentraeth*: This was a clash in Anglesey between two brothers for the control of Gwynedd.

1194 *Aberconwy*: Llywelyn the Great (Llywelyn ap Iorwerth) defeated his uncle Dafydd ab Owain Gwynedd in a struggle over Gwynedd.

1196 *Radnor*: A victory for the Lord Rhys (Rhys ap Gruffudd) against the Anglo-Normans.

1198 *Painscastle*: A crushing defeat of the Welsh of Powys under Gwenwynwyn by the Justiciar, Geoffrey Fitzpeter. Some 3,000 Welsh were reputed killed.

1228 *Ceri*: In Powys, Llywelyn the Great defeated the Justiciar, Hubert de Burgh.

1255 *Bryn Derwin*: In Gwynedd, Llywelyn ap Gruffudd defeated his brothers Dafydd and Owain over the succession to Gwynedd. Owain was imprisoned for 20 years.

1257 *Coed Llathen*: In the Tywi Valley, Llywelyn ap Gruffudd achieved a major victory with some 3,000 English reputed killed. This was one of the most serious defeats of an English army in Wales during the thirteenth century.

1282 *Dinefwr*: In June an English army under Gilbert de Clare was defeated.

1282 *Menai Strait*: In November an English army under Luc de Tany was destroyed trying to cross to Anglesey in flat-bottomed boats.

1282 *Irfon Bridge*: Llywelyn ap Gruffudd (Llywelyn the Last) was killed in a skirmish near Builth Wells on 11 December.

1295 *Maes Moydog*: Near Welshpool, Madog ap Llywelyn was defeated by the Earl of Warwick in the last rising against Edward I after the conquest of 1282. The longbow was first recorded as being used in this battle.

1401 *Hyddgen*: Near Pumlumon, Owain Glyndŵr achieved a victory in the first battle of his rebellion. About 22 English and Flemings were killed.

1404 *Campston Hill*: Near Grosmont, Gwent, Owain Glyndŵr's forces were defeated by Richard Beauchamp, Earl of Warwick.

1404 *Craig y Porth*: Near Monmouth, an English force was routed by Owain Glyndŵr with great loss of life.

1405	*Grosmont*: In this battle in Gwent in May, Owain Glyndŵr was defeated and over 1,000 Welshmen were reported killed.
1405	*Pwll Melyn*: Near Usk, Owain Glyndŵr suffered a further defeat, his brother Tudor was killed and his son Gruffudd was taken prisoner.
1406	*Gwent*: At an unidentified site on St George's Day (23 April), Owain Glyndŵr suffered another defeat and one of his sons was among some 1,000 Welsh reputed killed.
1461	*Twthill*: Near Caernarfon, during the Wars of the Roses, a Lancastrian force under Jasper Tudor was defeated by the Yorkists.
1464	*Dryslwyn*: A Lancastrian army was defeated by Yorkists in south Wales.
1597	*Second Spanish Armada*: A ship was driven ashore near Aberdovey and two Spaniards were killed with four taken prisoner before it was able to set sail again. Two other ships were driven ashore in Pembrokeshire but managed to get away without any effective local interference.
1644	*Montgomery*: In this first battle of the Civil War on Welsh soil, involving about 9,000 troops, some 500 Royalists and 40 Parliamentarians were killed in a Parliamentary victory.
1644	*Siege of Laugharne Castle*: During a five-day siege, 43 men were killed in a Parliamentary victory.
1644	*Machynlleth*: A Parliamentary force defeated the Royalists.
1645	*Newcastle Emlyn*: About 150 Parliamentary troops were killed in a Royalist victory.
1645	*Colby Moor*: In a Parliamentary victory near Winston, Dyfed, about 150 Royalist troops were killed and about 700 taken prisoner in a battle involving about 2,500 men.
1645	*Denbigh Green*: A Parliamentary victory in an encounter involving about 4,500 men.
1646	*Cardiff*: According to Parliamentary sources, some 250 Royalists were killed fighting for control of Cardiff Castle.
1648	*St Fagans*: In this last major battle ever fought in Wales, involving some 11,000 men, about 200 soldiers, mainly Royalist, were killed in a Parliamentary victory.
1648	*Y Dalar Hir*: In a Parliamentary victory near Bangor, about 30–40 men were killed on each side.
1648	*Red Hill*: Near Beaumaris, Parliamentarians gained another victory in a skirmish with Royalists.
1775–1783	*American War of Independence*: In 1778, John Paul Jones, founder

of the United States Navy, was active off the Welsh coast and watered on Caldey Island. In 1780, an American privateer captured two packet boats off Holyhead and held them to ransom.

1797 *Fishguard*: The last attempted invasion of mainland Britain occurred when some 1,400 French troops under an American general, William Tate, landed but surrendered after three days. At least one Frenchman was killed – four according to some sources. The Cardigan Militia (later the Pembrokeshire Yeomanry) won the only Honour ever granted for an engagement in the British Isles.

1914–1918 *First World War*: German U-boats sank many ships around the Welsh coast causing about 700 deaths. (See separate listings.) In 1916 a Zeppelin bombed Buttington, Powys, without causing any injuries or damage in the only German air raid on Wales during the war.

1939–1945 *Second World War*: German U-boats, mines and aircraft sank over 30 ships around the Welsh coast causing over 200 deaths. (See separate listings.) During the same period almost 1,000 people were killed during German air raids on Wales and some 30 German planes were brought down over Wales. (See separate listings.)

WARS, BATTLES AND CAMPAIGNS INVOLVING THE WELSH OUTSIDE WALES

945 Strathclyde was attacked by an English army including Welshmen from Dyfed.

1167 Some 300 Welsh archers, with 90 Norman knights, crossed to Ireland with Robert Fitz Stephen at the request of Diarmait Mac Murchada, King of Leinster, and more three years later with Richard, Earl of Pembroke ('Strongbow').

1173 The Lord Rhys (Rhys ap Gruffudd) led 1,000 men to fight for Henry II in France.

1242–1243 Hundreds of Welshmen fought in Henry II's campaign in Gascony.

1297 Over 5,300 Welshmen accompanied Edward I to Flanders of a total of 7,800 infantry and in Scotland 300 Welsh soldiers were killed at Stirling in Edward's service.

1298 Over 10,000 Welshmen accompanied Edward I on a campaign in Scotland and took part in the victory of the Battle of Falkirk.

1300s–1400s Many hundreds of Welsh mercenary soldiers found employment on the Continent and fought in France, Italy, Switzerland and Spain.

1314	Edward II's army, including thousands of Welsh troops, was defeated at the Battle of Bannockburn by the Scots under Robert the Bruce.
1322	Over 6,000 Welsh soldiers – a half of Edward II's army – campaigned for the King in Scotland.
1326	About 4,000 Welsh soldiers were in the English army campaigning in Gascony.
1334–1335	Again, about a half of Edward II's army campaigning in Scotland was Welsh with 500 archers contributing to the English victory in the Battle of Halidon Hill, Berwick.
1342	Some 600 Welsh troops took part in Edward III's invasion of Brittany.
1345	Jacob von Artevelde, leader of the Flemings against the French, had a bodyguard of some 500 Welshmen, many of whom were killed when he was assassinated this year.
1346	At the Battle of Crécy during the Hundred Years War, some 3,500 Welsh soldiers – possibly 5,000 – played a crucial role in the French defeat.
1356	At the Battle of Poitiers, Welsh soldiers again played an important role in the French defeat.
1415	At the Battle of Agincourt, Welsh troops played an important part in the defeat of the French. About 4,700 Welshmen served in Normandy alone.
1461	At the Battle of Mortimer's Cross, Edward IV's largely Welsh army defeated the Lancastrians.
1469	At the Battle of Banbury (Edgecote) as many as 5,000 Welsh Yorkist soldiers may have died.
1486	In the Battle of Bosworth, Henry Tudor defeated Richard III after marching through Wales from Dale, Dyfed. About a half of his 6,000–7,000 troops were Welsh.
1487	Lambert Simnel's revolt.
1497	Blackheath
1549	Cornwall
1554	Sir Thomas Wyatt's rebellion
1588–1602	Of some 100,000 troops recruited by Elizabeth I for service abroad, some 9,000 were Welsh. About 1,600 were recruited for the Earl of Essex's Cadiz campaign of 1596 and about 6,600 served in Ireland suffering heavy casualties at the Battle of the Yellow Ford.
1639–1640	Wales sent 600 troops in the first year and 700 in the second to join the Royal Army in preventing an invasion of England by Scottish Covenanters.

Welsh troops were used to put down these rebellions in Tudor England

1641–1643 Welsh troops were involved in putting down an Irish rebellion.

1642 In the Battle of Tewkesbury some 2,500 Royalist Welsh troops were killed.

1642 In the Battle of Edgehill about 5,000 Welshmen fought on the Royalist side with about 2,500 killed according to Parliamentary sources.

1645 During the Battle of Naseby about 100 Welsh women in the Royalist camp were reputedly killed by Parliamentary troops of the New Model Army.

1689, 1719 The first three Welsh regiments in the British army were formed. (For Honours of Welsh regiments in the British army, see Chapter 11.)

1899–1902 Some 200 Welshmen were killed in the Boer War in South Africa.

1914–1918 The First World War saw about 35,000 Welsh service personnel and members of the Merchant Navy killed.

1936–1939 During the Spanish Civil War, 33 of the 177 Welshmen who joined the International Brigades were killed.

1936–1945 During the Second World War, about 20,000 Welsh service personnel and members of the Merchant Navy were killed.

1951–1952 1st battalion, Welch Regiment, served with the United Nations in Korea during the 1950–53 war there.

1982 During the Falklands War, 39 Welsh Guardsmen were killed and 79 injured on the *Sir Galahad*.

1991 During the Gulf War, the 1st The Queen's Dragoon Guards ('The Cavalry Regiment of Wales') served as part of the Allied Forces, and two Welsh soldiers, one in the SAS and one in REME, were killed.

1993–1994 Two Welsh soldiers serving with the United Nations in Bosnia during the civil war in former Yugoslavia were killed – the first British soldiers to be killed there.

RIOTS, CIVIL DISTURBANCES, MUTINIES AND ESCAPES (from the early eighteenth century)

1715, 1716 Anti-Hanoverian riots by Jacobite mobs took place in Wrexham and a number of Dissenting chapels were damaged.

1728 Angry and hungry women in Beaumaris tried to stop corn being shipped out.

1740 There were riots in Rhuddlan by 400 armed miners from Mostyn and by lead miners over low wages and high corn prices. Troops were called in from Chester to maintain order. There were also food riots in Pembroke and Wrexham.

1742   William Seward, a Methodist preacher, was stoned to death by a mob in Hay-on-Wye.

1755   In November and December Carmarthen was terrorized by Jacobite anti-Whig mobs and several people were killed and injured.

1758   Cilgwyn quarrymen marched to Caernarfon to seize corn and two deaths occurred.

1783   Lead miners rioted in Aberystwyth in protest at high corn prices.

1793–1801   Food riots took place in many towns in Wales: at Abergele, Aberystwyth, Bala, Bangor, Bridgend, Barmouth, Caernarfon, Carmarthen, Carno, Conwy, Chepstow, Denbigh, Dowlais, Fishguard, Haverfordwest, Hay, Holywell, Machynlleth, Merthyr Tydfil, Mold, Narberth, Pembroke, Rhuddlan, Rhuthun, St David's, Swansea, Towyn and Wrexham.

Two miners were hanged in Cardiff after the Merthyr disturbances.

1809   There was a riot in Llanddeiniolen, Gwynedd, over land enclosures.

1812   A riot occurred at Nefyn, Llŷn, over enclosures.

1816   The Riot Act was read in Merthyr Tydfil during a miners' strike.

Soldiers fired warning shots in Aberystwyth during protests over enclosures.

1817   There were four weeks of lawlessness in Amlwch during January caused by high food prices.

1818   Cavalry were used in Carmarthen to stop a mob attempting to prevent the export of cheese.

1821   King George IV's visit to Carmarthen sparked off a riot in support of Queen Caroline.

1822–1826   Sporadic disturbances known as 'Rhyfel y Sais Bach' ('War of the little Englishman') took place on Mynydd Bach, Dyfed, over enclosures.

1822   Scots Greys opened fire in Gwent during industrial disturbances and several people were injured.

1830   The Riot Act was read in Rhosllanerchrugog to disperse striking miners. The yeomanry fired during a skirmish called the 'Battle of Chirk Bridge'.

1831   A riot took place in Mold. In Carmarthen a riot led to a parliamentary election being postponed from April to August. There were also election riots in Caernarfon, Montgomery,

Llanidloes and Haverfordwest. During the Merthyr Riots, 2–5 June, at least 16 people were killed and 70 injured when soldiers of the Argyll and Sutherland Highlanders opened fire.

1832–1834   This was the height of 'Scotch Cattle' disorders in south Wales, especially Monmouthshire, in the early days of trade-unionism in the area.

1839   A Chartist riot in Llanidloes led to the town being taken over by Chartists for a week in June. In November a Chartist march on the Westgate Hotel, Newport, resulted in the deaths of about 28 people as troops of the 43rd Regiment opened fire when crowds tried to storm the hotel.

1839–1842   During the Rebecca Riots, concentrated in south-west Wales, about 500 toll-gates were destroyed and one person was killed at Hendy, Dyfed.

1846   The Riot Act was read in Penmaenmawr and troops were brought in after some 300 local men attacked Irish navvies building a railway line.

1850   In Aberdare, during a miners' strike, the homes of strike-breakers were attacked with guns and explosives.

1856   Troops were sent into Talargoch, Flintshire, during a lead miners' strike.

1857   Troops were sent into the Aberdare area during a seven-week miners' strike.

1868   The Riot Act was read in Cardiff during general election disturbances.

1869   One man was killed during anti-Irish riots in Pontlottyn, Rhymney Valley. During riots in Mold caused by a miners' wages dispute, four men were shot dead by soldiers.

1882   Anti-Irish disturbances in the Tredegar area caused considerable damage to property and troops had to be sent in.

1886–1891   'Tithe War' disturbances took place in the Vale of Clwyd and the Riot Act was read at Mochdre in June, 1887. Troops had to be brought in to enforce the sale of farms in Denbigh and Bodfari in May, 1888, and disorders took place at Llangwm and Llanefydd.

1893   Troops were sent into south Wales during a 16-week hauliers' strike. English and Scottish 'blacklegs' were attacked during a miners' strike at Tumble.

1902   The Riot Act was read in Bethesda during the three-year Penrhyn Quarry lock-out. Troops were brought in to maintain order.

1910   During the Tonypandy Riots in November, considerable damage was done to property and one man died. Infantry and cavalry as well as police reinforcements from Bristol and London were brought into the Rhondda and to Aberdare. There were also disturbances at Cwmllynfell.

1911   In Cardiff in July, there were riots during a strike by dockers, seamen and others and Chinese laundries were attacked. About 500 troops had to be drafted into the city.

There was rioting in the Bargoed, Brynmawr, Cwm, Ebbw Vale and Tredegar areas for a week in August and Jewish-owned businesses were attacked. Troops were brought in to maintain order.

Also in August, during riots in Llanelli, two men were shot dead by soldiers during a strike and four men were killed when a rail truck exploded.

There were also several days of rioting in Swansea during September and October caused by industrial discontent, including protests against the use of 'blackleg' labour to break a strike at Port Tennant.

1915   Three German prisoners-of-war escaped from a camp at Llansannan, Gwynedd, but were recaptured within a few days after failing to rendezvous with two U-boats off the north Wales coast.

1919   During four days of serious race riots in Cardiff, three people were killed. There was a mutiny aboard the patrol vessel HMS *Kilbride* at Milford Haven over demobilization delays but no damage or injuries occurred. However, in a mutiny at Kinmel Camp, Rhyl, by Canadian soldiers awaiting repatriation, five men were killed and 28 injured.

1925   There was a riot at Ammanford during a strike by anthracite miners who controlled the town for 10 days; 58 men were sent to prison.

1926   During the last eight weeks of this year's miners' lock-out, 18 serious clashes occurred between miners and police in south Wales.

1929   At Cwmfelinfach, Gwent, over 700 people rioted over the employment of 'blackleg' labour at Nine Mile Point Colliery.

1931   A riot at Maerdy, Rhondda, led to 29 men and four women being given gaol sentences.

1933   A riot at Bedwas near Caerphilly led to seven men and four women receiving gaol sentences.

1935   Ten people received gaol sentences after disturbances in Blaina, Gwent. Rioting at Bedlinog during the Taff Merthyr Colliery 'stay in' strike led to the trial of 53 men and three women, all of whom were found guilty. Twenty-one were bound over and the rest imprisoned. In Merthyr Tydfil many women attacked the National Assistance Board offices and damaged its records.

1936 Following anti-Fascist demonstrations in Tonypandy, six men and one woman received gaol sentences.

1945 There was a mass break-out by 67 German prisoners-of-war from Island Farm camp, Bridgend – the biggest POW break-out ever in Britain. All the men were quickly recaptured.

1963–1969 Sabotage explosions and bomb attacks by an extremist nationalist organization, Mudiad Amddiffyn Cymru (Movement for the Defence of Wales), took place throughout Wales. Two of its members were killed by their own explosive devices at Abergele, Clwyd, in 1969, while a child was injured at Caernarfon and a warrant officer seriously injured at RAF Pembrey. Six members of the Free Wales Army were found guilty of Public Order and firearms offences in June, 1969, and three were given immediate prison sentences. In 1970 an army sergeant received a ten-year sentence and another man a six-year sentence for causing explosions.

1979 Start of the Meibion Glyndŵr (Sons of Glyndŵr) arson campaign. The extremist nationalist organization attacked English-owned property and businesses in many parts of Wales and also in England. Over 200 incidents had occurred by the end of 1992.

1991 There were four consecutive nights of rioting on the Ely estate in Cardiff in late August to early September following which 23 people received prison sentences. The riots were sparked off by a dispute between two local shopkeepers but hot weather and youth unemployment were considered to have been factors contributing to the violence.

NOTABLE WELSH EXECUTIONS

1283 On 3 October, Dafydd ap Gruffudd, the last native prince of Wales, was hanged, drawn and quartered at Shrewsbury for treason.

1292 Rhys ap Maredudd was executed at York following a revolt against Edward I he had led in south Wales.

1316 Execution at Cardiff of Llywelyn Bren (Llywelyn ap Rhys) for rebelling against Edward II.

1410 Rhys Ddu, Rhys ap Tudor and Philip Scudamore were executed for treason for supporting Owain Glyndŵr.

1461	Owen Tudor, husband of Henry V's widow, Catherine, and grandfather of the future King Henry VII, was beheaded for treason at Hereford during the Wars of the Roses.
1471	Sir Roger Vaughan, a Yorkist supporter, was beheaded by Jasper Tudor, a leading Lancastrian, at Chepstow after the Yorkist victory at the Battle of Tewkesbury.
1531	Sir Rhys ap Gruffudd was beheaded on Tower Hill and William Hughes was hanged at Tyburn for plotting the overthrow of Henry VIII.
1534–1543	Bishop Rowland Lee, President of the Council for Wales and the Marches, claimed he hanged some 5,000 people in Wales to eliminate chronic disorder there.
1539	For refusing to accept the supremacy of Henry VIII, John Eynon, priest of St Giles, Reading, was hanged in Reading, and John Griffith, chaplain to the Marquis of Exeter, was executed at Southwark.
1540	Edward Powell of Powys, a Catholic theologian and former headmaster of Eton, and Richard Featherstone, Archdeacon of Brecon, were hanged, drawn and quartered for treason at Smithfield, London.
1542	Thomas Capper, a Protestant, was burned at the stake in Cardiff for heresy. He was the first religious martyr in Wales.
1554	William Thomas, a Protestant from Powys, was executed in London for plotting the death of Queen Mary.
1554	Lewis Owen, Sheriff of Merioneth, was reputed to have hanged 80 of 'the red-haired bandits of Mawddach' on Christmas Eve.
1555	Bishop Robert Ferrer in Carmarthen and Rawlins White in Cardiff, both Protestants, were burned at the stake for heresy.
1558	William Nichol, a Protestant, was burned at the stake in Haverfordwest for heresy.
1584	Richard Gwyn, a Catholic, was hanged, drawn and quartered in Wrexham for heresy.
1585	William Parry of Northop, Clwyd, was executed in London for conspiring to kill Elizabeth I.
1586	Thomas Salusbury of Denbigh and Edward Jones of Wrexham were executed in London for their parts in the Babington plot to assassinate Elizabeth I.
1588	William Gunter, a Catholic priest from Raglan, was hanged in London for heresy.
1588	Richard Lloyd, a Catholic layman from Anglesey, was hanged at Tyburn, London, for heresy.

1589	Humphrey Pritchard, a Catholic layman, was hanged at Oxford for heresy.
1590	Edward Jones, a Catholic from Llanelidan, Dyffryn Clwyd, was hanged in London for harbouring a priest.
1593	John Penry of Llangammarch, Powys, a Puritan martyr, was beheaded in Surrey for heresy.
1593	William Davies, a Catholic priest from Croes yr Eirias, Gwynedd, was hanged, drawn and quartered at Beaumaris for treason.
1598	John Jones, a Catholic priest from Clynnog Fawr, Llŷn, was hanged at Southwark for heresy.
1601	Sir Gelly Meyrick of Pemrokeshire was executed in London for treason.
1610	John Roberts, a Benedictine monk from Trawsfynydd, Gwynedd, was hanged at Tyburn for treason, and Roger Cadwaladr, a Jesuit from the Welsh-speaking part of Herefordshire, was hanged, drawn and quartered at Leominster for treason.
1642	Edward Morgan, a seminary priest from Bettisfield, Clwyd, was hanged at Tyburn.
1646	Colonel John Poyer, the Royalist governor of Pembroke Castle, was executed by a Parliamentary firing squad at Covent Garden.
1646	Philip Powell, a Catholic priest from Trallong, Powys, was hanged, drawn and quartered at Tyburn for treason.
1651	Christopher Love, a Presbyterian minister from Cardiff, was hanged on Tower Hill for treason.
1660	Colonel John Jones of Maes-y-garnedd, Gwynedd, one of the signatories of Charles I's death warrant and brother-in-law of Oliver Cromwell, was executed at Covent Garden.
1679	Philip Evans of Monmouth and John Lloyd of Brecon, both Catholic priests, were hanged, drawn and quartered in Cardiff for treason.
1679	David Lewis, a Jesuit from Abergavenny, was hanged and disembowelled at Usk. He was the last person in Wales to suffer religious martyrdom.
1746	David Morgan, a barrister from Penygraig Taf near Quakers' Yard, Mid Glamorgan, was hanged, drawn and quartered in London for his part in Bonnie Prince Charles's Jacobite rebellion of 1745.
1801	At Cardiff Assizes, Samuel Hill and Aaron Williams were sentenced to death for their parts in food riots in Merthyr Tydfil.
1831	Dic Penderyn (Richard Lewis) was hanged in Cardiff for his alleged part in the Merthyr Rising and became regarded as Wales's first 'working-class martyr'.

1835	Edward Morgan was hanged at Monmouth for a 'Scotch Cattle' murder in Bedwellty.
1866	Robert Coe was hanged at Swansea for murder. This was the last public execution in Wales.
1915–1918	In France and Belgium, 13 men serving with Welsh regiments were executed by firing squad, nine for desertion and four for murder.
1958	Vivian Frederick Teed was hanged in Swansea for murder. This was the last execution to take place in Wales.

Unlike England and Scotland, there is no record of any witches or Lollard heretics (Wycliffites) being put to death in Wales.

15

WALES AND THE WELSH IN EUROPE AND THE REST OF THE WORLD

FACTS ABOUT WALES AND THE WORLD

- The names of the three oldest geological divisions in the Palaeozoic era are derived from Wales: the Cambrian (the Latin name for Wales) and the Ordovician and the Silurian (from the names of Celtic tribes in Wales).
- Milford Haven is the deepest natural waterway in Europe.
- The Bristol Channel has the second largest tidal range in the world – 40.1 ft. mean spring tide at New Passage.
- Merthyr Mawr, South Glamorgan, has the second tallest sand dunes in Europe.
- The gannetry on Grassholm, Dyfed, is the third largest in Europe and the fourth largest in the world.
- One-third of the world's population of grey seals is found on the Pembrokeshire coast of Dyfed.
- The largest Iron Age fort in north-west Europe is Tre'r Ceiri on Yr Eifl, Llŷn.
- St David's Head, Dyfed, appears on the oldest known map of the world – Ptolemy's map of the second century AD.
- Of the 30 forts in the Roman Empire, two were built on the Welsh borderland, at Caerleon and Chester.
- The remains of the Roman legionary barracks at Caerleon, Gwent, are the only ones on view anywhere in Europe.
- Offa's Dyke, 150 miles long, was the longest man-made boundary in Western Europe in the Middle Ages.
- In medieval Christendom, St David's had the same status as Santiago de Compostela, Galicia, in that two pilgrimages to either of them equalled one to Rome.
- Roger Barlow of Slebech, Pembrokeshire, was in Sebastian Cabot's second voyage of 1526 and later translated the Spanish *Suma de Geographie* – the first account of the New World in English.

- The main benefactor of Yale University was Elihu Yale. He was born in Boston of Welsh immigrant parents and in Wales became High Sheriff of Denbigh in 1704. He is buried in St Giles Church, Wrexham.
- The Skull and Crossbones flag was reputedly first flown by the Welsh pirate Bartholemew Roberts ('Black Bart' or 'Barti Ddu') from Little Newcastle, Dyfed, who was killed by the Royal Navy off West Africa in 1722.
- After copper was found there in 1768, Parys Mountain, Anglesey, soon became the largest copper mine in Europe.
- Morgan Edwards of Pontypool who died in Delaware in 1795 was joint founder of Brown University, Rhode Island.
- In the 1830s at Ynyscedwyn, Powys, iron was smelted with anthracite for the first time anywhere in the world.
- The Malagasy language of Madagascar was first put into writing by David Jones, a missionary educated at Neuadd Lwyd, near Aberaeron, who died in Mauritius in 1841.
- The first grammar and dictionary of Tahitian were written by John Davies, a missionary from Llanfihangel-yng-Ngwynfa, Powys, who died in Tahiti in 1855.
- Beijing (Peking) University developed from a language school in the city established by the missionary Professor Hopkyn Rees, born at Cwmafan, West Glamorgan, in 1869.
- The major coalfield in Queensland, Australia, was developed from the 1870s by Lewis Thomas from Llanfihangel Genau'r-glyn, Dyfed.
- Large areas of Central Africa were explored in the second half of the nineteenth century by Denbigh-born Sir Henry Morton Stanley (born John Rowlands).
- One of the greatest patriotic poems in Magyar, 'A Welesi Bardok' by Janos Arany (1817–72) is based on the tradition that Edward I ordered the execution of all captured Welsh bards after the conquest of 1282.
- The Welsh Cup, first won in 1878, is the world's third oldest football competition after England (1872) and Scotland (1874).
- Tredegar-born James T. Davis, was United States Secretary for Labour 1921–30 and US Senator from 1930 to 1945.
- At the outbreak of the First World War, Welsh coal made up one-third of world coal exports.
- The longest serving head of any United Nations agency was Sir Arthur Davies of Barry at the World Meteorological Office (Geneva) 1955–79.
- With some 11 million sheep, Wales is the most important sheep-rearing area in Europe with about 15 per cent of the sheep in the European Community.
- Welshpool's Monday sheep-market is reputed to be the largest in Europe.

- Bethesda slate quarry, 1,140 ft. (347.5 m.) deep, is reputed to have been the second largest quarry in Europe after the Carrara marble quarry in Italy.
- Dinorwic pump-storage power station is the biggest of its kind in Europe.
- Watwick Point lighthouse, Milford Haven, 157 ft. (48 m.) high, is the world's third tallest lighthouse.
- The longest railway station name in the world is Llanfair-pwllgwyngyll-gogerychwyrndrobwyll-llantisiliogogogoch, Anglesey.
- About 300 books are published in Welsh every year – more than in any other European minority language except Catalan.
- Hay-on-Wye, Powys, is reputed to be the largest centre in the world for the sale of second-hand books.

DATES OF SIGNIFICANCE AND INTEREST

*c.*1100 Henry I introduced Flemish settlers into south Pembrokeshire and possibly to Gower as well.

1346 At the Battle of Crécy, Welsh soldiers in Edward III's army were dressed in green and white, thought to be the first troops from Britain to appear on a continental battlefield in medieval Europe in uniform.

*c.*1550 Robert Recorde of Tenby invented the mathematical sign for equality (=).

1612– Sir Thomas Button of Duffryn near Cardiff, called the 'First White Man
1613 in Manitoba', commanded an expedition to search for Henry Hudson's expedition, lost in 1610, and to discover a north-west passage to Asia. He explored a large part of Hudson Bay (now Manitoba province) where Button Island is named after him.

1617 An attempt to found a Welsh colony, Cambriol, in Newfoundland, was made by Robert Vaughan but was abandoned after some 20 years.

1620 Of the 41 Pilgrim Fathers aboard the *Mayflower*, five are claimed to be Welsh.

1631– Thomas James of Abergavenny explored and chartered Hudson Bay
1632 while searching for a north-west passage to Asia. James Bay there is named after him.

1706 William Jones from Lanfihangel Tre'r-beirdd, Anglesey, became the first person to use the symbol π (pi) to denote the ratio of the circumference of a circle to its diameter.

1769 The first written record of the Maori language was made at Queen Charlotte Sound in New Zealand by Dr David Samuel of Nantglyn, Clwyd, while serving on board Captain Cook's ship *Endeavour*.

1771   The first accurate and reliable actuarial statistics, forming the basis of life insurance, were calculated by Dr Richard Price of Llangeinor, Glamorgan.

1776   The American Declaration of Independence was signed by five men who were definitely of Welsh origin including one, Francis Lewis, who was born at Newport, Gwent, and represented New York.

1778   During the American War of Independence, John Paul Jones, founder of the United States Navy, was active off the Welsh coast and watered on Caldey. He is commemorated by Jones Bay on the island.

1787   Between this year, when the 'First Fleet' of convicts sailed, and 1868, some 2,200 people from Wales – almost 300 of them women – were transported to Australia.

1793   Over 50 Quakers from Nantucket Island, USA, settled at Milford Haven to establish a whaling industry there.

1796–   John Evans of Waunfawr, Gwynedd, became the first man to map the
1797   2,000 miles of the Missouri River above its confluence with the Mississippi.

1798   The earliest known use of the term 'tramroad' was in the minutes of the Brecon and Abergavenny Canal Company.

1804   The world's first steam locomotive ran the 9¼ miles between Penydarren and Abercynon, Glamorgan, on 21 February carrying 10 tons of iron and 70 men at 5 m.p.h.

1807   The world's first fare-paying passenger railway (horse drawn) began operating between Swansea and Mumbles.

1811   The world's first free-standing rail bridge of metal was built at Robertstown near Aberdare.

1819   A Welsh settlement was established at Cardigan, New Brunswick, Canada.

1824   Captain William Davies Evans of St Dogwell's, Dyfed, invented the Evans Gambit – a popular chess move.

1830   The rails for the world's first steam railway between Liverpool and Manchester were made at Penydarren, Merthyr Tydfil.

1835   The steam whistle was invented by Adrian Stephens of Dowlais.

1836   Two Welshmen, Lewis Johnson and William Lewis, were killed in the Battle of the Alamo, Texas.
       The world's first narrow-gauge railway, the Blaenau Ffestiniog Railway, was opened.

1837   Rails made in south Wales were used in the construction of the Warsaw–Vienna railway.

1838–   Muntz Metal (Yellow Metal), a copper–zinc alloy, was invented in
1842   Swansea.

1841 Thomas Jones, born near Meifod, Powys, became the first of some 160 Welsh Calvinistic Methodist missionaries to work in the Khasia Hills of Assam, India, and was the first person, as far as is known, to put the Khasia language into writing.

1842 Hamburg was largely re-roofed with Welsh slate after this year's great fire in the city.

1848 The oldest named train in the world, the *Irish Mail*, began operating between London Euston and Bangor (extended to Holyhead in 1850).

1849 Some 250 converts from the Merthyr Tydfil area were among the first Mormon settlers at Salt Lake City, Utah, founded two years earlier by Brigham Young. (A further 700 Welsh Mormons arrived in 1856.)

1850 The world's first tubular bridge, designed by Robert Stephenson, was opened across the Menai Strait.

1850–
1851 An unsuccessful attempt was made to establish a Welsh settlement, Nova Cambria, to mine gold in Rio Grande do Sol, Brazil, by Evan Evans with about 100 people from Gwent.

1851 George Jones, the son of a Welsh immigrant from Llanwyddelan, Powys, was one of the two founders of the *New York Times* this year.

1852 The largest three-decked ship in the world, HMS *Duke of Wellington*, was launched at Pembroke Dock and became the flagship of Admiral Napier during the Crimean War.

1854 Lord Tredegar (Charles Morgan) and at least three other Welshmen survived the Charge of the Light Brigade.

1856–
1866 Samuel Roberts, of Llanbrynmair, unsuccessfully attempted to establish a Welsh colony in eastern Tennessee.

1859 The world's first mail-order business was opened by Sir Pryce Pryce-Jones at Newtown, Powys.

1861 The deepest rock-cutting in the world (120 ft./36 m.) was made on the Newtown–Machynlleth railway line at Talerddig, Powys.

1865 Mount Everest, the world's highest mountain, was named after Sir George Everest of Gwernvale near Crickhowell, Powys, the former surveyor-general of India.

   The Ffestiniog Railway became the first narrow-gauge railway in the world to carry passengers.

   A Welsh colony was successfully established in Chubut, Patagonia, and became the first community to give the vote to women.

1867 The Queensberry Rules governing boxing were revised by John Graham Chambers from Llanelli.

1868 The first Norwegian Seamen's Mission church outside Norway was opened in Cardiff.

1869   Williams Siemens invented the open-hearth method of steel production at Landore.

John Hughes of Merthyr Tydfil founded the first major ironworks in the Russian Empire, at Donetsk in the Ukraine – originally named Yuzovka (Hughesovka) after him.

1871   Lewis Jones became the only Welshman to be appointed governor of Chubut by the Argentine government.

Dr Livingstone was located by H. M. Stanley at Ujiji, Lake Tanganyika.

1873   At Nantclwyd Hall, Llanelidan, Clwyd, Major Walter Wingfield invented and patented nets for an outdoor game he called 'sphairistike' – now known as lawn tennis.

1875   Wheat from the North American prairies was first imported into Britain through Cardiff as well as Liverpool.

The United States Immigration Service became the first state institution anywhere in the world to recognize the Welsh as a distinct nationality.

1877   The death occurred in Hobart, Tasmania, of Dolgellau-born Thomas Richards, known as 'the father of Tasmanian journalism'.

1878   The open-hearth method of steel-making using phosphoric ores, which revolutionized steel production, was developed at Blaenafon, Gwent.

1880   The world's first mechanically propelled submarine, the *Resurgam*, sank off Llandudno.

1883   Sir Samuel Griffith from Merthyr Tydfil became Premier of Queensland.

1885   The world's first passenger-carrying ropeway came into service across the River Aeron at Aberaeron.

1889   The first-ever substitution in a football match was during the Wales v. Scotland game at Wrexham when, with the agreement of both sides, the Welsh goalkeeper was replaced after an injury.

1890   Sealyham Terriers were first bred at Sealyham Hall, Haverfordwest by Captain John Owen.

1895   The world's first hockey international was played between Wales and Ireland at Rhyl with Ireland winning 3–0.

1896   The first single-handed crossing of the Atlantic was completed by the Dane, Alfred Johnson, at Abercastle, Pembrokeshire, on 11 August.

1897   Guglielmo Marconi transmitted the world's first radio message across water from Flat Holm to Lavernock Point, South Glamorgan.

1899–   During the Boer War in South Africa, some 200 Welshmen
1902   were killed.

1900	The US Bureau of Census figures showed an all-time high Welsh population of 93,744 immigrants and 173,416 children of Welsh immigrants.
	The Royal Welch Fusiliers comprised the largest contingent of British troops involved in relieving the siege of Beijing (Peking) during the Boxer Rebellion.
1905	The International Bowling Board, the premier governing body of the sport throughout the world, was formed in Cardiff.
	Thomas Pryce from Brymbo, Clwyd, became the first Labour Prime Minister of South Australia.
1906	The only tennis Davis Cup Final ever played in Wales – between the USA and Australia at Newport – was won by the USA.
1908	The world's first-ever rugby league international was played at Aberdare where Wales beat New Zealand 9–8.
1909	Members of Sir Edward Shackleton's Antarctic expedition led by Sir T. W. E. David of St Fagans, became the first to reach the magnetic South Pole on 16 January.
1910	Henry Rolls of Monmouth became the first person to fly across the English Channel and back non-stop.
	Ernest Thompson Willows of Cardiff became the first person to fly an airship – the *City of Cardiff* – across the English Channel from England to France.
1914	Wales produced two world boxing champions this year: Freddie Welsh (Frederick Hall Thomas), Pontypridd, lightweight champion and Percy Jones, Porthcawl, featherweight champion.
1914–1918	During the First World War about 35,000 Welsh people were killed including merchant seamen and 19 women.
1915	William Morris Hughes, a Welsh-speaking Australian, became Prime Minister of Australia and held the position until 1923.
1916	Charles Evans Hughes, the Welsh-speaking son of a Tredegar immigrant, was only narrowly beaten by Woodrow Wilson in the United States presidential election. (9,129,606 to 8,538,221 popular votes; 277 to 254 electoral college votes).
	Jimmy Wilde, Tylorstown, Rhondda, became the world flyweight champion – he was the first holder of the title.
1920	Billy Meredith of Chirk, Clwyd, became the oldest man ever to play in a football international at 45 years 8 months (v. England).
1924	David Ifon Jones of Aberystwyth, founder member of the South African Communist Party, became the only Welshman to be given a state funeral in the (then) Soviet Union in Moscow.

Malcolm Campbell established a new world land-speed record of 146.16 m.p.h. at Pendine, Dyfed.

1925 The first Urdd Gobaith Cymru peace message to the world was broadcast by the BBC.

Malcolm Campbell set a new world land-speed record of 150.87 m.p.h. at Pendine.

Amelia Earhart became the first woman to fly the Atlantic when her seaplane *Friendship*, piloted by Wilmar Stultz, landed off Burry Port, Dyfed, after a 20 hour 49 minute flight from Newfoundland.

1926 J. G. Parry Thomas of Wrexham set a new world land-speed record of 171.02 m.p.h. beating the 169.30 m.p.h. he had set earlier in the year – both at Pendine.

1927 Malcolm Campbell set a new world land-speed record of 174.88 m.p.h. at Pendine.

1929 The first non-stop flight from Britain to India was accomplished by two Welsh airmen – Squadron Leader A. G. Jones-Williams and Flight Lieutenant N. H. Jenkins.

British Movietone News shot the first-ever sound film of a shipwreck – that of the *Molesey* wrecked on Skomer Island, Dyfed.

1931 Harold Gatty and Wiley Post refuelled at RAF Sealand, Clwyd, after flying non-stop from Newfoundland during their record-breaking eight-day flight around the world.

1933 Amy Johnson and Jim Mollison made the first non-stop flight across the Atlantic from the UK to the USA in 34 hours after taking off from Pendine on 22 July in their seaplane *Seafarer*.

1935 Felinfoel Brewery, Llanelli, became the first in Europe to market beer in cans.

1939– During the Second World War some 20,000 Welsh servicemen and women and members of the Merchant Navy were killed; almost 1,000 civilians were killed in German air raids on Wales. Milford Haven was the assembly point for convoys during the war involving some 17,000 vessels.

1942 Cardiff Docks were used in a mock attack in preparation for the successful assault on German-occupied St Nazaire, Brittany.

1943 About 100,000 Allied troops took part in a rehearsal of the D-Day landings in 'Operation Jantzen' on the south Wales coast between Amroth and Saundersfoot, Dyfed.

1944 About one-third of the ships in the Normandy landings sailed from Welsh ports.

1942–45 The German Deputy Führer Rudolf Hess was a prisoner at Abergavenny.

1946   Neath-born Ray Milland won the Hollywood Oscar for Best Actor for his role in *The Lost Weekend.*

In the first world title fight ever staged in Wales, Ronnie James, Pontardawe, lost the lightweight title contest to Ike Williams, USA, in Cardiff.

1947   The first Llangollen International Musical Eisteddfod was held.

1949   The last governor-general of an independent Newfoundland before it became a Canadian province was Lord MacDonald of Gwaunysgor.

1950   The world's worst air disaster up to that time occurred at Llandow, South Glamorgan, when an Avro Tudor V Plane returning from a rugby international in Ireland crashed killing 75 of 78 passengers and the crew of five.

Wales competed in football's World Cup for the first time.

The Tal-y-llyn railway became the world's first privately preserved railway.

The world's first scheduled helicopter service began between Cardiff, Wrexham and Liverpool. (It ended in 1951.)

1951   A world record crowd for an ordinary club rugby match (48,500) attended the game between Cardiff and Newport at Cardiff Arms Park.

1955   An expedition led by Sir Charles Evans was the first to conquer the world's third highest mountain, Kinchinjunga, in the Himalayas. (Sir Charles had been deputy leader of the successful Mount Everest expedition of 1953.)

1958   Wales reached the quarter-finals of the football World Cup in Sweden.

1959   Jimmy Wilde, Tylorstown, Rhondda, world flyweight champion 1916–23, became the first European to be elected to the American Boxing Hall of Fame.

Hugh Griffith of Marian-glas, Anglesey, won the Hollywood Oscar for Best Supporting Actor in *Ben Hur.*

1961   The world's first zinc blast furnace, at Llansamlet, began operating.

1962   The world's first commercial hovercraft service began on 20 July between Rhyl and Wallasey. The world's first hovercraft wreck followed the same year off Rhyl.

Llanwern steelworks near Newport opened at a cost of £48 million – Europe's most expensive civil engineering construction scheme to that date.

1963   The Ffestiniog power station was opened – the first pumped-storage scheme in Europe.

Abertysswg-born Jack Howells won the Hollywood Oscar for the Best Short Documentary Film, *Dylan Thomas.*

1966   Lynn Davies, Nantymoel, became the first person to hold the European, Commonwealth and Olympic long-jump titles at the same time.

1967   Paul Radmilovic, Cardiff, became the first Briton to be elected to the American Swimming Hall of Fame.

1968   Howard Winstone, Merthyr Tydfil, won the world featherweight boxing title.

1970   Saunders Lewis was nominated for the Nobel Prize for Literature.

       The second world and the first European field championships in archery were held at Llwynypia, Rhondda.

1971   Nicolette Milnes-Walker of Cardiff became the first woman to sail single-handed non-stop across the Atlantic – from Dale, Dyfed, to Newport, Rhode Island.

1972   In Skopje, Macedonia, Wales competed in the World Chess Olympiad for the first time.

1973   Japan played its first rugby match in Europe at Penygraig, Rhondda.

       The Nobel Prize for Physics was won by Cardiff-born Professor Brian Josephson.

1977   The first darts World Cup was won by Wales.

       Holywell-born Jonathan Pryce won a Broadway 'Tony' for his role in *The Comedians*.

1979   A world record for a powered hang-glider flight was set by Gerry Breen of Crickhowell, Powys, in a 202-mile flight from Tredegar to Norwich.

       Wales won the snooker World Cup and retained it in 1980.

1981   The World White Water Championships were held for the first time in Wales, at Trawsfynydd.

1982   With the launch of S4C, Welsh became the first European minority language with its own television channel.

       Wales became the first nuclear-free country in Europe when all eight county councils agreed never to allow nuclear weapons on their soil.

1983   The Cardiff 'Singer of the World' biennial competition began.

       Colin Jones, Gorseinon, drew the world welterweight title fight in Reno, Nevada.

1984   Ian Rush became the first Welshman to win the European Golden Boot Award as the leading league scorer with 32 goals in the 1983–4 season.

1987   Wales won the golf World Cup in Hawaii – the first of the British Isles countries to do so.

       Wales finished third in the first rugby union World Cup played in Australia and New Zealand.

1988   *Pobl y Cwm* became the first European-made 'soap opera' to be broadcast daily.

Steve Jones became the first Briton to win the New York Marathon.

The European Centre for Traditional and Regional Cultures opened in Llangollen.

The first Welsh sites were placed on UNESCO's World Heritage List: the castles at Beaumaris, Caernarfon, Conwy and Harlech.

1990   Griffith P. Williams of Llithfaen, Gwynedd, became the world's oldest author with the publication of his autobiography *Cofio Canrif* ('Remembering a Century') on his 102nd birthday.

The European Minority Languages centre was opened at Nant Gwrtheyrn, Llŷn, Gwynedd.

At Carmarthen Bay, Europe's largest vertical wind turbine was inaugurated.

1991   The first women's rugby union World Cup was held in Wales with the USA winning the final in Cardiff.

Holywell-born Jonathan Pryce won a Broadway 'Tony' for Best Actor in a Musical in *Miss Saigon*.

Ian Woosnam became the first Welshman to win a major golf tournament – the US Masters at Augusta, Georgia.

Eric Jones of Tremadoc, Gwynedd, was one of a party of four which made the first hot-air balloon flight over Mount Everest.

1992   The Wales Europe Centre was opened in Brussels.

Sir Anthony Hopkins (b. Port Talbot) won the Hollywood Oscar for Best Actor for his role in *The Silence of the Lambs*.

1993   The world featherweight title of the World Boxing Organization was won by Steve Robinson of Cardiff.

Europe's largest wind farm, at Llandinam, Powys, with 103 turbines, began operating.

WALES IN THE ROMAN EMPIRE

Place-names in Wales

Forts and Settlements:

Abergavenny	*Gobannium*	Caerwent	*Venta Silurum*
Brecon (Y Gaer)	*Cicutio*	Carmarthen	*Moridunum*
Caerhun (Conwy Valley)	*Conovium*	Caersws	*Mediomanum*
Caerleon	*Isca Silurum*	Cowbridge	*Bovium* (probably)
Caernarfon	*Segontium*	Dolaucothi (Dyfed)	*Luentinium*
Caersws	*Mediomanum*	Forden Gaer (Powys)	*Lavobrinta*

Holt (Clwyd)	*Bovium*	Neath	*Nidum*
Llandovery	*Alabum*	Llanio, Tregaron	*Bremia*
Loughor	*Leucarum* (possibly)	St Asaph	*Varae* (probably)
Monmouth	*Blestium*	Usk	*Burrium*

Geographical Features:

Anglesey	*Mona Insula*
Braich y Pwll (Llŷn)	*Ganganorum Promontorium*
St David's Head	*Octapitarum Promontorium*

Rivers:

Ewenny	*Aventio*	Towy (Tywi)	*Tuvius*
Loughor	*Levca*	Usk	*Isca*
Severn	*Sabrina*	Wye	*Vaga*
Glaslyn	*Tisobis*	Ystwyth	*Estucia*

Latin Borrowings

About 1,000 words in modern Welsh can be traced back to borrowings from Latin in the Celtic language spoken in Britain during the Roman occupation from the first to the fourth centuries AD.

WALES IN MODERN CELTIC EUROPE – Some Significant Dates

1707   Edward Lhuyd's *Archaeological Britannica* was published and became the basis of future study of Celtic languages.

1838   A Pan Celtic meeting was held at Abergavenny and is regarded as the first modern Celtic association.

1867   A Celtic congress was held at St Brieuc, Brittany – the second modern Celtic association.

1877   A Chair of Celtic Studies was established at Oxford University with Sir John Rhys appointed the first professor.

1888   A Pan Celtic Society was formed in Dublin.

1900   The Celtic Congress was formed in Dublin following a meeting the previous year at Cardiff during the National Eisteddfod there.

1904   The second Celtic Congress, held at Caernarfon, recognized language as being the criterion of a Celtic nation.

1920   The Board of Celtic Studies of the University of Wales was founded.

1961   The Celtic League was formed at the Rhosllanerchrugog National Eisteddfod with Gwynfor Evans the president until the position was abolished in 1972.

1963	The International Congress of Celtic Studies was held in Wales for the first time.
1971	In the Carlyon Bay agreement, the Archdruid of Wales was recognized as the head of the Celtic *gorseddau*, those of Brittany and Cornwall as well as Wales.
	The first Celtic Festival was held at Killarney.
1974	The 'Celtic Sea' was given an official definition as the area bounded by Ushant, Land's End, Hartland Point, St Govan's Head and Rosslare.
1980	The first Celtic Film and Television Festival was held on South Uist, Hebrides.
1985	A Centre for Advanced Welsh and Celtic Studies was established at University College, Aberystwyth, with permanent buildings from 1992.
1987	The International Congress of Celtic Studies was held in Wales for a second time.
1991	'Celtica' celebrations were held throughout Wales.
	The building of a Celtic resources centre at Machynlleth was announced.

COUNTRIES WITH CONSULATES IN WALES

Belgium	389 Newport Road, Cardiff, CF2 1RP.
Brazil	100 Newport Road, Cardiff, CF2 1DG.
Denmark	68 James Street, Cardiff, CF1 6SP.
Finland	Mount Stuart House, Mount Stuart Square, Cardiff, CF1 6QC.
France	Dumfries House, Dumfries Place, Cardiff, CF1 4YF.
Germany	Pencoed House, Capel Llanilltern, nr. Cardiff, CF5 6JH.
Italy	14 Museum Place, Cardiff, CF1 3BH.
Japan	1 Dumfries House, Dumfries Place, Cardiff, CF1 4BN.
Netherlands	4th Floor, 113–16 Bute Street, Cardiff, CF1 6TE.
Norway	Empire House, Mount Stuart Square, Cardiff, CF1 6UT.
Portugal	35 West Bute Street, Cardiff, CF1 5LH.
Sweden	4 Dunraven Crescent, Forest Hills, Talbot Green, Mid Glamorgan, CF1 1SE.
Thailand	38 Station Road, Llanishen, Cardiff, CF4 5LG.
Tunisia	Churchill House, Churchill Way, Cardiff, CF1 4HH.
Turkey	Empire House, Mount Stuart Square, Cardiff, CF1 6QZ.

WELSH SOCIETIES AND TWINNING ASSOCIATIONS

Welsh Societies Abroad

Information about Welsh exiles' organizations may be obtained from Cymru a'r Byd (formerly called Undeb y Cymry ar Wasgar), 'Hiraethog', Llannor, Pwllheli, Gwynedd, LL53 5UR.

Twinning Associations

For Welsh twinning arrangements with overseas regions, cities and towns, see chapter 3.

16

WALES AND THE WELSH IN BRITAIN

FACTS ABOUT WALES AND THE WELSH IN BRITAIN

- Wales is the main stronghold of the raven in Britain.
- The red kite is the only British bird found solely in Wales.
- The polecat is now found only in Wales, mainly in Tregaron Bog.
- The British black adder is found only in Tregaron Bog.
- A type of whitefish, the *gwyniad*, is found only in Lake Bala.
- Yellow whitlowgrass (*Draba azoides*) is found only in Gower and nowhere else in Britain.
- The Tenby daffodil (*Narcissus obvallaris*) is found only in a small area around Tenby.
- Craig Cerrig-gleisiad national nature reserve in the Brecon Beacons has the most southerly arctic-alpine plants in Britain.
- The Snowdonia National Park is the only place in southern Britain where the pine marten is found.
- The Dysynni Valley in Gwynedd is the only inland site in Britain where cormorants breed.
- The deepest cave in Britain is Ogof Ffynnon Ddu, Powys – 1,010 ft. (300 m.) deep and at 28 miles (48 km.) the second longest cave in Britain.
- The River Usk is the deepest river in the British Isles at its mouth.
- The only known self-generating lake (turlough) in Britain is at Druids Crag near Llandeilo.
- The second oldest known humanoid (Neanderthal) remains in Britain – some 230,000 years old – were found in Ponterwyd cave, Elwy Valley, Clwyd, in 1980.
- Some of the oldest remains of *Homo sapiens* found in Britain are those of 'the Red Lady of Paviland' (Gower) – actually a male – dated to some 23,000 years ago. Human artefacts dating back some 28,000 years have also been found at Paviland.

- The oldest known human footprints in Britain were found in 1986 at Uskmouth, Gwent, dating to about 5,000 BC.
- The 80 Bluestones at Stonehenge appear to have been transported from the Preseli Mountains, Dyfed, about 2,500 BC.
- The 40-tonne capstone on the neolithic burial chamber at Tinkinswood, South Glamorgan, is the largest capstone in Britain and dates to about 2,000 BC.
- Barclodiad y Gawres and Bryn Celli Ddu, both on Anglesey, are the only megalithic tombs in Britain with mural decorations.
- The Gop-y-Goleuni Bronze Age cairn at Trelawnyd, Clwyd is the second largest in Britain, some 36 ft. (11 m.) high with a 320 ft. (100 m.) maximum diameter.
- In the Neolithic period, hand axes made at Craig Llwyd, Penmaenmawr, Gwynedd, were traded all over the British Isles.
- The oldest iron artefact found in Britain is part of a sword found in Llyn Fawr, Rhondda, in 1911.
- The only fully excavated Roman amphitheatre in Britain is at Caerleon, Gwent.
- The Dolaucothi gold mine, Dyfed, is the only known Roman gold mine in Britain.
- The oldest monument to any British king – dated to about 500 AD – is to Voteporix and is now in Carmarthen Museum, Abergwili.
- The earliest secular stone building in Britain is the hall keep of Chepstow Castle dated to the decade after 1066.
- Wales was the only one of the main political units of the British Isles which avoided yielding substantial areas of land to the Scandinavian Vikings.
- Caerphilly Castle (30 acres or 12 hectares) is the second largest castle site in Britain after Dover (34 acres or 14 hectares) and was the first concentric castle to be built in Britain.
- Castell Dinas near Talgarth, Powys, is the highest castle site in Britain at 1,476 ft. (449 m.).
- The last major Romanesque church to be built in Britain was St David's Cathedral.
- Monmouth has the only bridge fortified with a gatehouse in Britain – thought to have been built in 1290.
- Conwy's medieval walls and 22 towers are the best preserved of any in the British Isles.
- Three kings of England were born in Wales: Edward II (Caernarfon, 1284), Henry V (Monmouth, 1387), and Henry VII (Pembroke, 1457).
- Carew tidal mill near Pembroke is one of only three in Britain and the only one in Wales.
- The oldest organ case in Britain, dating to the early sixteenth century, is in St Stephen's Church, Old Radnor, Powys.

- The term 'British Empire' is generally thought to have been coined by John Dee – London Welshman, mathematician, astronomer and alchemist (1527–1608).
- The name 'Great Britain' is reputed to have been suggested to King James I on his becoming king of both England and Scotland in 1603 by Sir William Maurice, MP for Caernarfon.
- The greatest weights ever lifted in Britain before the twentieth century were the four large girders of Britannia Bridge (across the Menai Strait), each weighing 1,250 tons, which had to be jacked into place.
- The Monmouthshire canal is the only canal in Britain to run through a national park and it has the longest stretch of water without locks of any canal in Britain – 25 miles from Llangynidr to Pontymoel.
- The wooden treadmill in Beaumaris Gaol is thought to have been the last in Britain to have been used.
- The Snowdon Summit Hotel is the highest building in England and Wales.
- Gwylfa Hiraethog, near Pentrefoelas, Clwyd, is reputed to be the highest private house in Britain at 1,600 ft. (496 m.).
- Llechwedd slate mine, Blaenau Ffestiniog, has Britain's steepest passenger railway, with a 1 in 1.8 (30°) gradient in the Deep Mine.
- The deepest hole in Britain before the Second World War was the Dorothea slate quarry in Gwynedd, 600 ft. (182 m.) deep.
- The Barmouth Viaduct is the longest timber estuarine bridge in Britain at 800 ft. (224 m.) long.
- Britain's first planned civic centre was that of Cardiff.
- The Royal Welch Fusiliers' goat mascot is the oldest known mascot tradition in the British army dating from at least 1717.
- Powys is the most sparsely populated county in England and Wales with only some 0.2 persons per hectare.
- Britain's smallest house is in Conwy – 6 ft. (182 cm.) wide, 8 ft. 4 in. (254 cm.) long and 9 ft. 4 in. (300 cm.) high.
- During the First World War there were more recruits per head of population from Wales than from either England, Scotland or Ireland.
- During the Second World War, the Royal Ordnance Factory at Bridgend, Mid Glamorgan, was the largest munitions factory in Britain with some 37,000 people employed – 35,000 of them women.
- The Dunlop Rubber Factory, Brynmawr, Gwent, was the first post-war building to be 'listed' for its architectural interest.
- The federal University of Wales with over 30,000 undergraduates and postgraduates is the second largest university in the United Kingdom after London University.

- Gold for royal wedding rings has traditionally come from the Clogau gold mine, Gwynedd.
- Holyhead is the third busiest passenger port in the UK.
- The only British politician to have held all four major offices of State was the Cardiff South East MP from 1945–87, James Callaghan: Chancellor of the Exchequer 1964–67; Home Secetary 1967–70; Foreign Secretary 1974–76; Prime Minister 1976–79.
- Britain's largest secular stained-glass window is in St David's Hall, Cardiff – a present from the twinned city of Stuttgart, Germany.
- The army's training area at Sennybridge, Powys, is the third largest in Britain covering 12,164 hectares.

DATES OF SIGNIFICANCE AND INTEREST

1326   The first Welsh representatives were summoned to an English Parliament by Edward II.

1405   A French army, which had landed at Milford Haven in support of Owain Glyndŵr, invaded England and penetrated to within eight miles of Worcester before being halted.

1485   Formation of the 250-strong Yeomen of the Guard, largely composed of trusted Welsh supporters of Henry VII, as the personal bodyguards of the first Tudor king.

1507   What is thought to have been the last medieval style tournament ever held in Britain took place at Carew Castle, Pembrokeshire.

1561   Thomas Young of Hodgeston, Pembrokeshire, became the first Welsh Archbishop of York.

1583   Thomas Pryce and William Middleton, both of Clwyd and both widely travelled adventurers, are said to have been the first to smoke tobacco publicly in London.

1610   The Manx language was first put into writing by the Welsh Bishop of Sodor and Man, John Phillips, with his translation of the Book of Common Prayer.

1613   London's first efficient water supply was created by Sir Hugh Middleton of Gaich Hill, Clwyd, with his 39-mile-long New River Scheme. Also in this year, his brother Sir Thomas Middleton, became Lord Mayor of London.

1638   Lewis Roberts of Beaumaris wrote *The Merchantes Map of Commerce*, the first systematic study of British trade.

1650   The Act for the Propagation and Preaching of the Gospel in Wales led to the establishment of some 63 schools – the first example of state education in Britain.

1680   Sir William Williams, MP for Chester, became the first Welsh Speaker of the House of Commons.

1686   James II made the last royal pilgrimage in the British Isles when he visited St Winifred's Well, Holywell.

1703   The first successful commercial production of tinplate in Britain was at Pontypool.

1747   The first known underground canal in Britain was dug at the Clyn-Du Colliery near Swansea.

1755   The longest single-span arch in Britain at the time – 140 ft. (42.7m.) – was built over the River Taff at Pontypridd by William Edwards.

1765   Lloyds Bank was founded in Birmingham by the Quaker Sampson Lloyd II of Dolobran, near Meifod, Powys.

1775   Morris Castle was completed at Morriston, Swansea, by Robert Morris to provide accommodation for his workforce and is thought to be the first example of workers' flats in Britain.

1778   The Smalls lighthouse, 21 miles (33.8 km.) west of St David's, was completed – at that time the most remote lighthouse in the British Isles.

1797   At Fishguard, the last attempted invasion of the British mainland took place by a French force of some 1,400. The only Honour ever awarded for an engagement in the British Isles was won by the Cardigan Militia on this occasion.

1801   At the Kymin, Monmouth, the only Naval Temple in Britain was built.

1802   The first recorded camping holiday in Britain was by Thomas de Quincey who toured Wales with a tent.

1805   Pontcysyllte Aqueduct was opened, the longest aqueduct in Britain at 1,007 feet (307 m.).

1815   The longest tramway tunnel in Britain at the time was built at Blaenafon, Gwent, just over one mile long.

1816   A party of soldiers from the 55th Regiment was conveyed in tramway waggons 15 miles from Newport to quell disturbances – the first time troops had been carried by this form of transport.

        The Irish Sea was crossed by balloon for the first time – from Dublin to Holyhead by Windham Sadler.

1822   The first known circulating hot water system in Britain was installed in a greenhouse by Anthony Bacon, ironmaster, at Aberaman, Mid Glamorgan.

1824   John Williams of Ystrad Meurig became the first rector of Edinburgh Academy.

A triumphal arch was erected at Holyhead at the end of the A5 road making it the only road in Britain with a triumphal arch at each end – it starts at Marble Arch, London.

1825   The rails for the pioneering Stockton–Darlington Railway were made at Ebbw Vale.

1832   Britain's first workmen's brass band was formed at Brown's Ironworks, Blaina, Gwent.

1834   The Royal Navy's first steam-powered man-of-war, HMS *Tartarus*, was launched at Pembroke Dock.

1839   At Newport, Gwent, the Chartist Rising took place – the last insurrection in Britain.

1841   The Skerries lighthouse, Anglesey, the last privately owned lighthouse in Britain, was sold for almost £500,000.

1843   The first Royal steam yacht the *Victoria and Albert*, was launched at Pembroke Dock.

1844   The first county road boards in Britain were established in south Wales following the Rebecca Riots against tolls on turnpike roads.

1846   The first Royal Navy ship to be driven by a screw propellor, HMS *Conflict*, was launched at Pembroke Dock.

1857   Owen Jones, superintendent of the works at the Great Exhibition of 1851, became the first Welsh holder of the gold medal of the Royal Society of British Architects.

       Crumlin Viaduct was opened – the highest railway bridge in Britain at 200 ft. (61 m.).

1861   Japanese knot grass (or knot weed) was first recorded as having 'gone wild' in Britain at Maesteg.

1863   The Torpantau Tunnel on the Merthyr Tydfil to Brecon line was opened – the highest railway tunnel in Britain at 1,313 ft. (400 m.).

1865   The first comprehensive dictionary of Cornish was compiled by a Welshman, Robert Williams.

       At Swansea, in the only outbreak of Yellow Fever ever to occur in Britain, 15 people died.

       Whitford Point Lighthouse, Gower, was built – the only cast-iron lighthouse ever constructed in Britain.

1872   The last recorded use of stocks in Britain was at Adpar, Dyfed, when Jack Foster was imprisoned for three hours for drunkeness.

1873   Britain's first sheep-dog trials took place at Bala.

       Construction of the longest breakwater in Britain – Holyhead break-water, 1½ miles (2.4 km.) long – was completed after being started in 1845.

1877   The Albert Medal was awarded to 25 rescuers for bravery at the

Tynewydd Colliery, Porth, Rhondda – the first time the medal had been awarded for a land rescue.

1879   The first ballroom in Britain to be lit by electricity was in the Lord Nelson Hotel, Milford Haven.

1880   The greatest ever 30-minute rainfall in Britain was recorded at Cowbridge in July – 2.9 in. (73.6 mm.).

1884   The result of the trial of Dr William Price at Cardiff Assizes made cremation legal in Britain and in British possessions abroad.

1888   The first agricultural department in a British university was opened at University College, Bangor.

1889   Barry Dock was opened covering 73 acres (29.6 hectares) – the largest dock in Britain.

1891   The first Salvation Army Shelter for women outside London was opened in Cardiff.

1894   The first major masonry dam in Britain was completed on the Afon Vyrnwy, Powys.

1895   In Anglesey, the last toll on the last turnpike road in Britain was paid.
         The National Trust acquired its first property in Britain - 4½ acres (1.8 hectares) at Dinas Oleu, Barmouth.

1896   The first moving pictures of the Prince of Wales, later King Edward VII, were shot in Cardiff.
         The Snowdon Mountain Railway was opened – the only rack-and-pinion railway in Britain and the highest piece of track at 3,493 ft. (1,064 m.).

1898   Construction of Weaver's Mill, Swansea, was completed – the first reinforced concrete building in Britain.
         The first British club devoted to rock-climbing, the Climbers' Club, was founded in north Wales.

1900   Keir Hardie, Merthyr Tydfil, became the first Labour MP to be elected in Britain.

1900–   Britain's longest major industrial dispute took place – the lock-out at
1903   Penrhyn Quarry, Gwynedd.

1906   Newport Transporter Bridge was opened – one of only two such bridges ever built in Britain. (The other is at Middlesborough.)

1908   Frank Mason, owner of the *Tenby Observer*, won a High Court case which established in Britain the right of the press to attend local council meetings (Admission of the Press Act, 1908).

1909   Freddie Welsh (Frederick Hall Thomas) of Pontypridd became the first holder of a Lonsdale Belt on winning the British lightweight title in London.

A record monthly rainfall in Britain occurred at Llyn Llydaw, Snowdonia, in October – 56.5 in. (1,435 mm.).

1910   Henry Rolls of Monmouth became the first Briton to be killed in an aircraft accident.

1912   The Irish Sea was crossed by plane for the first time, in a flight lasting 1 hour 40 minutes from Goodwick, Pembrokeshire to Enniscorthy, Wexford, by Denys Corbett Wilson.

1913   Britain's worst-ever mining disaster took place at Senghenydd, Mid Glamorgan, in October when 439 men and boys were killed.

1914   Britain's first flag-day – a development of street collections – took place at Griffithstown and Pontypool, Gwent, in aid of the National Relief Fund.

1914–   Two of the most popular songs of the First World War were written by
1918   Welshmen: 'Keep the Home Fires Burning' by Ivor Novello (born in Cardiff in 1893) and 'Pack Up Your Troubles in Your Old Kitbag' by Felix Powell (born in St Asaph in 1878).

1915   The first branch of the Women's Institute in Britain was opened at Llanfair PG, Anglesey.

        At Gallipoli, Able Seaman William Williams of Chepstow became the first member of the Royal Navy ever to be awarded the Victoria Cross posthumously.

1916   The south Wales coalfield became the first in Britain to be placed under government control.

        David Lloyd George became the United Kingdom's first Welsh Prime Minister.

1918   The last British serviceman to die in the First World War was Able Seaman Richard Morgan of Devauden, Gwent, on HMS *Garland* on 11 November – Armistice Day.

1922   The first Communist Party Parliamentary candidate anywhere in Britain contested a by-election at Caerphilly.

1923   Britain's longest narrow-gauge railway was completed – the Welsh Highland Railway 21.25 miles (36 km.) long.

1924   James Ramsey MacDonald, MP for Aberavon, became Britain's first Labour Prime Minister.

        At 49 years 8 months, Billy Meredith of Chirk became the oldest man ever to play in a FA Cup semi-final (for Manchester City v. Newcastle United).

1925   The last dam disaster in Britain occurred when the Llyn Eigiau Dam, Dolgarrog, Gwynedd, collapsed killing 16 people.

1926   The first parachute jump from an RAF plane was made by Pilot Officer Eric Pentland at RAF Sealand, Clwyd.

David Lloyd George became the first Welsh leader of the Liberal Party.

1927   The first-ever radio commentary on a team game in Britain was the England v. Wales rugby union game at Twickenham.

The FA Cup left England for the first and only time when Cardiff City beat Arsenal 1–0 in the Cup Final. This was also the first final to be broadcast.

The last horse-drawn tram on the British mainland – between Pwllheli and Llanbedrog – ceased operating after a storm destroyed the track.

Frank Moody, Pontypridd, won two British boxing titles – middleweight and lightweight.

A narrow-gauge railway, built for the construction of the Grwyne Fawr Reservoir, Powys, reached a height of 1,800 ft. (549 m.) – the highest of any adhesion-worked railway in the British Isles.

1928   Sir William Llewellyn became the first Welsh President of the Royal Academy.

1929   The first broadcast of an SOS appeal for a vessel in distress was for the steamer *Molesey* wrecked on Skomer.

The largest electric tramway cabs in Britain – double-deck 102 seaters – came into service on the Mumbles railway.

1930   Maurice Turnbull became the first Welsh cricketer to be capped for England – v. New Zealand at Christchurch. (Charles Prytherch Lewis of Abergavenny, an Oxford Blue, was once picked for England v. Australia in the 1880s but failed to make the journey.)

The first youth hostel in Britain was opened at Pennant Hall, Conwy Valley.

1932   Jack Petersen of Cardiff won two British boxing titles – heavyweight and light heavyweight.

1933   Britain's first bird observatory was set up on Skokholm.

Britain's first air service operated by a railway company, the Great Western Railway, began operating between Cardiff, Torquay and Plymouth.

1934   Bedlinog-born Cyril Frederick Walters became the first Welshman to captain an English Test team – v. Australia at Trent Bridge, Nottingham.

Sir Walford Davies was appointed Master of the King's Music.

1935   Britain's first 'stay down' strikes took place at a number of mines in the south Wales coalfield.

Swansea became the first club side in Britain to beat a New Zealand All Blacks touring rugby union side.

1936   The largest mass trial ever to take place in Britain was at Cardiff when 52 men and three women faced charges of rioting in Bedlinog during a mining dispute.

1938   The first scheduled night flight service within the UK began in October between Cardiff and Weston-super-Mare.

1939– About 350,000 evacuees were received in Wales during the Second
1945   World War.

1940   At Narvik, Norway, Captain Bernard Warburton-Lee of Maelor, Clwyd, became the first to receive a VC (posthumous) in the Second World War.

1943   The first mountain rescue service in Britain was established at RAF Llandwrog, Gwynedd.

1944   At Aberdovey, Gwynedd, Britain's first Outward Bound School was opened.

        Britain's first mass radiography unit for chest X-rays was set up by the Welsh National Memorial Association.

1945   The greatest-ever escape of prisoners-of-war in Britain took place from Island Farm Camp, Bridgend, when 67 German POWs escaped.

1946   The highest November temperature ever recorded in Britain was on 4 November at Prestatyn, Clwyd: 71°F (21.7°C).

1948   The last sailing lifeboat in Britain, the *William Cantrell Ashley*, was taken out of service at New Quay, Dyfed.

1949   Britain's first international Moslem conference was held in Cardiff.

        The first comprehensive school in England and Wales was opened at Holyhead.

1951   The first British Chess Federation Congress to be held in Wales was at Swansea.

        The British amateur golf championship was held in Wales for the first time at Royal Porthcawl.

1952   The Queen's Park South Estate, Wrexham, became the first in Britain to separate pedestrians from vehicular traffic.

1955   Anglesey became the first place in Britain to have a fluoridated water supply. (This ended in 1991.)

1956   Gower was designated the first Area of Outstanding Natural Beauty in England and Wales.

1957   Dai Rees won the BBC's Sports Personality of the Year Award.

1959   Harry Secombe was voted Show Business Personality of the Year.

1960   Mike Davies, Swansea, became the first Welsh tennis player to win the British hard courts title.

        The first Welsh actress to win the BAFTA award for Best British

Actress of the Year was Rachel Roberts for her role in *Saturday Night and Sunday Morning*.

1961   The last rugby union match played on a Football League ground was one between Cardiff and Bristol under floodlights at Ninian Park, Cardiff.

1962   Welsh National Opera launched a training scheme for singers – the first such scheme in Britain.

The first co-ordinated cliff, beach and inshore rescue service in Britain was established at Atlantic College, St Donat's, South Glamorgan.

1965   The first football match on closed-circuit television in Britain was a Second Division game between Cardiff City and Coventry City at Ninian Park shown on four screens at the Coventry ground.

1966   The first Welsh actor to win the BAFTA award for Best British Actor of the Year was Richard Burton for his role in *Who's Afraid of Virginia Woolf?*

The first special award for journalism of the British Press Awards was won by David Rhys Davies of the *Merthyr Express*.

The M4 Port Talbot by-pass was opened – the first length of urban motorway in Britain.

1967   Sir Morien Morgan became the first Welsh President of the Royal Aeronautical Society.

The first postbus in Britain ran between Llanidloes and Llangurig, Powys.

The Royal Mint was moved from London to Llantrisant, Mid Glamorgan.

1968   Tom Jones was voted Show Business Personality of the Year.

1969   Llandudno cabin lift opened – the longest cable-car system in Britain at one mile 40 feet.

1970   The Cardiff equitation centre opened – the first municipally owned riding-school in Britain.

Britain's first dial-a-poem service was launched in Wales.

1971   The highest January temperature ever recorded in Britain was at Aber, Gwynedd, on 10 January – 65°F (18.3°C).

The University Hospital of Wales opened – Britain's first completely integrated general hospital, dental hospital and medical school.

1972   Tony Lewis became the first Welshman currently playing for Glamorgan to captain an English test side – against India at New Delhi.

Llyn Brianne Dam was opened – at 288 ft. (87 m.) the highest dam in Britain.

1974   The Cory Band became the first Welsh brass band to win the British National Championship.

1976   Ogof Ffynnon Ddu, Powys, became the first cave in Britain to be designated a national nature reserve.

1977   The first UK athletics championships were held at Cwmbran.

1979   Britain's first and only Communist mayor took office – Mrs Annie Powell, Rhondda.

The Court of Appeal sat for the first time outside London, in Cardiff.

1981   The first Enterprise Zone to be established in Britain was at Swansea.

The women's peace march left Cardiff with 36 women to establish the camp at Greenham Common.

1982   Neil Kinnock became the first Welsh leader of the Labour Party.

1986   *Rhosyn a Rhith* (*Coming Up Roses*) was the first film in Welsh to be given a general release in Britain.

1988   The last British Rail steam train ran on regular service on the Vale of Rheidol Line.

1989   The first all-seat football international ever played in Britain was the Wales v. West Germany game at the National Stadium, Cardiff Arms Park which was a 0–0 draw.

Cardiff Rugby Club became the first club side in Britain to provide hospitality suites.

1990   John Evans, Britain's oldest man whose age could be authenticated, died at Fforestfach, Swansea, aged 112 years 292 days.

Following a referendum, Vaynor Community Council, Merthyr Tydfil, was abolished – the first time any local council in Britain had been abolished in this way.

1991   In the first floodlit rugby union international ever played in Britain, France beat Wales 22–9 at the National Stadium.

Wyn Calvin became the first Welshman to be elected King Rat of the entertainers' organization, the Order of Water Rats.

The first chairman of the UK's Radio Authority was Lord Chalfont (Alun Gwynne Jones).

1992   Britain's first Centre for Sports Science and Sports Medicine was opened in Cardiff.

A barrage across the River Tawe at Swansea was completed, the first of its kind in Britain.

1994   Sir Anthony Hopkins won the BAFTA Award for Best Leading Actor in a film for his role in *The Remains of the Day*.

PRINCES OF WALES

Welsh Princes of Wales

Although Owain ap Gruffudd (Owain Gwynedd), who died in 1170, had styled himself 'Prince of the Welsh', the first ruler to seek the title of 'Prince of Wales' was Dafydd, son of Llywelyn ab Iorwerth (Llywelyn the Great). He later settled for the title of 'Prince of North Wales' and then 'Prince of Aberffraw and Lord of Snowdonia'.

Llywelyn ap Gruffudd (Llywelyn the Last) was the first and only Welsh ruler to be recognized as Prince of Wales by an English king – by Henry III in the Treaty of Montgomery of 1267, after having adopted the title in 1258. Following Llywelyn's death in 1282, his brother Dafydd briefly assumed the title. Madog ap Llywelyn, who led the last revolt against Edward I in 1294–95, also took the title of Prince of Wales.

Owain Glyndŵr was proclaimed Prince of Wales at Glyndyfrdwy in 1400 at the beginning of his rebellion. He was crowned with the title in 1404 before representatives of Castille, France and Scotland with the Bishops of Bangor and St Asaph recognizing his position.

Other Princes of Wales

Edward (later Edward II)	1301*
Edward (the Black Prince)	1343
Richard (later Richard II)	1376†
Henry (later Henry V)	1399*
Edward	1454
Edward (later Edward V)	1471
Arthur Tudor	1489†
Henry Tudor (later Henry VIII)	1504
Henry Stuart	1610
Charles Stuart (later Charles I)	1616
Charles Stuart (later Charles II)	1640†
James Francis Edward Stuart (the Old Pretender)	1688†
George Augustus (later George II)	1714†
Frederick Lewis	1729†

*Edward II was born in Caernarfon and Henry V was born in Monmouth.
†None of these princes was ceremonially invested with the title. The dates shown against their names are those when they were created Prince of Wales and are not necessarily the same as investiture dates.

George William Frederick (later George III)	1751†
George Augustus Frederick (later George IV)	1762†
Albert Edward (later Edward VII)	1841†
George (later George V)	1901†
Edward (later Edward VIII)	1911
Charles Philip Arthur George	1958

Princesses of Wales

Joan (the 'Fair Maid of Kent')	1361	Caroline of Brunswick	1795
Catherine of Aragon	1501	Alexandra of Denmark	1863
Caroline of Ansbach	1714	Mary of Teck	1893
Augusta of Saxe-Coburg	1736	Lady Diana Spencer	1981

17

WALES AND THE WELSH

WELSH FIRSTS AND LASTS

445AD The first entry in *Annales Cambriae* ('The Welsh Annals') (Text A) – a prime source of Welsh medieval history.

682 First entry in *Brut y Tywysogion* ('Chronicle of the Princes') – a monastic record of mainly Welsh events.

c.830 The first recorded use of the red dragon representing Wales occurred in Nennius' *Historia Brittonum*.

850 The first recorded Viking attack on the Welsh coast occurred.

854 First known pilgrimage to Rome of a Welsh ruler by Cyngen of Powys.

878 Rhodri the Great, the first High King of Wales (the first ruler to unite the three principal kingdoms of Wales), was killed in battle.

c.890 The first ceremonial visit by a Welsh king – Anarawd, King of Gwynedd – to an English court, that of Alfred the Great, King of Wessex.

1052 The Battle of Llanllieni (Leominster) – the first time Normans and Welsh met in battle.

1063 Gruffudd ap Llywelyn, briefly King of Wales and the only monarch to extend his rule over the whole country, was killed by treachery.

1081 William the Conqueror visited St David's on his first and only expedition into Wales.

c.1115 The first earthwork and timber castle constructed by the Welsh themselves was built at Welshpool.

1125 First recorded visit of a Papal legate to Wales – Cardinal John of Cremona.

1138 The last recorded Viking attack on Wales – at St Dogmael's, Dyfed.

1170 Death of Owain Gwynedd (Owain ap Gruffudd), the first ruler to style himself 'Prince of the Welsh'.

1171 The first Welsh-built stone and mortar castle, Cardigan Castle, is thought to have been begun this year by the Lord Rhys (Rhys ap Gruffudd).

1174   The first marriage between members of Welsh and English royal houses – Dafydd ab Owain Gwynedd and Emma of Anjou, half-sister of Henry II.

1176   At Cardigan the first recorded eisteddfod was held, under the patronage of the Lord Rhys.

1201   The oldest recorded treaty between England and Wales which has survived dates from this year – it was between Llywelyn the Great and King John.

1216   What has been called 'the first Welsh parliament' was summoned by Llywelyn the Great and met at Aberdyfi.

1250   The oldest manuscript in Welsh, *Llyfr Du Caerfyrddin* ('The Black Book of Carmarthen'), is thought to date from this year.

      The first reference to coal-mining in Wales – at Margam, West Glamorgan.

1267   The first recognition by an English king of a Welsh ruler as Prince of Wales – Llywelyn ap Gruffudd (Llywelyn the Last) by Henry III in the Treaty of Montgomery.

1277   Construction of the last native Welsh castle – Caergwrle (Hope).

1291   The first English tax was imposed on newly conquered Wales.

1295   The first recorded use of the Welsh longbow was at the Battle of Maes Moydog.

1317   Aberffraw was the last Welsh royal palace to be demolished.

1322   The first Welsh representatives were summoned to an English Parliament, at York, by Edward II.

1349   The Black Death first affected Wales.

1404   Owain Glyndŵr summoned his first Welsh Parliament at Machynlleth.

1408   The first use of cannon in Wales was at the sieges of Harlech and Aberystwyth castles during the Glyndŵr rebellion.

1430   Construction began of the last castle to be built in Wales – Raglan Castle, Gwent.

1528   The earliest printed sheet relating to Wales was an indulgence issued with the authority of the Pope and Cardinal Wolsey by the Abbot of Strata Florida to raise funds for the monastery.

c.1534   First reference to gypsies in Wales.

1542   Thomas Capper was burnt at the stake in Cardiff for heresy, so becoming the first religious martyr in Wales.

1546   The first book to be printed in Welsh appeared – *Yn y lhyvyr hwnn* ('In this book' – its first words).

1567   Construction of the first brick house in Wales since the Roman occupation – 'Bachegraig' at Tremeirchion, Clwyd, by Sir Richard Clough.

1573   The first published map of Wales – by Abraham Ortelius of Antwerp.

c.1596 The first North American coniferous trees were brought to Wales.

1639   The first Noncomformist chapel in Wales was opened at Llanfaches, Gwent.

        The first recorded ascent of Snowdon was made by the botanist Thomas Johnson.

1648   The last major battle in Wales was fought involving about 11,000 soldiers – the Battle of St Fagans in which about 200 men, mainly Royalists, were killed.

1649   The first Baptist chapel in Wales was opened at Ilston, Gower.

1662   The first lighthouse on the Welsh coast was at St Ann's Head, Milford Haven.

1679   David Lewis, a Catholic priest from Abergavenny, was hanged and disembowelled at Usk for treason. He was the last Welsh religious martyr.

1692   First recorded use of gunpowder in mining in Wales – at a lead mine in Llanymynech, Powys.

1694   Death of the last known household bard in Wales – Siôn Dafydd Las (John Davies), family poet of the Nannau family of north-west Wales.

1697   The first known tramway in Wales was constructed by Sir Humphrey Mackworth for a coal mine he owned at Neath.

1708–   The first public libraries in Wales were established by the Society for
1711   the Promotion of Christian Knowledge at Bangor, Carmarthen, Cowbridge and St Asaph.

1724   The first Masonic lodge in Wales seems to have been founded in Carmarthen.

1737   Lewis Morris drew the first navigational charts of the Welsh coast.

1744   The Wrexham Neighbourly Society was founded – the first 'sick club' in Wales.

1752   The first turnpike road to serve Wales was opened between Wrexham and Shrewsbury.

1762   Banc y Llong (The Ship Bank) was founded in Aberystwyth – possibly the first bank in Wales.

1766   The first Welsh Canal Act was passed for the construction of a canal from Kidwelly to Carway.

1799   The first public park in Wales was opened by Philip Yorke at Erddig, Wrexham.

1804	The first newspaper in Wales was published – the *Cambrian* of Swansea.
1810	The *Carmarthen Journal* was first published – the oldest surviving newspaper in Wales.
1813	The first permanent military barracks in Wales were opened in Brecon.
1816	The first Royal Navy ships to be built in Pembroke Dock were launched.
1821	Swansea became the first place in Wales to have gas street lighting.
1822	The first passenger rail service in the south Wales valleys began operating between Tredegar and Newport on a horse-drawn tramway.
1824	The first gasometers in Wales were erected at Greenfield, Clwyd.
1830	The general election held this year was the last in which not a single seat was contested in Wales.
1832	The first temperance society in Wales was formed in Holyhead.
1835	The first museum in Wales was founded in Swansea by the Royal Institution of South Wales.
1836	The first friendly society in Wales was formed in Wrexham – the Philanthropic Order of True Ivorites. The last known duel took place in Wales – fought with pistols – at Gumfreston Hall near Tenby between Sir John Owen, MP, and William Richards, former Mayor of Tenby, who was severely wounded.
1839	In Pembrokeshire the last county yeomanry (volunteer cavalry) in Wales was disbanded. The first railway in Wales was opened between Llanelli and Pontardulais.
1840	The first major railway in Wales was opened – the Taff Vale Railway from Cardiff to Abercynon, extended to Merthyr Tydfil in 1841.
1841	The first known photograph to be taken in Wales and which has survived was of Margam Castle by the Reverend Calvert Jones.
1843	The first pier in Wales was opened at Beaumaris. Gold was first discovered in the Dolgellau area.
1850	Rugby was first played in Wales at St David's College, Lampeter.
1851	The first medical officer of health in Wales was appointed at Towyn, Clwyd.
1852	The first degrees were awarded to students in Wales – the BD (Bachelor of Divinity) at St David's College, Lampeter.
1853	The first art schools in Wales were opened at Caernarfon and Swansea. At Inkerman during the Crimean War, Captain Hugh Rowland of Llanrug, Gwynedd, became the first Welshman to be awarded the Victoria Cross.
1860	The first bowls club in Wales was founded at Abergavenny.

The first co-operative shop in Wales was opened at Cwmbach, Aberdare.

1866	The last public execution in Wales took place outside Swansea Gaol.
1870	The first football club in Wales was formed – the Druids of Rhiwabon.
1871	The first senior rugby side in Wales was formed at Neath.

Mrs Rose Crawshay became the first woman in Wales to be elected to membership of a public body – the Merthyr Tydfil School Board.

1874	The first Salvation Army mission in Wales was opened in Cardiff.
1875	The Ordnance Survey published its first complete maps of Wales.
1878	The first Welsh Cup Final was won by Wrexham.
1879	The first tennis club in Wales was formed at Newport.
1881	The first piece of modern legislation dealing only with Wales was passed – the Sunday Closing Act.
1885	The first electric tram service in Wales came into operation in Neath.
1886	William Abraham ('Mabon'), Liberal, Rhondda, was elected the first working-class MP in Wales.

The first Welsh opera, *Blodwen* by Joseph Parry, was first performed.

1889	Queen Victoria made her last visit to Wales.
1895	At Ely Racecourse, Cardiff, the first Welsh Grand National was run.
1896	The first indoor swimming pool in Wales was opened in Cardiff.
1898	The first motor buses in Wales came into service at Llandudno.
1900	The last pier to be opened in Wales was at Colwyn Bay.
1904	The last major religious revival in Wales began led by Evan Roberts.
1905	The first Labour Mayor in Wales was Enoch Powell, Merthyr Tydfil.
1906	The first hydro-electricity was generated in Wales at Cwm Dyli, Gwynedd.
1907	The first women's suffrage movement in Wales was formed in Llandudno.

In Cardiff, the first aircraft to be designed and built in Wales – the *Robin Goch* – was constructed by C. H. Watkins.

The first six rugby league sides in Wales were formed.

1908	In the first rugby league international played in Wales, New Zealand lost 9–8 at Aberdare.

The first Boy Scout troops in Wales were formed in Cardiff and Carmarthen.

1909	The first mines rescue station in south Wales was opened at Aberaman.
1910	The first Girl Guides company in Wales was formed in Carmarthen.
1911	The first seaside miniature railway in Wales was opened at Rhyl.
1912	Petty Officer Edgar Evans of Rhosili, Gower, became the first Welshman to reach the South Pole as a member of Scott's ill-fated expedition.

The first aviator's certificate to be issued in Wales was to Victor Hewitt at Rhyl flying a Bleriot monoplane.

1914 The first trolley-bus service in Wales began operating in Aberdare.

1915 The first airship base in Wales was opened by the Admiralty at Mona (Anglesey).

The first pit-head baths in Wales were at Deep Navigation Colliery, Treharris.

1917 The first Rotarian clubs in Wales were formed in Cardiff and Llanelli.

1918 The first woman parliamentary candidate in Wales stood for election.

1922 The first car to be produced in Wales, the 'Gwalia', was manufactured in Cardiff.

1923 The first Welsh-language broadcast was made.

Glamorgan County Cricket Club first defeated a touring side – the West Indies were beaten at Swansea by 43 runs.

1927 The first royal broadcast from Wales was by King George V opening the National Museum of Wales in Cardiff.

The first game on which a radio commentary was broadcast from Wales was the Wales v. Ireland rugby union international in Cardiff.

1928 Newport Round Table was established – the first in Wales.

1929 The first woman MP in Wales was elected – Megan Lloyd George (Liberal), Anglesey.

1930 Maurice Turnbull became the first Welsh cricketer to be capped for England – against New Zealand at Christchurch.

1931 Ted Tuck of Aberavon became the first person to swim the 16 miles from Mumbles to Aberavon.

1934 Bedlinog-born Cyril Walters of Worcestershire became the first Welshman to captain an English test side – against Australia at Trent Bridge.

1935 The first RAC Welsh rally was held.

The first Welsh-language film was made – *Y Chwarelwr* ('The Quarryman') by Urdd Gobaith Cymru.

1936 Arthur Horner was elected first Communist president of the South Wales Miners' Federation.

1940 The first deaths from German air raids on Wales occurred at RAF Penrhos, Gwynedd, and in Cardiff Docks in July.

1944 The last deaths in Wales during a German air raid occurred in Cardiff in March.

1945 This year saw the last general election in Wales in which a candidate was returned unopposed – Will John (Labour), Rhondda West.

The last manganese mine in Wales, the Benallt mine near Aberdaron, Llŷn, was closed.

1948	The first individual Olympic athletics medal was won by a Welshman – Tom Richards of Risca, Gwent, won the silver medal in the marathon in London.
1949	The first new town in Wales was designated – Cwmbran.
1951	Sir David Maxwell Fyfe was appointed the first Minister for Welsh Affairs.
	The first national park in Wales was designated – Snowdonia National Park.
1952	The first television transmitter in Wales was installed at Wenvoe near Cardiff.
1954	The first Welshman to hold a position of ministerial responsibility for Wales was appointed – Gwilym Lloyd George, Home Secretary and Minister for Welsh Affairs.
1955	The first national nature reserve in Wales was designated – Cwm Idwal, Snowdonia.
1958	The last execution in Wales took place in Swansea Gaol.
1961	The first referendum on the Sunday opening of pubs in Wales was held.
1963	Caernarfon became the first royal borough in Wales.
1964	The first individual Olympic gold medal won by a Welshman – Lynn Davies, Nantymoel, Mid Glamorgan, in the long jump.
	The Welsh Rugby Union made its first overseas tour – to South Africa.
	The first Secretary of State for Wales was appointed – James Griffiths.
1966	The first Plaid Cymru MP was elected – Gwynfor Evans, Carmarthen.
1969	The first North Sea (natural) gas reached Wales.
1970	Mair Leonard of Swansea became the first woman to swim from Mumbles to Porthcawl.
1972	The first company to be registered in Welsh was the Bala Lake Railway.
1973	The first *papur bro* (local Welsh-language community newspaper) was launched – *Y Dinesydd* of Cardiff.
1974	The first commercial radio station in Wales, Swansea Sound, was launched.
1976	The last iron-ore mine in Wales, at Llanharry, Mid Glamorgan, was closed.
	The first annual 10-mile race was held on Snowdon.
1977	David Jones of Baglan became the first Welshman to swim the Bristol Channel.
1982	The first ever papal visit to Wales – Pope John Paul II in Cardiff.
1986	The first annual Welsh proms were held at St David's Hall, Cardiff.

1990   The last coal mine in the Rhondda Valleys, Maerdy Colliery, closed.

1994   Tony Curtis became the first Professor of Poetry to be appointed in Wales (at the University of Glamorgan).

Tower Colliery, Hirwaun, Mid Glamorgan, became the first pit in Wales to be bought out by its miners.

1995 ANNIVERSARIES

25 Years Ago – 1970

The Port Talbot ore terminal, the Business Statistics Office, Newport, and the Driver and Vehicle Licensing Centre, Morriston, were opened. The last pit in the Afan Valley, at Glyncorrwg, and the Dorothea slate mine in Gwynedd, were closed.

There was a mass evacuation of people from Maerdy, Rhondda Fach, when the Lluest Wen reservoir began to leak; four men were killed when the Cleddau Bridge collapsed; the Britannia rail bridge across the Menai Strait was badly damaged by fire.

The Polytechnic of Wales was created.

The Pembrokeshire Coast Path was opened.

Saunders Lewis was nominated for the Nobel Prize for Literature, Bernice Rubens of Cardiff won the Booker Prize, and the literary magazine *Planet* was launched.

An army sergeant, John Jenkins, was sentenced to ten years in prison for causing explosions in Wales; in London, 14 members of the Welsh Language Society were imprisoned for disrupting the High Court; Adfer was founded to help preserve Welsh-speaking communities.

The deaths occurred of Sir Ifan ab Owen Edwards, founder of Urdd Gobaith Cymru, Jack Jones, novelist and playwright, Sir Albert Evans-Jones (the former Archdruid 'Cynan'), and the philosopher Bertrand Russell.

In Rome, six Welsh Catholic martyrs were canonized.

Plaid Cymru contested all Welsh seats in a general election for the first time; the first Conservative Secretary of State for Wales, Peter Thomas, was appointed.

David Broome won the world show-jumping championship in Brittany and Ray Reardon won the first of his six world snooker championships.

50 Years Ago – 1945

The controversial writer Caradoc Evans died in January. The former Prime Minister, David Lloyd George, died in March and Clement Davies became leader of the Liberal Party.

A mass break-out by 67 German prisoners-of-war occurred at Island Farm Camp, Bridgend in March.

In April the Victoria Cross was won by Captain Ian Liddell of Chepstow and by Corporal Edward Thomas of Pontlottyn.

In August, in the first post-war Labour government, Aneurin Bevan was appointed Minister of Health and James Griffiths Minister of National Insurance.

In the General Election a Welsh MP, Will John, Rhondda West (Labour), became the last person to be returned unopposed from Wales.

The Fforestfach Industrial Estate, Swansea, was opened by King George VI; near Aberdaron, Llŷn, the last manganese mine in Wales was closed.

There was a record crowd of 30,000 for a rugby league international in Wales as England were beaten 11–3 in Swansea.

A record gust of wind of 113 m.p.h. was recorded at St Ann's Head, Dyfed, in January.

75 Years Ago – 1920

Over 290,000 miners were employed in the coal mines of Wales, a record figure.

The Church in Wales was disestablished and University College, Swansea, was founded.

Queen's Dock, Swansea, the Plant Breeding Station at University College, Aberystwyth, and the largest sanatorium in Britain – at Talgarth, Powys – were opened.

Five members of the Rhoscolyn lifeboat were drowned in an accident off Llanddwyn Island, Anglesey.

Sir Pryce Pryce-Jones, the mail-order pioneer of Newtown, died and the writer Dick Francis and the politician Roy Jenkins were born.

The Board of Celtic Studies of the University of Wales was established.

100 Years Ago – 1895

In October in Anglesey, the last tollgate in Britain was removed.

The National Trust purchased its first property in Britain at Dinas Oleu near Barmouth.

Lady Charlotte Guest, translator of *The Mabinogion*, the industrialist H. A. Bruce (Lord Aberdare), and the novelist Daniel Owen died.

Sir Albert Evans-Jones ('Cynan') and Sir Ifan ab Owen Edwards were born.

The first Welsh Grand National was run at Ely Racecourse, Cardiff; at Rhyl, Ireland beat Wales 3–0 in the world's first hockey international.

150 Years Ago – 1845

In an explosion at Cwmbach, Aberdare, 26 miners were killed.
The literary magazine *Y Traethodydd* was launched by Thomas Gee.
The Afghan War hero, General Sir William Nott, died at Carmarthen.

200 Years Ago – 1795

The Neath Canal was opened between Neath and Glynneath.
Troops were called in to quell riots by miners in Denbigh in April.

250 Years Ago – 1745

The Forest Copper Works were founded, the first in the Swansea Valley.

300 Years Ago – 1695

The poet and hymnwriter Henry Vaughan ('The Silurist') died at Llansantffraed, Powys.

400 Years Ago – 1595

The distinguished Elizabethan soldier, Sir Roger Williams, died.

700 Years Ago – 1295

In the Battle of Maes Moydog near Welshpool in March, Madog ap Llywelyn was defeated by the Earl of Warwick in the last uprising against Edward I after the conquest of 1282.

750 Years Ago – 1245

The Franciscans founded a friary at Llanfaes, Anglesey.

800 Years Ago – 1195
Flemings recaptured Wiston Castle from the Lord Rhys.

1996 ANNIVERSARIES

25 Years Ago – 1971

The University Hospital of Wales, Cardiff, and the Rio Tinto zinc smelter, Holyhead, were opened (but ship-repairing at Holyhead ended after 134 years).

Mudiad Ysgolion Meithrin, the Welsh-language nursery schools movement, was launched in Aberystwyth.

Six miners were killed in an explosion at Cynheidre Colliery, Llanelli.

The deaths occurred of the artists Brenda Chamberlain and Ceri Richards, the writer Kate Roberts and the socialist poet and preacher T. E. Nicholas (Niclas y Glais).

Offa's Dyke Path was opened.

Geoff Lewis became the first Welsh jockey to win the Derby – on 'Mill Reef'; Nicolette Milnes-Walker of Cardiff became the first woman to sail single-handed, non-stop across the Atlantic; the Welsh Sports Council was established.

50 Years Ago – 1946

Welsh National Opera's first fully staged productions, *Cavalleria Rusticana* and *I Pagliacci* were performed at the Prince of Wales Theatre, Cardiff.

A Pneumoconiosis Research Unit was established at Llandough Hospital, Cardiff.

This was the peak year for fish landings at Milford Haven – 60,000 tons – but the last slate cargo was shipped from Porthmadog.

In August, Princess Elizabeth, now the Queen, was made a member of the Gorsedd of Bards at Mountain Ash.

The first world title fight ever staged in Wales took place in Cardiff in September when Ronnie James, Pontardawe, lost the lightweight fight to Ike Williams, USA.

The nationalist politician Lord Dafydd Elis-Thomas was born.

75 Years Ago – 1921

The Sunday closing of pubs was extended to Monmouthshire and the new diocese of Monmouth was created in the Church in Wales.

In the second worst train crash in Welsh history, 17 people were killed at Abermule, (Abermiwl), Powys, in January.

Coney Beach amusement park, Porthcawl, was opened.

Sir Harry Secombe and the rugby and athletics star, Ken Jones, were born.

Glamorgan was admitted to the county cricket championship.

Cyfarthfa Ironworks closed.

There were 186,635 horses on Welsh farms this year – a record.

100 Years Ago – 1896

The first graduate of the University of Wales was Maria Dawson.

At Tylorstown, Rhondda, 57 miners died in an explosion in January.

The Snowdon Mountain Railway was opened in April but was closed almost immediately for a year following a fatal accident.

Bangor Pier was opened and the Aberystwyth Cliff Railway began operating.

Shotton steelworks were opened by John Summers and in September an 11-month lock-out began at Penrhyn Quarry.

The Central Welsh Board was established as an inspectorate and examining body for intermediate schools.

The Roman Catholic diocese of Cardiff was created.

The first news film ever shot in Britain showed the Prince and Princess of Wales arriving at the Cardiff Exhibition in June.

On 17 December, a severe earthquake shock was felt all over Wales.

Lady Llanover, champion of Welsh folk culture, died aged 94, and the distinguished Welsh language scholar, Stephen J. Williams was born.

150 Years Ago – 1846

The Taff Vale Railway was extended into the Cynon Valley.

The Royal Navy's first screw-propeller ship, HMS *Conflict*, was launched at Pembroke Dock.

John Whitehead Greaves struck the Merioneth 'Old Vein' of slate at Llechwedd, Blaenau Ffestiniog.

A colliery explosion at Risca, Gwent, killed 35 miners.

The Cambrian Archaeological Society was formed.

The first Mormon missionaries arrived in Wales.

200 Years Ago – 1796

The Monmouthshire Canal was opened from Newport to Pontnewynydd in March.

John Jones (Talsarn), preacher and hymnwriter, and Hugh Williams, Chartist and supporter of Rebecca, were born; the prominent Methodist, Peter Williams, died.

250 Years Ago – 1746

David Morgan, a barrister of Penygraig Taf near Quakers' Yard, was executed in London for his support of Bonnie Prince Charlie's Jacobite Rebellion of 1745.

500 Years Ago – 1496

Sir Rhys ap Thomas was made justiciar of south Wales by Henry VII.

750 Years Ago – 1246

The deaths occurred of Dafydd ap Llywelyn and of Llywelyn the Great's chief administrator, Ednyfed Fychan, ancestor of the Tudors.
An English army penetrated beyond the River Conwy for the first time since 1100.

800 Years Ago – 1196

The Lord Rhys (Rhys ap Gruffudd) gained a victory over the Anglo-Normans at the Battle of Radnor.
The Cistercians founded Aberconwy Abbey.

900 Years Ago – 1096

William II led an unsuccessful expedition into Wales.

1100 Years Ago – 896

Danish Vikings attacked the palace of the King of Brycheiniog on an island in Llan-gors Lake. Llantwit Major and Llancarfan were also attacked by them.

1200 Years Ago – 796

Offa, King of Mercia, died having seen the completion of his massive 150 mile dyke marking the border between England and Wales.

1997 ANNIVERSARIES

25 Years Ago – 1972

Wylfa nuclear power station on Anglesey was opened.
St David's College, Lampeter, became a constituent college of the University of Wales.
Cardiff's first dock, the Bute West, was filled in and Port Talbot Dock closed.
In the first national coal strike since 1926, Welsh pits were closed for seven weeks.

The veteran socialist and former MP for Merthyr Tydfil, S. O. Davies, died.
Bilingual road signs began to be introduced and the Bala Lake Railway became
the first company to be registered in Welsh.
Tony Lewis of Glamorgan captained England against India; Richard Meade won
individual and team gold medals at the Munich Olympic Games; Mal Evans won
the world singles outdoor bowls championship; Llanelli beat the New Zealand
All Blacks and Neath won the first WRU Cup.

50 Years Ago – 1947

In April, on Sker Point, Porthcawl, the steamer *Samtampa* was wrecked with the
loss of her entire crew of 41 and all eight members of the Mumbles lifeboat were
drowned going to her assistance.
On St David's Day, the first local-authority Welsh primary school was opened in
Llanelli.
In January and February, blizzards and sub-zero temperatures caused chaos
throughout Wales.
The first Llangollen International Eisteddfod was held.
The conductor Owain Arwel Hughes and the actor Jonathan Pryce were born.
The deaths occurred of the distinguished historian, Sir John Lloyd, the novelist
Arthur Machen, and the south Wales miners' leaders, William Brace and Frank
Hodges.

75 Years Ago – 1922

David Lloyd George resigned as Prime Minister after a government defeat in a
by-election at Newport and in the following general election Labour became the
largest party in Wales for the first time.
Llandarcy oil refinery was opened.
Urdd Gobaith Cymru (The Welsh League of Youth) was founded.
The operatic star, Sir Geraint Evans, was born.
The Rhondda miners' leader and former Liberal MP, William Abraham
('Mabon'), died.

100 Years Ago – 1897

Aneurin Bevan and Ness Edwards, leading Labour politicians, Lord Miles Thomas,
military aviation pioneer, and Victor Earl Nash-Williams, archaeologist, were born.
In May Guglielmo Marconi transmitted the world's first ever radio message
across water from Flat Holm to Lavernock Point, South Glamorgan.
Private Samuel Vickery of Cardiff won the Victoria Cross at Tirah, Sudan.

The Grand Theatre, Swansea, was officially opened by the famous operatic soprano Adelina Patti.

150 Years Ago – 1847

The highly controversial *Report of the Commission of Inquiry into the State of Education in Wales* was published in April – 'The Treason of the Blue Books'.
In January the Point of Ayr lifeboat capsized drowning its entire crew of 13.
The third Marquis of Bute, restorer of Cardiff Castle and Castell Coch, was born.
Aberaman Ironworks, the last in the Cynon Valley, were opened.

200 years ago – 1797

At Fishguard in February the last attempted invasion of the British mainland took place. Some 1,400 French troops under an American general, William Tate, surrendered after three days.
The Montgomery Canal was opened from Frankton Junction to Garthmyl and the Breconshire Canal was opened from Gilwern to Llangynidr.

250 Years Ago – 1747

Edward Williams (Iolo Morganwg), scholar, forger and creator of the Gorsedd of Bards, was born at Llancarfan, Vale of Glamorgan.
The notorious smuggler, Owen Williams, was hanged in Cardiff.

300 Years Ago – 1697

The first known tramway in Wales was built by Sir Humphrey Mackworth at Neath.

400 Years Ago – 1597

A ship of the second Spanish Armada was driven ashore near Aberdyfi. Two Spaniards were killed and four taken prisoner before it made its escape.
Two other ships were driven ashore in Pembrokeshire but got away after meeting no effective local opposition.

500 Years Ago – 1497

A Yorkist revolt against Henry VII (Henry Tudor) led by Sir Thomas Vaughan of Tretower, Brecon, was put down by Sir Rhys ap Thomas.

700 Years Ago – 1297

Over 5,000 Welsh soldiers were recruited to fight for Edward I in Flanders.

750 Years Ago – 1247

After a successful expedition into Wales, Henry III imposed humiliating conditions on the Welsh in the Treaty of Woodstock.

800 Years Ago – 1197

The Lord Rhys (Rhys ap Gruffudd), ruler of Deheubarth and the dominant figure in Wales for half a century, died, and Owen Cyfeiliog, the 'Poet Prince' of Powys, also died.

900 Years Ago – 1097

William II led a second unsuccessful expedition into Wales.

1998 ANNIVERSARIES

25 Years Ago – 1973

Sony became the first major Japanese company to open a factory in Wales.
The Wales Trade Union Council was founded.
The Llyn Brianne Dam in Powys was completed, a fourth oil refinery was opened on Milford Haven and drilling for oil and gas began in the Celtic Sea.
Alan Llwyd became only the second person to win Chair and Crown at a National Eisteddfod.
The Wlpan method of intensive Welsh-language teaching was introduced and the first Welsh-language local community newspaper (*papur bro*) *Y Dinesydd*, was launched in Cardiff.
The Nobel Prize for Physics was won by Cardiff-born Professor Brian Josephson.
There were 424 deaths on the roads of Wales – a record.
The popular singer Donald Peers died in Australia.

50 Years Ago – 1948

New factories were opened by Hoover at Merthyr Tydfil and by British Nylon Spinners at Pontypool.

The first annual Miners' Eisteddfod was held at Porthcawl.
At St Fagans the Welsh Folk Museum was opened.
At the London Olympic Games, on finishing second in the marathon, Tom Richards became the first Welshman to win an individual Olympic athletics medal.
In August, Glamorgan won the county cricket championship for the first time.
The last sailing lifeboat in Britain, the *William Cantrell Ashley*, was taken out of service at New Quay, Dyfed.
Gwenllian Parry, widow of the cremation pioneer Dr William Price, died.
Ten Cardiff players were selected for Wales – a record international representation for any British rugby club.

75 Years Ago – 1923

The North Wales Quarrymen's Union merged with the Transport and General Worker's Union.
The first radio station in Wales, Station 5WA, began broadcasting from Cardiff.
The Church in Wales created a new diocese of Swansea and Brecon.
The Welsh Highland Railway, the longest in Britain, was completed between Porthmadog and Dinas near Caernarfon.
Jimmy Wilde lost the world flyweight title he had held since 1916.
The poets Danny Abse and John Ormond were born.
Talygarn Convalescent Home for miners was opened.

100 Years Ago – 1898

The South Wales Miners' Federation (the 'Fed') was formed, the first Welsh-language socialist newspaper, *Llais Llafur*, was launched, and the first Labour councillor in Wales was elected to Swansea town council.
New docks were opened at Port Talbot and Swansea; Mumbles Pier was completed.
The Roman Catholic diocese of Menevia at Wrexham was created.
Slate production in north Wales reached a peak.
The first reinforced concrete building in Britain – Weaver's Mill, Swansea – was built.
The first motor buses in Wales were introduced in Llandudno and the Glamorganshire Canal between Abercynon and Merthyr Tydfil was closed.
The deaths occurred of the publisher Thomas Gee and the nationalist advocate of a Welsh colony in Patagonia, Michael D. Jones.

150 Years Ago – 1848

In August the American emigrant ship *Ocean Monarch* caught fire off Colwyn Bay killing 178 people.

The Conwy rail bridge and the Chirk rail viaduct were opened while the world's first named train *The Irish Mail* ran between London Euston and Bangor. At Newport the 1,200 ft. rail viaduct was destroyed by fire.

Trinity College, Carmarthen, was founded by the Anglican Church and Llandovery School was opened.

The second Marquis of Bute, 'founder of Cardiff', died; Thomas Price ('Carnhuanawc'), the leading Celtic scholar, died.

200 Years Ago – 1798

The Swansea Canal was opened between Swansea and Ystradgynlais.

The deaths occurred of Thomas Pennant, noted traveller and naturalist, and Dr David Samuel who had sailed with Captain Cook.

In July, William Wordsworth wrote 'Lines Composed a Few Miles Above Tintern Abbey'.

250 Years Ago – 1748

Lewis Morris published the first detailed charts of the Welsh coast.

600 Years Ago – 1398

Archbishop Roger Walden of Canterbury agreed that henceforth 1 March was to be celebrated as the Feast of St David.

700 Years Ago – 1298

About 10,000 Welshmen fought for Edward I in the English victory over the Scots in the Battle of Falkirk.

800 Years Ago – 1198

Some 3,000 Welshmen were reputed killed in a victory over the Welsh of Powys by the Justiciar, Geoffrey Fitzpeter, at the Battle of Painscastle.

The rebuilding of St David's Cathedral, after a disastrous fire, was completed and Gerald of Wales became bishop-elect of St David's but was never consecrated.

900 Years Ago – 1098

In a battle off Anglesey, Vikings under King Magnus Barefoot of Norway killed Earl Hugh of Shrewsbury.

1999 ANNIVERSARIES

25 Years Ago – 1974

Local government reorganization reduced the number of Welsh counties from 13 to eight and definitely placed Gwent (Monmouthshire) in Wales.

MPs were allowed to take the oath in Welsh for the first time and the first Welsh-speaking university hall of residence, Neuadd Pantycelyn in Aberystwyth, was opened.

The Centre for Alternative Technology was opened at Machynlleth.

The first commercial radio station in Wales, Swansea Sound, began broadcasting.

The record-breaking BBC Wales 'soap opera', *Pobl y Cwm*, began.

Four archaeological trusts were established for rescue digs in Wales.

The Cory Band was the first Welsh brass band to win the British National Championship.

50 Years Ago – 1949

The first comprehensive school in England and Wales was opened at Holyhead, the Welsh Joint Education Committee was established, and the Cardiff (later Welsh) College of Music and Drama was founded.

The first meeting of the advisory Council for Wales was held in May.

Cwmbran became the first 'new town' in Wales.

The Wales Gas Board took over 105 local gas undertakings as the industry was nationalized.

On Boxing Day the Gwyn Nicholls Memorial Gates at Cardiff Arms Park were opened.

In September the largest meteorite ever to fall in Wales landed at Beddgelert, Gwynedd, and weighed 25½ ounces (723 grammes).

Wales's most capped rugby player, J. P. R. Williams, the snooker star, Terry Griffiths, the nationalist politician, Ieuan Wyn Jones, and the writer, Ken Follett, were born.

The deaths occurred of the writers T. Rowland Hughes and T. Gwyn Jones, and the Labour politician J. H. ('Jimmy') Thomas.

The Welsh Grand National was run at Chepstow for the first time.

75 Years Ago – 1924

Ramsay MacDonald, MP for Aberavon, became the first Labour Prime Minister.
Radio Station 5SX began broadcasting from Swansea.
Cardiff City provided both captains for a Wales v. Scotland international, Fred
Keenor (Wales) and Jimmy Blair (Scotland).
A new world land speed record of 146.16 m.p.h. was set by Malcolm Campbell
at Pendine.
In the Rhondda, the Pendyrus Male Choir was formed.

100 Years Ago – 1899

A French barque *Le Marechal Lannes*, was wrecked on Grassholm in March,
drowning her crew of 25.
An explosion at the Lluest Colliery, Garw Valley, killed 19 miners in August.
The leading Liberal politician T. E. Ellis died and the poet and critic David James
Jones ('Gwenallt') was born.
The pier at Tenby was opened.

150 Years Ago – 1849

An outbreak of cholera killed many people throughout Wales including 1,700 in
Merthyr Tydfil, 750 in Cardiff and 730 in Neath.
At the Lletty Shenkin Colliery, Aberdare, 52 men and boys were killed in an
explosion in August.
Lady Charlotte Guest finished her translation of *The Mabinogion*.
Some 250 Mormon converts left the Merthyr Tydfil area for Salt Lake City,
Utah, where they were among the first settlers.
The planned development of Llandudno by Lord Mostyn began after the
Chester–Holyhead Railway reached the town.

200 Years Ago – 1799

In November the Dutch ship *Valk* was wrecked on the Dutch coast drowning 247
men of the Royal Welch Fusiliers (23rd Regiment of Foot) together with 25
wives and children.
The first public park in Wales was opened at Erddig near Wrexham.
John Evans of Waunfawr, Gwynedd, who first mapped the course of the River
Missouri for almost 2,000 miles above its confluence with the Mississipi, died in
New Orleans.

300 Years Ago – 1699

The first attempt to improve commercial river transport in Wales took place with the building of a pound lock on the River Neath at Aberdulais.

400 Years Ago – 1599

Holyhead was designated a permanent posting station for Royal Mail to Ireland.

600 Years Ago – 1399

Richard II was betrayed to his enemy, Henry of Lancaster, at Conwy Castle – not Flint Castle as Shakespeare had it – and he died mysteriously the next year.

800 Years Ago – 1199

The Cistercians founded Cymer Abbey, Gwynedd.

1000 Years Ago – 999

The Bishop of St David's, Morgenau, was killed in a Viking raid.
The death occurred of Maredudd ab Owain, grandson of Hywel Dda, who had re-united Gwynedd and Deheubarth during his reign.

2000 ANNIVERSARIES

25 Years Ago – 1975

In a June referendum, Wales voted two to one to remain in the European Community.
The Cleddau Road bridge was opened.
The Land Authority for Wales was created.
The deaths occurred of the veteran Labour leader and first Secretary of State for Wales, James Griffiths, the poet and critic, Sir Thomas Parry-Williams, and the historian A. H. Dodd.
Gowerton won the Village Championship Trophy at Lords, the first Welsh cricket club to do so.

50 Years Ago – 1950

In Wales's worst air disaster, 78 passengers and crew were killed at Llandow,

South Glamorgan, when a plane carrying rugby supporters home from Ireland crashed.

The world's first scheduled helicopter service began operating between Cardiff, Wrexham and Liverpool.

A record number of three women MPs was elected in Wales.

The first 'all-Welsh' National Eisteddfod was held at Caerphilly.

Wales reached the quarter finals of the football World Cup in Sweden.

The last coal mine in Pembrokeshire, Wood Level Pit, closed.

Swansea became the first major town in Wales to allow the Sunday opening of cinemas.

The Tal-y-llyn Railway became the world's first privately preserved railway.

75 Years Ago – 1925

A riot at Ammanford during a miners' strike led to 58 people being gaoled.

Copper smelting in Swansea ended after 200 years.

Plaid Cymru was founded and the first Urdd Gobaith Cymru peace message to the world was broadcast.

The Llyn Eigiau Dam at Dolgarrog, Gwynedd, collapsed killing 16 people in November.

Amelia Earhart became the first woman to have flown the Atlantic when her seaplane *Friendship* landed off Burry Port in June.

Malcolm Campbell set a new world land speed record of 150.58 m.p.h. at Pendine.

The American press tycoon, William Randolph Hearst, bought St Donat's Castle, South Glamorgan.

Cardiff City were beaten by Sheffield United in the FA Cup Final.

The fashion designer, Laura Ashley, and the actor, Richard Burton, were born.

The former British, European and Commonwealth featherweight boxing champion, Jim Driscoll, died.

100 Years Ago – 1900

At Merthyr Tydfil, Keir Hardie was elected the first Labour MP in Britain.

Two major strikes began – at Penrhyn Quarry, Gwynedd, and on the Taff Vale Railway.

In three major disasters off the Welsh coast, 73 lives were lost.

The Aberdare Canal was closed and the last pier to be built in Wales, at Colwyn Bay, was opened.

The Royal Welch Fusiliers made up the largest British contingent in the relief of Peking (Beijing) during the Chinese Boxer Rising.

David Wynne, the composer, and Richard Hughes, the novelist, were born.
The third Marquis of Bute died. Sarah Jane Rees of Llangrannog founded the
Women's Temperance Movement.
Tredegar Iron and Steelworks closed.

150 Years Ago – 1850

The Britannia bridge over the Menai Strait was opened.
The South Wales Railway reached Neath and Swansea from Chepstow.
The first Welsh women's magazine, *Y Gymraes*, was founded.
The hierarchy of the Roman Catholic Church in Wales was restored.
Rugby was first played in Wales at St David's College, Lampeter.
An unsuccessful attempt was made to found a Welsh settlement in Brazil.

200 Years Ago – 1800

Tredegar Ironworks and Dorothea Quarry, Blaenau Ffestiniog, were opened.
The Brecon Canal was opened from Brecon to Tal-y-bont.
The cremation pioneer, Dr William Price, and the publisher and reformer,
Samuel Roberts ('S. R.'), were born.
Mary Jones walked 25 miles from Llanfihangel-y-pennant to Bala to buy a Bible,
so inspiring the formation of the British and Foreign Bible Society.

250 Years Ago – 1750

Howell Harris was expelled from the Methodist movement for heresy.

300 Years Ago –1700

The Welsh Baptist Association was formed.
Sir Humphrey Mackworth formed the Company of Mines Adventurers to exploit
the lead mines of Cardiganshire and he opened the first works charity school in
Wales at Esgair Hir.
The death occurred of the first Welsh Speaker of the House of Commons, Sir
William Williams.

500 Years Ago – 1500

The distinguished soldier, Sir William Herbert, was born.

600 Years Ago – 1400

Owain Glyndŵr's rebellion, the third Welsh war of independence, began.

900 Years Ago – 1100

By tradition, an eisteddfod is said to have been held at Caerwys under the patronage of Gruffudd ap Cynan.

1500 Years Ago – 500

At the Battle of Mount Badon, attributed to this year, the British, possibly under Arthur, defeated the Saxons and halted their advance for 50 years.

NOTABLE PEOPLE FROM WALES

This list of some 700 names cannot claim to be exhaustive but may be considered a fair representation of individual Welsh achievements across a wide range of activities over many centuries.

Academics, Scholars (see also Educationists, Scientists)

Adam of Usk (1352?–1430), chronicler
Sir John Ballinger (1860–1933), librarian
Sir Idris Bell (1879–1967), literary academic
Emrys George Bowen (1900–93), geographer and anthropologist
Glyn Daniel (1914–86), archaeologist
Wendy Davies (born 1942), historian
Sir William Llewelyn Davies (1887 –1952), librarian
A. H. Dodd (1891–1975), historian
Arthur Wade Evans (1875–1964), historian
Daniel Silvan Evans (1818–1913), lexicographer
Emyr Iestyn Evans (1905–1989), geographer
George Ewart Evans (1909–88), oral historian
Theophilus Evans (1693–1767), historian
J. Gwyn Griffiths (born 1911), classical scholar
James Howell (1594–1666), historiographer Royal
Arthur Lloyd James (1884–1943), phonetician
Geraint H. Jenkins (born 1946), historian
R. T. Jenkins (1881–1969), historian

Richard Robert Jones (Dic Aberdaron), (1780–1843), linguist
Sir William Jones (1746–94), philologist
Edward Lhuyd (1660–1709), historian
J. E. Lloyd, (1861–1947), historian
Angharad Llwyd (1780–1866), antiquarian
Bedwyr Lewis Jones (1933–92), Welsh-language scholar
Ieuan Gwynedd Jones (born 1920), historian
Kenneth O. Morgan (born 1934), historian
T. J. Morgan (born 1907), Welsh-language scholar
Lewis Morris (1701–65), cartographer
Sir John Morris Jones (1884–1929), grammarian
Victor Earle Nash-Williams (1897–1955), archaeologist
Edward Thomas Nevin (1925–92), economist
Bob Owen ('Croesor') (1885–1962), antiquarian and book collector
George Owen (c.1551–1613), historian and antiquarian
Sir David Hughes Parry (1893–1973), legal academic
Thomas Parry (1904–85), literary academic
Iorwerth Peate (1901–82), folk historian
Thomas Price ('Carnhuanawc') (1787–1848), historian and Celtic scholar
William Rees (1887–1978), historian
Sir John Rhys (1840–1915), philologist
Bertrand Russell (1872–1970), philosopher
David Smith (born 1945), historian
Brinley Thomas (1906–1994), economist
Trevor Thomas (1907–93), art historian
Alfred Wallace (1823–1913), naturalist
John Walters (1721–97), lexicographer
David Williams (1738–1816), philosopher
David Williams (1900–78), historian
Glanmor Williams (born 1920), historian
Gwyn A. Williams (born 1925), historian
G. J. Williams (1892–1963), historian and literary academic
Sir Ifor Williams (1881–1965), Welsh-language scholar
J. E. Caerwyn Williams (born 1912), literary academic
Stephen J. Williams (1896–1992), Welsh-language scholar

Actors

Sir Stanley Baker (1928–76)
Richard Burton (1925–84)

Timothy Dalton (born 1944)
Windsor Davies (born 1930)
Meredith Edwards (born 1917)
Hugh Griffith (1912–80)
Kenneth Griffith (born 1921)
Sir Anthony Hopkins (born 1937)
Donald Houston (1923–91)
Glyn Houston (born 1926)
Nerys Hughes (born 1941)
Dafydd Hywel (born 1946)
Emrys James (1930–89)
Griff Rhys Jones (1953)
Terry Jones (born 1942)
Charles Kemble (1775–1854)
Ronald Lewis (1928–82)
Philip Madoc (born 1934)
Ruth Madoc (born 1943)
Ray Milland (1908–86)
Beth Morris (born 1949)
John Ogwen (born 1944)
Siân Phillips (born 1934)
Jonathan Pryce (born 1947)
John Rhys-Davies (born 1944)
Rachel Roberts (1927–80)
Sarah Siddons (1755–1831)
Ray Smith (1936–91)
Victor Spinetti (born 1933)
William Squire (1920–89)
Madeline Thomas (1890–1990)
Naunton Wayne (1901–78)
Emlyn Williams (1905–87)

Architects, Builders

William Edwards (1719–89), bridge builder
Sidney Colwyn Foulkes (1884–1971)
Inigo Jones (1573–1652)
Owen Jones (1809–74)
Alwyn Lloyd (1881–1960)
John Nash (1752–1835)

John Prichard (1817–86)
Dewi Prys Thomas (1916–85)
Sir Percy Thomas (1883–1969)
Sir Clough Williams-Ellis (1883–1978)

Artists, Sculptors

Sir Frank Brangwyn (1867–1956)
Sir Edward Burne-Jones (1833–98)
Brenda Chamberlain (1912–71)
John Elwyn (born 1916)
Merlyn Evans (1910–73)
John Gibson (1790–1866)
Moses Griffiths (1747–1819)
Allan Gwynne-Jones (1892–1982)
Hugh Hughes (1790–1863)
Joseph Murray Ince (1806–59)
James Dickson Innes (1887–1914)
Augustus John (1878–1961)
Gwen John (1876–1939)
Sir William Goscombe John (1860–1952)
David Jones (1895–1974)
Jonah Jones (born 1919)
Thomas Jones (1742–1803)
Sir William Llewellyn (1863–1941)
Arthur Miles (1905–87)
John Petts (1914–1991)
Edward Pugh (c.1761–1813)
Ceri Richards (1903–71)
Will Roberts (born 1910)
Ivor Roberts-Jones (born 1913)
David Tinker (born 1924)
Evan Walters (1893–1951)
Kyffin Williams (born 1918)
Richard Wilson (1713–81)
Ernest Zobole (born 1927)

Broadcasters

Donald Baverstock (born 1924)

Teleri Bevan (born 1931)
James Cellan-Jones (born 1931)
Owen Edwards (born 1933)
John Humphreys (born 1943)
Geraint Stanley Jones (born 1936)
Martyn Lewis (born 1945)
Angus McDermid (1921–88)
John Morgan (1929–88)
Mavis Nicholson (born 1930)
Roy Noble (born 1942)
Anneka Rice (born 1958)
Wynford Vaughan-Thomas (1908–87)
Aled Vaughan (1920–89)
Sir Hugh Wheldon (1916–86)
Alun Williams (1920–92)
G. V. Wynne-Jones (1911–85)

Composers

Sir Walford Davies (1869–1941)
Alun Hoddinott (born 1929)
Arwel Hughes (1909–88)
Robert Jones (c.1485–1535)
Daniel Jones (1912–93)
William Matthias (1934–92)
Joseph Parry (1841–1903)
Brinley Richards (1819–88)
Mansel Thomas (1909–86)
Thomas Tomkins II (1572–1656)
Grace Williams (1906–77)
David Wynne (1900–85)

Educationists, Social Reformers, Philanthropists

Bridget Bevan (1698–1779)
Gwendoline Davies (1882–1951)
Margaret Davies (1884–1963)
Sir Ifan ab Owen Edwards (1895–1970)
Sir Owen M. Edwards (1858–1920)
Lady Charlotte Guest (1812–95)

Sir David James (1887–1967)
Tom Jones (1870–1955)
John Viriamu Jones (1856–1901)
Lady Llanover (Augusta Waddington Hall) (1802–96)
Sir Lewis Morris (1833–1907)
Sir Hugh Owen (1804–81)
Robert Owen (1771–1858)
William Price (1800–93)
Sir Ben Bowen Thomas (1899–1977)
Sir Daniel Lleufer Thomas (1863–1940)
Jac L. Williams (1918–77)
John Williams (1792–1858)
Elihu Yale (1649–1721)

Explorers, Sailors, Mountaineers, Travellers, Buccaneers/Pirates

John Callice (*fl.* 1570s), pirate
Sir T. W. E. David (1858–1934)
Elizabeth Davies (Betsi Cadwaladr) (1789–1860), the 'Welsh Florence Nightingale'
Hywel Davies (died 1719), pirate
Sir Charles Evans (born 1918)
Edgar Evans (1876–1912)
John Evans (Waunfawr) (1770–99)
Sir George Everest (1790–1866)
Hugh Griffith (died 1602), pirate
Thomas James (*c.*1593–*c.*1635)
Tristan Jones (born 1924)
Anna Harriette Leonowens (1834–1914), tutor to the royal children in Siam
Sir Henry Morgan (*c.*1635–88)
Bartholemew Roberts ('Black Bart') (*c.*1682–1722), pirate
David Samuel (1751–98)
Sir Henry Morton Stanley (John Rowlands) (1841–1904)

Industrialists, Financiers, Business Innovators

Laura Ashley (1925–85), fashion designer
Anthony Bacon I (1718–86), ironmaster
Crawshay Bailey (1789–1872), ironmaster
Jeff Banks (born 1943), fashion designer
H. A. Bruce (Lord Aberdare) (died 1895), coalowner

Second Marquis of Bute (1793–1848), coalowner
Third Marquis of Bute (1847–1900), coalowner
Walter Coffin (1784–1864), coalowner
John Cory (1828–1910), coalowner
Richard Crawshay (1739–1810), ironmaster
William Crawshay II (1788–1867), ironmaster
David Davies (1818–90), coalowner and railway and docks builder
David Emmanual (born 1952), fashion designer
Josiah John Guest (1785–1852), ironmaster
John Hanbury (1664–1734), tinplate pioneer
Anthony Hill (died 1862), ironmaster
Sir Julian Hodge (born 1904), financier
Samuel Homfray (died 1822), ironmaster
John Hughes (1814–89), ironmaster
Sir William Lewis (Baron Merthyr) (1837–1914), coalowner
William Alexander Madock (1773–1828), land reclamation pioneer
Sir Hugh Middleton (*c.*1560–1631), early industrialist
Tommy Nutter (1943–92), leisure industry magnate
Sir Henry Mackworth (1657–1727), early industrialist
Owen Owen (1847–1910), department store owner
Richard Pennant (Lord Penrhyn) (1737–1808), slate magnate
Thomas Powell (1779–1863), coalowner
Sir William Price (died 1938), dairy magnate
Sir Pryce Pryce-Jones (1834–1920), mail-order pioneer
Mary Quant (born 1934), fashion designer
Charles Rolls (1877–1910), car maker
Thomas Assheton Smith (1752–1828), slate magnate
David Thomas (1794–1882), ironmaster and coalowner
Lewis Thomas (1832–1913), Welsh-Australian coal owner
Richard Thomas (1836–1916), steel magnate
Sidney Gilchrist Thomas (1850–85), steel innovator
Henry Hussey Vivian (Baron Swansea) (1821–94), copper magnate
Thomas Williams (1737–1802), 'The Copper King'

Journalists, Publishers, Newspaper Proprietors

James Gomer Berry (Lord Kemsley) (1883–1968)
William Ewart Berry (Lord Camose) (1879–1954)
Hugh Cudlipp (1913–90)
Percy Cudlipp (1905–62)

Reginald Cudlipp (born 1910)
Charles Curran (1903–72)
Aneurin Talfan Davies (1909–80)
Sir Trevor Evans (1902–81)
Paul Ferris (born 1929)
Thomas Gee (1815–98)
Joseph Harris ('Gomer') (1773–1825)
Thomas Jones (1648–1713), Welsh almanack compiler
Sir David Nicholas (born 1930)
William Rees ('Gwilym Hiraethog') (1802–83), 'father of the Welsh press'
Samuel Roberts ('S. R.') (1800–85)
Margaret Haig Thomas (Viscountess Rhondda) (1883–1958)

Military, Naval and Air Leaders

Dafydd ab Ieuan ab Einion (*fl.* 1440–1468), soldier
Sir Thomas Button (died 1634), admiral
Sir Hugh Evans-Thomas (1862–1928), admiral
Dafydd Gam (died 1415), soldier
Mathew Gough (Goch) (died 1450), soldier
Sir Hywel ap Gruffudd ('Y Fwyall' – 'The Axe') (died c.1381), soldier
Sir Rhys ap Gruffudd (died 1536?), soldier
Sir William Herbert (1500–70), soldier
Maurice Kyffin (*c.*1555–98), soldier
Rowland Laugharne (died 1767), soldier
T. E. Lawrence (Lawrence of Arabia) (1888–1935), soldier
Sir Charles Lloyd (*c.*1602–1661), military engineer
Henry Lloyd (*c.*1720–83), soldier
Sir Hugh Pughe Lloyd (1894–1981), airman
Huw Llwyd (*c.*1573–1630), soldier
Sir Robert Mansell (*c.*1573–1656), admiral
William Middleton (*c.*1550–*c.*1600), soldier and sailor
Charles Morgan (1575?–1643), soldier
Charles Morgan (Lord Tredegar) (1830–1913), soldier
Sir Thomas Myddleton (1586–1666), soldier
Sir William Nott (1782–1845), soldier
Owain Glyndŵr (c.1354–1416), soldier
Owain Lawgoch (Owain ap Thomas ap Rhodri) (*c.*1330–78), soldier
Sir John Owen (1600–1666), soldier
Sir Thomas Picton (1758–1815), soldier

Sir Gregory Sais (died 1390), soldier
Lord Miles Thomas (1897–1980), military aviator
Sir Sackville Trevor (died 1634), sailor
Sir Roger Williams (*c.*1549–95), soldier

Musicians

John Cale (born 1942), guitarist
John Cynan Davies (1905–91), conductor
Osian Ellis (born 1928), harpist
Alun Francis (born 1943), conductor
Ann Griffiths (born 1935), harpist
Owain Arwel Hughes (born 1942), conductor
Rae Jenkins (1903–83), conductor
Edward Jones (1752–1824), 'The King's Harpist'
Dill Jones (1923–84), jazz pianist
Geraint Jones (born 1917), conductor and organist
Griffith Rhys Jones ('Caradog') (1834–97), conductor
Grant Llewellyn (born 1960), conductor
Wyn Morris (born 1929), conductor
David Owen ('Dafydd y Garreg Wen') (1711?–1741), harpist
John Parry (1710?–82), harpist
John Parry ('Bardd Alaw') (1776–1851), harpist
Nansi Richards-Jones (1888–1979), harpist
Alec Templeton (1909–63), jazz pianist
John Thomas ('Pencerdd Gwalia') (1826–1912), harpist to Queen Victoria
Thomas Thomas (1829–1913), harpist
Maria Jane Williams (1794–1873), collector of Welsh airs and folk songs.

Opera Singers

Stuart Burrows (born 1933)
Zoe Creswell (1910–92)
Arthur Davies (born 1950)
Ben Davies (1858–1943)
Ryland Davies (born 1943)
Tudor Davies (1892–1958)
Sir Geraint Evans (1922–92)
Rebecca Evans (born 1964)
Helen Field (born 1951)

Eiddwen Harry (born 1949)
Gwynne Howell (born 1938)
Anne Howells (born 1941)
David Hughes (1863–1921)
Della Jones (born 1948)
Dame Gwyneth Jones (born 1936)
Parry Jones (1891–1963)
Dennis O'Neill (born 1948)
Margaret Price (born 1941)
Robert Tear (born 1939)
Bryn Terfel (born 1963)
Helen Watts (born 1928)

Politicians and Lawyers

Leo Abse (born 1917), Labour
Kenneth Baker (born 1934), Conservative
Aneurin Bevan (1897–1960), Labour
Ann Clwyd (born 1937), Labour
Idris Cox (1900–89), Communist
Clement Davies(1884–1962), Liberal
S. O. Davies (1886–1972), Labour
Lord Edmund-Davies (1906–1992), lawyer
Huw T. Edwards (1892–1970), Labour and Plaid Cymru
Ness Edwards (1897–1968), Labour
T. E. Ellis (1859–99), Liberal
Gwynfor Evans (born 1912), Plaid Cymru
John Frost (1784–1877), Chartist
David Lloyd George (1863–1945), Liberal
Gwilym Lloyd George (1889–1968), Conservative
Lady Megan Lloyd George (1902–66), Liberal and Labour
James Griffiths (1890–1975), Labour
Ray Gunter (1909–77), Labour
Sir Benjamin Hall (1802–67), Liberal
Vernon Hartshorn (1872–1931), Labour
Michael Heseltine (born 1933), Conservative
Michael Howard (born 1941), Conservative
Lord Geoffrey Howe (born 1926), Conservative
Lord Geraint Evans (born 1925), Labour
Lord Cledwyn Hughes (born 1916), Labour

Lord Barnett Janner (1892–1982), Labour, Liberal and Zionist
George Jeffreys (1645–89), ('The Hanging Judge')
Sir Leoline Jenkins (1625–85), lawyer
Will John (1878–1955), Labour
Aubrey Jones (born 1911), Conservative
Lord Elwyn Jones (1909–1989), Lawyer
Michael D. Jones (1822–98), Nationalist
Robert Armstrong Jones (Emrys ap Iwan) (1851–1906), Nationalist
Lord Roy Jenkins (born 1920), Labour and Liberal Democrat
Neil Kinnock (born 1942), Labour
Sir George Cornewall Lewis (1806–63), Liberal
David Watts Morgan (1867–1933), Labour
Rhodri Morgan (born 1938), Labour
John Morris (born 1931), Labour
T. E. Nicholas ('Niclas y Glais') (1878–1971), socialist
Morgan Phillips (1902–63), Labour
John Prescott (born 1938), Labour
Henry Richard (1812–88), Liberal
Lord Ivor Richard (born 1932), Labour
Lord Dafydd Elis-Thomas (born 1946), Plaid Cymru
George Thomas (Viscount Tonypandy) (born 1909), Labour
J. H. ('Jimmy') Thomas (1874–1949), Labour
Dafydd Wigley (born 1943), Plaid Cymru
Hugh Williams (1796–1874), Chartist
Sir William Williams (died 1700), first Welsh Speaker of the House of Commons

Popular Entertainers and Songwriters

Shirley Bassey (born 1937)
Max Boyce (born 1943)
Wyn Calvin (born 1927)
Tommy Cooper (1922–84)
Harry Parr Davies (1914–55)
Ryan Davies (1937–77)
Maudie Edwards (1906–91)
Ivor Emmanuel (born 1926)
Mary Hopkin (born 1950)
Dafydd Iwan (born 1943)
Tom Jones (born 1940)
Ivor Novello (1893–1951)

Tessie O'Shea (born 1918)
Donald Peers (1910–1973)
Sir Harry Secombe (born 1921)
Shakin' Stevens (Michael Barratt) (born 1948)
Dorothy Squires (born 1917)
Stan Stennett (born 1927)
Donald Swann (1923–1994)
Bonnie Tyler (born 1953)
Edith Wynne (1842–97)

Religious Leaders and Hymnwriters

David Charles (1762–1834)
Thomas Charles (1755–1814)
Morys Clynnog (c.1525–81)
Thomas Coke (1947–1814)
Walter Craddock (1610–59)
E. Tegla Davies (1880–1967)
Howell Davies (c.1716–70)
Richard Davies (c.1501–81)
Alfred George Edwards (1848–1937), first Archbishop of Wales
John Elias (1774–1841)
William Erbery (1604–54)
Christmas Evans (1766–1838)
Rhys ('Arise') Evans (c. 1607–60)
Gerald of Wales (c.1146–1223)
Ann Griffiths (1776–1801)
Richard Gwyn (c.1557–84)
Howell Harris (1714–73)
John Hughes (1873–1932)
John ap John (1625?–97)
Dan Jones (1811–61)
Griffith Jones (1683–1761)
John Jones (1796–1857)
Morgan Llwyd (1619–59)
John Mills (1621–83)
Bishop William Morgan (c.1545–1604)
William Owen (1813–93)
John Penry (1563–93)
Vavasor Powell (1617–70)

Rees Pritchard ('The Old Vicar') (1579–1644)
Evan Roberts (1878–1951)
Daniel Rowland (1713–90)
William Salesbury (c.1520–84)
Thomas Wallensis (or Walfys) (died c. 1350)
Isaac Williams (1802–65)
Archbishop John Williams (1582–1650)
John Williams (1740–1821)
Peter Williams (1723–96)
William Williams (Pantycelyn) (1717–91)
William Wroth (c.1576–1641)
Jubilee Young (1887–1962)

Scientists, Technologists, Inventors

John Dee (1527–1608), Mathematician, astronomer, alchemist
Sir Horace Evans (1903–63), Royal physician
Calvert Jones (1802–77), photographic pioneer
Ernest Jones (1879–1958), psychoanalyst
Sir Robert Jones (1858–1933), orthopaedic surgeon
Sir Robert Armstrong Jones (1917–43), psychiatrist
William Jones (1675–1749), mathematician
Brian Josephson (born 1940), physicist, Nobel Prize winner
Lewis of Caerleon (fl. 1490s), royal physician
John Dilwyn Llewelyn (1810–82), photographic pioneer
Lord Walter Marshall (born 1932), physicist
Sir Morien Morgan (1912–78), aeronautics engineer
Sir William Henry Preece (1834–1913), radio pioneer
Robert Recorde (died 1558), mathematician and physician
Sir Clement Price Thomas (1893–1973), thoracic surgeon
Hugh Owen Thomas (1834–1891), orthopaedic surgeon
Sir James William Tudor Thomas (1893–1976), ophthalmic surgeon
Sir Ifor Williams (born 1937), chemist
Sir John Williams (1840–1920), royal physician
Ernest Thompson Willows (1886–1926), airship pioneer

Sports Personalities

Eddie Avoth (born 1945), boxing
Ivor Allchurch (born 1929), football
Jack Anthony (1890–1954), horse racing

W. J. Bancroft (1871–1959), rugby union
Phil Bennett (born 1948), rugby union
Billy Boston (born 1934), rugby union and rugby league
David Broome (born 1940), equestrianism
Percy Bush (1879–1955), rugby union
John Graham Chambers (1843–83), athletics and rowing
John Charles (born 1931), football
Mel Charles (born 1935), football
J. C. Clay (1898–1973), cricket
W. J. Cleaver (born 1921), rugby union
Brian Curvis (born 1937), boxing
Cliff Curvis (born 1927), boxing
Claude Davey (born 1908), rugby union
Dai Davies (1897–1976), cricket
Dai Davies (born 1948), football
Emrys Davies (1904–75), cricket
Gerald Davies (born 1945), rugby union
Hywel Davies (born 1956), horse racing
Jonathan Davies (born 1962), rugby union and rugby league
Phil Davies (born 1963), rugby union
John Dawes (born 1940), rugby union
John Disley (born 1928), athletics
Dai Dower (born 1933), boxing
Jim Driscoll (1880–1925), boxing
Gareth Edwards (born 1947), rugby union
Joe Erskine (1934–90), boxing
Ieuan Evans (born 1964), rugby union
Tommy Farr (1914–86), boxing
Steve Fenwick (born 1951), rugby union and rugby league
Trevor Ford (born 1923), football
Rhys Gabe (1880–1967), rugby union
Ryan Giggs (born 1974), football
Arthur Gould (1864–1919), rugby union
Tanni Grey (born 1969), paraplegic athletics
Terry Griffiths (born 1949), snooker
Neil Haddock (born 1964), boxing
Terry Holmes (born 1957), rugby union and rugby league
Colin Jackson (born 1967), athletics
Carwyn James (1929–83), rugby union
Leighton James (born 1953), football

Ronnie James (born 1917), boxing
Albert Jenkins (1895–1953), rugby union
Neil Jenkins (born 1971), rugby union
Debbie Johnsey (born 1957), equestrianism
Cliff Jones (1914–1990), rugby union
Colin Jones (born 1959), boxing
Jeff Jones (born 1941), cricket
Joey Jones (born 1953), football
Ken Jones (born 1921), athletics and rugby union
Percy Jones (1892–1922),rugby union
Steve Jones (born 1955), athletics
Jack Kelsey (1929–92), football
Tony Lewis (born 1938), cricket
Willie Llewellyn (1879–1973), rugby union
Sir Harry Llywellyn (1879–1973), equestrianism
Jack Matthews (born 1920), rugby union
Mathew Maynard (born 1966), cricket
Richard Meade (born 1938), equestrianism
Cliff Morgan (born 1930), rugby union
Griffith Morgan ('Guto Nyth Bran') (1700–1737), athletics
Hugh Morris (born 1963), cricket
Doug Mountjoy (born 1942), snooker
Gwyn Nicholls (1874–1939), rugby union
Peter Nicholas (born 1959), football
Robert Norster (born 1957), rugby union
Mel Nurse (born 1937), football
Johnny Owen (1956–80), boxing
Jack Petersen (1911–90), boxing
Nicky Piper (born 1966), boxing
Terry Price (1946–93), rugby union and rugby league
Tom Pryce (1949–77), motor racing
Paul Radmilovic (1886-1968), swimming
Ray Reardon (born 1932), snooker
Dai Rees (1913–83), golf
Leighton Rees (born 1940), football
Robbie Regan (born 1968), boxing
Dick Richardson (born 1934), boxing
Gus Risman (1911–94), rugby union and rugby league
John Roberts (1823–93), billiards
Keith Rowlands (born 1936), rugby union

Ian Rush (born 1961), football
J. G. Parry Thomas (1884–1927), motor racing
Leighton Phillips (born 1949), football
Steve Robinson (born 1934), boxing
Dean Saunders (born 1964), football
Austin Savage (born 1941), hockey
Alf Sherwood (1923–90), football
Neville Southall (born 1950), football
Jim Sullivan (born 1903), rugby union and rugby league
John Taylor (born 1943), rugby union
Haydn Tanner (born 1917), rugby union
John Toshack (born 1949), football
Eddie Thomas (born 1926), boxing
W. J. Trew (1878–1920), rugby union
Maurice Turnbull (1906–44), cricket
Nigel Walker (born 1965), athletics and rugby union
Cyril Frederick Walters (born 1905), cricket
Steve Watkin (born 1964), cricket
Alan Watkins (born 1922), cricket
David Watkins (born 1942), rugby union and rugby league
Freddie Welsh (Frederick Hall Thomas) (1886–1927), boxing
Ossie Wheatley (born 1935), cricket
Jimmy Wilde (1892–1969), boxing
Bleddyn Williams (born 1933), rugby union
J. J. Williams (born 1948), rugby union
J. P. R. Williams (born 1949), rugby union
Rhys Williams (1930–93), rugby union
Rex Willis (born 1924), rugby union
Howard Winstone (born 1939), boxing
Martin Woodroffe (born 1950), swimming
Wilfred Wooller (born 1912), cricket and rugby union
Ian Woosnam (born 1958), golf
Terry Yorath (born 1950), football

Trade Union Leaders

Noah Ablett (1883–1935) – Miners
William Abraham ('Mabon') (1842–1922) – Miners
George Barker (1858–1936) – Miners
Richard Bell (1859–1930) – Railwaymen

William Brace (1865–1947) – Miners
A. J. Cook (1884–1932) – Miners
Moss Evans (born 1925) – Transport workers
Dai Dan Evans (1898–1874) – Miners
Dai Francis (1911–81) – Miners
Arthur Horner (1894–1968) – Miners
Frank Hodges (1887–1947) – Miners
Edward Hughes (1897–1925) – Miners
Tom Jones (1908–90) – Transport workers
Clive Jenkins (born 1926) – Technicians
W. H. Mainwaring (1884–1971) – Miners
Alfred Onions (1858–1921) – Miners
W.J. Parry (1842–1927) – Quarrymen
Will Paynter (1903–84) – Miners
Tom Richards (1859–1931) – Miners
Jack Roberts (1899–1979) – Miners
C. B. Stanton (1873–1946) – Miners

Writers

Dannie Abse (born 1923)
Ewart Alexander (born 1931)
Ron Berry (born 1920)
Euros Bowen (1904–88)
Dilys Cadwaladr (1902–79)
Brenda Chamberlain (1912–71)
Irma Chilton (born 1930)
Gillian Clarke (born 1937)
Bert Coombes (1894–1974)
Tony Curtis (born 1946)
Idris Davies (1905–53)
Gareth Alban Davies (born 1926)
James Kitchener Davies (1902 –52)
Pennar Davies (born 1911)
Rhys Davies (1903–78)
T. Glynn Davies (1926–88)
Tom Davies (born 1941)
W. H. Davies (1871–40)
Dafydd ap Gwilym (*c.*1320–*c.*1370)
Robert Jones Derfel (1824–1905)

John Dyer (1701–57)
Marion Eames (born 1921)
Maurice Edelman (1911–75)
Dorothy Edwards (1903–34)
Islwyn Ffowc Elis (born 1924)
Sir Albert Evans-Jones ('Cynan') (1895–1970)
Caradoc Evans (1878–1945)
Ellis Humphrey Evans ('Hedd Wyn') (1887–1917)
E. Eynon Evans (1904–89)
Hugh Evans (1854–1934)
Margiad Evans (1909–58)
Peter Finch (born 1947)
Ken Follett (born 1949)
Dick Francis (born 1920)
J. O. Francis (1882–1956)
Menna Gallie (1920–90)
Raymond Garlick (born 1926)
Geoffrey of Monmouth (c.1090–1155)
Geraint Goodwin (1903–41)
Wyn Griffith (1881–1954)
W. J. Gruffydd (1881–1954)
Harri Gwynn (1913–85)
George Herbert (1593–1633)
James Howell (1593–1666)
Cledwyn Hughes (1920–78)
John Ceiriog Hughes (1833–87)
Richard Hughes (1900–76)
T. Rowland Hughes (1903–49)
Emyr Humphreys (born 1919)
Bobi Jones (born 1929)
David James Jones ('Gwenallt') (1899–1968)
Glyn Jones (born 1905)
Gwyn Jones (born 1907)
Jack Jones ('Jac Glan-y-Gors') (1766–1821)
Jack Jones (1884–1970)
John Gwilym Jones (1904–88)
Lewis Jones (1897–1939)
R. Brinley Jones (born 1929)
Sally Roberts Jones (born 1935)
T. Gwynn Jones (1871–1949)

Iolo Goch (*c*.1328–1405)
Lewis Glyn Cothi (*c*.1420–89)
Alun Lewis (1915–44)
Eiluned Lewis (1900–79)
Saunders Lewis (1893–1985)
Richard Llewellyn (1906–1983)
Benjamin Heath Malkin (1769–1842)
Arthur Machen (1863–1985)
Walter Map (*c*.1140–*c*.1209)
Roland Mathias (born 1915)
Julian Mitchell (born 1935)
Dyfnallt Morgan (1917–94)
Elaine Morgan (born 1920)
Eluned Morgan (1870–1938)
Jan Morris (born 1926)
Leslie Norris (born 1921)
John Ormond (1923–90)
Alun Owen (born 1925)
Daniel Owen (1835–95)
Goronwy Owen (1723–69)
Wilfred Owen (1893–1918)
Gwenlyn Parry (1932–91)
Thomas Pennant (1726–98)
R. Williams Parry (1884–56)
Sir Thomas Parry-Williams (1887–1975)
John Cowper Powys (1872–1963)
Alwyn Rees (1911–74)
Ernest Rhys (1859–1962)
Keidrych Rhys (1915–87)
Alun Richards (born 1929)
Kate Roberts (1891–1985)
Lynette Roberts (born 1909)
Dafydd Rowlands (born 1938)
Bernice Rubens (born 1928)
Howard Spring (1889–1965)
Meic Stephens (born 1938)
Craig Thomas (born 1942)
Dylan Thomas (1914–53)
Edward Thomas (1878–1917)
Gwyn Thomas (1913–81)

Leslie Thomas (born 1931)
Ned Thomas (born 1936)
R. S. Thomas (born 1913)
William Thomas ('Islwyn') (1832–78)
John Tripp (1927–86)
Aled Tudur (c.1465–1528)
Henry Vaughan (1622–95)
Hilda Vaughan (1892–1985)
Richard Vaughan (1904–83)
Frank Vickery (born 1951)
Vernon Watkins (1906–67)
Harri Webb (born 1920)
D. J. Williams (1885–1970)
Edward Williams (Iolo Morganwg) (1747–1826)
Gwyn Williams (1904–91)
Herbert Williams (born 1932)
Huw Menai Williams (1885–1961)
Islwyn Williams (1903–57)
Raymond Williams (1921–85)
Rhydwen Williams (born 1916)
Waldo Williams (1904–71)
Ellis Wynne (1671–1734)

WOMEN AND WALES – DATES OF SIGNIFICANCE AND INTEREST

1850   *Y Gymraes*, the first Welsh women's magazine, was founded.
1865   The Welsh colony in Chubut, Patagonia, gave the vote to women of 18 and over.
1871   Rose Crawshay became the first woman to be elected to membership of a public body – the Merthyr Tydfil School Board.
1872   The first teacher training college for women in Wales was opened in Swansea.
1883   University College, Cardiff, became the first in Wales to admit women undergraduates.
1885   The first woman doctor in Wales, Frances Hoggan, was registered.
1886   The Association for Promoting the Education of Girls in Wales was founded.
1891   The first Salvation Army shelter for women outside London was opened in Cardiff.
1896   The first graduate of the University of Wales was Maria Dawson.

1901   Sarah Jane Rees of Llangrannog founded the Women's Temperance Movement.

1907   The first women's suffrage movement in Wales was founded in Llandudno.

1912   In the Stockholm Olympic Games, Irene Steer of Cardiff became the first Welsh woman to win an Olympic medal – a gold in the 4 × 100 metres swimming relay.

1915   The first branch of the Women's Institute in Britain was founded at Llanfair PG, Anglesey.

1918   The first woman parliamentary candidate in Wales was Mrs. Millicent Mackenzie standing for the University of Wales seat.

1929   The first woman MP elected in Wales was Megan Lloyd George (Liberal) for Anglesey.

1950   A record number of three women MPs was elected in Wales: Megan Lloyd George (Liberal), Anglesey; Dorothy Rees (Labour), Barry; and Eirene White (Labour), Flint East.

1964   Eirene White became the first Welsh woman MP to be given a ministerial appointment – Parliamentary Under Secretary at the Colonial Office.

1967   Merched y Wawr, (the Welsh-language women's movement) was founded.

1971   Nicolette Milnes-Walker of Cardiff became the first woman to sail single-handed non-stop acros the Atlantic.

1972   The zoologist Gwendolen Rees became the first woman Fellow of the Royal Society.

1974   Publication of Elaine Morgan's *The Descent of Woman*.

1978   Welsh Women's Aid was established.

1979   The first women MEPs in Wales – Beata Brookes (Conservative), North Wales, Ann Clwyd (Labour), Mid and West Wales, were elected.
        Annie Powell, Rhondda, became the first and only Communist mayor to take office anywhere in Britain.

1981   Greenham Common women's peace camp was established after a march which started from Cardiff with 36 women.

1983   The Welsh Assembly of Women was founded.

1984   The Women's Advisory Council of the Wales TUC was established.
        Ann Clwyd became the first woman MP for a south Wales mining constituency.

1984–   Women's support groups were set up during the year-long miners'
1985   strike in south Wales and the seven-month Ffestiniog quarrymen's strike in north Wales.

1987   Honno Welsh Women's Press was founded.

1991   Two of the three major prizes at the National Eisteddfod were won by women for the first time: Einir Jones (Crown) and Angharad Tomos (Prose Medal).

1992   A record number of 24 women candidates stood in the general election.

          An unsuccessful attempt was made to get Eluned Phillips elected as the first woman Archdruid.

          Tanni Grey of Cardiff won four medals at the Paraplegic Games in Barcelona.

1993   The first annual Women in Wales awards were made.

TRAVELLERS' ACCOUNTS OF TOURS IN WALES

(From Gerald of Wales to George Borrow)

Gerald of Wales	1188	Henry Wigstead	1797 and 1800
John Leland	1535–1543	William Bingley	1798
William Camden	1586	Henry Skrine	1798
John Aubrey	1650s	Richard Warner	1798
Duke of Beaufort	1684	George Liscomb	1799
Lady Celia Fiennes	1698	William Coxe	1801
Daniel Defoe	1724–1725	Thomas de Quincy	1802
Lord Lyttleton	1755	J. T. Barber	1803
Arthur Young	1768	Richard Fenton	1803
William Gilpin	1770	Benjamin Heath Malkin	1804
Dr Samuel Johnson	1774	Edward Donovan	1805
Richard Warner	1778 and 1799	William Mayor	1805–1806
Henry Penruddocke		Duke of Rutland	1805
Wyndham	1781	Richard Fenton	1810
Thomas Pennant	1784	Walter Davies	1810
Sir Richard Colt Hoare	1793 and 1810	Michael Faraday	1819
Joseph Hucks	1795	Thomas Roscoe	1837 and 1844
Arthur Aiken	1797	George Borrow	1862

FORMATION OF WELSH NATIONAL INSTITUTIONS, PRESSURE GROUPS, POLITICAL BODIES AND OTHER ORGANIZATIONS

1473–1689   Council of Wales and the Marches (Ludlow)

1543–1830	Courts of Great Sessions
1715	The Society of Ancient Britons (London)
1751	The Honourable Society of Cymmrodorion (London)
1792	Gorsedd of Bards (first meeting, Primrose Hill, London)
1807	The Red Dragon won heraldic recognition as the royal badge for Wales
1826	Presbyterian Church of Wales
1846	Cambrian Archaeological Association
1856	'Hen Wlad Fy Nhadau' composed
1857	South Wales Institute of Engineers founded
1861	First modern National Eisteddfod (Aberdare)
1866	Welsh Baptist Union
1871	Welsh Congregational Union
1872	Union of Welsh Independents
1874	North Wales Quarrymen's Union
1886	Cymru Fydd (Liberal Party home rule movement)
1886	Welsh Land League
1888	Welsh Parliamentary Party formed by the Liberals
1893	University of Wales
1896	Central Welsh Board (education)
1898	South Wales Miners' Federation
1904	Royal Welsh Agricultural Society
1907	Welsh Department, Board of Education
1907	National Museum of Wales, Cardiff
1907	National Library of Wales, Aberystwyth
1908	Ancient and Historical Monuments Commission in Wales
1911	Welsh School of Social Services
1912	Welsh Health Insurance Commission
1916	Welsh Housing Aid Association
1919	Welsh Board of Health
1919	Welsh Department, Ministry of Agriculture
1920	Board of Celtic Studies
1920	Disestablishment of the Church in Wales
1922	University of Wales Press
1922	Welsh Council of the League of Nations Union
1922	Urdd Gobaith Cymru
1925	Plaid Cymru
1925	Welsh School of Architecture
1928	Council for the Protection of Rural Wales
1934	Cymdeithas Cerdd Dant
1937	BBC Welsh Home Service 1937

1941	Undeb Cymru Fydd (New Wales Union)
1942	Welsh Reconstruction Advisory Council
1944	First Welsh Day debate in the House of Commons
1946	Welsh Regional Hospital Board
1948	Wales Tourist Board
1948	Undeb y Cymry ar Wasgar (Welsh exiles' organization, later Cymru a'r Byd)
1948	Welsh Folk Museum
1948	Welsh Joint Education Committee (replaced CWB of 1896)
1948–1966	Council for Wales and Monmouthshire (advisory)
1950–1957	Parliament for Wales Campaign
1951	Minister for Welsh Affairs
1952	Broadcasting Council for Wales
1953	Historic Buildings Council for Wales
1954	First *Digest of Welsh Statistics* published
1955	Cardiff officially recognized as capital
1955	Farmers' Union of Wales
1957	Minister of State for Welsh Affairs
1959	Yr Academi Gymreig
1959	Red Dragon recognized as the national flag of Wales
1960	Welsh Grand Committee in the House of Commons
1961	Welsh Books Council
1962	Welsh Language Society
1962	Welsh Association of Male Choirs
1964	Secretary of State for Wales: Welsh Office
1965	Development Corporation for Mid Wales (in 1977 the Development Board for Rural Wales)
1966–1968	Welsh Economic Council (replaced the Council for Wales)
1967	Merched y Wawr (Welsh women's organization)
1967	Welsh Arts Council
1968	Welsh Council (advisory)
1968	Countryside Commission for Wales
1970	Adfer (to preserve Welsh-speaking local communities)
1971	University Hospital of Wales
1972	Welsh Film Board
1972	Welsh Sports Council
1972	Bank of Wales (originally the Commercial Bank of Wales)
1973	Welsh Centre for International Affairs
1973	Wales TUC
1975	Labour Party – Wales (formerly the Welsh Regional Council of Labour)

1975	Welsh Consumer Council
1975	Land Authority for Wales
1976	Welsh Development Agency
1977	Welsh Industrial and Maritime Museum
1977	Cofiwn (to commemorate events of national Welsh significance)
1977	Wales Craft Council
1978	Wales CBI first annual conference
1978	National Language Centre, Nant Gwrtheyrn, Llŷn
1979	Select Committee on Welsh Affairs in the House of Commons
1982	S4C (Welsh-language television channel)
1982	St David's Hall, National Concert Hall, Cardiff
1983	Welsh Assembly of Women
1984	Cadw (Heritage in Wales)
1985	Cefn (Welsh language rights movement)
1987	Health Promotion Authority for Wales
1987	Institute of Welsh Affairs
1988	Welsh Language Board (advisory but statutory from 1993)
1989	Welsh Film and Television Archive, Aberystwyth
1991	Countryside Council for Wales (replaced the Countryside Commission)

CONSUMER AND ADVISORY BODIES

Welsh Consumer Council (Cyngor Defnyddwyr Cymru)
Castle Buildings, Womanby Street, Cardiff, CF1 2BN

Community Relations Councils
Gwent Racial Equality Council, Gloucester Chambers, Skinner Street, Newport.
South Glamorgan Racial Equality Council, Unit 8, Williams Court, Trade Street, Cardiff, CF1 5DQ.
West Glamorgan Community Relations Council, c/o 94 Angel Chambers, Walter Street, Swansea.

Citizens Advice Bureaux
Clwyd Abergele, Colwyn Bay, Denbigh, Flint, Holywell, Mold and Buckley, Prestatyn, Rhyl, Ruthin, Shotton, Wrexham.
Dyfed Aberystwyth, Ammanford, Cardigan, Carmarthen, Llanelli, Pembroke Dock.
Gwent Abergavenny, Abertillery, Blackwood, Blaenavon,

	Brynmawr, Caldicot, Chepstow, Cwmbran, Ebbw Vale, Monmouth, Newport, Pontypool, Risca, Tredegar.
Gwynedd	Bangor, Caernarfon, Dolgellau, Holyhead, Llandudno.
Mid Glamorgan	Aberdare, Bargoed, Bridgend, Caerphilly, Maesteg, Mountain Ash, Pontypridd, Porthcawl, Rhymney.
Powys	Brecon, Machynlleth, Montgomery, Llandrindod Wells, Ystradgynlais.
South Glamorgan	Barry, Cardiff (Butetown, City Centre, Ely, Grangetown, St Mellons, Trowbridge), Cowbridge, Llantwit Major, Penarth.
West Glamorgan	Neath, Port Talbot, Swansea

EARLY CLOSING DAYS AND MARKET DAYS IN 90 WELSH TOWNS

Town	*Early closing day*	*Market days*
Aberdare	Thursday	Saturday
Aberdyfi	Wednesday	–
Abergavenny	Thursday	Tuesday, Friday
Abertillery	Wednesday	Thursday, Saturday
Aberystwyth	Wednesday	Monday
Amlwch	Wednesday	Friday
Ammanford	Thursday	Friday
Bala	Wednesday	Thursday
Bangor	Wednesday	Friday
Bargoed	Wednesday	Thursday
Barmouth	Wednesday	Thursday
Barry	Wednesday	–
Beaumaris	Wednesday	–
Beddgelert	Wednesday	–
Benllech	Thursday	–
Betws-y-coed	Thursday	–
Blackwood	Thursday	Friday
Blaenau Ffestiniog	Thursday	–
Brecon	Wednesday	Tuesday, Friday
Bridgend	Wednesday	–
Builth Wells	Wednesday	Monday, Friday
Caernarfon	Thursday	Saturday
Caerphilly	Wednesday	–
Capel Curig	Wednesday	–
Cardiff	Wednesday	–

Town	Early closing day	Market days
Cardigan	Wednesday	Monday, Saturday
Carmarthen	Thursday	Monday (sheep only)
		Tuesday, Wednesday, Friday, Saturday
Chepstow	Wednesday	–
Colwyn Bay	Wednesday	–
Conwy	Wednesday	Tuesday, Saturday
Cowbridge	Wednesday	Tuesday
Cricieth	Wednesday	–
Crickhowell	Wednesday	Thursday
Cwmbran	Wednesday	Friday, Saturday
Denbigh	Thursday	–
Dolgellau	Wednesday	Friday
Fishguard	Wednesday	Thursday
Flint	Thursday	Friday
Harlech	Wednesday	–
Haverfordwest	Thursday	Tuesday, Saturday
Hay-on-Wye	Tuesday	Thursday
Holyhead	Tuesday	Saturday
Holywell	Wednesday	Thursday, Friday, Saturday
Kilgetty	Wednesday	Friday
Knighton	Wednesday	Thursday
Lampeter	Wednesday	Alternate Tuesdays
Llandeilo	Thursday	Friday
Llandovery	Thursday	Friday
Llandrindod Wells	Wednesday	Friday
Llandudno	Wednesday	–
Llanelli	Tuesday	Thursday, Saturday
Llangefni	Tuesday	Thursday, Saturday
Llanidloes	Thursday	Alternate Fridays
Llangollen	Thursday	–
Llanrwst	Thursday	Tuesday
Llanwrtyd Wells	Wednesday	–
Llanybyther	Wednesday	Alternate Mondays: horse sales last Thursday of the month.
Machynlleth	Thursday	Alternate Wednesdays
Menai Bridge	Wednesday	Monday
Merthyr Tydfil	Thursday	Tuesday, Saturday
Milford Haven	Thursday	Friday
Mold	Thursday	Wednesday, Saturday

Town	Early closing day	Market days
Monmouth	Thursday	Friday, Saturday
Neath	Thursday	Wednesday
Newcastle Emlyn	Wednesday	Friday
Newtown	Thursday	Tuesday
Newport(Gwent)	Thursday	Wednesday
Pembroke	Wednesday	–
Pembroke Dock	Wednesday	Friday
Pontypridd	Thursday	Wednesday, Saturday
Porthcawl	Wednesday	–
Porthmadog	Wednesday	Friday
Port Talbot	Wednesday	Tuesday, Saturday
Prestatyn	Thursday	Tuesday, Friday
Pwllheli	Wednesday	Wednesday
Rhayader	Thursday	Alternate Wednesdays
Rhondda	Thursday	–
Rhuddlan	Thursday	–
Rhyl	Thursday	Wednesday, Saturday
Rhuthun	Thursday	Tuesday, Thursday, Friday
St Asaph	Thursday	Thursday
Swansea	Thursday	Saturday
Talgarth	Wednesday	Friday
Tenby	Wednesday	–
Tregaron	Thursday	Alternate Tuesdays
Usk	Wednesday	–
Welshpool	Thursday	Monday
Wrexham	Wednesday	Monday

THE TWENTY TOP TOURIST ATTRACTIONS

(*Figures for 1992*)

Attraction	Number of visitors
1. Ocean Beach Amusement Park, Rhyl	700,000(estimate)
2. Padarn Country Park, Llanberis	380,400
3. Pembrey Country Park	377,200(estimate)
4. Welsh Folk Museum, St Fagans	349,000
5. Oakwood Leisure Park, Narberth	314,400
6. Portmeirion, Penrhyndeudraeth	266,600

7.	National Museum of Wales, Cardiff	255,600
8.	Swallow Falls, Betws-y-coed	245,900
9.	Llechwedd Slate Caverns	238,700
10.	Rhyl Sun Centre	234,900
11.	Caernarfon Castle	228,200
12.	Royal Welch Fusiliers Regimental Museum, Caernarfon Castle	201,200
13.	Loggerheads Country Park	200,000(estimate)
14.	Anglesey Sea Zoo	186,200
15.	Conwy Castle	180,300
16.	Penscynnor Wildlife Park, Neath	175,900
17.	Brecon Beacons Mountain Centre	166,500
18.	Margam Country Park	160,000
19.	Welsh Mountain Zoo	157,400
20.	Cardiff Castle	148,200

STRUCTURES OF INTEREST

(Not listed elsewhere)

- The only known prehistoric lake dwelling (crannog) in Wales has been found at Llan-gors Lake (Llyn Safaddan), Powys.
- Some 500 masonry and earthwork castles were constructed in medieval Wales, about 50 of them by the Welsh.
- Abbey Cwm-hir, Powys, now in ruins, had a 242 foot (73.8 m.) nave – the longest in Wales and the fourth longest in Britain.
- Some 34 sets of town walls have been recorded in Wales.
- There are two tiers of arrow slits in Tenby town walls – the only example of this in Wales.
- Chirk Castle is the only castle in Wales which has been lived in continuously since the thirteenth century.
- The first post-Reformation Catholic church in Wales was built in Monmouth.
- Over 200 windmills are known to have been built in Wales. In nineteenth century Wales there were 90 still working, 50 of them on Anglesey and five of them on Holy Island. The only working windmill left in Wales is at Llanddeusant, Anglesey.
- The smallest church in Wales is at Rhos-on-Sea, Gwynedd. Dedicated to St Trillo, it is 15 ft. by 9 ft and holds six people.
- The highest railway station in Wales was Cwmbargoed in the Rhymney Valley at 1,250 feet (381 m.).

- Cadw (Heritage in Wales) manages some 125 ancient monument sites.
- There are over 16,000 buildings in Wales 'listed' as being of outstanding historical or architectural interest; there are over 400 conservation areas and 2,600 scheduled monuments.
- The tallest building in Wales is the smokestack of Pembroke power station, 700 ft. (213 m.) high.
- The Castle Arcade, Cardiff, is the only arcade in Britain with three storeys.
- Ten piers were built in Victorian Wales:

Beaumaris	1843	Bangor	1896
Aberystwyth	1865	Rhos on Sea	1896
Rhyl	1867	Mumbles	1898
Llandudno	1876	Tenby	1899
Penarth	1894	Colwyn Bay	1900

ANIMAL EXTINCTIONS IN HISTORIC TIMES

Brown bear Possibly survived into medieval times but may have become extinct during the Roman Occupation.

Beaver Probably became extinct in the twelfth century, possibly earlier.

Roe deer Probably became extinct in the medieval period.

Red deer Probably survived to the early eighteenth century, possibly became extinct earlier. Both deers have been re-introduced into parks during this century.

Wolf Probably survived to the sixteenth century.

Wild boar Probably became extinct during the seventeenth century, possibly earlier.

Golden eagle Possibly survived until the eighteenth century, probably became extinct earlier.

Wild cat Appears to have survived until the nineteenth century.

Black rat Thought to have disappeared during the 1960s after having been introduced about the fourteenth century.

SELECT BIBLIOGRAPHY

William Condry, *The Natural History of Wales* (Bloomsbury Books, 1981).

John Cule (ed.), *Wales and Medicine* (British Society for the History of Medicine, 1975).

Cymdeithas Llyfrgelloedd Cymru, *Enillwyr Prif Wobrau Llenyddol yr Eisteddfod Genedlethol* (1978).

John Davies, *History of Wales* (Penguin Books, 1993).

R. R. Davies, *Conquest, Co-operation and Change: Wales 1063–1415* (Oxford University Press/University of Wales Press, 1986).

Edward Doylerush *A Guide to Aircraft Crashes in Snowdonia* (Midland Counties Publications, 1985) and *A Guide to Aircraft Crashes in North-West and Mid Wales* (Midland Counties Publications, 1990).

Charles Hocking, *Dictionary of Disasters at Sea During the Age of Steam 1824–1962* (Lloyds Register of Shipping, 1969).

Honourable Society of Cymmrodorion, *Dictionary of Welsh Biography* (1959).

Arnold J. James and John E. Thomas, *Wales at Westminster: A History of Parliamentary Representation of Wales 1832–1979* (Gomer Press, 1981) and *Union to Reform: A History of Parliamentary Representation of Wales 1536–1832* (Gomer Press, 1986).

Geraint H. Jenkins, *The Foundations of Modern Wales 1642–1780* (Oxford University Press/University of Wales Press, 1987).

David J. V. Jones, *Before Rebecca: Popular Protest in Wales 1793–1835* (Allen Lane, 1973).

J. E. Lloyd, *A History of Wales from the Earliest Times to the Edwardian Conquest* (2 volumes) (Longman Green, 1911).

Dillwyn Miles, *The Royal National Eisteddfod of Wales* (Christopher Davies, 1978).

Kenneth O. Morgan *Rebirth of a Nation: Wales 1880–1980* (Oxford University Press/University of Wales Press, 1981).

Meic Stephens (ed.), *Oxford Companion to the Literature of Wales* (Oxford University Press, 1986).

Paul Weller (ed.), *Religions in the UK: A Multi-Faith Directory* (University of Derby, 1993).

Glanmor Williams *Recovery, Reorientation and Reformation: Wales c.1415–1642* (Oxford University Press/University of Wales Press, 1987).

John Williams, *Digest of Welsh Historical Statistics* (Welsh Office, 1985).

Welsh Office, *Digest of Welsh Statistics* (annually).